TREATMENT OF
Posttraumatic Stress Disorder
in Special Populations

TREATMENT OF

Posttraumatic Stress Disorder in Special Populations

A COGNITIVE
RESTRUCTURING
PROGRAM

Kim T. Mueser, Stanley D. Rosenberg,
and Harriet J. Rosenberg

AMERICAN PSYCHOLOGICAL ASSOCIATION

WASHINGTON, DC

Published by
American Psychological Association
750 First Street, NE
Washington, DC 20002
www.apa.org

To order
APA Order Department
P.O. Box 92984
Washington, DC 20090-2984
Tel: (800) 374-2721; Direct: (202) 336-5510
Fax: (202) 336-5502; TDD/TTY: (202) 336-6123
Online: www.apa.org/books/
E-mail: order@apa.org

In the U.K., Europe, Africa, and the Middle East, copies may be ordered from
American Psychological Association
3 Henrietta Street
Covent Garden, London
WC2E 8LU England

Typeset in Goudy by Circle Graphics, Inc., Columbia, MD
Printer: Edwards Brothers, Inc., Ann Arbor, MI
Cover Designer: Minker Design, Sarasota, FL
Technical/Production Editor: Harriet Kaplan

The opinions and statements published are the responsibility of the authors, and such opinions and statements do not necessarily represent the policies of the American Psychological Association.

Library of Congress Cataloging-in-Publication Data

Mueser, Kim Tornvall.
    Treatment of posttraumatic stress disorder in special populations : a cognitive restructuring program / Kim T. Mueser, Stanley D. Rosenberg, and Harriet J. Rosenberg. — 1st ed.
      p. ; cm.
    Includes bibliographical references.
    ISBN-13: 978-1-4338-0464-9
    ISBN-10: 1-4338-0464-6
    1. Post-traumatic stress disorder. 2. Cognitive therapy. 3. Dual diagnosis. I. Rosenberg, Stanley D. II. Rosenberg, Harriet J. III. American Psychological Association. IV. Title.
    [DNLM: 1. Stress Disorders, Post-Traumatic—therapy. 2. Cognitive Therapy—methods. 3. Program Development. 4. Stress Disorders, Post-Traumatic—complications. 5. Vulnerable Populations. WM 170 M9468t 2009]
    RC552.P67M84 2009
    616.85'210651—dc22
                                2008055055

British Library Cataloguing-in-Publication Data
A CIP record is available from the British Library.

Printed in the United States of America
First Edition

To my mother, Sonja T. Mueser

—*Kim T. Mueser*

To our grandchildren, Hannah Marks, Emma Marks, Ian Marks,
and Rebeca Rosenberg Martinez

—*Stanley D. Rosenberg and Harriet J. Rosenberg*

CONTENTS

FOREWORD

This volume is a welcome addition to the literature on how to help people with posttraumatic disorders. The authors' practical cognitive approach and their variations of it with special populations are especially valuable because the chapters address different obstacles to progress in treatment, characteristic of different comorbidities. The authors are well attuned to the complexity.

Traumas cause mismatches between information from the traumatic event and generalized information, or *schemas*, which were pre-event expectations of what the world would be like. After trauma, the prior sense of identity and connection with the world is fractured in many ways. New information does not match old information and persisting attitudes. These mismatches evoke alarm and can activate intense emotional and undermodulated states of mind. Treatment helps ameliorate these symptoms as well as those of conditioned avoidances to prevent reminders of the mismatch in sets of information.

The mind seems to have intrinsic survival properties for assimilating new information in a way that can increase adaptation to changed circumstances. This functions as if it were a completion tendency. Information processing is carried forward, even if this means intrusions into awareness of memories of trauma, until that information is more or less successfully processed, becoming a part of the person's life story rather than an artifact stored in an active, repetitive type of peremptory memory.

A completion tendency maintains and re-presents to information processing channels the active memory until processing is complete. Completion, at least relatively speaking, has occurred when new realities mesh well enough with inner meaning systems and capacities for coping. The treatments proposed in this volume foster that kind of process.

An intrusive episode from a mismatch is alarming, and many repetitions without progress in processing emotional information can produce affects such as self-loathing or despair. The techniques offered in this book aim at helping patients reach a sense of such completion of trauma processing by identifying and modifying these beliefs and schemas.

A vital ingredient for the patient to feel safe in the process of attempting to change is development of a good enough therapeutic alliance. Safety in the relationship makes it possible to keep on processing emotionally difficult information. It takes more than one dose of effort to modify beliefs and pre-existing enduring schemas. Until then, recall of trauma and its meanings to an endangered self activate, or can activate, various inhibitory or information-distorting control maneuvers. These operations might be used to avoid dreaded, undermodulated states of mind such as searing shame, unending guilt, despairing sadness, or revengeful rage. Approaches in this book deal with these control processes in the patient as obstacles to treatment, obstacles addressed with respect and trust-building.

Trauma has an impact on identity. It can cause a shift from competent to incompetent and attractive to unattractive images of self, from a solid sense of strength to a sense of weakness. Trauma can evoke a shift away from having a coherent identity. Dissociative experiences may result, and a person may feel like a totally different individual at different points in time. Through the process of coping with trauma a person may grow. This beneficial result is called *posttraumatic growth in personality*. It is hoped that many of the approaches described in this collection will lead to patients who not only recover their equilibrium but also gain a sense of strengthening and posttraumatic growth as well.

Mardi Horowitz, MD
Professor of Psychiatry
School of Medicine
University of California at San Francisco

ACKNOWLEDGMENTS

The help and support of numerous people have been critical in shaping our understanding of posttraumatic disorders, the needs of special populations, and the development and testing of the Cognitive Restructuring for Posttraumatic Stress Disorder (PTSD) program. First, we are indebted to Edna B. Foa, whose pioneering work has provided some of the strongest evidence for cognitive–behavioral treatment of PTSD and hope to survivors of trauma. Dr. Foa's earlier treatment model, which included cognitive restructuring as a secondary treatment element, served as the nucleus for our program. We have also benefited from the support and insights of numerous other colleagues in the trauma field, including Brock Chisolm, David M. Clark, Judith A. Cohen, Anke Ehlers, Julian D. Ford, David W. Foy, Matthew J. Friedman, B. Christopher Frueh, Shirley M. Glynn, Lisa B. Goodman, Jessica L. Hamblen, Lib Hembree, Judith Herman, Lee Hyer, Ann Jennings, Kristina Muezenmaier, Pallavi Nishith, Fran H. Norris, Paula P. Schnurr, Nicholas Tarrier, and Claudia Zayfert. We also thank the many clinicians and program leaders we have worked with who have been critical to the development and implementation of our treatment model, including Elisa Bolton, Delia Cimpean, Rachael Fite, Lisa Fortuna, Jennifer Gottlieb, M. Kay Jankowski, Ed Kim, Weili Lu, Stephanie Marcello, Katie McDonnell, Mark

P. McGovern, Annabel Prins, Rosemarie Risoti, Michelle Salyers, Stephen M. Silverstein, and Phil Yanos.

In particular, we thank the following colleagues who contributed chapters in their areas of expertise:

Arthur I. Alterman, PhD, University of Pennsylvania School of Medicine, Philadelphia, Pennsylvania

Elisa E. Bolton, PhD, Manchester Veterans Affairs Medical Center, Manchester, New Hampshire

Delia Cimpean, MD, Dartmouth Medical School, Lebanon, New Hampshire

Amanda P. Dauten, BA, Dartmouth Medical School, Lebanon, New Hampshire

Keith M. Drake, BA, Dartmouth Medical School, Lebanon, New Hampshire, and Connecticut College, New London

Rachael A. Fite, PhD, Associates in Psychological Services, Somerville, New Jersey

Lisa R. Fortuna, MD, MPH, University of Massachusetts Medical School, Worcester, Massachusetts

Jessica L. Hamblen, PhD, Dartmouth Medical School, Lebanon, New Hampshire, and Veterans Affairs National Center for PTSD, White River, Vermont

M. Kay Jankowski, PhD, Dartmouth Medical School, Lebanon, New Hampshire

Mark P. McGovern, PhD, Dartmouth Medical School, Lebanon, New Hampshire

Fran H. Norris, PhD, Dartmouth Medical School, Lebanon, New Hampshire, and Veterans Affairs National Center for PTSD, White River, Vermont

Annabel Prins, PhD, San Jose Sate University, San Jose, California

Paula P. Schnurr, PhD, Dartmouth Medical School, Lebanon, New Hampshire, and Veterans Affairs National Center for PTSD, White River, Vermont

We are also indebted to the numerous trauma survivors with whom we have worked over the years. These individuals have taught us about the meaning of trauma and ways of coping with its effects and have inspired us with their strength, courage, and determination to take back their lives and overcome their traumatic experiences.

A special thanks goes to Glenda Madden and Beth Dickinson for their help in preparing this book for publication. Finally, we thank our editors, Susan Reynolds, Beth Hatch, and Harriet Kaplan, without whose help, support, and patience this book would not have been possible.

TREATMENT OF
Posttraumatic Stress Disorder
in Special Populations

INTRODUCTION

KIM T. MUESER, STANLEY D. ROSENBERG,
AND HARRIET J. ROSENBERG

Over the past several decades, there has been a growing awareness, and concern, about the widespread problem of emotional trauma. Common traumatic events have ranged from child physical and sexual abuse, to rape and domestic violence, to war and displacement, to accidents, natural disasters, and terrorist attacks. These events inflict psychological wounds on those exposed, including a heightened vulnerability to posttraumatic stress disorder (PTSD). Although trauma takes a huge toll on the functioning and quality of many peoples' lives, we now know that special populations of individuals, such as persons with comorbid psychiatric, substance use, or medical conditions; cultural/ethnic minorities; those exposed to disaster or mass violence; and youth, are at even greater vulnerability. The burden of trauma is magnified in special populations by a confluence of factors, including increased exposure to traumatic events, low detection of posttraumatic disorders, and barriers to access to validated treatments for these disorders. A recent review of the research literature concluded that "true advancement of the field will require a deliberate process of evaluation and adaptation of efficacious treatments with less restricted more clinically representative PTSD samples" (Spinazzola, Blaustein, & van der Kolk, 2005, p. 427).

Treatment approaches for special populations need to be sufficiently flexible to address the broad range of traumatic events these individuals are exposed to, impose minimal stress on their already difficult lives, and be standardized with easy-to-follow guidelines. To fulfill these goals, we developed the Cognitive Restructuring (CR) for PTSD program.

This book explains the concepts, techniques, research background, and specific procedures of the CR for PTSD program so that readers can deliver the program in their own setting. We include step-by-step instructions and sample dialogues to demonstrate techniques as well as handouts that can be photocopied and distributed to clients during sessions. We explain all concepts in user-friendly language so that a broad range of helping professionals can understand and provide the program.

The CR for PTSD program is flexible in its ability to both address the psychological effects of any traumatic event and accommodate a broad range of individual differences, such as different comorbid disorders, level of education and intellectual functioning, and ethnic or cultural background. The program minimizes stress related to treatment by relying on cognitive restructuring as the main active ingredient and eschewing the use of exposure techniques. Most special populations require 12 to 16 weekly sessions to complete the program, although a 6-session format is available for clients treated in primary care settings. As mentioned previously, the program also includes a wealth of educational handouts that are readily accessible to all traumatized individuals.

The CR for PTSD program is based on evidence and modern theories of posttraumatic reactions that place a premium on the importance of individuals' appraisals of traumatic events, their own reactions and those of others, and the meaning of the experience in terms of oneself and one's place in the world. The program uses cognitive restructuring to teach individuals how to examine and challenge their trauma-related appraisals—an approach based on research showing that cognitive restructuring is just as effective as exposure therapies for posttraumatic disorders (Marks, Lovell, Noshirvani, Livanou, & Thrasher, 1998; Resick, Nishith, Weaver, Astin, & Feuer, 2002; Tarrier, Pilgrim et al., 1999) and more effective than any alternatives (Chard, 2005; Ehlers, Clark, et al., 2003; Marks et al., 1998; Monson et al., 2006). Consequently, a growing research base indicates that the program has high acceptability to vulnerable individuals from special populations, poses low stress, and is clinically effective.

The effectiveness of the CR for PTSD program has been demonstrated in two pilot studies, one randomized clinical trial, and one randomized trial currently in progress for persons with severe mental illness, as well as several pilot studies for other special populations (see chap. 1, this volume). Because this work was a team effort involving many of our collaborators over a period of years, we have invited these colleagues to write chapters for this book relating most strongly to their own expertise and their contributions to the overall development of the treatment model (see Acknowledgments, p. xii, and chaps. 10–16). As the program spreads to new settings, further studies are being conducted.

This book is organized into three parts. Part I provides a broad historical perspective on theories and research on psychological trauma and the treatment of posttraumatic disorders, including a description of the CR for PTSD treatment program (chap. 1), followed by the practicalities of assessing trauma exposure and PTSD in vulnerable individuals (chap. 2) and an overview of the treatment program (chap. 3).

Part II provides a detailed explication of the different steps of the treatment program, replete with numerous case examples and sample dialogues that can be used with any person from a special population. Specifically, chapter 4 describes how to initiate treatment after someone has been diagnosed with PTSD, including therapeutically engaging the client, orienting him or her to the program, developing a crisis plan to minimize possible threats to completing the program, and teaching breathing retraining to manage high levels of anxiety. Chapter 5 describes strategies for educating clients about PTSD and associated problems, such as interpersonal problems and substance abuse. Chapters 6 through 8 describe in detail the strategies for teaching clients cognitive restructuring. In these chapters, the primary emphasis is placed on teaching a simple, five-step approach to cognitive restructuring as a skill for first coping with any negative feelings, and then later applying that skill to addressing and correcting trauma-related thoughts and beliefs that lead to posttraumatic symptoms. Chapter 9 describes generalized training for the program and how to terminate it at the end of the 16-session period. All clinicians will benefit from reading the chapters in Parts I and II.

Part III describes how to use the treatment program with a variety of special populations. Each of the chapters in this part provides background into the nature of trauma problems in the special population, adaptations of the program, and clinical examples. Separate chapters address the unique needs and adaptations of a different special population, including individuals with psychosis (chap. 10); borderline personality disorder (chap. 11); addiction (chap. 12); adolescents (chap. 13); survivors of disaster, terrorism, and other mass violence (chap. 14); minorities and refugees (chap. 15); and individuals in primary health care settings (chap. 16).

The book also includes an appendix, which contains an extensive array of easy-to-use handouts for clients, all formatted to facilitate photocopying and use in routine clinical practice.

More than 20 years ago, the first efficacious treatments were developed for PTSD, and although substantial progress has been made in developing and validating treatment models for the general population, there have been few advances in treatments for vulnerable populations. The CR for PTSD program described in this book is a state-of-the art, research-based model that includes the flexibility, low stress, and high acceptability required for people in special populations. It holds the promise of helping people rebuild their lives, their sense of self, and their connections to their communities.

I

BACKGROUND AND ASSESSMENT

1

TRAUMA AND POSTTRAUMATIC STRESS DISORDER IN VULNERABLE POPULATIONS

KIM T. MUESER, STANLEY D. ROSENBERG,
AND HARRIET J. ROSENBERG

Between one half and two thirds of all people in the United States have been exposed to at least one traumatic event, even when the term *trauma* is used narrowly to denote a highly threatening and emotionally severe incident (Kessler, Sonnega, Bromet, Hughes, & Nelson, 1995; Norris, 1992; Stein, Walker, & Forde, 2000). Time-limited psychological symptoms of varying intensity are common following such events, and a significant minority of people who experience trauma develop severe and persistent symptoms. About one person in 10 in the United States suffers from posttraumatic stress disorder (PTSD) in his or her lifetime (Kessler et al., 1995). Although for many people the disorder is time limited, for others it exhibits a waxing and waning course over many years. At any one point, between 3 and 4 people in 100 of the U.S. population met criteria for a PTSD diagnosis over the past 12 months (Kessler, Chiu, Demler, & Walters, 2005). PTSD is thus a fairly common psychiatric disorder, and it is one—particularly in its chronic forms—that can carry a high burden of disability. Early treatment has been shown to be beneficial in reducing both chronicity and severity of the disorder. External factors, such as the availability of social supports immediately following exposure, help to reduce one's risk of developing a disorder, but factors such as the number and the severity of trauma exposures increase risk. Moreover, as researchers have mapped the occurrence of traumatic events and the emotional problems that often follow in their wake, it has become clear that trauma exposure is far more common among vulnerable subgroups in our country.

This chapter provides a broad historical, conceptual, and scientific overview of trauma and of posttraumatic disorders (including PTSD) and their treatment. This overview underlies the development and rationale of the Cognitive Restructuring (CR) for PTSD treatment program for special populations. First, we discuss the definition of trauma and describe its correlates. We then demonstrate the increased vulnerability of special populations to trauma. Next, we discuss the evolving conceptualization of posttraumatic disorders, from the earliest recorded Western literature, through medical and psychiatric concepts from the U.S. Civil War era, through modern times, culminating in the definitions and current theories and research on PTSD found in the fourth edition of the *Diagnostic and Statistical Manual of Mental Disorders* (*DSM–IV*; American Psychiatric Association, 1994) and the International Classification of Diseases (ICD; World Health Organization, 2004). The two most common treatments for PTSD—exposure and CR—are then compared, with research supporting a preference for CR. Finally, we discuss the development of the CR for PTSD program. Several clinical trials of the program have demonstrated its effectiveness and feasibility, and we summarize these trials at the end of the chapter.

TRAUMA AND ITS CORRELATES

Obviously, the term *trauma* is part of everyday language and has many shades of meaning. For example, people may discuss the impact of divorce, financial setbacks, or getting fired from a job as "traumatic." These sorts of stressors are discussed in the mental health literature as "adverse life events," and there is little question that the accumulation of such experiences can negatively impact physical health, mental health, and overall functioning (Avison & Gotlib, 1994; Lovallo, 2005). However, as used in this book, the term *trauma* refers to a more limited and extreme class of events: the experience of an uncontrollable event perceived to threaten a person's sense of integrity or survival. This usage follows the definition adopted by the *DSM–IV*, in which a traumatic event is defined as involving direct threat of death, severe bodily harm, or psychological injury, which the person at the time finds intensely distressing (i.e., the person experiences intense fear, helplessness or horror). Common traumatic experiences include sexual and physical assault; combat exposure; and the sudden, unexpected death of a loved one.

Trauma exposure has been associated with a wide range of negative effects, including increased use of medical and mental health services (Drossman et al., 1990; Freedy, Resnick, Kilpatrick, Dansky, & Tidwell, 1994; Golding, Stein,

Siegel, Burnam, & Sorenson, 1988; Moeller, Bachman, & Moeller, 1993; Rapkin, Kames, Darke, Stampler, & Naliboff, 1990; H. J. Rosenberg, Rosenberg, Williamson, & Wolford, 2000; H. J. Rosenberg, Rosenberg, Wolford, et al., 2000); substance use disorders; and psychological distress, including PTSD (Beitchman et al., 1992; Polusny & Follette, 1995; Widom, 1999). Negative psychiatric and health outcomes are associated with the total number of exposures to traumatic events and also with their intensity. Sexual assault and other forms of interpersonal violence in which the victim suffers actual physical harm, along with childhood sexual abuse, represent the forms of trauma most likely to lead to persistent psychiatric disorders, including PTSD, which are described more fully subsequently, and depression, which is often found to be comorbid with PTSD.

TRAUMA AND SPECIAL POPULATIONS

So-called *special populations* (people faced with special or multiple challenges, such as discrimination or poverty, or with handicaps or deficits, such as chronic mental or physical illness) are also more likely to experience trauma and PTSD. In recent years, it has become clear that many clients entering various medical, psychiatric, and substance abuse treatment services experience undiagnosed and untreated posttraumatic symptoms, whether or not their primary complaint appears to be trauma related. In this context of significant unmet need, it is important that providers working with clients in various treatment settings, particularly those working with high-risk and vulnerable populations (e.g., homeless people, the urban poor) become more knowledgeable about trauma, its psychological effects, and methods of treating posttraumatic disorders.

For example, studies of people with severe mental illness have shown that trauma exposure is virtually universal in this group and multiple traumas are common (Brady, Rierdan, Penk, Losardo, & Meschede, 2003; Mueser, Salyers, et al., 2004). Although the rate of current PTSD in the population is about 2 to 3 per 100 (Cuffe et al., 1998; Kessler et al., 1999), the rate among people with severe mental illness appears to be 20 to 40 per 100 clients. At the same time, people with chronic and severe psychiatric illness are unlikely to have their posttraumatic disorders assessed and even less likely to receive treatment for them. Women in prisons (Dixon, Howie, & Starling, 2005) or in substance abuse treatment (J. P. Read, Brown, & Kahler, 2004) also show very high rates of past abuse and other traumas, as do high medical services users, including people in treatment for complex medical disorders such as nonepileptic seizures (Bowman, 1993). Runaway and homeless youth (Burton, Foy, Bwanausi, Johnson, & Moore, 1994; S. J. Thompson, 2005); youth in substance abuse treatment (Deykin & Buka, 1997); and refugees from conflict-ridden environments, such as the former Yugoslavia, Southeast Asia, and Somalia (Berthold, 1999; Stein, Comer, Gardner, & Kelleher, 1999) also have high rates of trauma and PTSD. The high rates of current PTSD in four of these special populations are illustrated in Figures 1.1 through 1.4. The studies depicted in these figures are just a representative sampling of the published research on PTSD in each group, with many more studies in the literature. Although proven techniques for the treatment of PTSD have developed dramatically in the past decade, effective practices for these special populations have not yet progressed to the same point.

It is thus crucial that psychiatric, medical, and other human services providers recognize the complex and often confusing ways in which people with posttraumatic disorders present to care. People suffering from trauma-related disorders are also quite likely to be struggling with other problems, including poverty, depression, substance use disorders, and chronic medical illness. All of these factors can mask and divert attention from these clients' intense and disabling trauma-related symptoms. Ironically, the people who are most likely to be traumatized and most likely to develop severe and persistent PTSD are also the least likely to be correctly diagnosed and treated. People in most special populations are generally underserved medically and psychiatrically, and if they do receive services, are much more likely to be

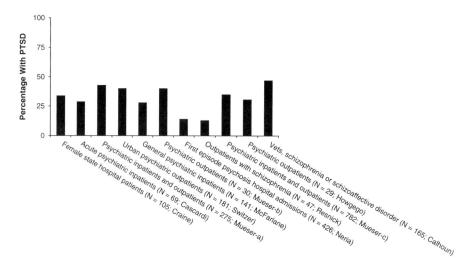

Figure 1.1. Rates of posttraumatic stress disorder (PTSD) in surveys of clients with severe mental illness. Studies are shown in chronological order. Craine = Craine, Henson, Colliver, and MacLean (1988); Cascardi = Cascardi, Mueser, DeGiralomo, and Murrin (1996); Mueser-a = Mueser et al. (1998); Switzer = Switzer et al. (1999); McFarlane = McFarlane, Bookless, and Air (2001); Mueser-b = Mueser et al. (2001); Neria = Neria, Bromet, Sievers, Lavelle, and Fochtmann (2002); Resnick = Resnick, Bond, and Mueser (2003); Mueser-c = Mueser, Rosenberg, Jankowski, Hamblen, and Descamps (2004); Howgego = Howgego et al. (2005); Calhoun = Calhoun et al. (2007).

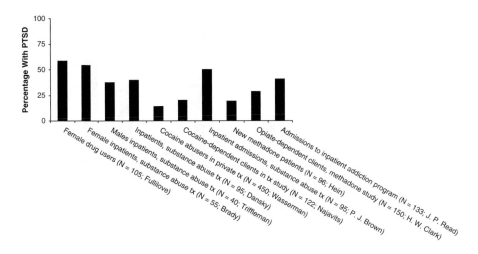

Figure 1.2. Rates of posttraumatic stress disorder (PTSD) among clients in substance abuse treatment. Studies are shown in chronological order. Fullilove = Fullilove et al. (1993); Brady = Brady, Killeen, Saladin, and Dansky (1994); Triffleman = Tiffleman, Marmar, Delucchi, and Ronfeldt (1995); Dansky = Dansky, Roitzsch, Brady, and Saladin (1997); Wasserman = Wasserman, Havassy, and Boles (1997); Najavits = Najavits, Weiss, Shaw, and Muenz (1998); P. J. Brown = P. J. Brown, Stout, and Mueller (1999); Hein = Hein, Nunes, Levn, and Fraser (2000); H. W. Clark = H. W. Clark, Masson, Delucchi, Hall, and Sees (2001); J. P. Read = J. P. Read, Brown, and Kahler (2004). tx = treatment.

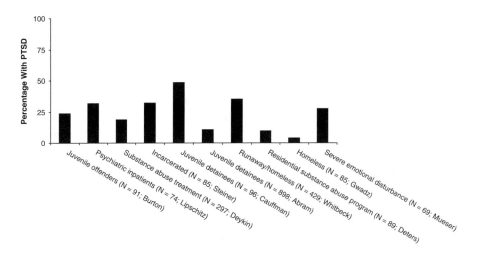

Figure 1.3. Rates of posttraumatic stress disorder (PTSD) in special adolescent populations. Studies are shown in chronological order. Burton = Burton, Foy, Bwanausi, Johnson, and Moore (1994); Lipschitz = Lipschitz et al. (1996); Deykin = Deykin and Buka (1997); Steiner = Steiner, Garcia, and Matthews (1997); Cauffman = Cauffman, Feldman, Waterman, and Steiner (1998); Abram = Abram et al. (2004); Whitbeck = Whitbeck, Adams, Hoyt, and Chen (2004); Deters = Deters, Novins, Fickenscher, and Beals (2006); Gwadz = Gwadz, Nish, Leonard, and Strauss (2007); Mueser = Mueser and Taub (2008).

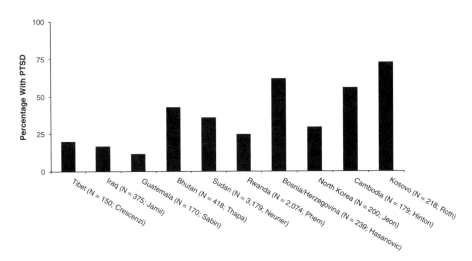

Figure 1.4. Rates of posttraumatic stress disorder (PTSD) in refugee populations. Studies are shown in chronological order. Crescenzi = Crescenzi et al. (2003); Jamil = Jamil et al. (2003); Sabin = Sabin, Cafdozo, Nackerud, Kaiser, and Varese (2003); Thapa = Thapa, Van Ommeren, Sharma, de Jong, and Hauff (2003); Neuner = Neuner et al., 2004; Pham = Pham, Weinstein, and Longman (2004); Hasanovic = Hasanov, Sinanovi, and Pavlovic (2005); Jeon = Jeon et al. (2005); Hinton = Hinton et al. (2006); Roth = G. Roth, Ekblad, and Agren (2006).

offered care for other problems rather than treatment for posttraumatic disorders per se.

One reason that posttraumatic disorders have gone undetected in these special populations is that individuals may present for treatment many years, even decades, after the most damaging events have occurred. They often present to providers with multiple problems that may have no obvious relation to the earlier traumas, and clients themselves may not make the connection between current symptoms and previous life events that may have a persistent negative impact. Moreover, treatment providers in busy mental health, addiction treatment, and medical practice settings are often pressed to deal adequately even with clients' presenting symptoms, like substance abuse relapse, increased mood problems, or high blood pressure. Even though considerable evidence demonstrates that these presenting problems may be strongly influenced by trauma reactions and that current distress and functional problems are made worse by posttraumatic symptoms, few providers have been trained to assess or treat posttraumatic disorders in these populations.

Social isolation may be viewed, for example, as sign of depression, as part of a pattern of negative symptoms in schizophrenia, or as a manifestation of paranoid thinking. Only careful assessment of posttrauma history can reveal, alternatively, the relation between phobic avoidance of social settings, or types of people, and early trauma. These fear-based responses (part of the avoidant symptoms that characterize PTSD) may have become so much a part of the person's adaptation that he or she no longer thinks consciously about what he or she is avoiding. These trauma-based schemas become part of implicit memory (e.g., rules such as "Stay away from crowded places" or "No one can be trusted").

Assessment of trauma history and symptoms can reveal that such cognitive distortions derive from actual past experiences but now have become overgeneralized and function as if they are still useful rules for conducting one's life. Indeed, posttraumatic disorders, as understood from a variety of perspectives, have been characterized as disorders of memory, leading to intrusion of the past into the current moment with often highly disturbing and puzzling impact. As Freud and Brewer (1895) observed well over a century ago, people with posttraumatic disorders "suffer mainly from reminiscences" (p. 7). The most graphic symptom of this sort is termed a *flashback,* in which the survivor actually experiences him- or herself as being back in the earlier traumatic moment, even when the trauma occurred years before. There is no "statute of limitations" on such symptoms. World War II veterans, for example, have reported flashbacks 20 and 30 years after the actual traumatic event. Flashbacks, like other posttraumatic symptoms, may also wax and wane over time. Trauma memories more commonly intrude into present functioning in more subtle ways (e.g., as preoccupations about past events or readiness to anticipate negative events), distorting or blocking awareness of the current environment. Even when not fully articulated in consciousness, trauma experiences may influence the way survivors engage and think about the world, leaving them with a legacy of fear, distrust, profound loss of confidence, and pessimism. Janoff-Bulman (1992) has described many of the cognitive changes that occur following trauma exposure as representing "shattered assumptions" about the world and the self.

To recognize, assess, and treat special-population trauma survivors, it can be useful to understand the evolving, and sometimes competing, conceptualizations of PTSD, including the etiology, symptomatic presentation, patient experience, and paths to recovery. In the following pages, we provide a broad historical, cross-cultural, and theoretical overview of posttraumatic disorders and their treatment.

HISTORICAL PERSPECTIVES ON POSTTRAUMATIC DISORDERS

Controversies remain over the boundaries of PTSD and its robustness as a diagnostic entity (Brewin, 2003; McNally, 2003). In this section, we attempt to illustrate the broad, multiperspective consensus about the basic elements of posttraumatic reactions.

Literary and Journalistic Accounts

Although PTSD was not formally recognized as a diagnosis until the third edition of the *Diagnostic and Statistical Manual of Mental Disorders* (*DSM–III*; American Psychiatric Association, 1980), awareness of the emotional disorders associated with extreme forms of trauma exposure has a long history across historical eras and cultures. Such traumatic stress symptoms as agitation, stupor, and nightmares have been noted as part of warfare and other catastrophes since ancient times. There are a number of excellent articles and books dealing with the historical evolution of the concept and use of the ideas of emotional trauma and its impact (e.g., Birmes, Hatton, Brunet, & Schmitt, 2003).

The traumas of war, and their enduring imprint on participants, are recognizable as central themes in some of the earliest written literature and have a continuous presence in literature to the current period. Mumford (1992) examined the concept of emotional distress as it appeared in the Hebrew Bible, which was composed between the 13th and the 2nd centuries BCE. Trauma reactions are frequently noted, as in Psalms 55:5: "Fearfulness and trembling come upon me, and horror overwhelms me" (quoted in Mumford, 1992, p. 93). In general, heart-related sensations are the primary set of metaphors for expressing emotional states, and the heart is used to signify the self or the inner person (p. 95).

This combination of overwhelming fear-related responses and somatic, particularly cardiac sensations and related metaphors, will continue to figure prominently in the evolving concepts of posttraumatic responses from antiquity to modern times. One of the earliest recorded legends or sagas, the epic of Gilgamesh (carved on stone tablets in approximately 2000 BCE), provides evidence that the Babylonians, as well as the ancient Hebrews, were well aware of the complex and enduring impact of trauma exposure (Sandars, 1972). Gilgamesh, who likely reigned in about 2700 BCE, was the king of Uruk, now Iraq. In the legend, Gilgamesh journeys with his friend Endiku to do battle with the demon Humbaba. As they approach this combat, Gilgamesh is troubled with nightmares, and at the time of the encounter with the demon, becomes temporarily overwhelmed with terror. He overcomes his weakness and paralysis and eventually defeats the monster. However, Endiku soon becomes mysteriously ill and dies, precipitating a crisis for Gilgamesh that bears the hallmarks of a traumatic grief reaction. He persistently reexperiences his friend's death and ruminates about his own mortality, becomes detached and fatalistic, feels increasingly helpless, and begins a period of seemingly aimless wandering.

The two great epic poems of Homer, *The Iliad* and *The Odyssey*, dated to approximately 850 BCE, are also sagas of war and its aftereffects. Like Gilgamesh, the major protagonists, Achilles and Odysseus, are heroes of superhuman dimension. However, both exhibit dramatic shifts in emotion and behavior following their combat experiences, with the death of comrades as the triggering events. Achilles, for example, suffers intrusive memories of Patroclus, his friend lost in combat, and suffers sleep disturbance associated with these memories. Shay (1995, 2000), in his reanalyses of *The Iliad* and *The Odyssey* based on our modern understanding of the impact of war, argued that the emotional wounds borne by Achilles and Odysseus bear striking similarity to symptoms seen in Vietnam veterans.

More modern fiction, from Shakespeare on, also provides clear and compelling imagery of the impact of trauma on human emotion and cognition. In *King Henry IV*, Hotspur, a veteran anticipating combat, suffers sleep disturbance, nightmares, social withdrawal, startle responses, and melancholy. In *Romeo and Juliet*, Shakespeare has a dream fairy visit soldiers in their sleep, making them reexperience bloody combat episodes. Lady Macbeth, following the murder of Duncan, the king, becomes dissociative, reexperiences the event intensely, and suffers flashbacks. Many war novels, including depictions of the Civil War (e.g., Crane's [1895] *The Red Badge of Courage*), both World Wars (e.g., Remarque's [1929] *All Quiet on the Western Front*; Hemingway's [1940] *For Whom the Bell Tolls*), and the Vietnam war (e.g., O'Brien's [1990] *The Things They Carried*), have depicted protagonists experiencing what would now be recognized as acute stress reactions and suffering more enduring psychological wounds associated with exposure to repeated traumatic events.

Journalistic and autobiographic accounts of the 17th, 18th, and 19th centuries, such as the diary of Samuel Pepys, a survivor of the Great Fire of London in 1666, also included reports of intense fear, recurrent nightmares about the event, sleep disturbance, and suicidal wishes (Daly, 1983; Trimble, 1985). The story of Florence Nightingale, seen as a heroic figure for her sacrifices in caring for the wounded of the Crimean War in 1854–1855, is filled with posttraumatic malaise following the war and intrusive memories of the wounded and dying (Birmes et al., 2003).

Medical and Psychiatric Accounts

Although literary and autobiographical treatments of trauma and its impact have been continuous from the earliest literature to the present, medical and psychiatric interest in and conceptualizations of posttraumatic symptoms date back at least as far back as the U.S. Civil War. In the last half of the 19th century, the concept of *Da Costa syndrome* or *irritable heart* appeared in the medical literature. Seen first in combat veterans, it was characterized by anxiety (fearfulness, chest pain mimicking heart attack), "fits of hysterics with excessive emotionality" (Birmes et al., 2003, p. 20), extreme fatigue, and arousal symptoms (palpitations, sweating). These symptoms were attributed to physical factors (exhaustion) and also to psychological processes (nostalgia).

Historically overlapping with the Civil War, the expansion of passenger travel on railroads in both the United States and Europe entailed an increase of high-impact accidents and saw the labeling of syndromes manifest by crash survivors (e.g., "spinal concussion" and "railway spine"; Erichsen, 1866). In England at the same time, physicians were reporting cases in which symptoms developed in persons involved in railroad accidents but who had reported no immediate physical injury. Symptoms were a mixture of psychological and physical reactions, including sleep disturbance, nightmares, avoidance of trauma-related stimuli, headaches, spine tenderness, paralysis, and cognitive changes (Cohen & Quintner, 1996). Physicians at the time saw these as a form of organic pathology, related to the sympathetic action of the nervous system (Trimble, 1985). In cases in which significant organic findings were absent, the primary explanation offered for these disorders related to malingering and secondary gain, issues that continue to shadow the concept of posttraumatic disorders to the present time. That is, the railroads were the corporate "deep pockets" of their day, and there was suspicion on the part of many that those suffering multiple symptoms (physical and psychological), but with little identifiable organic injury, were exaggerating symptoms to pursue compensation. A third view that began to emerge was that these disorders did not represent malingering but instead psychological sequelae of trauma exposure that could be understood as a subclass of the increasingly important psychiatric category of hysteria (Trimble, 1985).

Indeed, 19th-century philosophic, psychiatric, and neurological theorizing gave great weight to the role of trauma in the etiology of so-called neurotic disorders, including hysteria and conversion reaction (e.g., paralysis), as well as neurasthenia (e.g., pain, weakness) and somatization. As we have outlined, such reactions had long been part of the array of symptoms observed in trauma survivors and in people who had experienced overwhelming fear. These symptoms were highly prevalent in the neuropsychiatric patients of the day. Although the tendency for biogenetic explanation was the dominant trend in the medical community, psychological theorizing was beginning to become more prominent. In Paris, Charcot (1872–1873) and Janet (1898) introduced the idea that many of their neuropsychiatric patients at Salpêtrière, considered "hysterics" in the nosology of the day, suffered from the effects of psychic trauma. For Charcot (1895), hysteria, the "Great Neurosis" of his day, was the outcome of severe trauma and genetic disposition to psychiatric disorder, whereas Janet (1925) emphasized the mechanisms by which early traumatic events, such as violent assaults, are split off from consciousness and then, functioning as unconscious memories, become the basis of the traumatic symptoms. Janet estimated that half of the hysteric, neurasthenic, and obsessive patients seen at Salpêtrière exhibited this common history and were characterized by the inability to process traumatic memories. The patient developed hysteria (the posttraumatic disorder) when he or she could not deal with the fear and horror provoked by the instigating event and exhibited no emotional response to it. This reflected or predisposed one toward a more long-term inability to incorporate the events and associated emotions into basic schemas and set the stage for dissociative processes, including what Janet described as flash-backs to the traumatic event (Birmes et al., 2003).

These views laid the foundation for the emerging field of psychoanalysis, one of the primary influences of 20th-century European and American psychiatry. During 1885 and 1886, Freud worked under Charcot in Salpêtrière to learn more about his theories and techniques and became acquainted there with Janet's ideas. This period of intense study and learning was an intellectual turning point for Freud, who was originally trained in neurology. After his time in Paris, Freud (1893–1899/2001) focused his interest on psychopathology as opposed to neuropathology. In the *Aetiology of Hysteria*, Freud (1896/1962) acknowledged Charcot's influence in shaping his and Breuer's explorations of the etiology and treatment of hysteria. In this work he declared (citing Breuer), "The symptoms of hysteria are determined by certain experiences of the patient's which have operated in a traumatic fashion and which are being reproduced in his psychical life" (pp. 192–193).

Like Janet, Freud saw the development of the psychiatric disorder as arising from the splitting off of the trauma memory, and its persistence not in conscious thought but in symbolized, often bodily symptoms (e.g., nausea, paralysis). He also concluded that these traumatic events were primarily sexual in nature and dated from early childhood rather than the more recent past. This hypothesis wove through, and was frequently modified in, Freud's work, has been extensively discussed by other writers (Herman, 1992b; Masson, 2003). The formula Freud annunciated in 1896 was based on a series of cases of adult women presenting with primarily "hysterical" symptoms. In the process of the treatment, Freud and Brewer (1895) came to infer (based on more or less spontaneous descriptions and recollections) that these women had suffered childhood sexual exploitation. Of course, current empirical research has shown that women survivors of childhood sexual abuse are at extremely high risk of developing PTSD but that this group is far from the majority of those exhibiting posttraumatic disorders. We also know that amnesia for the events of childhood is not a precondition for the development of PTSD but that partial amnesia (or at least decayed memory) for early events is common and that dissociative responses at the time of the trauma experience are correlated with later symptomatology.

Although Freud significantly modified his theory of the etiology of hysteria, he continually returned to the issue of trauma and its emotional impact. He clearly recognized that the experience of combat also produced post-traumatic symptoms, and he argued for the importance of psychological as opposed to neurologic (concussive) etiology. Freud ultimately differentiated the traumatic neuroses (exogenous in origin) from the actual neuroses (determined by intrapsychic conflict and developmental processes). For Freud, the traumatic neuroses, or neuroses of war, produced symptoms that were analogous to those of actual neuroses. However, he argued that "a fixation at the moment of the trauma lies at their root" (Freud, 1917/1989, Lecture XVIII). This fixation is commonly manifest in the reliving of the traumatic moment in the patient's dreams, which represents an unsuccessful attempt at mastery of trauma (Freud, 1933/1954). The basic formula for cure of traumatic neuroses was succinctly described by Freud (1914/1957) in his article "Remembering, Repeating, and Working Through": The therapist must help patient to remember the dissociated memory and translate the (unconscious) symptom back to its historical meaning at the moment of the trauma. This step allows both emotional and cognitive changes, including an understanding by the patient of his or her own symptoms, character, and of neurotic disorders generally.

To understand this formula, it must also be remembered that Freud's trauma psychology was part of his larger theoretical enterprise of understanding and treating all forms of neurosis. A key element of the overall theory was that unconscious conflict lay at the root of all psychological disturbances (i.e., all symptoms were the result of conflicts between unconscious desires and expectations that the patient could neither articulate nor resolve). In testifying about the treatment of World War I veterans, Freud (1920/1956) wrote,

> The immediate cause of all war neuroses was an unconscious inclination in the soldier to withdraw from the demands, dangerous or outrageous to his feelings, made upon him by active service. Fear of losing his own life, opposition to the command to kill other people, rebellion against the ruthless suppression of his own personality by his superiors—these were the most important affective sources on which the inclination to escape from war was nourished. (p. 17)

During the period when Freud's views were becoming increasingly influential in the treatment of limited classes of patients (often privileged women), European and American psychiatry was attempting to deal with the massive psychiatric casualties of World War I. It was estimated, for example, that the British Army suffered "mental breakdown" in 7% to 10% of the officer corps and in 3% to 4% of other ranks (Gersons & Carlier, 1992). Competing with the Freudian concept of psychogenic origins of the war neuroses were two other models. First, military commanders (and to some extent, the general public) saw most cases of shell shock as simply malingering or "moral cowardice" in the face of danger and expected duty to country. The British response to panic—for example, entailing paralysis or flight from the battlefield—included court martial or "Field Punishment Number One": tying the offender to a stationary object for hours at a time, often in range of enemy fire. In other cases, the dominant worldview of psychiatry and military medicine entailed primarily neurobiological explanations.

The term *shell shock* was introduced in military medicine and psychiatry as a label for the effects of prolonged trauma observed in men serving in the front lines in France, Flanders, and Gallipoli. The syndrome included—along with panic—fatigue, slowed reactions, heightened startle responses, irritability, confusion, disconnection from the environment, somatic reactions (e.g., paralysis, seizures), sleep disturbance, ruminations, and guilt. These symptoms were generally thought to result from the effects of shell blasts on the central nervous system or from a form of monoxide poisoning. However, military psychiatrists of the day, working intensely with many psychiatric casualties, were already beginning to understand the complexity of the etiologic factors and psychological processes underlying the disorder. In the midst of the conflict, such observers as W. H. Rivers (1918) and Grafton Smith (1917) were already noting the involvement of such factors as prolonged stress and sleep deprivation, the horrific nature of the immediate traumas, guilt, shame, and other troubling factors in the etiology of the disorder.

In 1917, Smith and Pear referred to the common knowledge in military medicine that many of the soldiers exhibiting the symptoms of shell shock had not been directly exposed to concussive blasts. They noted that these soldiers might have instead been exposed to "appalling experiences," such as "the sight and sound of his lacerated comrades," and experienced reactions not only of intense fear but also "sympathetic pain" and "disgust or nausea at the happenings in the trenches" (p. 2). Smith and Pear noted further that although symptoms might well have been disabling, these survivors were neither malingerers nor "madmen." Rather, they described them as being afflicted by unstable and exaggerated emotion rather than loss of reason and observed that they sometimes recovered rapidly and totally from extreme symptoms when placed in a safe environment. Smith and Pear also described the often prolonged and complex array of symptoms and personality changes observed in these veterans, many of whom were sent to convalesce in special hospitals for "nerve cases." It is interesting that they focused on cognitive changes, notably alterations of self-concept including loss of self-efficacy.

Rivers (1918), after carefully observing and treating multiple cases of shell shock, was also struck by the cognitive aspects of both the development and relief of the disorder. Without referring to Freud directly, he drew a clear distinction between combat-related trauma reactions and Freud's conceptualization that the trauma behind hysterical symptoms is sexual in nature, that it derives from early childhood, or that it must be "repressed" in the sense that it is no longer available to conscious recall. He argued instead that the symptomatic veterans make their emotional problems worse by actively trying to forget and not think about (suppress) trauma-related memories, even though family, friends, and medical personnel generally believed that such forgetting was necessary to recovery and encouraged the soldiers to do so. He described cases in which ideational avoidance (thought suppression) or forms of occupational therapy ("keeping too busy" to think about the trauma) were attempted but did not help the soldiers with sleep disturbance, nightmares, and diverse somatic complaints. Rivers, who was far ahead of his day in recognizing the ineffectiveness of such strategies for the more symptomatic veterans, described a therapeutic approach that appears to share basic elements with current treatments for PTSD: disclosure of trauma experiences (exposure) and finding new ways to think about traumatic events and what they signify for and about the patient (CR).

In World War II, the term *shell shock* was replaced by alternative terms such as *combat fatigue* and *gross stress reaction*. Combat fatigue, thought to be brought on by prolonged and severe exposure to war trauma, was typically characterized by several symptom types: hyperarousal, irritability, and sleep disturbance or nightmares. It was thought of as a neurotic disorder, with the stressors of war revealing underlying character weakness or vulnerability, leading to symptom formation. In some of the more dangerous military occupations (e.g., flying bombers, where the fatality rate was very high), rates of "flying fatigue" were so high that the military had to set limits on the total number of expected missions to keep pilots in the cockpit. Still, the emphasis in the diagnosis was on the vulnerability of the person rather than on the nature of the stressor.

The gross stress reaction construct, as developed in the diagnostic manual of the Veterans Administration (Hout, 2000), influenced the American Psychiatric Association in the development of the *Diagnostic and Statistical Manual of Mental Disorders* (DSM; American Psychiatric Association, 1952), which included the same disorder. Although psychiatrists of the post–World War II era clearly were aware that concentration camp survivors, prisoners of war, and survivors of plane crashes and natural disasters all exhibited stress reactions similar to those described in combat veterans, the second edition of the *DSM* (American Psychiatric Association, 1968) did not further develop (or even include) the term. It was thus the Vietnam War, and its multiple levels of fallout, that led to the inclusion in *DSM–III* of the diagnosis of PTSD in the basic form that is now used. From *DSM–III* on, much greater emphasis was placed on the nature of the stressor rather than any vulnerability of the host. Indeed, we are now much more aware that anyone is vulnerable to PTSD if the trauma exposure is sufficiently extreme or ongoing.

CURRENT PSYCHIATRIC DEFINITIONS OF POSTTRAUMATIC STRESS DISORDER

An authoritative definition of trauma is found in the Axis I (A1) and Axis II (A2) criteria in the current *DSM–IV* (American Psychiatric Association, 1994). The A1 criteria refer directly to the nature of the traumatic event the person must undergo, specifying that it must involve threat to life; serious physical injury; or threat to physical or psychological integrity (e.g., physical assault, sexual assault or abuse), either the patient's or someone else's if directly witnessed. The trauma should constitute a type of event so severe as to be beyond the capacity of usual psychological defenses to cope adequately. Not only must the event be severe but the person must also exhibit A2 criteria: At the time of the event, the person's response must involve intense fear, helplessness, or horror.

Once the A1 and A2 criteria are met (a clear trauma has been identified), PTSD is defined by three types of symptoms: (a) reexperiencing the trauma; (b) avoidance of trauma-related stimuli, and (c) overarousal. These symptoms must be related to a specific trauma (e.g., being shot during a robbery) or class of traumas, such as being physically abused as a child (even if that abuse occurred a number of times over a period of years). It is common to have these symptoms immediately following a particular traumatic event, but to qualify for a *DSM–IV* diagnosis of PTSD, the symptoms must persist for or develop at least 1 month after exposure to that trauma and be associated with actual impairments of function. Examples of reexperiencing include intrusive, unwanted memories of the event; nightmares; flashbacks; and distress when exposed to reminders of the traumatic event (e.g., being in the vicinity of the trauma or meeting someone with similarities to the perpetrator). Avoidance symptoms include efforts to avoid thoughts, feelings, or activities related to the trauma; inability to recall important aspects of the traumatic events; diminished interest in significant activities; detachment; restricted affect; and a foreshortened sense of future. Overarousal symptoms include hypervigilance, exaggerated startle response, difficulty falling or staying asleep, difficulty concentrating, and irritability or angry outbursts. *DSM–IV* criteria require that a person must have at least one intrusive, three avoidant, and two arousal symptoms to be diagnosed with PTSD. A simple way to remember this formula is known as the "one-three-two rule."

ICD criteria are similar but somewhat less specific:

Posttraumatic stress disorder arises as a delayed or protracted response to a stressful event or situation (of either brief or long duration) of an exceptionally threatening or catastrophic nature, which is likely to cause pervasive distress in almost anyone. Typical symptoms include episodes of repeated reliving of the trauma in intrusive memories ("flashbacks"), dreams or nightmares, occurring against the persisting background of a sense of "numbness" and emotional blunting, detachment from other people, unresponsiveness to surroundings, anhedonia, and avoidance of activities and situations reminiscent of the trauma. There is usually a state of autonomic hyperarousal with hypervigilance, an enhanced startle reaction, and insomnia. Anxiety and depression are commonly associated with the above symptoms and signs, and suicidal ideation is not infrequent. The onset follows the trauma with a latency period that may range from a few weeks to months. The course is fluctuating but recovery can be expected in the majority of cases. In a small proportion of cases the condition may follow a chronic course over many years. (World Health Organization, 2004, p. 67)

CURRENT RESEARCH AND THEORY

Facilitated by the increased public concerns about the health and well-being of a number of types of trauma survivors (e.g., veterans, survivors of child abuse or domestic violence), careful, broad-based research on posttraumatic disorders has accelerated. In more recent years, the psychological and psychophysiological components of posttraumatic disorders have been better characterized through empirical studies, and the affective, cognitive, and interpersonal alterations associated with trauma exposure extensively described in the literature. Neuroimaging techniques have been used to examine the neurobiological alterations seen in those who develop PTSD, including hippocampal changes (atrophy) and alterations in amygdala function. Both lines of research have been associated with advances in treating PTSD. A variety of psychotherapeutic interventions (primarily based on cognitive behavioral techniques) have now been well established through multiple clinical trials, and effective treatments are now available for a variety of trauma populations, including children, combat veterans, sexual assault survivors, and women who experienced abuse in childhood. Biological treatments, which build on the similarities between the neurobiology of PTSD and the neurobiology of depression, have also shown utility in reducing symptoms. However, until recently, no proven treatments for clients with severe psychiatric, substance abuse, and other special needs and/or comorbid posttraumatic disorders have been available.

The exact boundaries of PTSD as a syndrome continue to receive challenge and criticism and undergo gradual modification. Whereas some have argued that posttraumatic disorders are as old as civilization, others have argued that PTSD is a modern construct with only limited validity across time periods, cultures, populations, or even trauma types (Bracken, 2001; Herbert & Sageman, 2004). For many who have studied survivors of the most extreme and prolonged sorts of trauma (e.g., concentration camp survivors, children suffering chronic physical and sexual abuse), the catalog of symptoms constituting PTSD in *DSM–IV* or the ICD criteria does not fully capture the profound alterations to the organization of self that such trauma entails. Authors like Krystal (1988), Lifton (1967), and Herman (1992b) have provided compelling historic and clinical data regarding the relentless impact of such brutalization in destroying the human sense of aliveness, purposiveness, meaning, trust, and capacity for relatedness. The syndrome associated with such exposure is sometimes referred to as *complex PTSD* (Herman, 1992a; S. Roth, Newman, Pelcovitz, van der Kolk, & Mandel, 1997), although this disorder has not been formally recognized in *DSM–IV*. An important idea to consider is that although complex PTSD as described in the literature entails multiple symptoms, these certainly include as well the core symptoms included in the basic syndrome of PTSD.

For the purposes of this volume, it is not crucial that we resolve these ongoing debates about fine-tuning definitions of PTSD. Most basically, we have attempted to summarize the core features of posttraumatic syndromes as they have been recognized for thousands of years. Throughout recorded history, people have reported how horrific, brutal, and life-altering events can trigger extreme fear reactions. The intense, often sudden nature of the trauma is such that people are overwhelmed by forces they cannot control, and they find that their ways of coping with stress or challenge are insufficient to the circumstance. Such events are profoundly disruptive and can challenge or even undo the most basic schemas that allow the person to organize reality and to act in the world. In some instances, the trauma survivor shuts down cognitively: He or she "dissociates," "represses," or becomes "amnesic." That is, the person uses mechanisms of defense or extreme coping strategies in an attempt to find relief from events and feelings he or she finds unendurable. At the same time, survivors often somehow become fixated or stuck in the moment of greatest fear and paralysis (physical and/or psychological). Although they might wish to never experience (or even remember) the event again, they are paradoxically drawn to "reliving" the event over and over: sometimes by conscious rumination; sometimes by nightmares; sometimes by a delusion-like state of "reliving" the event as if it were happening all over again, in whole or in part; and other times by developing symptoms that symbolize their feelings at the time of the event (e.g., paralysis without organic etiology). Over many thousands of reported cases from disparate backgrounds and trauma types, these emotions, reactions, and symptoms, in somewhat varying combinations, have been documented.

COGNITIVE DIMENSIONS OF POSTTRAUMATIC STRESS DISORDER

Associated with any or all of these symptoms are trauma-distorted cognitions, including overestimates of danger in the current environment; pervasive distrust and pessimism; somatic concerns or worries about body integrity; and, often, self-blame and self-doubt. In the moment of traumatic reaction, and the days and weeks following, the person who develops a posttraumatic stress reaction feels forever altered, as if he or she cannot go on with life with any sense of purpose or confidence. For some, these feelings come to be reduced or resolved over time, and the person can return to a more sustainable way of being. For others, the symptoms, and the resultant changes in basic assumptions about themselves and the world, do not easily resolve. Although the impact of trauma can be conceptualized on many levels, it is clear that the cognitive alterations associated with posttraumatic response can be a key for understanding and for treating these disorders. Extensive work in cognitive psychology has demonstrated that changing the trauma-related cognitions can have profound impact on the full range of posttraumatic symptoms, impacting PTSD itself, subdiagnostic posttraumatic disorders, and related conditions (Ehlers, Clark, Hackmann, McManus, & Fennell, 2005; Halligan, Michael, Clark, & Ehlers, 2003).

It is in the conceptualization of trauma-related disorders, PTSD, or so-called "traumatic neuroses" that cognitive psychology and psychodynamic approaches share important commonalties in understanding of the syndromes and the requirements for recovery. Both of these perspectives are meaning based, emphasizing that the role of appraisal, interpretation, and attribution of significance to the events strongly influences long-term adaptation following trauma exposure. For example, both cognitive and dynamic therapists frequently must deal with one of the most painful aspects of childhood sexual abuse for many survivors: feelings of guilt, self-blame, and "badness." All of these involve complex attributions and interpretations of early experiences, events that often occurred when the child's own emotional development, cognitive abilities, and moral reasoning were at a very early developmental level and when reasoned attribution of responsibility for events would not have been possible. Yet, like fixation on the event itself, such early cognitions, and their contributions to self-schema, often endure into adulthood and influence adult problems with self-worth, self-care, and social relatedness.

As we have seen, as early as World War I, clinicians attempting to help traumatized patients explicitly noted both the affective and cognitive components of the posttraumatic disorders. Case report after case report in the clinical literature has shown how both emotional and cognitive elements of trauma response have conscious and unconscious components, the survivors only intermittently being able to articulate the ways they experienced and subsequently processed the traumatic event. Whether conscious or implicit, there is enormous evidence of the complex interactions between the traumatic event, the emotional states produced immediately and over the long term, and the trauma-related cognitions. For example, the objective level of danger associated with an event (e.g., the likelihood of severe injury or death occurring) does not in and of itself determine the person's appraisal of the event or the person's assessment of whether he or she has the opportunity and ability to influence the outcome. Thus, a man driving a car on an icy road, seemingly headed for an imminent collision, may feel that he can steer or brake the car to avoid contact. Conversely, he might in that same instant feel incompetent behind the wheel and then panic, feeling helpless and terrified. The passenger beside him might be oblivious, or confident in the driver, or even more panicked than the driver because there would be nothing the passenger could do to alter events. Whether or not the car crashes, and regardless of the severity of injuries, posttraumatic reactions are likely to be worse for the person who feels helpless to change events at the moment of impact or who feels guilty and inadequate because he or she "caused" the accident. Nor would such cognitions stand as isolated (albeit painful) ideas. Rather, they would represent severe challenges to self-schema, undermining the person's implicit belief in his or her competence to manage daily tasks, to deal with challenges effectively, and to be worthy of trust by others.

In recent years, clinicians and researchers have attempted to more precisely delineate these relationships between posttraumatic symptoms, emotion, and cognitions. One of the most influential models of posttraumatic disorder is found in the work of Mardi Horowitz (1975, 1979, 1986) and is known as the *two-factor model*. Horowitz's conceptualization of stress responses is based on an information processing (cognitive) model but also is informed by his early training in Freudian psychoanalysis. Horowitz argued that trauma disrupts the survivor's mental models or schema, confronting him or her with events or realities that are incompatible with the schemas he or she has used previously. Such schemas have both conscious (active memory) and unconscious (implicit) components. These schemas are more than handy assumptions or organizing devices; they also go to the core of who the person experiences him- or herself to be and frame important interactions with the world, especially relationships with other people. The incompatibility between the traumatic reality and these enduring schemata often requires radical revision, and the person is caught between recognizing this need for altering core schemas and being unable or unwilling to change the felt essence of who and what they are. This inability to incorporate the traumatic events and their meaning into implicit memory means that the immediate traumatic memories and associated ideas and feelings remain in active memory, where they continue to be a focus of conscious thought and where they are easily aroused by multiple cues and reminders. Given how painful and potentially disruptive the trauma-related memories and ideas can be, the person attempts to suppress and avoid them and oscillates between the symptoms of intrusion (unwanted memories, nightmares, rumination) and attempts at denial or suppression of trauma-related stimuli (avoidance, amnesia, dulling of emotion).

ALTERNATIVE AND CONVERGENT MODELS

More recent theories continue to ascribe a central role to the appraisal of the traumatic event, which is a multidimensional process of perception, evaluation, and integration of information into personal schemas and factors such as motives or goals. The appraisal of the trauma, and one's response to it, can influence the development of posttraumatic symptoms or "hardiness" in the face of severe stressors (Brewin & Holmes, 2003; Ehring, Ehlers, Cleare, & Glucksman, 2008; Kindt & Engelhard, 2005). For example, Foa's emotional processing theory (Foa & Riggs, 1993; Foa & Rothbaum, 1998; Foa, Steketee, & Rothbaum, 1989) posits that posttraumatic symptoms emerge when a traumatic event is perceived as fundamentally overriding prior beliefs of safety, requiring a radical reorganization of beliefs and behaviors.

Although traumatic events can fundamentally challenge how individuals perceive others and the world (e.g., "I never imagined people could be so vicious"), the person's evaluation of how they responded to those events (e.g., "I thought of myself as strong, not someone who would freeze up if threatened") can also be a contributing factor. Ehlers and Clark (2000) built on the work of Foa by developing a model that expands the role of appraisal in influencing the nature and intensity of reactions to external events. They have enumerated a wide range of trauma-based appraisals that are predictive of the development of posttraumatic symptoms. These appraisals are not limited to concerns about safety but also address threats to the individual's future (e.g., "I'll never be able to live a normal life again"), his or her worth (e.g., "I'm no good if I could let this happen to me"), sanity (e.g., "I must be going crazy because I keep having these flashbacks"), resilience (e.g., "I am defeated"), capacity for close relationships and love (e.g., "I'll never be able to trust someone again"), vulnerability (e.g., "I'm an easy target"), autonomy (e.g., "I have no control over my life"), and even his or her humanity (e.g., "I'm a robot—I feel nothing"; Dunmore, Clark, & Ehlers, 2001; Ehlers, Maercker, & Boos, 2000; Ehlers, Mayou, & Bryant, 1998, 2003; Halligan et al., 2003).

Thus, how individuals construe their traumatic experiences is broadly accepted as critical to whether they develop posttraumatic symptoms. Interventions developed for PTSD vary in the extent to which they overtly focus on individuals' appraisals of their traumatic events. In the following section we briefly review research on the treatment of posttraumatic disorders and discuss its implications for treating these disorders in special populations.

COGNITIVE–BEHAVIORAL TREATMENT OF POSTTRAUMATIC SYMPTOMS

Over the past several decades a broad range of psychotherapeutic treatments have been developed for PTSD and related posttraumatic syndromes. Among the different approaches that have been evaluated, the preponderance of research has examined, and supported, the efficacy of cognitive–behavioral interventions (Benish, Imel, & Wampold, 2008; Bisson et al., 2007; Bradley, Greene, Russ, Dutra, & Westen, 2005). Two specific cognitive–behavioral treatment methods have demonstrated the greatest efficacy: *exposure therapy* and *cognitive restructuring*. These two approaches are described next, as well as the evidence supporting them and their applicability to special populations.

Exposure Therapy

Exposure therapy (formerly called *flooding* or *implosion therapy*) is at the core of a wide range of programs that have been developed for the treatment of anxiety disorders, including PTSD (Foa, Hembree, & Rothbaum, 2007; Smyth, 1999), social phobia (Heimberg & Becker, 2002), panic disorder (Craske, Barlow, & Meadows, 2000), obsessive–compulsive disorder (Steketee, 1999), and simple phobia (Bourne, 1998). Avoidance of feared but objectively safe stimuli, such as reminders of traumatic experiences, social situations, or potential contaminants, is a defining feature of anxiety disorders. Exposure therapy, which is often combined with teaching relaxation or anxiety management skills, involves helping people overcome their avoidance by systematically exposing them to feared situations while minimizing their natural tendency to immediately escape from any anxiety-provoking situation. As people are exposed to feared but safe stimuli, they gradually learn that these stimuli do not in fact pose a real threat and their anxiety habituates and along with it their avoidance of those situations. Although exposure therapy approaches were first developed on the basis of theories of learning (Stampfl & Levis, 1967), the mechanisms underlying their treatment effects have been conceptualized using cognitive models based on information processing theory (Foa & Kozak, 1986).

Exposure therapy for PTSD usually involves exposure to two types of trauma-related reminders: imaginal stimuli (such as memories of traumatic experiences) and real-life situations (e.g., returning to the scene of an accident). *Imaginal exposure* to distressing memories of traumatic events is typically conducted by having the client in therapy sessions close his or her eyes, focus on recalling one event at a time, and describe in detail exactly what happened and how he or she reacted. Although anxiety usually starts out high when individuals first begin to talk about their traumatic experiences, it typically goes down over time, both within and across treatment sessions, as people learn that their memories cannot hurt them. Imaginal exposure therapy sessions are sometime audiotaped so the client can conduct additional exposure as homework on his or her own between sessions. Exposure to feared but safe real-life situations (or *in vivo exposure*) is conducted by having the client construct a hierarchy of feared situations and gradually expose him- or herself to those situations for long enough periods of time that the individual's initial anxiety subsides.

Exposure therapy for PTSD has been more extensively studied than any other treatment approach, and evidence supports its efficacy, with the bulk of research on survivors of sexual assault, combat, and accidents (Benish et al., 2008). Although exposure therapy is most often combined with relaxation training, it has also been combined with other methods, such as social skills training, teaching problem solving, stress management training, and CR (Cloitre, Cohen, & Koenen, 2006; Foa & Rothbaum, 1998; Kubany & Ralston, 2008; Scott & Stradling, 2006). Despite the evidence base for exposure therapy, several limitations of the approach raise concerns, especially when using the methods with vulnerable individuals from special populations. These limitations include questions about the acceptability of the approach, the high stress involved in confronting feared memories and situations, and reduced effectiveness when anxiety is not the dominant upsetting emotion.

Exposure therapy has problems with acceptability to both client and clinicians. By definition, exposure therapy requires individuals to directly face and deal with memories and situations related to their traumatic experiences. Because avoidance of trauma-related stimuli is a defining characteristic of PTSD, it can be difficult or impossible to engage some clients in exposure therapy (Scott & Stradling, 1997; Zayfert & Becker, 2000). In addition, many clinicians are uncomfortable or openly skeptical about the benefits of exposure therapy because of concerns such as retraumatizing the client, exacerbating PTSD symptoms, or worsening other symptoms (Becker, Zayfert, & Anderson, 2004; Boudewyns & Shipley, 1983; Kilpatrick & Best, 1984; Pitman et al., 1991). Furthermore, the presence of comorbid disorders and other problems common to vulnerable populations, such as psychosis, substance abuse, suicidality, and self-injurious behavior, is widely accepted as a counterindication for exposure therapy (Becker et al., 2004; Foy et al., 1996; Litz, Blake, Gerardi, & Keane, 1990). As a result of these concerns, despite more than 20 years of research on exposure therapy, it is still not widely provided to people with PTSD (Becker et al., 2004; Foy et al., 1996); even experts on exposure therapy report using it with only 58% of their cases with PTSD (Litz et al., 1990).

A second limitation of exposure therapy is the presumed stress associated with participation in the treatment. Confronting trauma-related memories and situations is a frightening, stressful experience (Jaycox & Foa, 1996). Perhaps partly because of the inherently stressful nature of exposure therapy, research has routinely excluded special populations with a high sensitivity to stress (Spinazzola, Blaustein, & van der Kolk, 2005). As a result of the consensus that exposure therapy is inappropriate for vulnerable individuals, few efforts have been reported on implementing the approach in special populations, although Brady et al. (2001) reported a high dropout rate in an open clinical trial of exposure therapy for people with PTSD and cocaine dependence.

A third problem with exposure therapy is its limited effectiveness in addressing posttraumatic symptoms in individuals for whom anxiety is not the dominating negative emotion. Several studies have that shown clients with strong feelings of guilt, shame, or anger benefit less from exposure therapy than people for whom anxiety is their most troubling emotion (Foa, Riggs, Massie, & Yarczower, 1995; Pitman et al., 1991; Resick et al., 2002; Smucker, Grunert, & Weis, 2003). This is an important concern considering that, as previously reviewed, non–fear-related appraisals of traumatic events are often strongly predictive of PTSD and lead to emotions other than anxiety (Ehlers & Clark, 2000).

Cognitive Restructuring

Cognitive restructuring (also called *cognitive therapy* or *cognitive–behavior therapy*) was originally developed for the treatment of depression (A. T. Beck, Rush, Shaw, & Emery, 1979) but has since been applied to anxiety disorders (D. A. Clark, 2004), including PTSD (Resick & Schnicke, 1993), and a range of other disorders (Kingdon & Turkington, 2004). CR is based on the premise that depression, anxiety, and other negative feelings are mediated by individuals' thoughts and beliefs about events, themselves, and the world. These thoughts and beliefs may or may not be factually accurate. To the extent that negative, self-defeating thoughts or beliefs are inaccurate, correcting them can reduce or eliminate the associated upsetting feelings. CR involves systematically teaching people how to identify, examine, challenge, and change thoughts associated with negative feelings.

Treatment programs using CR for posttraumatic disorders involve helping clients examine and modify inaccurate trauma-related beliefs about other people in general, the world, and themselves. Some programs are primarily based on CR but also include a more circumscribed exposure component, such as writing an account of the traumatic event or limited discussion of the traumatic experience (Ehlers et al., 2005; Resick & Schnicke, 1993). CR is often integrated into multicomponent programs for PTSD that include a range of other methods, such as exposure and skills training (Cloitre et al., 2006; Kubany & Ralston, 2008).

Similar to exposure therapy, CR for PTSD has strong empirical support (Benish et al., 2008; Bradley et al., 2005). Aside from studies demonstrating that CR is more effective than either wait-list or attention control treatments (Chard, 2005; Duffy, Gillespie, & Clark, 2007; Ehlers, Clark, et al., 2003; Marks et al., 1998; Monson et al., 2006), several studies have directly compared CR with exposure therapy and found them to be of comparable effectiveness (Marks et al., 1998; Resick et al., 2002; Tarrier, Pilgrim, et al., 1999). In fact, two of these studies reported some advantage of CR over exposure therapy.

The 5-year follow-up of Tarrier and Sommerfield (2004) found that clients who had received CR maintained their gains more than those who received exposure therapy, whereas Resick et al. (2002) found that CR was more effective at reducing guilt than exposure therapy.

Several studies have also compared the effectiveness of combining CR with exposure therapy versus either exposure therapy alone or CR alone. In general, the combination of the two approaches has not been found to be more effective than either exposure therapy alone (Foa et al., 2005; Marks et al., 1998; Paunovic & Öst, 2001) or CR alone (Marks et al., 1998), although two studies suggested modest benefits of combination therapy over exposure therapy alone (Bryant et al., 2008; Bryant, Moulds, Guthrie, Dang, & Nixon, 2003). Finally, a dismantling study of Resick's cognitive processing model compared her full model, which is based mainly on CR but also includes exposure in the form of writing about the traumatic experience, with CR without the writing assignments or with writing assignments alone (Resick et al., 2008). Although all three conditions were effective, clients who received CR alone tended to have the best outcomes.

Considering the centrality of disturbed appraisals to all modern theories of posttraumatic symptoms, CR would appear to be the more elegant treatment approach because it can alter not only appraisals regarding safety (like exposure therapy) but also the wide range of other posttraumatic appraisals, including guilt, self-worth, and sense of future.

COGNITIVE RESTRUCTURING FOR POSTTRAUMATIC STRESS DISORDER IN SPECIAL POPULATIONS

Research on the treatment of posttraumatic symptoms in the general population indicates that exposure therapy and CR are of comparable effectiveness and that the combination of the two methods is no more effective than either one alone, suggesting that the most parsimonious approach to treatment would include one but not both of these methods. However, most of this research has excluded vulnerable individuals from special populations (Spinazzola et al., 2005), providing little empirical guidance to inform the choice as to which approach to use.

There are several reasons for developing a program for special populations primarily on the basis of CR rather than exposure therapy. First, CR can be expected to have both higher acceptability to clients and clinicians than does exposure therapy and to be less stressful because it does not require direct confrontation of feared memories and situations. Second, considering the evidence that exposure therapy is less effective in treating PTSD when feelings of anger, guilt, or shame dominate (Foa et al., 1995; Pitman et al., 1991; Resick et al., 2002; Smucker et al., 2003), CR may be a more useful approach for treating the broad range of negative feelings that accompany PTSD in either the general or special populations. Third, there is abundant experience using CR to successfully treat other problems in special populations such as psychosis (A. T. Beck, Rector, Stolar, & Grant, 2009; Chadwick, 2006; Kingdon & Turkington, 2004; Morrison, Renton, Dunn, Williams, & Bentall, 2004), self-injurious behavior (Linehan, 1993), and addiction (A. T. Beck, Wright, Newman, & Liese, 1993), in contrast to scant experience with exposure-based methods in these populations.

The CR for PTSD program was designed to treat the broad population of persons with PTSD while accommodating to the special needs of vulnerable populations. The program includes teaching breathing retraining, a common anxiety management strategy, education about PTSD and other trauma-related problems, and a primary focus on CR for addressing posttraumatic symptoms. Approximately 75% to 80% of the program is devoted to teaching CR as a skill for managing negative feelings and modifying posttraumatic appraisals underlying PTSD symptoms.

The theoretical underpinnings of the program are based on cognitive models of posttraumatic disorders reviewed in this chapter that posit effects of traumatic experiences on altering or introducing conflict into individuals' schemas about themselves, other people, and the world (Brewin & Holmes, 2003; Dalgleish, 2004; Ehlers & Clark, 2000; Horowitz, 1979, 1986). CR uses explicit techniques to help those with posttraumatic symptoms complete, and sometimes correct, the process of incorporating traumatic events into schemata that organize the self and the world. Because posttraumatic symptoms are defined partly in terms of their intrusive and upsetting effects on individuals' normal lives, teaching CR as a way of coping with negative feelings naturally leads to addressing trauma-related thoughts and beliefs.

Focusing on teaching CR as a general self-management skill for dealing with any negative feeling rather than using it solely to target cognitions believed to be related to traumatic experiences simplifies the teaching process for therapists and clients alike because it requires no distinction to be made between which thoughts or feelings are (vs. are not) related to the trauma. In contrast, cognitive processing therapy requires clients to elucidate an "impact statement" early in treatment about the effects of trauma on their lives and then uses CR to address "stuck points" regarding conflicts between prior beliefs and how the person explains the traumatic event, necessitating different treatment manuals for different traumatic events or populations, such as rape (Resick & Schnicke, 1993), childhood sexual abuse (Chard, Weaver, & Resick, 1997), or veterans (Resick, Monson, & Chard, 2006). In addition, by teaching CR as a self-management skill for dealing with any negative feelings, the treatment program described here obviates the need to formally incorporate potentially stressful exposure work into CR, in comparison with some CR programs developed for the general population (Ehlers et al., 2005; Resick & Schnicke, 1993).

CLINICAL TRIALS OF THE COGNITIVE RESTRUCTURING FOR POSTTRAUMATIC STRESS DISORDER PROGRAM

Research supports the acceptability and feasibility of the CR for PTSD program across a range of special populations. Two pilot studies have shown that the program can be successfully implemented in persons with severe mental illness (Hamblen, Jankowski, Rosenberg, & Mueser, 2004; Mueser, Rosenberg, Jankowski, Hamblen, & Descamps, 2004; S. D. Rosenberg, Mueser, Jankowski, Salyers, & Acker, 2004), including minorities with severe mental illness (Lu et al., 2009). One randomized controlled trial of 108 persons with severe mental illness and PTSD, including individuals with borderline personality disorder, compared the program with usual services and reported significant effects favoring the CR program on PTSD symptom severity, depression, anxiety, overall psychiatric symptoms, and posttraumatic cognitions (Mueser et al., 2008). Furthermore, changes in posttraumatic cognitions were found to mediate improvements in PTSD symptoms, supporting the cognitive model of PTSD. In addition, completion of homework assignments, which focused mainly on practicing CR, was associated with greater improvements in distressing symptoms, suggesting beneficial effects of teaching CR as a skill. Finally, one open clinical trial of a group-formatted approach to the CR for PTSD program demonstrated its feasibility and promising clinical outcomes (Mueser et al., 2007).

In addition, open clinical trials have demonstrated the feasibility and positive clinical effects of implementing the CR for PTSD program with a range of other special populations. Positive effects of the program for survivors of disasters or terrorism have been reported for survivors of the 9/11 terrorist attacks (Hamblen, Gibson, Mueser, & Norris, 2006) and Hurricane Katrina (Hamblen et al., in press). Similarly, the program has been successfully implemented in several addiction settings and shown to improve PTSD and substance abuse outcomes (McGovern, Lambert-Harris, Acquilano, Weiss, & Xie, in press). Open clinical trials have further shown promise regarding the effects of the program on improving PTSD in adolescents (Rosenberg & Jankowski, chap. 13, this volume), with ethnic/cultural minorities (Fortuna, chap. 15, this volume), and in primary care settings (Prins, Cimpeon, & Schnurr, chap. 16, this volume). Multiple randomized controlled trials of the program in special populations are either planned or under way.

SUMMARY AND CONCLUSIONS

The specific ideas or cognitions underlying posttraumatic symptoms that the client is helped to appraise and modify in the CR for PTSD program may appear limited or atomistic (e.g., "Riding in a car is too dangerous"). However, the process of doing this work can help to illuminate the nature of the client's implicit beliefs, how these have been impacted by trauma, and what repair or new alterations of schemata might be available to reduce symptoms and open up possibilities for more adaptive and gratifying ways of being. Although the language and some aspects of technique may be different, the psychodynamic formula of remembering, repeating, and working through shares many basic similarities with the process the client goes through in CR. In dynamic therapy, the trauma survivor is also helped to put into words his or her beliefs and the meanings associated with the trauma and is invited to step back to examine those beliefs and meanings on their merits. As in cognitive approaches, the dynamic therapist helps the client to reassess the inferences he or she has made about the world and themselves and to ask whether earlier events are clouding perceptions of current reality and future possibilities. In current understandings of the process of change in dynamic therapy, schemas are ultimately organized around larger narrative structures, most notably the patient's "life story."

As the reader learns the techniques of CR described in this book and reads about working with a variety of trauma survivors, it will become clear how clients can learn to feel a renewed sense of self-efficacy by understanding the genesis of their posttraumatic symptoms, appraising their impact on ongoing adaptation, and learning ways in which they have the power to reduce their symptoms by actively examining and altering the cognitive schemas that support and maintain them. Beginning modestly by dealing with specific situations and related cognitive distortions, clients can become empowered to challenge more fundamental assumptions underlying their distress. They can thus rewrite life stories in ways that recognize that their basic worth and humanity have endured the hardship of trauma and that instill hope and confidence in their ability to shape their own future as they would like it to be.

2

ASSESSMENT OF TRAUMA AND POSTTRAUMATIC DISORDERS

KIM T. MUESER, STANLEY D. ROSENBERG,
AND HARRIET J. ROSENBERG

As discussed in chapter 1 of this volume, the most common and carefully delineated psychiatric disorder found in trauma survivors is posttraumatic stress disorder (PTSD). The best available information suggests that in the U.S. population, about 5% of men and 10% of women will develop PTSD over their lifetime. Whereas PTSD is thus one of the more common psychiatric problems in the general population, a much higher percentage of people in special populations will develop the disorder. For example, among refugees from war-torn regions, PTSD rates ranging from more than one half to approximately two thirds have been reported, and studies have shown that runaway and homeless youth in the United States have PTSD rates exceeding 80%. Among people with severe mental illness, more than one third develop PTSD at some point in their lives.

Whereas most psychiatric disorders are defined by a given symptom or combination of symptoms, PTSD is one of a smaller group of syndromes that, by definition, must be triggered by a specific *precipitant* or etiologic agent. For example, the *Diagnostic and Statistical Manual of Mental Disorders* (4th ed.; *DSM–IV*; American Psychiatric Association, 1994) diagnosis of *bereavement* requires the death of a loved one as the precipitant, whereas the diagnosis of *substance-induced psychotic disorder* depends on ingestion of a psychoactive substance as a required etiologic agent. In both of these diagnoses, the symptoms must develop very shortly after the precipitating event (e.g., in substance-induced psychotic disorder, the symptoms develop during or within 1 month of intoxication or withdrawal). In addition to the specified precipitant, both also require a particular set of symptoms directly related to the exogenous factor. Similarly, PTSD diagnosis entails two major parts: assessment of the presence of a traumatic event or events (including specific types of emotional responses at the time of the event); and assessment of the three categories of symptoms that constitute the disorder—re-experiencing, avoidant, and arousal symptoms. In addition, the symptoms must cause clinically significant distress or impairment in social, occupational, or other important areas of functioning. PTSD symptoms may develop rapidly following an event, or they may alternatively present after some period of time has elapsed (i.e., *delayed-onset PTSD*). Even if posttraumatic symptoms develop immediately following a traumatic event, they must persist for at least 1 month to meet the criteria for a PTSD diagnosis. Severe symptoms within the immediate 1-month window following trauma exposure can be diagnosed as *acute stress disorder*. For an unfortunately high percentage of trauma survivors, acute stress disorder persists beyond 30 days and progresses to PTSD. Other people exposed to trauma may not meet the criteria for acute stress disorder but may have a more delayed response to the events and later develop symptoms. In either sequence, PTSD is the most common and directly attributable psychiatric disorder to develop following trauma exposure, although depression and substance use disorders may also ensue, with or without diagnosable PTSD symptoms.

The steps by which PTSD develops after a trauma exposure have been well documented. During and immediately following the event, the survivor experiences an intense emotional response, such as fear, anxiety, grief, helplessness, and often a complex mixture of all of these. Memories of the event may be associated with reexperiencing all of these emotions and subsequently elaborated emotions and ideas (e.g., guilt, sense of loss) as the person continues to process the implications of the trauma. Because these recollections are so charged and distressing, the person attempts to avoid memories or situations that are reminders of the trauma, leading to further vigilance and avoidant behavior. In addition, some traumatic events are so overwhelming that the survivor's assumptions abut the world (e.g., "People are mostly okay") and him- or herself ("I know how to look out for danger as well as the next person") can be shattered. The survivor may construct new cognitive frames or internal scripts that keep him or her locked in aspects of the traumatic moment (e.g., "I could be attacked at any moment," "No one can be trusted"). The severity of the trauma, the number of traumas the person has been exposed to in a lifetime, the nature of social supports available, and the quality known as *psychological hardiness* or *resilience* all influence the likelihood of developing PTSD following exposure, as well as influencing the severity and chronicity of this disorder.

The process of determining the presence and intensity of the precipitant (i.e., the traumatic event) can be somewhat complex, as can be the process of determining that the presenting symptoms and problems are related to the effects of the specific trauma or class of traumas (e.g., child physical abuse) to which the person has been exposed. One reason for this complexity is that each component of the diagnosis entails elements of appraisal and subjective evaluation by the person who experienced the trauma. Assessment must rely on the capacity of the person to accurately recall, report, and evaluate events and emotions, often from many years past, that may have been confusing and overwhelming at the time of occurrence. The validity of people's accounts of traumatic events has been a topic of much controversy, especially regarding reports by adults of childhood sexual abuse (Brandon, Boakes, Glaser, & Green, 1998; D. Brown, Scheflin, & Hammond, 1998; Herman, 1992b; Loftus & Ketcham, 1994; McNally, 2003; Pope & Hudson, 1995). In addition, resistance to screening for traumas such as sexual abuse has also come from care providers who are unsure of both how to ask questions about such sensitive topics and how to deal with the information that might be revealed by the assessments. For example, Friedman, Samet, Roberts, Hudlin, and Hans (1992) found that the great majority of primary care patients would prefer that their physician routinely inquire about past history of physical and sexual abuse, but only a minority of physicians believe that such questions should be asked, and inquiries are rarely made at initial evaluations and annual exams (less than 7%). As we discuss in this chapter, a number of efficient, reliable assessment measures can be used by both trained and untrained personnel and are well accepted by multiple populations.

TRAUMA ASSESSMENT IN SPECIAL POPULATIONS

Advocacy groups representing vulnerable populations have been explicit that trauma assessment be part of routine care, since the needs of trauma survivors can only be served if providers are aware of past experiences and how they might affect current needs (e.g., how a client might react to seclusion and restraints). However, in the past, the need for accuracy in reporting traumatic experiences was thought to be a significant barrier to assessing groups, such as people with severe mental illness, whose disorders may result in psychotic distortions or delusions with themes involving sexual or physical abuse (Coverdale & Grunebaum, 1998). One concern was that the psychotic processes would produce invalid and unreliable responses to trauma-related questions. Another concern was that inquiring about past trauma might be clinically inadvisable (leading to a worsening of symptoms) and might be experienced as intrusive and distressing to the client. However, research has shown that such concerns are exaggerated, misplaced, or based on the anxieties of service providers rather than on clients' actual preferences or vulnerabilities. Fortunately, the past decade has provided evidence that valid assessments of trauma and its effects can be obtained for people from a variety of special populations and that these assessments are well tolerated.

Given the private nature of many interpersonal traumas, such as sexual abuse, reports of victimization are not always easy to verify externally. The reliability of reports over time can be more easily determined. The few studies of the temporal stability of trauma exposure measures in the general population report fair to moderate test–retest reliability (Goodman et al., 1999; Green, 1996; Lauterbach & Vrana, 1996; Norris & Kaniasty, 1996). People with severe psychiatric, substance abuse, and neurocognitive symptoms can also respond to standard assessment instruments in a reliable and valid way, particularly if given appropriate supports. For example, levels of test–retest reliability comparable with those found in the general population have been reported in studies of clients with severe mental illness (Meyer, Muenzenmaier, Cancienne, & Struening, 1996). Goodman et al. (1999) showed that the internal and test–retest reliability of self-reports of PTSD symptoms over 2 weeks was high. Mueser et al. (2001) found high internal and interrater reliability and moderate test–retest reliability over 2 weeks for the Clinician-Administered PTSD Scale (CAPS; Blake et al., 1995), and moderate convergent validity with the self-report PTSD Checklist (PCL; Blanchard, Jones-Alexander, Buckley, & Forneris, 1996). Wolford et al. (2008) compared expert interviewer versus computer-assisted interview formats in a large sample of clients with severe mental illness and found high test–retest correlations for both reported number of traumas and PTSD score, as well as good convergent validity between self-report (PCL) and interview (CAPS) measures of PTSD. Taken together, the evidence indicates that reliable and valid assessments of both trauma exposure and PTSD can be conducted in persons with severe mental illness. Similar evidence supports the validity of trauma and PTSD assessments in other special populations.

TRAUMA AND POSTTRAUMATIC STRESS DISORDER ASSESSMENT

As we discuss in this chapter, PTSD assessment usually proceeds in a two-part process: (a) documenting the precipitating traumatic event or events and (b) evaluating whether the frequency and intensity level of posttraumatic symptoms meet the criteria for PTSD diagnosis.

Overview

The choice of assessment measures depends first of all on the specific purpose or use for the data gathered. For example, people can be evaluated as part of an intake process to determine eligibility for trauma treatment. Assessment can also be used to survey prevalence of trauma and PTSD in clients or patients in an agency or to determine baseline rates and levels of PTSD when beginning a clinical research trial. Selection of an appropriate measure also involves determining the skill set and experience of the assessor, the characteristics of the special population (e.g., refugees, psychiatric clients, adolescents), the preference for a self-report versus interview technique, and practical considerations such as time constraints, type of setting (private or public), availability of computer-assisted or Web-based surveys, and cost factors of using copyrighted materials versus measures available in the public domain. In addition to considering these variables, there are other choices to be made regarding the scope of the assessment (i.e., how narrow or comprehensive the survey of trauma history needs to be). In some situations, it is sufficient to assess for and identify a single trauma. In other cases, a more comprehensive survey of both the types and numbers of traumatic events experienced is warranted.

A number of self-report scales and structured interviews have been developed for each of these two major assessment tasks. There are many scales available in English and Spanish, as well as a number in other languages. Several of the most practical are brief and low-cost and have shown to be reliable and valid with multiple populations. In general, we recommend the use of brief, self-report approaches to determine trauma exposure, particularly for special populations, either through paper-and-pencil procedures (with help for those with literacy problems) or computer-assisted interviewing. Depending on the circumstances and the level of precision needed, it is possible to get a fairly accurate assessment of trauma exposure in 10 or 15 minutes using well-validated self-report measures. People can be reasonably well screened for PTSD in even less time, with some valid self-report screening instruments being as brief as 5 minutes. If more intensive, in-depth evaluation is needed, either of trauma history or PTSD symptoms, there are many well-researched and well-validated diagnostic measures. These measures are described in more detail later in this chapter.

A range of trauma and PTSD screening and diagnostic measures are described in the following subsections, as well as procedures for assessing other related areas (e.g., trauma-related cognitions, common comorbid conditions such as depression or substance abuse) that may be useful in selecting clients for treatment, in monitoring change or progress during treatment, and in evaluating overall outcomes or benefit from trauma-focused treatments. While some specific instruments for assessing trauma exposure and PTSD are described here, two resources are recommended for a comprehensive overview of available measures: (a) a Web site created by the National Center for Posttraumatic Stress Disorder (http://www.ncptsd.va.gov), which has a thorough listing of instruments, target populations, time of administration, and related data; and (b) *Assessing Psychological Trauma and PTSD*, a book edited by J. P. Wilson and Keane (2004). Although some instruments are designed to assess both trauma exposure and PTSD, we first discuss instruments used only to assess for trauma exposure.

Assessing Trauma Exposure

There are multiple trauma exposure assessment tools to choose from, ranging from very brief and general to rather lengthy and detailed. Research has made clear, however, that very general, abstract questions (e.g., "Have you ever been traumatized?") often do not uncover many forms of trauma, such as child physical or sexual abuse. Questions about traumatic experiences must be asked in a neutral and factually specific way and avoid use of emotionally loaded language that is open to interpretation. For example, asking, "Were you physically abused as a child?" requires inferences to be drawn about the boundaries of abuse versus discipline and may be experienced as stigmatizing one's family or may call forth denial in other ways. Asking specific questions such as, "When you were a child, did a parent or other caretaker hit, kick, or punch you in a way that caused bruises or bleeding?" is much more likely to elicit a useful response and, indeed, will be endorsed by people who claim to never have been abused. Although much concern has been generated by possible overreporting of traumatic events (e.g., *false memory syndrome*; Loftus & Ketcham, 1994), the best available research suggests that underreporting of past traumas is far more common (L. W. Williams & Banyard, 1998). The specificity of questions, and even the use of some redundancy in the content of items, will likely enhance the utility of a trauma screen.

When selecting a trauma history measure to use as part of a PTSD assessment in a particular population, it is important to keep a number of things in mind. Clearly, there are many extremely stressful events in life that people experience as quite terrible and will refer to as "traumas" (for example, getting divorced, having a miscarriage, or suddenly being fired with no job prospect in sight). Some of the available trauma exposure measures do include events such as these and can provide useful information for clinicians dealing with clients who have experienced them. However, not all types of distressing experiences can be characterized as "traumatic" according to the *DSM–IV* diagnostic requirements for PTSD. The characteristics of the precipitating traumatic event, according to the *DSM–IV*, require "experiencing, witnessing or being confronted by an event . . . that involves *actual or threatened death or serious injury, or a threat to the physical integrity of self or others* [italics added]" (American Psychiatric Association, 1994).

When screening for trauma as part of an assessment of PTSD, it is preferable that the screen be highly specific as to type of event and that it only include events that might qualify according to the *DSM–IV* criteria for PTSD. Even within this more specific category, it may be important to consider the types of trauma that the particular population has experienced and the kinds of traumas that are likely to lead to psychiatric problems. For example, one in four girls in the United States is sexually assaulted by age 18 (Finkelhor, Hotaling, Lewis, & Smith, 1990), and adolescents are the highest risk group for sexual assault in the U.S. population (Klaus & Rennison, 2002). Rates for minority women are higher than those for Caucasian women. Compared with nontraumatized peers, victims of sexual assault traumas are three times as likely to develop psychiatric disorders and four times as likely to develop substance abuse problems. A provider working with adolescent or young adult women from minority backgrounds, even when the focus of the intervention is on a totally different topic (e.g., mothering skills) and not explicitly trauma related, should consider how trauma issues may impact clients and the work of the program. If trauma screening is to be implemented, agencies should also be sensitive to choosing culturally appropriate sexual abuse and assault items in screening their client group for trauma exposure.

Some trauma history measures go beyond simple endorsement of exposure to a traumatic event or events and provide additional information, useful in subsequent PTSD screening and also in understanding the client's subjective and personal experience of the trauma. It is possible to screen for emotional responses to the event or events (e.g., "Did you think your life or the lives of others were in danger?" or "Did you feel intense fear, helplessness, or horror?"), for actual harm resulting from the trauma (e.g., "Were you seriously injured?"), and for age at time of the event(s) and the number of times the trauma(s) occurred.

The Brief Trauma Questionnaire (BTQ; Schnurr, Vielhauer, Weathers, & Findler, 1999) is a 10-item self-report trauma exposure screen that can be administered quickly and has shown suitability for special populations such as persons with severe mental illness as well as for general population groups. The BTQ asks respondents for a simple yes or no answer to the question, "Have you experienced this event?" for each of the 10 listed types of traumatic events. For each yes response, the respondent is also asked two additional yes or no questions: "Did you think your life was in danger or you might be seriously injured?" and "Were you seriously injured?" The BTQ is designed to quickly screen for many different and prevalent types of traumatic experiences, including war traumas, serious car accidents, natural disasters, exposure to violent death, life-threatening illness, and physical or sexual abuse. As with many of the self-report measures, the questions on the BTQ can be easily modified for presentation by a clinician to clients who might have difficulty with reading comprehension. Whereas the BTQ provides a screen for the *DSM–IV* Axis I (A1) criterion necessary to make a PTSD diagnosis (exposure to a specific type of traumatic event), it does not screen for the Axis II (A2) criterion (a response of fear, helplessness, or horror). Whether the client has the required emotional response to his or her trauma can be assessed by using either a different trauma exposure measure with an A2 question included (such as the Trauma History Screen or the Trauma History Questionnaire) or a second, subsequent measure that specifically assesses presence of PTSD.

Above all, the decision leading to choice of trauma exposure instrument should be framed by the following parameters: population characteristics, types of traumas that need to be covered, time constraints for the assessment, skill level of the administrators, and setting for the evaluation. The clinician's choice of instrument might be different if the population being treated is very specific, such as refugees, combat veterans, or abused women. Even if it is known that a certain type of trauma is most prevalent in the particular client base (e.g., war trauma or sexual abuse victims), the clinician might decide that a comprehensive, rather than a narrow, trauma screen could provide additional and useful clinical information. A busy clinic setting with limited privacy, nonclinical staff, or a limited time for assessment might argue for using a self-report measure rather than an interviewer. In summary, it is recommended that trauma assessment begin with the simplest and briefest screen that will meet the needs of the population. Many more details about the traumatic events and possible emotional reactivity can be uncovered during the next part of the evaluation process: screening for PTSD and PTSD symptoms. Table 2.1 provides the list of traumatic screens on the National Center for PTSD Web site as discussed previously and is a good starting point for examining possible screening instruments.

Screening for Posttraumatic Stress Disorder Symptoms

Some people who experience serious, life-threatening traumatic events are psychologically hearty and do not develop long-term symptoms or reactions that necessitate treatment. The trauma screen is a simply a first step, documenting that traumatic events have occurred and often also showing that there is emotional distress related to the exposure. People who are vulnerable to psychological traumatization can exhibit a variety of symptoms (e.g., severe depression) and reactions (e.g., substance abuse) but do not necessarily exhibit the particular constellation of symptoms and reactions that are necessary conditions for meeting the *DSM–IV* diagnosis of PTSD.

PTSD screening is a means of assessing (a) whether or not a client has an emotional disturbance related to the trauma and (b) the likelihood that the symptoms and emotional reactions to the trauma will meet criteria for a diagnosis of PTSD. Most PTSD screens are designed to be brief and to elicit intensity, frequency (or both) of symptoms and reactions to Criterion A (which includes Criteria A1 and A2, already described) traumas. Probably the most widely used and researched screen is the PCL (Weathers, Litz, Herman, Huska, & Keane, 1993). A self-report rating scale, the PCL has good psychometric properties, including internal and test–retest reliability, and convergent validity (Blanchard et al., 1996).

TABLE 2.1
Trauma Exposure Measures

Trauma exposure measure	Format	No. of items	Time to administer (minutes)	Assesses *DSM–IV* Criterion A?
Combat Exposure Scale (CES)	Self-report	7	5	No
Evaluation of Lifetime Stressors (ELS)	Self-report and interview	56	60–360	Yes
Life Stressor Checklist— Revised (LSC–R)	Self-report	30	15–30	Yes
National Women's Study Event History	Interview	17	15–30	A1 only
Potential Stressful Events Interview (PSEI)	Interview	62	120	Yes
Stressful Life Events Screening Questionnaire (SLESQ)	Self-report	13	10–15	No
Trauma Assessment for Adults (TAA)	Self-report and interview	17	10–15	A1 only
Trauma History Screen (THS)	Self-report	13	2–5	Yes
Trauma History Questionnaire (THQ)	Self-report	24	10–15	A1 only
Traumatic Events Questionnaire (TEQ)	Self-report	13	5	A1 only
Traumatic Life Events Questionnaire (TLEQ)	Self-report	25	10–15	A1 only
Trauma History Questionnaire (THQ)	Self-report	24	10–15	Yes
Traumatic Stress Schedule (TSS)	Interview	9	5–30	A1 only

Note. Target group for all measures is adults. Table reprinted from the U.S. Department of Veterans Affairs, National Center for PTSD Assessments (2007). *DSM–IV = Diagnostic and Statistical Manual of Mental Disorders* (4th ed.).

The PCL contains 17 questions that map onto the three *DSM–IV* PTSD symptom clusters: reexperiencing, avoidance, and arousal. Respondents are asked to look at a list of "problems and complaints that people sometimes have in response to stressful life experiences" and then decide how much each problem has bothered them over the past 3 months. The response choices are distributed on a 5-point intensity scale and range from 1 = *not at all* to 5 = *extremely*. For example, Question 1 asks the respondent if they have "repeated, disturbing memories, thoughts, or images of a stressful experience from the past?" Question 17 asks if the person is "feeling jumpy or easily startled." Several versions of the PCL are tailored for specific populations, and a short form for use in primary care contains only six questions (Lang & Stein, 2005). The PCL for civilians comes in two versions: in one (PTSD Checklist—Civilian), there is no specification required of the traumatic event; in the other (PTSD

Checklist—Specific), the respondent is asked to name the specific traumatic event before completing the symptom checklist. The PCL has proved feasible, practical, and reliable in both research studies and clinical applications in screening for PTSD in multiple military and civilian populations (Dobie et al., 2002; Grubaugh, Elhai, Cusack, Wells, & Frueh, 2007), including use for psychiatric inpatients and outpatients with multiple, severe disorders (Mueser et al., 1998; Mueser et al., 2008; Mueser, Salyers, et al., 2004). Moreover, in instances in which concerns such as staff time or the burden of scoring make automation desirable, the PCL has been successfully applied in a Web-based, computer-assisted format and used in special populations of clients with severe mental illness and adolescents seeking care in community mental health settings (Wolford et al., 2008).

Two common techniques are used for scoring the PCL. Because the scale allows respondents to report the degree to which each of the 17 criteria symptoms "bothers" them (on a scale of 1 = *not at all* to 5 = *extremely*), each respondent will have a score of 17 (no symptoms) to 85 (all symptoms present at an extreme level). Most research with civilian populations has shown that an efficient cutoff score for screening is a total of 45, but the score that is most useful in some special populations may be somewhat higher. The second method for scoring the PCL is to examine responses to determine whether the "1-3-2 rule" has been met. That is, did the respondent endorse one reexperiencing (Items 1–5), three avoidant (Items 6–12), and two hyperarousal symptoms (Items 13–17) at a moderate or greater level of severity?

Aside from identifying likely cases of PTSD, the PCL can serve as a useful tool for giving the clinician specific information about changes in the nature and severity of a client's PTSD symptoms over the course of treatment. If a client reports intrusive thoughts, sleep disturbance, or difficulty with concentration, these personal issues can represent a starting point for discussion, education about the disorder, and shared decision making about treatment. The PCL and other PTSD screening and self-report measures are listed in Table 2.2.

The information obtained from a brief PTSD screen enables the clinician to make a more informed decision about next steps in the assessment process. Unlike trauma history screens, the responses to screens for PTSD such as the PCL are scored. Both total score (level of symptom intensity) and the pattern of symptoms endorsed offer important data for deciding on readiness for therapeutic intervention and appropriateness of specific PTSD treatment. For example, presence of trauma exposure and a negative PTSD screen could lead the clinician to assess for alternative diagnoses associated with trauma such as depression. A low total score, but with responses indicating a worrisome symptom pattern, might mean that the client has a level of symptomatology that is currently manageable. A clinician might decide to delay entry into treatment to see whether the symptoms resolve or become exacerbated.

TABLE 2.2
Posttraumatic Stress Disorder (PTSD) Screens

Corresponds to PTSD screen	No. items	Time to admin. (min.)	Allows multiple trauma?	DSM–IV criteria?
Distressing Event Questionnaire	35	10–15	Yes	Yes
Impact of Events Scale—Revised	22	5–10	No	Yes
Los Angeles Symptom Checklist	43	10–15	Yes	No
Mississippi Scale for Combat-Related PTSD Modified PTSD Symptom Scale	17	10–15	Yes	No
Penn Inventory for Posttraumatic Stress Disorder	27	15–20	Yes	No
PTSD Checklist (PCL)—Civilian, Military, Specific Trauma	17	5–10	Yes	Yes
Purdue PTSD Scale	17	5–10	No	Yes
Revised Civilian Mississippi Scale for PTSD	30	5–10	No	Yes
Screen for Posttraumatic Stress Symptoms	17	10–15	Yes	Yes
Trauma Symptom Inventory	100	15–20	Yes	No
Trauma Symptom Checklist—40	40	10–15	Yes	No
Primary Care PTSD Screen	4	2	Yes	N/A
Short PTSD Rating Interview (SPRINT)	8	3	Yes	N/A
Beck Anxiety Interview—Primary Care	7	3	Yes	N/A
Short Form of the PTSD Checklist	6	2	Yes	N/A
Short Screening Scale for PTSD	7	3	Yes	N/A
SPAN (startle, physical upset, anger, numbness)	4	2	Yes	N/A
Trauma Screening Questionnaire	10	4	Yes	N/A

Note. Table adapted from the U.S. Department of Veterans Affairs, National Center for PTSD Assessments, (2007). DSM–IV = Diagnostic and Statistical Manual of Mental Disorders (4th ed.).

Diagnosis of Posttraumatic Stress Disorder

As discussed, PTSD is defined by three types of symptoms: (a) reexperiencing the trauma, (b) avoiding trauma-related stimuli, and (c) overarousal. These symptoms must be related to the index trauma, persist or develop at least 1 month after exposure to that trauma, and lead to impairment of function (DSM–IV). Examples of reexperiencing include intrusive, unwanted memories of the event, nightmares, flashbacks, and distress when exposed to reminders of the traumatic event, such as being in the vicinity of the trauma or meeting someone with similarities to the perpetrator. Avoidance symptoms include efforts to avoid thoughts, feelings, or activities related to the trauma; inability to recall important aspects of the traumatic events; diminished interest in significant activities; detachment; restricted affect; and a foreshortened sense of future. Overarousal symptoms include hypervigilance, exaggerated startle response, difficulty falling or staying asleep, difficulty concentrating, and irritability or anger outbursts. DSM–IV criteria require that a person must have at least one intrusive, three avoidant, and two arousal symptoms to be diagnosed with PTSD.

When a client screens positive for PTSD using a validated measure like the PCL, there is a markedly increased probability that he or she will meet the diagnostic criteria for PTSD. Multiple studies have shown that there is excellent correlation between scoring positive for PTSD on the PCL and PTSD diagnosis established with gold standard PTSD diagnostic measures.

By *gold standard measures*, we mean instruments that have been assessed in multiple rigorous studies and have demonstrated good reliability and validity for PTSD diagnoses. For this reason, they have garnered consensus support from experts in the field and are used in research studies and in forensic and insurance evaluations. They are much lengthier to administer than the PCL (often taking between 1 and 2 hours), require clinical expertise and training for the administrator, and are usually in interview format. They do provide much more detail about the nature of the trauma, the emotional response, and the possible associated problems in functioning. Probably the best established measure of this type is the CAPS.

The CAPS is a semistructured interview for the assessment of PTSD that takes between 1 and 2 hours to administer, depending on the characteristics of the population to be evaluated. Both frequency and intensity ratings are calculated for each of the 17 *DSM–IV* symptoms of PTSD. For example, if the respondent states that he or she has recurrent memories of the trauma, he or she is then asked, "How often?" Possible responses can range from once or twice a month to daily or every day. The respondent is then asked how much distress or discomfort the memories cause. Responses can range from mild distress or disruption of activities to extreme, incapacitating distress. Interviewers are also asked to judge whether each symptom described appears to be trauma related. This is an important distinction to make because in some populations, such as persons with severe mental illness, symptoms might be related to an ongoing psychotic process or a neurocognitive deficit rather than to exposure to a specific trauma. Symptoms are defined as *present* if they meet a minimum frequency and intensity level. Diagnosis of PTSD is computed by calculating the number of required reexperiencing, avoidant, and arousal symptoms endorsed by the client. The overall severity of PTSD is determined by adding all the intensity and frequency scores to yield the CAPS total score. In addition, responses to CAPS questions provide information on the duration of the disturbance and on level of functioning (self-care and independent living skills, subjective distress, impairment in social functioning, and impairment in occupation or life role functioning). Systematic research indicates that the CAPS is a reliable and valid instrument for assessing PTSD in persons with severe mental illness (Mueser et al., 2001) as well as for evaluating PTSD in general populations.

For any assessment, it is worth thinking about the practicality and cost–benefit issues of using an instrument like the CAPS, in terms of the value of its additional yield in precision and depth of information. As an alternative, clinicians may consider using a briefer instrument like the Posttraumatic Stress Diagnostic Scale (described in the next paragraph) or even relying on the PCL, which takes less than 10 minutes to administer and can be administered via computer, for diagnosis and severity assessment. For example, in one study the correlation between the PCL (using the "moderately severe" cut-point) and the CAPS was 0.929 (Wolford et al., 2008).

A leading alternative diagnostic measure for PTSD that might be useful to clinicians is the Posttraumatic Stress Diagnostic Scale (PDS; Foa & Tolin, 2000). This 49-item instrument includes a trauma history section and like the PCL, can be used to either screen for or diagnose PTSD. It can be administered to individuals from ages 17 to 65 years, and the questions are written at an 8th-grade reading level. The PDS is a self-report instrument (although it can be used as an interview), takes approximately 15 minutes to administer, and the questions parallel the DSM–IV criteria for PTSD. The PDS provides a diagnosis, number of symptoms, a symptom severity score, and level of impairment of functioning. It has four parts. Part 1 provides a trauma history. Part 2 asks which traumatic event bothers the respondent most, when the event happened, what was the level of danger and client's emotional response. Part 3 is a list of problems related to the trauma, frequency, onset time, and duration of symptoms. Part 4 asks the respondent to check off how much the PTSD problems have interfered with his or her work, relationships, leisure activities, and other areas of daily life. The CAPS and the PDS have been shown to correlate strongly with each other and thus perform about equally well for diagnosing as assessing change in PTSD symptoms.

ASSESSING OTHER DOMAINS IN CLIENTS WITH POSTTRAUMATIC STRESS DISORDER

Clinicians treating clients with PTSD should consider assessing several other related areas prior to therapeutic engagement. These measures can focus on important comorbid conditions and overall functioning, which impact treatment planning, or on process measures that can help to direct and monitor treatment progress.

The most common conditions that are comorbid with PTSD are depression and substance abuse. Assessing the level of depression and suicidal ideation is important in the clinician's preparation prior to initiating the cognitive restructuring (CR) for PTSD treatment program. The standardized CBT program described here has been shown to reduce depressive symptoms as well as PTSD symptoms in people with severe mental illness (Mueser et al., 2008).

However, as the clinician guides a client through the treatment modules, there might be some temporary increases in stress levels and emotional strain. Assessing depression prior to therapy and at points during the process is recommended for monitoring the level of distress, ensuring the client's safety, and optimal pacing of the sessions. In addition, because the primary clinical method for treating PTSD in this program is cognitive restructuring, which is one of the best-validated psychotherapeutic interventions for depression, assessing and monitoring depression over the course of the program provide opportunities for directly targeting thoughts, beliefs, and schemas that contribute to depression, whether or not they are related to the individual's traumatic experiences. The Beck Depression Inventory—II (A. T. Beck, Steer, & Brown, 1996) is a well-validated self-report scale for depression that has been used in a wide range of studies on different populations and disorders, including our research on the CR for PTSD program for persons with severe mental illness.

Screening for substance abuse or dependence is also recommended prior to enrolling a client in PTSD treatment. Alcohol and drugs are commonly used to avoid memories and cope with PTSD symptoms. A measure that has been used successfully in many trauma populations, including adolescents, is the CRAFFT (Knight, Sherritt, Shrier, Harris, & Change, 2002). The CRAFFT is a six-item screen that does not specifically ask the respondent to reveal exactly how much he or she uses substances. Instead, it is more indirect, for example, "Have you ever ridden in a car driven by someone (including yourself) who was 'high' or had been using alcohol?" and "Do you ever forget things you did while using alcohol or drugs?" In our experience, screening positive for substance abuse should not rule out a client engaging in the CR for PTSD program. However, dependence on substances can adversely affect attendance.

Many clients with posttraumatic disorders also grapple with a variety of other psychiatric problems and may have periods during which they exhibit poor or marginal overall adaptation. Overall psychiatric symptoms can be assessed with the expanded version of the Brief Psychiatric Rating Scale (BPRS; Lukoff, Nuechterlein, & Ventura, 1986), a widely used measure that taps a broad range of psychiatric symptoms (Shafer, 2005). Because there is overlap between PTSD symptoms and symptoms of other severe mental illnesses—for example, hypervigilance—it is often difficult for a clinician to determine how much a given symptom is related to the reported trauma. Information gathered by use of the BPRS can help clarify whether the symptoms presented by the client are more likely trauma related or a reflection of another underlying psychiatric condition.

As discussed in chapter 1 of this volume, a group of clients that has been the focus of much concern in the trauma literature are those people with so-called complex PTSD or disorders of extreme stress, not otherwise specified (DESNOS; Luxenberg, Spinazzola, Hidalgo, Hunt, & van der Kolk, 2001).

These clients have typically suffered early traumatization (generally before age 10) from multiple forms of abuse and neglect and are characterized by impairments and symptoms that go beyond the intrusive, avoidant, and arousal symptoms seen in simpler, less chronic forms of PTSD. Although not formally listed as a *DSM* diagnosis, the DESNOS construct was assessed as part of a large *DSM–IV* field trial and conceptualized as having seven primary symptom types: alterations in affect and impulses (e.g., self-destructiveness), alterations in attention of consciousness (e.g., amnesia, depersonalization), alterations in self-perception, alterations in perceptions of the perpetrator, alterations in relations with others, somatization, and alterations in systems of meaning (e.g., loss of faith, increased sense of hopelessness or despair). If early, severe abuse is known or suspected, complex PTSD can be assessed with a structured interview, the Structural Interview for Disorders of Extreme Stress (known as "SIDES"; developed by Pelcovitz, 1997, and available from the author). It may be crucial to the safety and potential clinical benefit of these clients that clinicians treating them for PTSD symptoms per se be aware of their multiple vulnerabilities and ways of coping (e.g., use of self-injurious behaviors to control anxiety or other unbearable affect).

Knowledge about the disorder of PTSD can be an important factor in preparing and motivating the client for treatment. It can help the client to understand the rationale for the elements and components of the therapy. It is often surprising how little clients may know, or how distorted their knowledge is regarding PTSD, even if they have suffered with the disorder for years. Level of knowledge about PTSD (the symptoms, reactions, and associated problems) can be assessed with the PTSD Knowledge Test. This test contains 15 multiple choice questions about PTSD. In one study of people with severe mental illness, the coefficient alpha for the test was .68 and the test–retest reliability over a 4- to 5- month no-treatment period was .65 (Mueser et al., 2008). In addition, the test has been shown to be sensitive to the effects of an education program about PTSD (Pratt et al., 2005), as well as the CR for PTSD program described in this book (Mueser et al., 2008). It can provide background information that can help shape the discussion when the clinician begins the psychoeducational module of this program.

As we have discussed, posttraumatic disorders manifest themselves on multiple levels: biological, affective, and cognitive. The CR for PTSD program focuses on helping clients challenge and alter the cognitive distortions believed to underlie PTSD. This approach is based on the theory (as well as empirical findings) that altering trauma-related cognitions can lead to reductions in affective and biological symptoms as well. In line with this theory and earlier findings, a recently completed randomized controlled trial of the CR for PTSD program in people with severe mental illness found that changes in posttraumatic cognitions mediated improvements in PTSD symptoms over the course of therapy and at follow-up (Mueser et al., 2008).

Thus, evaluating trauma-related cognitions before and during treatment can provide valuable information about potentially important beliefs to target with cognitive restructuring, and success at altering those beliefs.

Trauma-related cognitions can be evaluated with the Posttraumatic Cognitions Inventory (Foa, Ehlers, Clark, Tolin, & Orsillo, 1999), a self-report measure focusing on common negative thoughts and beliefs about oneself, other people, and the world that frequently occur in individuals with PTSD. This scale consists of 36 items that represent the cognitive changes seen in many trauma survivors. Items represent three major classes of cognition: negative cognitions about the self (e.g., "I feel like an object, not a person"); negative cognitions about the world (e.g., "People are not what they seem"); and self-blame (e.g., "Somebody else would not have gotten into this situation"). High scores correspond to greater endorsement of negative or trauma-distorted beliefs.

SUMMARY AND CONCLUSIONS

Trauma exposure and posttraumatic disorders are quite common in the U.S. population and much more common in special populations such as people with mental illness, refugees, inner city residents, and adolescents. It is worthwhile and relatively easy to screen people entering services for trauma exposure and posttraumatic symptoms. A number of good screens are available, and choice of instruments should depend on the particular issues in the population being studied (e.g., common types of trauma, literacy level, preferred language). In some cases, more precise diagnostic information may be required, and there are several gold standard assessments available for diagnosis of PTSD. The two most common comorbid disorders associated with PTSD are depression and substance use disorder. Brief, reliable tools for assessing these conditions are available, and it is often important to evaluate clients with posttraumatic symptoms for depression and substance abuse at the beginning of treatment and as treatment progresses. Less commonly, complex PTSD may be suspected, and assessment of these symptoms may be clinically useful.

3

AN OVERVIEW OF THE COGNITIVE RESTRUCTURING FOR POSTTRAUMATIC STRESS DISORDER PROGRAM

KIM T. MUESER, STANLEY D. ROSENBERG,
AND HARRIET J. ROSENBERG

This chapter provides an overview of the Cognitive Restructuring for Posttraumatic Stress Disorder (CR for PTSD) program, including the rationale and a brief description of each of the core program components. We also address the coordination of the program with other mental health or substance abuse treatment services the client may be receiving. Finally, we consider the role of social support for clients participating in treatment and how such support can be used to further the goals of the program.

CORE COMPONENTS OF THE COGNITIVE RESTRUCTURING FOR POSTTRAUMATIC STRESS DISORDER PROGRAM

Treatment begins with basic preparatory work, including an *orientation to the treatment program* and its components, followed by developing a *crisis response plan*. Next, *breathing retraining* is taught as a strategy for helping individuals cope with and reduce high anxiety levels. *Psychoeducation* is then provided about the nature of trauma, PTSD, and other problems commonly associated with trauma, such as interpersonal difficulties. *Cognitive restructuring* (CR) is then taught to help clients manage their negative feelings and to correct erroneous trauma-related beliefs about themselves, other people, and the world. *Generalization training* and *termination* are conducted toward the end of the program to ensure that clients are able to use CR on their own outside of sessions, to review treatment gains, and to discuss any plans to meet ongoing or potential needs that may arise in the future. Table 3.1 summarizes the approximate session numbers in which the different components of the program are covered. A brief description of each component is provided next.

Orientation to the Treatment Program

After assessments have been conducted to confirm that an individual has PTSD, a brief description of the program is usually provided to gauge the person's interest in treatment and to identify any obstacles that could interfere with his or her participation (e.g., transportation to sessions). If the person expresses interest, and no major obstacles are identified for which workable solutions cannot be found, the first session is scheduled.

The purpose of the orientation session is to provide the client with specific information about what will occur in the upcoming sessions and to set clear, positive expectations for active participation and change during and after the program. The orientation begins with the therapist addressing the purpose of the program (i.e., to help individuals cope with and overcome posttraumatic reactions), logistics (e.g., session frequency and length), the components of the program, other considerations (e.g., social support), and homework. Using a handout titled "Orientation to the CR for PTSD Program" (Handout #1; see Appendix) the therapist briefly reviews and explains each issue, eliciting and responding to clients' questions in an upbeat, positive manner. Potential problems or concerns are dealt with when they arise in this overview discussion (e.g., the client has limited reading or writing skills).

TABLE 3.1
Outline of Cognitive Restructuring for Posttraumatic Stress Disorder
Program Modules, Estimated Time, and Corresponding Session Numbers

Module	Approximate time	Session no.
Orientation to program	15–20 minutes	1
Crisis response plan	15–20 minutes	1
Breathing retraining	15–20 minutes	1
Psychoeducation	2 hours	2–3
Cognitive restructuring	8–12 hours	4–16
Generalization training and termination	2–4 hours	12–16

Crisis Response Plan

People with PTSD frequently have other disorders as well (e.g., mental illness, substance use disorder, medical illness) and may experience multiple challenges trying to navigate their lives. As a result of their posttraumatic reactions, which are often complicated by these other disorders, traumatized individuals are often vulnerable to crises that can threaten their well-being and their ability to participate in the program. Developing a crisis plan is a collaborative effort aimed at agreeing on what constitutes a crisis for that individual, on the early signs that a crisis might be impending, and on an action plan for what to do in case the early warning signs of a crisis appear or a crisis actually occurs. It also begins the work of the treatment in an active, collaborative manner.

The crisis plan is summarized on the Crisis Plan Checklist Worksheet (Handout #2; see the Appendix for this and other handouts). Crisis plans focus on common crises such as the reemergence or worsening of psychiatric symptoms (e.g., depression, self-injurious or suicidal thoughts or behavior); resumption or worsening of drug or alcohol use, abuse, or dependence; or loss of housing. Significant others, as well as other treatment providers, are often involved in the client's crisis response plan.

When developing a crisis plan, the therapist emphasizes that the top priority in treatment is to ensure the client's safety so that he or she can successfully complete the program and reclaim his or her life from traumatic experiences. By doing this, the therapist helps the client view the crisis plan as a "safety net" and not as something that could threaten or terminate his or her participation in the program. The crisis plan is written down and shared with any appropriate supportive persons.

Breathing Retraining

Most persons with posttraumatic disorders experience significant, and often debilitating, anxiety. Because the teaching of CR does not usually begin until the fourth session, clients can benefit immediately from learning a simple skill for reducing their anxiety—breathing retraining, which is a commonly taught skill for helping people manage and reduce their anxiety. The technique involves teaching the client to slow down the rate of breathing by taking normal breaths in and then exhaling slowly and gradually. Breathing retraining is taught through a combination of therapist modeling, in-session practice, and homework.

There are two advantages to teaching breathing retraining early in the program. First, the skill is relatively easy to learn and can provide rapid relief once the client has practiced it a number of times. Breathing retraining can then serve as a valuable tool for managing the anxiety clients experience in their daily lives before they become proficient at CR. Second, teaching this skill sends an important meta-message: "You [the client] can exert a lot more control over negative feelings than you have imagined. This treatment can teach you skills that you can use to make yourself less anxious and more in control." Third, once breathing retraining has been taught, the therapist can prompt the client to use the skill in the event that he or she becomes overwhelmed with anxiety during a treatment session. Because severe anxiety during a session can interfere with ability to learn, breathing retraining provides a useful remedy that can often bring quick relief and enable the client to resume working on trauma-related issues with the therapist after a brief break.

Psychoeducation About Posttraumatic Disorders

Psychoeducation involves teaching clients about the nature of post-traumatic disorders, such as how *trauma* is defined and the common symptoms of these disorders (e.g., nightmares), and serves to "normalize" a person's reactions to the events. Because many people with posttraumatic disorders have rarely or never talked about their reactions, it is not uncommon for a client, during an educational session, to utter something on the order of, "I thought I was crazy! You mean other people have these same problems?" By understanding that other people who are exposed to traumatic events experience the same kinds of problems, clients often feel validated and relieved that they are not alone in their trauma reactions.

In addition to normalizing the client's reactions to traumatic events, information about posttraumatic symptoms and associated problems can increase motivation to work on and overcome these characteristic difficulties. As clients learn about posttraumatic disorders, they often realize that many of their personal challenges are related to their traumatic experiences. For example, clients do not typically realize that problems trusting other people are common in people with posttraumatic disorders, and understanding this suggests to them that participation in the program could improve their interpersonal relationships.

Psychoeducation usually requires two sessions, with handouts guiding the discussion between the therapist and client. Information is taught interactively, with an emphasis on helping clients identify which symptoms they have experienced, what the symptoms are like, and how they are problematic. By the end of the psychoeducation module, the therapist should have a good grasp of how the posttraumatic disorder has had an impact on the client's life. In addition, the therapist and client should identify at least one area of functioning affected by the disorder that the client is motivated to improve, such as social relationships or caring for his or her children. Identifying functional goals for participation in the CR for PTSD program can further increase the client's motivation to change while providing a practical focus for some of the collaborative work.

Cognitive Restructuring

CR is the heart of the CR for PTSD program, and the majority of treatment sessions are focused on it. It is through the teaching, practice, and systematic application of this skill that most symptoms and problems associated with posttraumatic disorders can be reduced or eliminated. In addition, collaboration with other treatment providers or significant others is primarily focused on helping clients apply this skill in their daily lives.

CR is a strategy for identifying, evaluating, and changing inaccurate thoughts and beliefs that lead to negative feelings. Because life experiences, especially traumatic ones, affect how people view themselves, others, and the world, CR is a tool for systematically examining those thoughts and beliefs that result in posttraumatic symptoms and altering them accordingly. The primary emphasis is on teaching CR to clients as a skill for dealing with negative emotions such as anxiety, depression, guilt or shame, and anger, rather than the therapist using it as a method for changing the client's thoughts and perceptions. Maintaining the focus of therapy on the client learning CR as a self-management skill avoids the unnecessary conflict and alienation from treatment that can arise when the therapist attempts to persuade a client that his or her thoughts are inaccurate. Early sessions usually focus on teaching CR to help clients deal with any negative feelings they may experience, whereas later sessions focus more closely on thoughts, beliefs, and schemas related to traumatic events, if they have not been previously addressed.

Teaching CR begins with an introduction to the thought–feeling model to acquaint clients with the concept that emotions are influenced by specific thoughts and beliefs that may or may not be accurate. Next, clients are introduced to the common styles of thinking, which are based on the concept of cognitive distortions developed for cognitive–behavioral therapy for depression and anxiety by A. T. Beck (e.g., A. T. Beck, 1963; A. T. Beck et al., 1979). A handout is reviewed with the client that describes the common styles of thinking (Handout #7; see Appendix), and for each style clients are encouraged to see whether they can identify any examples of situations in which they engaged in that style of thinking. After some or all of the common styles have been reviewed in a session, the client is given homework to practice identifying thoughts related to negative feelings, determining whether the thoughts fit a common style of thinking, and if so, coming up with a more accurate thought. Between one and two sessions are usually devoted to the common styles of thinking, although additional sessions may be devoted to this skill later in therapy, as discussed later. By the end of the first session teaching common styles of thinking, many clients have enough of a grasp of the skill to begin using it and experiencing benefits in terms of relief from feelings of anxiety, depression, and guilt.

After clients have a basic understanding of the common styles of thinking, they are introduced to the 5 Steps of CR. The 5 Steps of CR concept makes it easier to link current negative feelings to trauma-related beliefs and schemas because clients are given guidelines for exploring how thoughts may be related to more fundamental beliefs and schemas. This allows for a closer examination and disputation of beliefs and schemas that stem from traumatic experiences and contribute to posttraumatic symptoms. Unlike the common styles of thinking, the 5 Steps of CR concept does not assume that all negative feelings result from inaccurate or distorted thoughts or beliefs. Instead, the 5 Steps of CR concept provides a structure for evaluating the accuracy of thoughts related to negative emotions and, when these thoughts are judged to be accurate, prompts clients to develop an action plan to deal with the situation and the negative feelings associated with it. This can be useful because it can help clients learn how to deal with genuine problem situations that cause distress rather than trying to avoid those situations, which often get worse in the long run.

The 5 Steps of CR are (a) describe the situation, (b) identify the strongest negative feeling, (c) identify the thought most strongly related to that feeling, (d) evaluate the thought by considering objective evidence supporting and not supporting the thought, and (e) take action. The final step involves either changing the thought to a more accurate one if it was not supported by the evidence or formulating an action plan to do something about the situation that is causing the negative feeling. As with the common styles of thinking, clients are taught that the cue for using the 5 Steps of CR is the experience of negative emotions.

Many clients have difficulty articulating specific thoughts related to their negative feelings. To help clients improve their skills at this, they are taught some basic strategies for identifying thoughts related to feelings, using a handout ("Guide to Thoughts and Feelings"; Handout #12; see Appendix). This handout describes common thoughts related to four major negative feelings (anxiety, depression, shame or guilt, and anger) and provides questions clients can ask themselves to pinpoint what thoughts or beliefs are related to a negative feeling.

When the 5 Steps of CR are introduced to the client, usually in Session 5 or 6, the therapist helps the client apply each skill to a current or recent feeling in the same session. This provides some immediate relief to the client, either in the form of reducing the negative feeling or coming up with a concrete plan for dealing with it, and reinforces the skill. As with the common styles of thinking, at the end of each session a homework assignment is collaboratively agreed on for the clients to practice the 5 Steps of CR.

Although using the 5 Steps of CR is the most powerful method for identifying and challenging thoughts and beliefs that contribute to negative feelings, it is also a complex skill that some clients have difficulty learning to do on their own. To overcome the difficulties, the therapist can simplify the CR skill to make it easier for clients to use on their own. For example, some clients find it more helpful to return to using the common styles of thinking as the preferred method of CR. Others may find it useful to simply brainstorm different ways of thinking about a problem situation to reinforce that there are multiple perspectives for any given situation, rather than formally weighing the evidence for and against a particular thought. Other modifications to CR are possible as well. The ultimate goal is to help the client develop a skill for dealing with negative emotions that involves examining his or her thoughts and beliefs related to those feelings, including trauma-related thoughts and beliefs, and either modifying them accordingly or weakening their impact on the individual.

Generalization Training and Termination

As with most cognitive–behavioral treatment approaches, clients are prepared for termination from the beginning of therapy. Generalization training is integral to termination because it focuses on ensuring that clients are able to use CR on their own following the termination of treatment. For most clients, a full course of 16 treatment sessions is provided, so that the client and therapist are both aware of when treatment will end, and this is discussed in previous sessions. For clients who demonstrate more rapid improvement in their posttraumatic symptoms, an earlier termination date can be agreed on.

In addition to discussing termination before the final session, another way of preparing for the end of therapy with clients who are in separate mental health or substance abuse treatment is for the therapist to arrange for a key provider (e.g., the client's case manager) to attend one of the later sessions and for the client to explain what he or she has found helpful in the program, including the CR skill. This session can serve to both reinforce the client for skills he or she has learned and treatment-related gains and to give the key provider some specific strategies that can be used to support the client after termination (e.g., prompting the client to use CR if he or she experiences significant distress).

The final session is mainly devoted to reviewing accomplishments made during prior sessions, talking about how to manage any ongoing posttraumatic symptoms, and anticipating possible needs the client may have in the future. It is not uncommon for clients to continue to experience posttraumatic symptoms at the end of therapy, despite having made gains in the program, including learning CR skills. Clients are informed that this often happens and that continued practice of their breathing retraining and CR skills after therapy ends often results in further improvements in and even recovery from their troubling symptoms.

Symptom Monitoring Throughout the Program

Monitoring PTSD and depression severity over the course of the program provides invaluable information to the clinician about the effectiveness of treatment and areas of client distress. We recommend using the PTSD Checklist (PCL) and Beck Depression Inventory—II (BDI; A. T. Beck, Steer, & Brown, 1996) to monitor symptoms at the beginning of every third session (e.g., Sessions 1, 4, 7, 10, 13, 16). It is most helpful if the clinician scores these self-report scales as soon as they are completed and briefly discusses them with the client afterward. Symptoms that are especially distressing can be the focus of some work during the session, such as using CR to address persistent PTSD or depressive symptoms.

Coordination of Treatment With Other Providers

People with posttraumatic disorders such as PTSD frequently have co-occurring disorders, including other mental illnesses and substance use disorders, and they may be receiving treatment for those disorders (Kessler et al., 1995; S. H. Stewart, Pihl, Conrod, & Dongier, 1998). People with severe mental illnesses in particular often receive treatment from a variety of different providers, who may function as a team working out of a local community mental health center. When the client is receiving treatment from other providers, it is crucial that the CR for PTSD program is provided in a coordinated, integrated fashion with the other services. To effectively treat posttraumatic disorders, it is important for the therapist to maintain the focus of therapy on those problems and to avoid allowing therapy to be diverted to addressing a wide range of client needs that are not directly related to these disorders. Housing, medical, legal, and pharmacological treatment needs can all interfere with maintaining the focus of the CR for PTSD program unless other treatment providers are attending to these needs.

Coordinating treatment with other providers, and informing them about the nature and goals of the CR for PTSD program, is essential if those individuals are to support the client's participation. Professionals often have mixed opinions and feelings about the importance of posttraumatic disorders in the lives of the clients whom they treat, and some of concerns may be related to their own histories of trauma. Many professionals are highly supportive of client participation in trauma-focused treatment, but some are concerned that treatment will be unduly stressful and could precipitate relapses or other deteriorations in functioning that could be their responsibility to attend to. These concerns may be especially prominent if the provider believes the treatment approach is based not on CR but on therapeutic exposure, which is often perceived as highly stressful. Addressing these concerns and developing strategies for jointly monitoring the client's symptoms and functioning throughout the program is critical to enlisting the support of other providers. Furthermore, informing other treatment providers about the CR for PTSD program, including the rudiments of CR, and keeping them up to date regarding the client's progress in the program create the opportunity for them to work in concert with the therapist to actively support the client's work on trauma-related issues, the skills taught in the program.

When the therapist's role in an agency places him or her in regular contact with other providers who are working with the client, there are many natural opportunities for integrating the trauma work with other mental health or substance abuse services being provided. However, if the therapist does not have regular contact with the other treatment providers, it is important to develop a routine in which this can be accomplished. This could be arranged by the therapist's attending treatment team meetings on a regular basis or having individual meetings with a critical provider (e.g., case manager, psychiatrist), either in person or on the phone. For most clients, it is recommended that some contact occur between the therapist and other treatment providers at least once every 2 or 3 weeks, although more frequent contact is needed for some clients, such as those who are prone to crises, whose symptoms are only tenuously stabilized or who have particular difficulty learning the skills taught in the CR for PTSD program.

Role of Social Support

A large body of research documents the importance of social support as both a protective factor from developing psychiatric disorders and as a moderating factor that can lessen the severity of a disorder (Callaghan & Morrissey, 1993; Cobb, 1976; Veiel & Baumann, 1992). In a similar vein, greater social support has been found to confer some protection from negative psychological consequences in traumatized individuals (Eriksson, Van De Kemp, Gorsuch, Hokke, & Foy, 2001; L. A. King, King, Fairbank, Keane, & Adams, 1998; Norris & Kaniasty, 1996; Romans, Martin, Anderson, O'Shea, & Mullen, 1995; Thompson et al., 2000). The importance of social support is underscored by the fact that exposure to trauma can also erode social support and worsen its impact on individuals, especially when disclosure is associated with negative reactions from others (Neria, Solomon, & Dekel, 1998; Ullman & Filipas, 2001).

Just as social support can help buffer people from the negative effects of stressful and traumatic events, social support can also play a crucial role in facilitating the ability of clients to benefit from the CR for PTSD program. The therapist needs to evaluate the extent and nature of the client's social support at the beginning of therapy. Before doing this, the therapist discusses with the client the importance of social support and the role it can play in helping him or her benefit from the program. Clients sometimes need to be assured that details of their traumatic experiences will not be the focus of work with significant others. Then, information can be gathered by inquiring whom the client has regular contact with; asking about whether these relationships are supportive; and identifying possible areas of conflict, which individuals might help him learn the information and skills, and how to enlist that support. Although the emphasis is on natural, nonprofessional supports such as family members and friends, paraprofessionals and professionals (e.g., case managers, drug and alcohol counselors, residential staff members) may serve as significant others for clients who lack natural supports. Supportive others can review educational materials about trauma and PTSD with clients, encourage (and help) them to complete homework assignments, and prompt them to use (or help apply) skills such as breathing retraining and CR. Such active support increases clients' opportunities for learning and using the information and skills taught in the program. This may be especially important for clients who have cognitive impairments that make it difficult for them to practice and use the skills taught in sessions on their own without special assistance.

Although lack of social support can clearly pose a barrier to improving posttraumatic symptoms for some clients, even more problems can occur when the client has a negative or stressful relationship with a significant other (Tarrier, Sommerfield, & Pilgrim, 1999). Close relationships characterized by high levels of conflict, as reflected by frequent arguments, raised voices, threats, or hostile acts, can inhibit or discourage people from practicing or using skills taught in the program. Often, for people to learn new skills they need a relatively safe environment in which they feel comfortable trying something new. Helping a client create such a safe space can be critical to the learning process. Sometimes significant others have a supportive relationship with the client, but because they may misunderstand the nature of posttraumatic reactions and the CR for PTSD program, they may discourage the client from participating in the program or practicing the skills at home.

There are multiple options for capitalizing on supportive relationships that clients have with significant others. Scheduling a brief meeting between the therapist, client, and significant other toward the beginning of the program can help orient the support person to the goals and nature of the program, address concerns, describe ways the person may be able to help, and build positive expectations for the client's change in the program. Some clients may benefit from having occasional follow-up meetings with the therapist and significant other to review new information and skills taught and progress made in treatment. If the client continues to experience some posttraumatic symptoms toward the end of treatment, it may be fruitful to have a meeting with the client and support person aimed at discussing how the significant other can help the client use the skills taught in the program, as well as to explore other strategies for reducing distress and interference related to those symptoms. It can be helpful to prepare for such meetings in advance with the client and for the client to take some or all of the lead in explaining new information and skills to his or her support person.

Most involvement of significant others includes activities like helping the client review handout material, facilitating homework completion and helping the person practice skills in appropriate situations. For some clients who are disorganized or forgetful, it may be helpful for the therapist to send the support person written materials related to the program (with the client's permission). In some situations, it may also be useful for the therapist to have occasional telephone contact with a support person (with the client's permission) to review the client's progress, troubleshoot problems, and consider ways the person can support the client's work in the program.

SUMMARY AND CONCLUSIONS

The CR for PTSD program is a time-limited (usually 12–16 weeks) individual therapy program for persons who want to work on coping with and overcoming the effects of trauma on their lives. The program was designed to meet the needs of a wide range of persons with posttraumatic disorders, including those facing multiple life challenges, such as severe mental illness, addiction, housing instability, and health problems. The program includes the following treatment components: orientation to the program, crisis planning, breathing retraining, education, CR, and termination. Home assignments are given regularly for clients to review material and practice targeted skills. Therapy is coordinated with other treatments the person may be receiving. The availability of social support for the client is evaluated, with efforts undertaken to harness such support in the service of the client's participation in the program.

The primary focus of the program is on teaching clients the skill of CR for dealing with negative emotions. As clients develop expertise in this skill, they become increasingly able to identify, challenge, and correct trauma-related beliefs and schemas about themselves, other people, and the world that lead to their posttraumatic reactions. Successfully challenging and changing trauma-related beliefs helps clients develop more adaptive and cohesive narratives about their life experiences and leads to reductions in posttraumatic symptoms such as reexperiencing, avoidance, and overarousal. As clients change their own negative and inaccurate perceptions about themselves and the world and become less fearful of living their lives and pursuing their goals, their quality and enjoyment of life can potentially grow.

II

TREATMENT

4

BEGINNING TREATMENT: ENGAGEMENT, ORIENTATION, CRISIS PLANNING, AND BREATHING RETRAINING

KIM T. MUESER, STANLEY D. ROSENBERG, AND HARRIET J. ROSENBERG

This chapter describes the first steps of initiating the Cognitive Restructuring for Posttraumatic Stress Disorder (CR for PTSD) program. These steps are (a) engaging the client in treatment and dealing with ambivalence about change, (b) orienting the client to the program, (c) making a plan for potential crises, and (d) teaching breathing retraining as an anxiety self-management skill.

Instilling motivation for treatment and providing information about the nature and goals of the program set the stage for clients being active learners and taking a lead role in overcoming the effects of PTSD on their lives. Developing a crisis plan both provides assurance regarding the client's safety and minimizes the chances of crises interfering with completion of the program. Breathing retraining is a skill that can be quickly taught and provide immediate relief from anxiety, which can facilitate participation in the program. The orientation, crisis plan, and breathing retraining can usually be covered in a single treatment session.

ENGAGEMENT

At the outset, the therapist informs the client about PTSD and engages him or her by setting clear and positive expectations for participation. For many clients, engagement in treatment is a straightforward process that flows naturally from the assessment of trauma and PTSD into discussion of the disorder and treatment options. The process of engagement includes providing information about PTSD, briefly exploring how PTSD has affected the person's life, and describing the CR for PTSD program and other treatment options. This can usually be accomplished in 15 to 30 minutes.

Providing Information About Posttraumatic Stress Disorder

When a diagnosis of PTSD has been established, the therapist should inform the client and provide some basic information about the disorder. The therapist's immediate goal is to help the client understand that the symptoms and difficulties he or she has experienced following the traumatic events are due to a common disorder or syndrome (i.e., PTSD). This understanding normalizes people's reactions to traumatic events by letting them know that they are not alone. This information can reduce feelings of shame traumatized people often have about how they have coped with their experiences and instill confidence that the disorder is well understood. For example:

> *Therapist:* We've spent some time talking together about your traumatic experiences and how they've affected you. Based on these discussions, it is clear that you have posttraumatic stress disorder, or PTSD. PTSD is a common disorder that people have after exposure to traumatic events, such as childhood physical or sexual abuse, being assaulted or raped, being in a bad accident or natural disaster, or being in combat. Some of the most common symptoms of PTSD include intrusive images of the experiences, difficulty sleeping, and avoiding things that remind you of the traumatic events.

> *Client:* Do you mean other people have these same experiences?

> *Therapist:* Yes, these problems are actually quite common among people who have experienced traumatic events. About 1 in 10 people develop PTSD at some point in their lives.

> *Client:* I didn't realize that. I used to think I was crazy because I would keep having those thoughts and pictures in my head coming back again and again.

> *Therapist:* Yes, that's a very common problem.

This amount of information about PTSD is sufficient for most clients, and the therapist can proceed to briefly explore how PTSD has affected the client's life. Some clients want to know more about PTSD. If so, the therapist should provide this information freely. If clients' desire for more information continues for more than 15 to 20 minutes, the therapist should inform them that they have many excellent questions and that these and other questions can be addressed in the program that the therapist is going to describe.

Exploring How Posttraumatic Stress Disorder Has Affected the Client's Life

After the therapist has explained the client's PTSD diagnosis, the focus shifts to exploring with the client how PTSD has affected his or her life. The purpose of this discussion is to identify how PTSD is a problem for the individual in order to harness the client's motivation to participate in treatment for it. The therapist can ask a few probative questions to explore how PTSD has affected the person, based in part on the completed assessment. A great deal of exploration is usually not necessary; 5 to 10 minutes is usually sufficient.

> *Therapist:* Let's spend a couple of minutes talking about how PTSD has affected you. One of the symptoms you described is having frequent memories of your abuse popping into your head. What's that like for you?
>
> *Client:* It's horrible, I hate it. I sometimes try to make them go away by cutting myself or drinking. But the relief is only temporary, and the memories keep coming back.
>
> *Therapist:* That must be very difficult to cope with. How about your sleep? How do your difficulties sleeping affect you?
>
> *Client:* Well, I'm awake most of the night, and then I usually drift off when it's finally morning. I get only a few hours every night, and I always feel groggy—like a zombie.
>
> *Therapist:* I understand, that sounds like a real struggle for you. How about avoiding things that remind you of your experiences? Is that a problem?
>
> *Client:* I avoid most public places. I do my shopping late at night because I don't like other people looking at me.
>
> *Therapist:* That makes you feel uncomfortable?
>
> *Client:* Yes, especially when men look at me.

Therapist:	I can see that these PTSD symptoms are a real problem for you. How have your symptoms interfered with doing things that you'd like to do and with enjoying life?
Client:	What life? I can't work. I'm a nervous wreck. It's even hard to feel close to the people I love, like my children.

Brief Description of Cognitive Restructuring for Posttraumatic Stress Disorder Program

The therapist next provides a brief introduction, explaining that there is a treatment program specifically designed to address PTSD and conveying hope that participation in the program will reduce or eliminate many of the client's symptoms and problems that are due to PTSD. The most critical information to provide at this early stage of engagement is that the program is time limited (12–16 weeks), that it focuses specifically on PTSD and related problems, that it has been shown to be helpful to other people with PTSD, and that it works by providing information about PTSD and teaching strategies for coping with anxiety and other trauma-related negative feelings.

Therapist:	Now that we've talked a little bit about how PTSD has affected you, I would like to describe a treatment program that you might find helpful. This program is the Cognitive Restructuring, or CR, for PTSD program. The program is provided in individual one-on-one sessions, once per week, for 12 to 16 weeks.
	The aim of the program is to help people overcome the effects of trauma on their lives. This includes reducing or eliminating PTSD symptoms or helping people manage symptoms so they don't interfere with their lives. The focus of this program is on providing you with basic information about PTSD, teaching strategies for dealing with anxiety, and teaching you skills for dealing with thoughts and beliefs related to your traumatic experiences. What do you think about this program?
Client:	Sounds interesting. Do you mean that the program can eliminate these problems?
Therapist:	Yes, for some clients, PTSD symptoms can be completely eliminated. For other clients, the severity of the symptoms can be reduced so they cause less distress and interference.
Client:	So can you really make those bad memories go away?
Therapist:	Nobody really knows how to make memories go away. The goal of this program isn't to make bad memories go away but rather to make it possible for people to live and enjoy their

lives, despite the traumatic experiences they have had and their memories of those experiences. It is possible to live a worthwhile and rewarding life, even if you have suffered much trauma in your life, without making the memories of those experiences go away. Those memories are part of you, and this program will help you learn to live with those memories and at the same time move forward in your life.

Dealing With Ambivalence

Some individuals are ambivalent about participating in any treatment program for PTSD. Often clients have struggled with their symptoms for years and have reached a precarious balance in their lives that they are afraid to upset. Some people lose hope for a better life and are reluctant to commit to the effort of participating in a new program. Still others are skeptical that a short-term program can help them overcome the effects of trauma they have endured for so many years.

Ambivalence or skepticism is a normal part of the change process. All people are hesitant about making significant life changes, even for the better (e.g., getting married, taking a new job), because change involves dislodging a person from his or her usual routine and facing uncertainty. Therefore, when encountering ambivalence about participating in the program, the therapist's efforts should focus on normalizing, understanding, and exploring the basis of the person's concerns rather than pathologizing those concerns as "resistance."

First and foremost, it is important to acknowledge and empathize with the natural fear the client has about dealing with disturbing memories of past events. The therapist can validate these concerns while also providing words of support and encouragement:

Therapist: I can understand how scary it is for you to think about confronting and dealing with your abusive experiences. These are memories that you've tried to keep tucked away for a long time, but they have somehow managed to keep intruding on your life. It's true that dealing with these experiences can be frightening. However, in this program I will be teaching you skills for coping with your anxious feelings and for emotionally processing your memories of traumatic experiences. I'll be here with you, supporting you every step of the way as you learn these skills and recover from your traumatic experiences.

Another useful strategy for dealing with ambivalence is to help the client make a list of the pros and cons of participating in the CR for PTSD program. When exploring the advantages of participation, attention should be given both to the potential benefits of reduced PTSD symptoms and distress as well as to reduced interference with other parts of the client's life, such as social relationships, work or school, or parenting. Reference to the client's symptoms, as reported on during the screening or diagnostic assessment, can be a good launch point or reminder for such discussions. Directly querying clients about their concerns is usually straightforward. The most common concerns include worry about focusing on past traumatic experiences, despair that renders the person hopeless about the future, and high levels of stress that make it difficult for the person to commit the effort to participating in the program.

The therapist can remind the client that the program is not an exposure-based approach to PTSD and that it is entirely up to the client how much he or she would like to talk about his or her traumatic experiences. The therapist can also explore how well the client's current efforts to cope with PTSD are working. Despite great efforts to avoid trauma-related stimuli, most people with PTSD continue to be bombarded by memories of these experiences. Helping clients see the limited effectiveness of their efforts to cope with their trauma responses can tip the balance in favor of participating in the program.

For some clients, the anguish and despair they experience make it impossible for them to conceive of a better future. Hopelessness is a common feature of depression, which is frequently compounded by the PTSD symptom of a foreshortened sense of future. In responding to such despair, the therapist needs to walk a fine line between validating the client's distraught feelings and not reinforcing beliefs of hopelessness. The therapist can explain that when people feel depressed they often have a bleak outlook on life and their future, but that outlook is not necessarily accurate. The therapist can also point out that some of the skills taught in the CR for PTSD program have been shown to be very helpful in dealing with and overcoming feelings of depression.

Special population clients often face multiple stresses in their lives, including ones not directly related to their PTSD, and it may be difficult to focus their energies on just one particular source of stress. For example, a person may have medical or financial problems or have other responsibilities, such as taking care of an elderly parent. The therapist should first explore whether the most pressing problems are likely to be resolved in the near future. For example, if a person is experiencing a housing problem, it may be preferable to postpone treatment until that situation has been resolved. If the stresses the client is facing appear unlikely to improve in the near future, the therapist can help the client explore the pros and cons of participating in the program. In this discussion, the therapist should also explore with the client whether effective treatment for PTSD might reduce stress in the long run. For example, PTSD often interferes with employment (Mueser, Essock, Haines, Wolfe, & Xie, 2004; Savoca & Rosenheck, 2000), and clients who are unable to work and are under great financial stress could explore whether the CR for PTSD program might help them return to work and reduce this strain.

The goal of explaining the CR for PTSD program is not strictly to persuade clients to participate but to enable them to make an informed decision about treatment. This explanation also involves discussing other treatment options, such as pharmacological treatment for PTSD (Schoenfeld, Marmar, & Neylan, 2004). After the client has weighed the advantages and disadvantages of participation and made a decision, this decision should be respected, and the option of trying the program at a later date should be discussed.

ORIENTATION TO THE COGNITIVE RESTRUCTURING FOR POSTTRAUMATIC STRESS DISORDER PROGRAM

When the client has decided to participate in the CR for PTSD program, the therapist provides a more detailed explanation of it to set clear and positive expectations. An orientation sheet is used to facilitate this discussion, which usually takes 10 to 15 minutes to complete (Handout #1; see Appendix).

The therapist reviews the orientation sheet with the client, briefly elaborating on the different points and responding to any questions that arise along the way. When discussing the goals of the program, the therapist can integrate the specific PTSD symptoms that the client experiences and the interference these symptoms cause in day-to-day functioning as important foci of treatment. The following is an example of how to introduce the topic of logistics to a client with severe mental illness who receives case management and other psychiatric services at the local community mental health center:

> *Therapist:* In the beginning, we'll meet once a week for a total of about 12 to 16 sessions. Toward the end, we may want to space out our sessions to every other week. The CR program is time limited, and when it is completed we will stop meeting for the program. You will be able to continue using the skills you've learned in the program with the support of your case manager, which will help you continue to improve your skills for dealing with difficult feelings and situations in your daily life.

When describing the components of the CR for PTSD program, the therapist's goal is to inform the client about the nature of and rationale for each component. After the previous discussions, the client will already have some familiarity with how the program works, but a brief review in the orientation session helps to ensure understanding. Before describing the treatment, the therapist reviews the focus of the program on posttraumatic reactions and reviews any other treatment services the client will continue to receive. An example of how to explain this to a client is provided below:

Therapist: We will be working together on difficulties you are having related to your traumatic experiences. This program is aimed at helping you manage your PTSD symptoms and reducing their effects on your life, not on retelling your experiences. There may be times when we talk about past upsetting events, but we will not discuss them in detail, and it will be up to you on how much you want to talk about them.

We will work together on three main things. First, I will teach you a technique for coping with anxiety called *breathing retraining*. This skill will help you manage anxiety and symptoms of physical tension. We will focus on this skill first so that you can begin using it right away.

Second, you will learn about PTSD and other common symptoms and problems people also experience. PTSD is a common disorder people experience after traumatic events. Being aware of and understanding your PTSD symptoms is an important step toward coping with them more effectively.

Third, I'll teach you a skill called *cognitive restructuring*. Traumatic experiences often lead to upsetting and distressed feelings, and these emotions can be difficult to handle. Cognitive restructuring is a skill that can help you identify and challenge unhelpful thoughts and beliefs that contribute to your upset feelings. You will learn how to use cognitive restructuring to help you change trauma-related thoughts about yourself and the world that contribute to your negative feelings and PTSD symptoms.

The importance of homework to success needs to be emphasized, and the differences between the CR for PTSD program and other therapy approaches may need to be explained. Some clients object to homework because it reminds them of school. It may be helpful to use another term, such as *home assignment* or *skill practice*. It is also useful to emphasize the collaborative nature of homework so clients understand that assignments are not imposed them but are determined jointly. For example,

Therapist: The CR program may be different from other types of therapy you have received. I will teach you new skills for managing difficult feelings related to your traumatic experiences. Because learning is so important in this program, part of it also involves you practicing the skills we cover in session when you are on your own, as homework assignments. In fact, practicing these skills on your own is just as important a part of the program as coming to the sessions. Therefore, at the end of each session we will work together to come up with an assignment you can do before the next session.

CRISIS PLANNING

A *crisis* is anything that could happen in the client's life that could threaten clinical stability or the client's ability to continue to participate in the CR for PTSD program. Trauma work can be emotionally challenging, and sometimes there are temporary increases in symptoms before improvements occur. Developing a crisis plan is primarily aimed at monitoring the signs of an impending crisis, preventing a crisis when such signs appear, and having a plan for minimizing or containing the effects of a crisis should it occur.

The most common types of crises include the reemergence or worsening of psychiatric symptoms (e.g., psychotic symptoms, depression), resumption of or increase in substance use problems, self-harming behavior (e.g., cutting), and suicidal thinking. The therapist initiates discussion of the crisis plan by explaining that learning how to take care of one's mental health is an important goal of the CR for PTSD program. One way of helping clients learn how to do this is to review past challenges they have had with their mental health and to develop a plan for preventing or responding to those problems in the future. Developing such a plan can make both the client and the therapist feel more confident about initiating the program.

If the client already has a crisis plan in place, it can be reviewed and modified as needed. If no plan exists, client and therapist should complete the Crisis Plan Checklist Worksheet (Handout #2; see Appendix) together. An example is provided next:

> *Therapist:* Before we begin with breathing retraining as a tool to decrease anxious feelings, I'd like to spend a few minutes with you helping you learn how to take better care of your own mental health. Now, we have all heard a lot about how we can, and should, take care of our *physical* health, like we should eat vegetables, get enough sleep and get exercise, and so on. But no one ever talks about how we should take care of our *mental* health. That's what I want to talk with you about now.
>
> You know from your own experiences that when things are really bad and you are in a stage in which your symptoms are really severe, you didn't get there overnight. Usually, what happens is that there is a slow increase of symptoms over a few days or weeks. For example, you might start feeling more anxious or sad or start noticing that you don't feel like going places or that you're missing appointments or that

you start wanting or using alcohol or drugs [*insert other symp-tom escalations that may be more appropriate to the client*]. It's important that we figure out what your specific pattern is, because if you know what your own warning signs are, you can learn to notice them earlier and to get help sooner. This can actually help you prevent a mental health crisis or even stop a hospitalization, giving you more control over your life.

I want us to think through together and write down all of the warning signs that you have experienced before other crises that you've had in your life. Let's start by understanding what I mean by *crisis*. Here is a worksheet for us to fill out together, which will guide us through the steps of figuring out your own unique warning signs and also what to do if you notice them and how to help avoid a hospitalization or crisis. [*takes out Crisis Plan Checklist Worksheet (Handout #2; see Appendix) and goes through the items with the client*]

This was an important thing for us to do together because while most people participating in this program get significant and lasting improvements in their symptoms and function-ing from the first session onward, sometimes PTSD symptoms don't get better immediately. It can take time and effort to learn the skills before finally experiencing relief from the symptoms of PTSD. This can be especially hard when you are dealing with thoughts and feelings related to traumatic events that you have tried to avoid thinking about for so many years. Therefore, having a plan, like the one we just did together, for dealing with any increases in symptoms or problem behaviors can help ensure your safety and help both of us feel confident and comfortable about your well-being as we work together in this program. Do you have any questions?

Sometimes it is helpful for other people to be involved in monitoring and helping the client respond to a crisis. This can be especially crucial for clients whose first signs of a crisis may involve the loss of insight, such as experiencing paranoid thoughts or social withdrawal and who have regular contact with a supportive person who could help take steps to avert the crisis. The involvement of other supportive persons may also be very useful when working with clients who have had significant substance abuse problems, for whom relapse into addiction may be accompanied by minimization or denial. Potential supports include family members or friends, a therapist, or a case manager.

Some clients can readily identify potential crises but are reluctant to communicate their distress and get help from others. Some of this reluctance can be understood as stemming from the mistrust traumatized individuals often have toward other people and hence their reluctance to disclose distressed feelings to them. The therapist should show understanding of these concerns but persist in helping the client develop some plan that both of them will feel comfortable with. The therapist can take responsibility for the need to develop a crisis plan by explaining that it is his or her duty to ensure the client's safety while participating in the program and that the plan will also maximize the client's ability to complete and benefit from the program.

BREATHING RETRAINING

Breathing retraining is a widely taught skill in the treatment of anxiety disorders (D. M. Clark, Salkovskis, & Chalkley, 1985; Craske & Lewin, 1998; Foa & Rothbaum, 1998; Rygh & Sanderson, 2004). The skill requires approximately 15 minutes to teach and can be taught at the end of the first session. By learning this skill at the beginning of the program, the client is able to start using it from the first session onward and to get some immediate relief from the intense anxiety that often accompanies posttraumatic reactions. As the client learns breathing retraining, he or she can use it to reduce distress that occurs in and outside sessions.

Teaching breathing retraining involves three basic steps. First, the therapist establishes the rationale for breathing retraining as an anxiety management strategy. Second, the therapist teaches the skill by actively demonstrating it and then engaging the client in practicing the skill in the session. Third, a plan is agreed on for the client to practice the skill as a homework assignment.

Rationale for Breathing Retraining

Before explaining how breathing retraining works, it can help to elicit any experiences the client has had using relaxation techniques. These experiences can often be built on when explaining the purpose of breathing retraining.

> *Therapist:* The first skill we're going to work on is called *breathing retraining*. People with PTSD often experience high levels of physical tension and anxiety. Breathing retraining is a strategy for reducing this tension and anxious feelings. By learning this skill today, and by practicing it on your own, you will have a skill that you can begin using immediately to deal with your distressed feelings.
>
> *Client:* Yes, I could use that.

Therapist:	Before I teach this skill, I'm wondering whether you've ever used any relaxation techniques before. If so, what have you used and have they helped?
Client:	Sometimes when I'm feeling really tense I like to listen to music.
Therapist:	Good. It sounds like you have one strategy for dealing with tension and anxiety that you sometimes find effective. I think you'll also find breathing retraining helpful because you can use it anywhere, even when other people are around.

Some clients report that they already know or use breathing retraining. The therapist should acknowledge this experience and explore whether the client found the skill helpful and currently uses it to deal with anxiety. Although clients sometimes report that they know breathing retraining, they are often not familiar with the skill as taught in the program. Therefore, it is important to review the skill with the client and practice it in session, even if the client reports familiarity with it.

The rationale for breathing retraining can be established by explaining that it is a skill for reducing the high flow of oxygen to the brain that occurs during periods of high tension and anxiety.

Therapist:	When people feel upset, they often breathe more quickly, or hyperventilate. What's it like for you when you feel upset?
Client:	I definitely breathe faster. My muscles feel tense, and I sometimes clench my jaw and fists.
Therapist:	Yes, those are very common reactions to feeling anxious. The problem with breathing more quickly is that it increases the amount of oxygen in the brain, which can make you feel lightheaded, even more stimulated, and even more anxious.
Client:	That happens to me, I begin to feel panicky.
Therapist:	Exactly. Sometimes people try to take a deep breath to calm down. Have you ever tried that?
Client:	Yes. It sometimes helps a little, but not much.
Therapist:	Right. The problem with taking a deep breath is that while it may slow your breathing down, you're still getting lots of oxygen to the brain, and that's responsible for those anxious feelings.
Client:	So what am I supposed to do? Stop breathing?
Therapist:	No [*laughing*], you can keep breathing. The idea is to slow down your breathing. Instead of taking a deep breath, take a

normal breath and then exhale slowly. While you exhale, say a soothing word like *relax* or *peaceful*. By taking normal breaths and exhaling slowly, you'll reduce the flow of oxygen to your brain, which will reduce your feelings of anxiety. Here, I'll demonstrate it, and then we can try it together.

After checking to make sure the client is using breathing retraining correctly, the therapist should encourage the client to practice the skill for a few minutes. When the client has finished, the therapist should check and find out what the experience was like for the client. Minor modifications at this time can be made to the method to suit the client's preferences. For example, some clients like to include imagery of a pleasant scene in the breathing retraining. Some clients have difficulty pausing between breaths and feel that they are always trying to catch their breath. For these clients, the pause between breaths can be shortened or eliminated. Some clients like to combine tensing and releasing their muscles with the breathing retraining.

The first time breathing retraining is practiced in the session, it often does not significantly reduce anxiety. The therapist should normalize this and explain that breathing retraining is a skill that requires practice for one to achieve proficiency. With practice, many people find that breathing retraining is very useful for reducing tension and anxiety and that they can use this skill anytime throughout the day.

Homework

At the end of the session, a homework assignment should be agreed on for the client to practice breathing retraining. For example, if agreeable to the client, a homework assignment could be created to practice breathing retraining (5–10 minutes) once a day for the next week. Initially, breathing retraining should be practiced in a calm setting to facilitate learning the skill, and the homework plan should address where and when this can take place. As the client becomes more skilled at breathing retraining, he or she can begin using it to cope with stressful or upsetting situations. The breathing retraining handout (Handout #3; see Appendix) should be given to the client and reviewed with him or her at this time.

At the beginning of the next session, the therapist should review with the client the homework assignment to practice the breathing retraining. Any difficulties the client has experienced using the skill should be problem-solved together, as well as any obstacles that interfered with practicing the skill. If the client reports practicing the skill, the therapist should reinforce this and plan with the client to continue practicing the skill during the following week and (if the client is game) to begin using it in more challenging situations. If the client becomes distraught during any subsequent sessions, the therapist may prompt him or her to use the breathing retraining to cope with those feelings.

SUMMARY AND CONCLUSIONS

When the client has been engaged and is motivated for treatment, the therapist prepares him or her by providing an orientation to the CR for PTSD program and setting positive expectations for active participation. Special population clients are often very sensitive to the stress of working on their traumatic experiences, and establishing a crisis plan to detect and respond to any increases in problematic symptoms or behaviors ensures the client's safety during the program and maximizes the chances of successful completion. Finally, teaching breathing retraining provides the client with a skill he or she can immediately begin to use to reduce anxious and other distressful feelings. These activities, which are usually accomplished in a session following engaging the client in treatment, set the stage for the subsequent sessions aimed at psychoeducation about PTSD and CR.

5

PSYCHOEDUCATION ABOUT POSTTRAUMATIC REACTIONS

KIM T. MUESER, STANLEY D. ROSENBERG,
AND HARRIET J. ROSENBERG

The steps of orienting the client to the Cognitive Restructuring for Posttraumatic Stress Disorder (CR for PTSD) program, developing a crisis plan, and teaching breathing retraining are followed by basic education about posttraumatic reactions, including the symptoms of PTSD, to inform clients about posttraumatic symptoms and to establish that PTSD is a common and treatable disorder. Providing this information can decrease the shame that people have when they believe their reactions to traumatic events reflect personal weaknesses, can instill hope for change, and can harness motivation to actively participate in treatment.

We recommend two sessions to teach the educational material, the first focused on the symptoms of PTSD and the second on associated problems. Therapists should strive to limit psychoeducation to two sessions even when working with clients who have significant cognitive impairments or severe symptoms that require the therapist to present the material more slowly and to review information more often (e.g., psychotic symptoms). With such clients, the therapist should highlight the key points of the educational topics and help the client identify his or her most severe symptoms or problems, on the basis of information already gathered during the assessment, and spend less time on other symptoms or problems. Additional sessions devoted to psychoeducation are unlikely to produce significant symptom relief, and the time is better spent teaching cognitive restructuring (CR), the most critical ingredient of the CR for PTSD program.

At the end of the second psychoeducational session, the therapist reviews with the client the impact of the traumatic events, the PTSD symptoms, and associated problems on the client's life. The purpose of this review is to identify one or two areas of functioning that have been affected by PTSD that the client would like to improve over the course of participating in the program. Identifying such functional goals can further increase motivation to participate in the program and can be a focus of collaborative work aimed at overcoming the effects of trauma. Work toward achieving these goals need not wait until PTSD symptoms have been reduced or eliminated but can occur concurrently, with CR used to help clients deal with the negative emotions and perceived obstacles they encounter when attempting to pursue them.

PSYCHOEDUCATIONAL TEACHING TECHNIQUES

Teaching people about their psychiatric illness and helping them relate this information to their own experiences is a widely used process called *psychoeducation* (Anderson, Reiss, & Hogarty, 1986; Ascher-Svanum & Krause, 1991; Goldman & Quinn, 1988). Psychoeducation involves helping clients understand and incorporate information about their psychiatric illness that has personal relevance and significance, according to the principles in Table 5.1.

Information about PTSD and associated problems is taught using two handouts containing worksheets that clients can use to identify specific symptoms or problems they have experienced. The therapist can give the relevant handout to the client at the beginning of the session, refer to it over the course of the session while paraphrasing the material, and pause frequently for the client to write down his or her experiences, symptoms, or problems. The therapist can also take turns with the client reading the handout, discussing points and exploring their relevance to the client's experiences. For clients who do not have good reading skills, the handout can be dispensed with during the session. It can be helpful if a supportive person can be identified who can review the information in the handout with these client as a homework assignment.

Teaching about symptoms and problems follows a general pattern. The therapist first describes a symptom or problem area, elicits the client's understanding and experience with that symptom, and then has the client record his or her experience on the pertinent worksheet in the handout.

TABLE 5.1
Psychoeducational Teaching Principles

Principle	Strategies
Interactive, not didactic	■ Strive for an active discussion. ■ Pause frequently to get client's input. ■ Ask open-ended questions (cannot be answered with yes or no) rather than closed-ended questions to stimulate discussion.
Provide factual information	■ Present critical facts about posttraumatic stress disorder and related problems. ■ Elicit questions and provide answers. ■ Be honest and straightforward. ■ Tell client you will get back to him or her later if you do not know the answer to any questions.
Explore relevance of facts to client's experiences	■ After explaining each symptom and problem area, explore client's experience with them. ■ Ask questions to understand impact of symptoms and problems on client's life.
Check comprehension and retention of information	■ For comprehension, pause occasionally and ask client to describe his or her understanding of key facts. ■ For retention, at beginning of next session ask a few questions about topics covered in last session. ■ Explain or review material again as needed.
Show empathy	■ Paraphrase client to demonstrate understanding. ■ Use good eye contact, body orientation, and minimal verbal encouragers ("uh huh", "I see") to show active listening. ■ Express empathy when client is distressed.

Common Reactions to Trauma I: Posttraumatic Stress Disorder Symptoms

The therapist should be familiar with the client's primary PTSD symptoms, as revealed in the assessment, before reviewing them with the client. The therapist should explore any major discrepancies that appear between the client's report on the assessment and the discussion of symptoms in the educational session. For example, some symptoms may have improved or worsened since the initial assessment or the client may have misunderstood a particular symptom during the assessment.

At the beginning of the session, after reviewing the breathing retraining homework from the prior session and describing the agenda for the current session, the therapist provides the client with the handout (Common Reactions to Trauma I: PTSD Symptoms: Handout #4; see Appendix) and begins the discussion. When reviewing the different PTSD symptoms with the client, the therapist should pay particular attention to those symptoms linked to the criterion traumatic event(s) on which the diagnosis of PTSD was based while also exploring symptoms related to other traumatic events.

> *Therapist:* Posttraumatic stress disorder, or PTSD, is a common psychiatric disorder that occurs after someone has been exposed to a traumatic event. A disorder is just a group of symptoms that often occur together. A trained professional makes the diagnosis of PTSD based on a careful interview. Do you remember when we did that interview?
>
> *Client:* Yes, I think I do.
>
> *Therapist:* Good. Today I would like to spend some time with you talking about the specific symptoms of PTSD, with a particular focus on the symptoms that you have experienced. Okay?
>
> *Client:* Okay.
>
> *Therapist:* The symptoms of PTSD can occur after the experience of any traumatic event. This could include physical or sexual abuse or assault, being in an accident or natural disaster, being in combat, or experiencing the sudden or unexpected death of a loved one. Regardless of the specific event, the same types of symptoms occur. For PTSD to be diagnosed, the symptoms have to be present and severe for more than a month after the event occurred. There are three types of symptoms that are used to diagnose PTSD: reexperiencing symptoms, avoidance symptoms, and overarousal symptoms. Let's spend some time talking about them. Any questions so far?
>
> *Client:* So does everybody who has had a traumatic event develop PTSD?
>
> *Therapist:* Good question! No, not everyone develops PTSD. But we know that it's a pretty common response to trauma. About 1 in 10 people develop PTSD at some time in their lives, and the more trauma they have been exposed to, and the more severe the trauma, the greater their chance of getting PTSD.
>
> *Client:* So, I guess I'm not alone?
>
> *Therapist:* No, certainly not.

Reexperiencing Symptoms

Reexperiencing symptoms are among the most pervasive of all PTSD symptoms. Common reexperiencing symptoms are intrusive memories of the traumatic event, distress when exposed to reminders of the event, and nightmares. Many clients mistake intrusive memories of an event for flashbacks.

The distinction can be made by explaining that flashbacks involve temporary loss of contact with the present reality and the momentary reexperiencing of the event as though it were occurring again. Flashbacks are rare compared with the other reexperiencing symptoms.

> *Therapist:* The first type of PTSD symptoms involves reexperiencing the traumatic event. The most common way people reexperience trauma is by having thoughts of the event or memories of the event just pop into their mind at odd times, like when they're doing regular things during the day. For example, a person could be fixing their car or doing dishes, and then out of the blue the memory pops into their mind or they just start thinking about what happened to them for no apparent reason. Have you had intrusive thoughts or memories of your traumatic experiences?
>
> *Client:* Yes, that happens a lot of the time.
>
> *Therapist:* What's that like for you?
>
> *Client:* Like you said, I'll be in the middle of doing something, or maybe nothing at all, and suddenly the memory comes out of nowhere.
>
> *Therapist:* And what's the memory that pops into your head? Is it just one memory, or several different ones?
>
> *Client:* It's usually a memory related to when my uncle was abusing me. Sometimes the memory is my uncle opening the door to my bedroom late at night. Sometimes the memory is him in my bed, making me do stuff.
>
> *Therapist:* I see. And what's it like for you when those memories come up?
>
> *Client:* Oh, it's bad [*shudders*]. I get all tense and anxious, and I just try to put the thoughts out of my head.
>
> *Therapist:* Well, your reaction to those memories is a very common one; most people find them very upsetting. Let's take out your handout on PTSD symptoms, and you can write some notes about your experience with intrusive memories or thoughts.

Avoidance Symptoms

Avoidance symptoms are usually related to situations that trigger trauma-related thoughts or beliefs. Most clients are aware of some of their avoidance, but for some people who experienced trauma early in their lives, it is so deeply ingrained into their habits and lifestyle that they are not aware they are avoiding thoughts, feelings, and situations that remind them of their traumatic experiences. For example, one woman who experienced sexual abuse from an early age chose to live an isolated lifestyle without ever consciously attempting to avoid situations that reminded her of those experiences.

Therapist:	The second set of PTSD symptoms is avoidance. People who have experienced trauma often try to avoid people, places, thoughts, and feelings that remind them of those experiences. It's easy to understand this because people naturally avoid things that make them feel uncomfortable or anxious.
	Let's talk about some of the specific ways people who have experienced traumatic events avoid things that remind them of those events. One way is that people may try to push thoughts out of their minds when a trauma-related thought pops into their head, such as trying to think of something else or trying distract themselves by listening to music or engaging in vigorous exercise. What things have you tried to do to get rid of thoughts about your trauma experiences?
Client:	Sometimes I just force myself to think of something different.
Therapist:	And is that effective?
Client:	A little bit, sometimes. But it seems like thoughts and memories always come back, no matter how hard I try to escape them.
Therapist:	Yes, that's a very common experience for people with PTSD. Is there anything else you've tried to do to avoid or get rid of those thoughts?
Client:	Sometimes I play with my dog. He takes my mind off things for a while.
Therapist:	Those are some good examples of how you try to avoid thoughts related to your trauma. Another kind of avoidance is avoiding activities or places that remind the person of their trauma.

Avoidance symptoms that involve emotional numbing and feelings of detachment require special explanation; for example:

Therapist:	People sometimes avoid thinking about their traumatic experiences without even trying to. For example, people may forget part of the traumatic event. People may also avoid upsetting thoughts and feelings about the experiences, leading them to feel emotionally numb. Sometimes people feel detached from others around them and can't experience close emotions, even with people they love. Have you ever had the feeling of being emotionally numb or detached from others?

Overarousal Symptoms

In contrast to reexperiencing and avoidance symptoms, overarousal symptoms often do not have an obvious relationship to the specific traumatic events experienced by the individual. However, these symptoms may be especially prominent in situations in which people are reminded of their traumatic experiences.

Therapist:	The third set of PTSD symptoms involves physical arousal or tension. People who have experienced traumatic events often have difficulty sleeping, feel irritable or easily angered, and may be jumpy and have trouble concentrating. Do you ever have these overarousal symptoms?
Client:	Lots of the time. My wife tells me I'm like a time bomb; she never knows what's going to set me off.
Therapist:	And what happens when you are set off?
Client:	It isn't pretty. Sometimes I yell at her or my kids, and then later I feel bad about it. When I know that I'm feeling that way, I just try to get away from everyone and isolate myself. There is no reason they should pay for what I've gone through.
Therapist:	That sounds very difficult. I can see that you care a lot for your family and are trying to protect them.
Client:	I try.
Therapist:	How about your sleep?
Client:	I'm up half the night. I just can't settle down and relax.
Therapist:	And what effect does that have on you?
Client:	I'm exhausted most of the time, and that also puts me in a bad mood.
Therapist:	I can understand how hard that must be. Some other common arousal symptoms include being easily startled and always feeling on guard or alert, like you're always looking over your shoulder to make sure you're safe.

Homework

By the end of the session, the therapist should be able to cover the symptoms of PTSD in sufficient detail so that the client can identify which symptoms he or she has. However, there often is not enough time in the session for the client to write down which symptoms he or she experiences and finds most problematic in the PTSD handout. One possible assignment is for the client to complete the worksheets contained in the handout. If those sheets were completed in the session, an alternative assignment might be to review the educational handout or have the client to review it with a supportive person, such as a family member. This assignment can be given in addition to a mutually agreed on plan for the client to continue practicing the breathing retraining exercise.

Common Reactions to Trauma II: Associated Problems

Psychoeducation about common problems associated with PTSD uses the same basic approach as for PTSD symptoms: It enables clients to understand that many other problems they may be experiencing are common among trauma survivors with PTSD. Again, this serves to normalize those problems and to instill hope that the program may decrease them. This discussion also paves the way for a more focused discussion on how PTSD has affected the person's life and which areas of functioning the client would most like to see improved. After reviewing homework from the previous session with the client, the therapist can give the client Handout #5 (see Appendix) and introduce the focus of this session as follows:

> *Therapist:* Many people with PTSD also experience other symptoms that interfere with their lives and cause them distress. Let's talk about some of these problems. First, people with traumatic experiences often have a range of different negative feelings, such as depression, guilt, and anger. Second, people often have difficulties in their relationships with other people. Third, people sometimes use drugs and alcohol to cope with their PTSD symptoms, which can lead to further problems.

Negative Feelings

When discussing common negative feelings associated with PTSD, the therapist should focus on the client's experience of those emotions in daily living, whether or not they are clearly related to PTSD symptoms. The discussion of fear and anxiety can be introduced as follows:

> *Therapist:* In the last session, we talked about fear and anxiety being common emotions that people have when they are reminded of their traumatic experiences. These feelings can be so strong that they persist even in situations that pose no danger at all. When have you felt fearful, tense, or anxious?
>
> *Client:* I feel tense and on guard whenever I'm out of my home. I feel that anything could happen and I have to be prepared.

Therapist: That sounds very hard. What's it like to have those feelings?

Client: It's very stressful. I can't enjoy things because I'm always so tense.

Depression is the most common comorbid disorder in people with PTSD (Breslau, Davis, Peterson, & Schultz, 2000; Kessler et al., 1995; Shalev et al., 1998). The pervasive avoidance and the high level of arousal associated with PTSD often make it difficult to enjoy activities the way the person used to. In addition, people may feel sad when they look back on their lives and consider the losses related to their traumatic experiences, such as the loss of innocence caused by childhood sexual abuse, loss or absence of love in a physically abusive environment, or the loss of a loved one.

Therapist: Other common reactions to trauma include sadness and depression. After a trauma, people often feel less interested in things and have a hard time having fun. People may feel hopeless or think about suicide. As we've talked about earlier, if it ever feels like that to you, I want you to tell me, so I can help you with those thoughts and feelings. Have you been feeling sad or depressed? Down or uninterested in things?

Client: Yes, quite a bit.

Therapist: What's that like for you? Can you tell me a little more about it?

Client: I feel like there is no hope, that I have no future.

Therapist: That must be very difficult to bear.

Client: It is. Sometimes it seems like the hardest thing to do to keep going on.

Therapist: I can understand how hard it must be for you. I want you to know that I think that you're taking a very courageous and important step in dealing with your traumatic experiences by participating in this program for your PTSD. The skills that we will be focusing on can be helpful not only for your PTSD symptoms, but your feelings of sadness and depression as well.

Feelings of shame and guilt are common in trauma survivors, especially those who have experienced childhood sexual abuse. It is important to identify these feelings as early as possible in treatment so that the therapist can, first, normalize them to the client and, second, be alert for opportunities when teaching CR to address and reexamine the beliefs that are responsible for those feelings.

Therapist:	Another type of upsetting feeling people often experience after trauma is guilt or shame. People may blame themselves for what happened. Or they may think that they are weak and inadequate because they were not stronger in dealing with the trauma. Do you ever have feelings of guilt or shame about what happened to you?
Client:	I think about that a lot. I look back on the night I was raped, if you can call it that, I mean. I knew the guy, it was a date, and I invited him up to my apartment. The next thing I knew, he was forcing himself on me. I didn't want sex, and I tried to say no, but he wouldn't listen.
Therapist:	So you blame yourself for what happened?
Client:	I should have been more forceful. I could have screamed.
Therapist:	But you didn't.
Client:	No. I was afraid.
Therapist:	Afraid of what?
Client:	That he was going to hurt me!
Therapist:	That's very understandable. Your reaction is a very common one people have after being assaulted—they blame themselves for not acting differently. Is there anything else about this experience that you blame yourself for?
Client:	I think I should have been stronger in dealing with it after it happened. I could have reported him, but I didn't. I could have just learned my lesson and gotten on with my life, but I didn't. Instead, I just broke down and went into a depression.
Therapist:	I understand. People often blame themselves for not coping with their traumatic experiences better. But just because you blame yourself, it doesn't mean that you did something wrong. When we begin work on cognitive restructuring in the next session, you'll find that not all of the thoughts that lead to negative feelings are accurate. And I'll be teaching you a skill for evaluating just how accurate those thoughts are.

Feelings of anger are very common in people with PTSD (Chemtob, Novaco, Hamada, Gross, & Smith, 1997). Sometimes anger is the dominant emotion, and it may consume the individual's thoughts about past traumatic experiences and characterize how they respond to any perceived threats in their day-to-day lives. Clients may oscillate between anxious and angry feelings. For some individuals, the processing of traumatic experiences involves helping them deal with unresolved anger so that they can move forward in their lives. Other clients may develop healthy and appropriate feelings of anger after their incorrect beliefs of responsibility for traumatic events have been challenged, and these feelings need to be dealt with.

> *Therapist:* Feeling angry is also a common reaction to traumatic events. People are angry about what happened to them, or with the person who hurt them, or with someone who didn't protect them. This anger can be stirred up during regular interactions with people, such as loved ones or even strangers. Have you experienced angry feelings?
>
> *Client:* Yes, I often feel consumed by feelings of rage. It clouds my entire life.
>
> *Therapist:* What's that about?
>
> *Client:* I don't see how my stepfather could have done that to a little girl. Me. It was so wrong of him. So selfish of him to take away my childhood.
>
> *Therapist:* Are you angry with anyone else?
>
> *Client:* My mother. She should have known. She should have protected me. Even when I told her after I had run away my first time, she didn't believe me.
>
> *Therapist:* I see. Sometimes angry feelings can be so strong that people swear, yell, or want to hit someone. For other people there is lots of anger, but it never comes to the surface or gets expressed. How do you respond to your angry feelings?
>
> *Client:* I'm pretty good at keeping it under control, and I try not to show it. But every once in awhile I lose control and shout at my husband or children. I've broken things, thrown dishes. Things get black when I get in a rage, and I do things I don't remember after. It feels awful to hear about it after it's happened.
>
> *Therapist:* Feeling angry can make it hard to get along with others. How does it affect your family?
>
> *Client:* I think they're afraid of me. Everybody is always tiptoeing around me, trying to make sure they don't "upset Mommy."

Relationship Difficulties

Relationship difficulties in people with PTSD can be attributable to a wide range of factors, such as distrust of other people; problems with intimacy because it triggers trauma-related memories; avoidance of people; or feelings such as anxiety, anger, or depression. Discussing the effects of trauma on close relationships both normalizes these difficulties and identifies areas that clients are often strongly motivated to change.

> *Therapist:* Another common reaction people experience after trauma is relationship difficulties. When people have had significant trauma, they often don't feel as close to others as they'd like. This can be the result of negative emotions related to PTSD: anxiety, sadness, guilt, or anger. Or it can be related to a numbing of feelings that makes it hard to connect with others. Sometimes people experience difficulties in their sexual relationship because it reminds them of their trauma, especially if it was sexual in nature. How have your traumatic experiences affected your relationships?
>
> *Client:* It causes a lot of problems for me. It's very hard for me to trust anyone. As soon as I start to get close, I get afraid and push them away. I want to get closer to people, but I don't know how. It stirs up so many feelings.
>
> *Therapist:* That happens to a lot of people. What kinds of feelings gets stirred up when you start to get close to someone?
>
> *Client:* I get afraid, I feel panicky. I'm sure I'm not good enough for the person, or I can't trust them.
>
> *Therapist:* And that's related to your experiences growing up?
>
> *Client:* I think so. My father punished me and beat me a great deal. He always used to tell me I was no good.

Drugs and Alcohol

Drug and alcohol problems are common in people with PTSD (K. T. Brady, Killeen, Brewerton, & Lucerini, 2000; S. H. Stewart et al., 1998), who often use substances to cope with disturbing symptoms (Nishith, Resick, & Mueser, 2001) or temporarily escape from the misery of their lives. However, there are numerous negative consequences of substance use, including addiction and retraumatization (Dansky, Saladin, Brady, Kilpatrick, & Resnick, 1995; Gearon & Bellack, 1999; Mueser, Rosenberg, Goodman, & Trumbetta, 2002). Discussion of substance use problems and PTSD can be initiated as follows:

> *Therapist:* Some people who have been through traumatic experiences have problems with alcohol or drugs. They may try to avoid thinking about their experiences by using substances too much, or they may use to take away strong negative feelings, like anxiety or sadness. However, using these substances actu-

ally makes these feelings worse over the long run. People with PTSD may also use drugs or alcohol to sleep better or deal with nightmares. This often seems helpful at first, but these substances interfere with the body's ability to sleep well and often lead to worse sleep problems. How often do you use alcohol or drugs?

Client: I like to have a drink now and then.

Therapist: Can you tell me a little more about that? How often?

Client: A few times a week usually. Maybe three or four times. Or five times.

Therapist: When do you usually like to drink?

Client: In the evening, before I go to bed.

Therapist: I see. What are your main reasons for wanting a drink?

Client: I have a lot of trouble falling asleep at night, and having a few drinks seems to help with that.

Therapist: Any other reasons?

Client: If my boyfriend wants sex. I have to be loaded because otherwise there is no way that I can relax.

Therapist: That's a common reaction to traumatic experiences. Does your boyfriend know about this?

Client: Yes, we usually drink together.

Therapist: And when you drink, how many drinks do you usually have?

Client: Before sex, five, six, or even more. Before going to bed, three or four.

Therapist: How about drug use?

Client: My boyfriend sometimes brings home some cocaine and we get high.

Therapist: What's that like for you?

Client: It feels good, like I can set aside my problems for a little while.

Therapist: How do you think your use of alcohol or cocaine is related to your traumatic experiences?

Client: I think my sexual and physical abuse has made me so that I always feel on edge, always on the lookout, never able to relax. That's gotten in the way of sleeping. I don't really enjoy sex. I've never enjoyed it, but wish I could. Well, I like the closeness, but that's all, because I just think about what happened to me. Drinking makes it not so bad—like I don't have to think about it.

Therapist:	And the cocaine?
Client:	I don't know. Maybe it's a way of having a good time every once in a while. Don't I deserve that? It's a relief to not have to think about my past.
Therapist:	That helps me understand. You should know that the reasons you gave for using alcohol and drugs are really very common for people with PTSD. One of the goals of this program is to teach you some new skills for dealing with your thoughts and feelings about your traumatic experiences. Many people find that as they learn new skills and emotionally process their memories, they no longer need to use substances to cope with their PTSD symptoms.

Other Associated Symptoms

Although psychoeducation for associated problems with PTSD focuses on negative emotions, relationship difficulties, and drug and alcohol use, clients are often curious about other symptoms they have and whether these could also be related to their trauma. One common associated symptom is *dissociation* (Cardena & Spiegel, 1993; Gershuny, Cloitre, & Otto, 2003; Lewis-Fernandez et al., 2002) during which people may feel temporarily disconnected from their bodies or the world around them and may "space out" during stressful times and not be aware of what's happening around them.

Difficulties in cognitive functioning are another common problem in people with PTSD (Barrett, Green, Morris, Giles, & Croft, 1996; Brandes et al., 2002; Buckley, Blanchard, & Neill, 1990). These problems may be apparent in areas such as attention and concentration, memory, and information processing. Distraction and preoccupation due to PTSD symptoms, such as intrusive trauma-related thoughts and exaggerated perceptions of danger, can make it difficult for people to perform important tasks such as work or school.

Although less common, hallucinations and delusions can also occur in people with PTSD (Butler, Mueser, Sprock, & Braff, 1996; Mueser & Butler, 1987; Sautter, Cornwell, Johnson, Wiley, & Faraone, 2002; Seedat, Stein, Oosthuizen, Emsley, & Stein, 2003). For example, a combat veteran may report hearing the voices of fallen comrades or a rape survivor may develop paranoid thoughts about men watching her. These symptoms can lead to odd or threatening behavior, social isolation, or suicide attempts and can be a source of considerable distress.

Some clients with bipolar disorder or schizophrenia-spectrum disorders who have recently also been diagnosed with PTSD wonder whether their initial diagnosis is incorrect and whether all of their problems stem from their traumatic experiences and PTSD. This is an understandable, but tricky, question to address. Trauma in childhood or adolescence can increase vulnerability to developing a wide range of psychiatric disorders (Edwards, Holden, Felitti, & Anda, 2003; Figueroa, Silk, Huth, & Lohr, 1997; J. Read, van Os, Morrison, & Ross, 2005; Saunders, Villeponteaux, Lipovsky, Kilpatrick, & Veronen, 1992), and of course it is possible to have both a major mood disorder or schizophrenia-spectrum disorder and PTSD. However, trauma history is frequently not assessed, and hence PTSD is often not diagnosed, in people with severe psychiatric disorders (Cusack, Frueh, & Brady, 2004; Mueser et al., 1998; Salyers, Evans, Bond, & Meyer, 2004). There is always a possibility that symptoms related to PTSD can be construed as due to another disorder, and the person misdiagnosed accordingly. For example, irritability and other arousal symptoms of PTSD can resemble the hypomanic or manic symptoms of bipolar disorder, leading to misdiagnosis. Similarly, social avoidance and emotional numbness in PTSD can resemble the negative symptoms of schizophrenia, while trauma-related hallucinations and delusions are easily construed as psychotic symptoms of schizophrenia (Oruc & Bell, 1995; Waldfogel & Mueser, 1988).

The most straightforward approach to this question is to acknowledge that PTSD is associated with a wide range of symptoms but also to point out that it is possible for people to have both PTSD and another psychiatric disorder. Participation in the CR program may be helpful in reducing symptoms of both PTSD and their other disorders. If the program is effective in reducing or eliminating the client's PTSD symptoms and other symptoms remit as well, this can be taken as evidence that those symptoms may have been part of the person's posttraumatic reaction.

Homework

Because the format and material covered in the session on associated problems related to traumatic experiences are similar to those in the previous session on PTSD, a similar homework assignment can be agreed on. This could include the client's completing any remaining worksheets from the handout, reviewing the handout, or sharing and reviewing the handout with a support person. Any problems the client had completing the homework assignment for the first psychoeducational session, such as feeling anxious and not wanting to write about PTSD symptoms, can be addressed when developing the assignment following the second session.

Exploring Functional Goals

At the end of the second psychoeducational session, before beginning CR, the therapist should explore the client's functional goals for treatment. This discussion should not emphasize thoughts or feelings, but behaviors that reflect the client's adjustment in his or her social context, including areas such as relationships, leisure activities, self-care, and role functioning. Examples of goals related to different areas of functioning are provided in Table 5.2. As previously noted, from the time that the client's PTSD is confirmed, the therapist is on the lookout for ways to understand how traumatic experiences and PTSD have influenced the client's functioning and adjustment. Once the client understands the nature of PTSD, the time is ripe to explore areas of functioning that the client would like to see improved as a result of treatment.

During the psychoeducational sessions, some clients talk openly about how their traumatic experiences and PTSD have affected their lives and inter-

TABLE 5.2
Examples of Goals for Different Areas of Functioning

Area	Examples of goals
Close relationships	■ Having friends, seeing friends more often, or getting closer to friends ■ Having an intimate partner ■ Enjoying sexual relations ■ Spending more time with a partner or family member ■ Being able to enjoy a casual conversation with a member of the opposite sex
Role functioning	■ Working a part-time or full-time job ■ Pursuing a more interesting or more demanding job ■ Getting a volunteer job ■ Trying to get a promotion for which one feels one is qualified ■ Returning to school to complete a degree
Leisure and recreation	■ Being able to concentrate while reading a book ■ Pursuing an activity outside of the home, such as an aerobics class, a dance class, or going to the movies ■ Being able to drive oneself to go desired places ■ Developing or rekindling a hobby or pastime, such as knitting, following sports, or making a scrapbook on a favorite topic ■ Being able to go to a store to purchase items related to an area of interest (such as knitting supplies) ■ Pursuing a form of self-expression, such as art, music, or poetry
Self-care and independent living	■ Attending to one's personal hygiene (bathing/showering, oral hygiene, grooming) ■ Doing household tasks, such as laundry, cooking, shopping, and budgeting ■ Maintaining one's living environment (such as cleaning, straightening up) ■ Maintaining stable housing and avoiding homelessness or having to crash with family or friends ■ Stopping one's use of alcohol or drugs ■ Attending to medical or dental needs ■ Avoiding having to go into the hospital for the treatment of mental health or substance abuse problems

fered with attaining personal life goals. Other clients may talk about their symptoms, but the effects of PTSD on their functioning or goals are less clear. Many clients with PTSD either do not appear to have any functional goals, or they believe they could never achieve them as long as they have PTSD symptoms. Encouraging clients to talk about which areas of functioning they most want to improve and informing them that progress toward these changes can be accomplished in the CR program while working on PTSD symptoms can be enlightening to clients who want a better life but have felt stymied by their PTSD.

There are many opportunities to talk about the effects of trauma and PTSD on the client's functioning during the psychoeducational sessions, and it is quite natural for the therapist to inquire how those symptoms and problems have interfered with important aspects of daily living. Even if a client reports impaired functioning in a particular area, the therapist should not assume that improving in this area is an important personal goal but should inquire as to which areas of functioning the client most wants to change.

Sometimes clients are afraid to set personal goals and cannot imagine pursuing such goals as long as they have PTSD symptoms. It may be helpful to ask these clients to talk about how their lives would be different if they had not experienced their traumas and did not have PTSD. Getting people to imagine their lives without PTSD can begin the process of identifying areas they care most about changing. Once they are identified, the therapist should review these areas with the client, and emphasize that the CR program can help them make progress toward these goals. In subsequent sessions, these goals should be followed up on, with progress toward them reinforced. Subsequent sessions should also address problems or obstacles the client may have encountered during the use of breathing retraining and CR.

SUMMARY AND CONCLUSIONS

Providing information about PTSD and associated difficulties both normalizes clients' reactions to traumatic events and helps them develop a fuller understanding of how these experiences have affected their lives. This knowledge can alleviate some of the self-blame that trauma survivors often have about their responses to trauma while instilling hope that the CR program may improve not only their PTSD symptoms but some of their other problems as well. This expectation is further reinforced at the end of the psychoeducational sessions by discussing functional goals the client would like to make progress toward over the course of the program. These sessions serve to solidify the therapeutic relationship with the client and as a foundation for beginning work on CR, the cornerstone of the CR for PTSD program.

6

COGNITIVE RESTRUCTURING I: THE COMMON STYLES OF THINKING

KIM T. MUESER, STANLEY D. ROSENBERG,
AND HARRIET J. ROSENBERG

Cognitive restructuring (CR) consists of a broad set of strategies aimed at helping people change inaccurate thoughts or beliefs that lead to negative feelings (A. T. Beck, Rush, Shaw, & Emery, 1979). The basic theory underlying the use of CR for posttraumatic reactions is that trauma, and how people respond to it, shapes their thoughts and beliefs about themselves, other people, and the world in general (Dalgleish, 2004; Ehlers & Clark, 2000). Trauma-related beliefs may develop gradually over a period of time during which multiple traumatization occurs (e.g., believing "men can't be trusted" over the course of childhood sexual abuse), soon after a traumatic event has occurred (e.g., believing "no situation is safe and I could be attacked at any time" after a violent robbery), or a long period following traumatic events (e.g., believing "I am shameful and did 'bad' things because I didn't prevent myself from being sexually abused as a child"). These beliefs, also called *schemas*, shape individuals' perceptions of the world and their associated emotional reactions, such as having a heightened perception of threat which then leads to chronic feelings of anxiety.

However, these trauma-related schemas are inaccurate, and they are often are destructive perspectives on the self and the world. In some cases, individuals cling to beliefs that were accurate at one point in time, but no longer are (e.g., the belief that "the world is an unsafe place" for a child raised in a physically abusive environment). In other cases, the schemas are understandable but exaggerated beliefs based on a traumatic experience that shattered the person's assumptions about the world (e.g., inflated perceptions of danger in a person who was the victim of a violent crime). For still others, the beliefs are wholly inaccurate and were formed in the aftermath of trauma as part of the individual's attempts to understand and create meaning out of the experience (e.g., a woman's belief that she was responsible for her childhood sexual abuse because she experienced some sexual pleasure from the abuse and did not try to stop it).

Teaching individuals how to identify and challenge trauma-related misperceptions can correct these beliefs and ameliorate the negative feelings associated with them. CR is taught to clients as a self-management skill for dealing with common negative emotions related to posttraumatic stress disorder (PTSD), such as anxiety, depression, guilt, or anger. The initial focus of CR is on helping clients learn how to use the technique to cope with any negative feelings they experience. As clients become more skilled at CR, the focus gradually shifts to identifying and challenging core trauma-related beliefs that underlie their PTSD symptoms.

Cognitive Restructuring I, discussed in this chapter, is aimed at first teaching clients about the relationship between thoughts and feelings and second at how to recognize and challenge what we refer to as *common styles of thinking* (i.e., common logical errors that occur when people draw conclusions about specific events, such as jumping to conclusions before there is sufficient evidence, sometimes referred to as *cognitive distortions*; A. T. Beck, 1963; A. T. Beck et al., 1979; Burns, 1999; Ellis, 1962; Leahy, 2003). Beginning CR with a focus on common styles of thinking gives clients a tool they can immediately grasp and begin using to cope with their negative feelings and challenge the thoughts associated with them.

Cognitive Restructuring II (chap. 7, this volume) builds on the common styles of thinking by teaching the 5 Steps of CR, a method for identifying core thoughts and schemas that contribute to negative feelings and systematically evaluating the evidence for and against those thoughts. This method is a more powerful CR tool because it helps people to pinpoint core beliefs related to their traumatic experiences and to correct them accordingly. Although all clients are taught the 5 Steps of CR, the most critical goal is for clients to be able to use some type of CR to deal with their negative feelings, either this approach, the common styles of thinking, or some other variant of the skill.

THE FIRST COGNITIVE RESTRUCTURING SESSION

We recommend that CR be started in the fourth session, after the client has learned breathing retraining and has gained an understanding of the nature of PTSD symptoms and associated problems. CR can be started earlier, if feasible, but should not be delayed past the fourth session unless the client is in crisis.

PTSD symptoms and depression should be routinely monitored with all clients, including administering the PTSD Checklist (PCL; Blanchard, Jones-Alexander, Buckley, & Forneris, 1996) and Beck Depression Inventory—II (BDI; A. T. Beck, Steer, & Brown, 1996) at the beginning of every three sessions, starting with Session 1. We specifically recommend beginning the first CR session with this assessment. This provides a good indication of the level of distress experienced by the client at the beginning of CR, which can be used to judge the effectiveness of the client's ability to use the skill over subsequent sessions. The review of recent PTSD and depression symptoms can also prove useful for teaching CR later in this session or subsequent ones. For example, the therapist may refer to specific items from the PCL or BDI ratings that the client endorsed in order to explore whether they reflect specific common styles of thinking.

When the client has completed the assessment forms, the therapist briefly reviews them with him or her and discusses whether any changes in symptoms have occurred since the previous administration of the measures (e.g., in Session 1). Lack of change in symptoms can be normalized, as the client has not yet learned CR. Improvements in symptoms can be briefly explored (e.g., has the use of breathing retraining reduced anxiety?). Occasionally clients report a mild increase in symptoms. This too can be normalized as an early effect of engaging in trauma work; as clients begin to confront their traumatic experiences and change their long-standing patterns of avoidance, some increase in anxiety and associated symptoms can naturally occur.

After the client's symptom self-ratings have been discussed, the therapist reviews the homework assignment from the previous week and answers any questions the client may have about associated problems related to PTSD. The remainder of the session is devoted to introducing the rationale for CR and then teaching the client how to recognize and challenge the common styles of thinking. At the end of the session, a homework assignment is developed for the client to practice using the common styles of thinking to cope with negative feelings.

Introducing Cognitive Restructuring

CR can be introduced as follows:

Therapist: Up to this point in the program, we have worked on two things to help you with your PTSD symptoms. First, you have learned breathing retraining as a way of dealing with anxiety and tension. Second, you have learned about the symptoms and associated problems of PTSD. By understanding that your reactions to traumatic events are common ones that other people have, you can begin to learn better ways of handling these problems. Today we are going to begin working on a skill called *cognitive restructuring*. This is a strategy for dealing with the upsetting feelings that often accompany traumatic reactions.

After laying the groundwork for CR, the therapist engages the client in a brief discussion of the most distressing negative feelings he or she experiences related to the trauma. This discussion makes those feelings salient and prepares the client for the discussion that follows about how thoughts can influence feelings. For example:

Therapist: We've talked about how people with PTSD often experience a wide range of negative feelings. Some of the most common upsetting emotions include fear and anxiety, sadness and depression, guilt and shame, and anger. Which of these negative feelings do you experience the most?

Client: That's a tough one. I think I have a lot of those feelings. I know I have a lot of anger, and I sometimes feel consumed with hate.

Therapist: What kinds of situations trigger those feelings?

Client: Sometimes I just think about it, what my brother did to me, and I know it's not right. Sexually abusing a little girl like that. And it makes me full of hate, even now, 5 years after he has been dead.

Therapist: Do other situations bring on those feelings?

Client: When somebody does something that affects me, I get angry. I sometimes overreact and have those same hateful feelings.

Therapist: What about the other negative feelings associated with PTSD?

Client: I'd like to get closer to someone, but I'm afraid.

Therapist: Afraid of what?

Client: Afraid of getting hurt again. Afraid of being vulnerable.

Therapist: Any other feelings?

Client: I feel guilty that I didn't tell my father about the abuse. He would have put his foot down. He would have done something to stop my brother.

Therapist: And when do you have those feelings?

Client:	Whenever I think about what he did to me.
Therapist:	Any other times?
Client:	When I was married. I used to have those feelings whenever I had sex. Like there was something wrong with me. Like I was dirty or bad.
Therapist:	As you now know, all of these feelings are very common in people with PTSD. Now let's spend some time understanding where those feelings come from. Upsetting feelings such as anxiety, guilt, or anger are usually related to what we think about a situation or an event. Let's use an example of how our thinking affects our feelings in a situation. Pretend you were sleeping at night and you were awakened by a sound of a scratching noise at your window. You think, "There must be a burglar trying to break into my bedroom." How would you feel?
Client:	I'd be afraid. I'd think he was going to hurt me.
Therapist:	Right. It would only be natural to be afraid if you thought someone was trying to break into your apartment. Now pretend that you were lying in bed and you heard that same scratching noise at your window. But this time you remember that you let the cat out before you went to bed, and you think, "Oh, that must be the cat. She wants to come in." Now how would you feel?
Client:	Maybe a little annoyed, if she'd woken me up. Or maybe I'd be happy to see her and know that she's okay.
Therapist:	Right. If you thought that sound was your cat scratching at the window, you'd respond differently, maybe by being a bit annoyed, or you might be glad to see her. This is an example of how your thoughts determine your feelings. Until you look at the window and know what's there, you don't know whether it's your cat, a burglar, or something else. If you thought it was a burglar you'd be afraid, but you would have a totally different reaction if you thought it was your cat.

An alternative example is the "walking down the street" scenario:

Therapist:	For example, let's imagine you are walking down the street and you see someone you know walking with a few other people, and you say hello to her. But she doesn't say anything back. How would you feel if that happened?

Client:	I think I'd be hurt. Why shouldn't she say hello to me? I said hello to her.
Therapist:	Okay, that's good. So you'd feel hurt. And why would you feel hurt? What would you be saying to yourself that would make you feel hurt?
Client:	Maybe that she doesn't like me. Or she thinks she's better than me.
Therapist:	Right. So if you thought your friend didn't like you or was deliberately ignoring you, you'd feel hurt. Now let's say when your friend didn't say hello to you that you noticed she was talking to the other people, and you thought, "She must not have heard me say hello." How would you feel then?
Client:	I'd probably just shrug it off. I don't think I'd feel anything in particular.
Therapist:	Would you feel hurt or offended?
Client:	No, there wouldn't be any reason to.
Therapist:	Right. If you didn't think your friend was deliberately ignoring you, you wouldn't feel bad about her not saying hello. This is an example of how thoughts determine your feelings. How people react in a situation depends on their thoughts about it. You'd feel bad if you thought your friend was ignoring you, but not if you thought she hadn't heard you.

Either of these examples usually helps clients understand the relationship between thoughts and feelings. If the client understands the first example, the therapist can move on to talking about how life experiences shape thoughts and feelings. If the client has difficulty grasping the first example, the second one should be used to illustrate the point.

In general, the more cognitively impaired the client is, the more important it is for the therapist to provide concrete examples of extreme and different thoughts in a particular situation, and the different feelings that would be associated with each thought. For clients with better cognitive functioning, the therapist may elect to brainstorm with the client a variety of different thoughts someone might have in a given situation (such as the "walking down the street" scenario) and then consider the different feelings associated with each thought. Encouraging clients to consider different possible thoughts for a particular situation establishes that there are multiple perspectives for any particular situation and different feelings associated with those perspectives.

When the relationship between thoughts and feelings has been established, the therapist next explains how personal life experiences, including traumatic ones, can affect the way people perceive and think about situations they experience throughout their lives:

Therapist: So, given any situation that you experience, your feelings depend on what you think about that situation. What makes people think the way they do?

Client: I don't know. Most of the time I'm not even aware that I'm thinking.

Therapist: That's a good point. Often the thoughts that we have in situations are automatic. You might not be aware that you're having these automatic thoughts, but you're having them nevertheless. One of the things that shape the thoughts we have, including our automatic thoughts, is our life experiences. Over the course of your lifetime, you've learned ways of understanding or thinking about things from your different experiences, including your traumatic experiences.

Client: You mean like what my brother did to me?

Therapist: Yes, exactly. Over time, those ways of thinking about yourself, other people, or the world grow stronger and develop into beliefs. And these beliefs continue to shape the way you look at things. You may not even be aware of your beliefs or how they influence your reactions to the world around you.

Everyone has thoughts and beliefs that affect the way he or she looks at the world. However, these beliefs are often not true, even though people may take them for granted because they've thought that way for so long. This can be particularly true when people have had traumatic experiences, which can lead to negative and unhelpful beliefs about themselves, other people, or the world. And of course these negative beliefs lead to the negative feelings that we've been talking about, such as anxiety, guilt, and depression. How do you think that your brother abusing you may have affected your beliefs and feelings?

Client: I'm not sure. I know that I felt afraid and ashamed.

Therapist: Okay. Let's talk about feeling afraid first. What are you afraid of?

Client: That I'm going to be hurt.

Therapist: Right. And why do you think that your brother abusing you as a child would make you afraid of being hurt as an adult?

Client: Someone's brother isn't supposed to hurt them or do bad things to them. He's family. But he hurt me. So I guess I'm afraid that other people will hurt me too.

Therapist: Okay, that helps me understand. You're afraid that other people will hurt you because your brother hurt you. Would you say that you believe that in general, people can't be trusted?

Client:	I think so. Or at least men can't be trusted.
Therapist:	Okay, so you can see how your traumatic experiences contributed to your belief that people can't be trusted. And your belief that no men can be trusted makes you feel afraid in a lot of situations.
Client:	I do feel afraid a lot.

When the therapist has helped the client identify some examples of how traumatic experiences have influenced his or her beliefs and the feelings associated with them, the common styles of thinking is introduced as a strategy for examining the thoughts underlying negative feelings, and changing them when they are inaccurate of unhelpful:

| Therapist: | So we know that thoughts and beliefs contribute to the feelings that we have in our everyday lives. And we know that traumatic and other life experiences affect these thoughts and beliefs. Last, we know that beliefs are sometimes not accurate. Learning how to examine and challenge thoughts and beliefs that lead to distressing feelings is an important tool for helping you deal with those feelings and for processing your life experiences. Our work together will involve helping you learn how to identify and challenge thoughts and beliefs that lead to upsetting feelings. |
| | I'd now like to teach you a helpful method for identifying when your thinking is leading to unpleasant feelings and evaluating whether your thoughts are accurate or not. This method involves learning about the "common styles of thinking" or common inaccurate, unhelpful ways of thinking that lead to distress. Everyone engages in these common styles of thinking sometimes, but some people who have had traumatic experiences are more prone to it than others. |

Using the Common Styles of Thinking handout (Handout #7; see Appendix), the therapist provides a brief explanation of each style and why it is inaccurate, and then helps the client identify examples of situations in which he or she engaged in that style. For each example, the therapist prompts the client to describe the feelings associated with the thought, why the thought was inaccurate in that situation, what a more accurate thought would have been, and whether that more accurate thought would have reduced his or her distress. The therapist can remind the client of previously mentioned upsetting trauma-related thoughts and client and therapist can explore together whether the thought reflects a common style of thinking. An example of introducing and discussing the common styles of thinking is provided next:

Therapist: Let's spend a few minutes talking about the common styles of thinking and why each one is inaccurate. One is *all-or-nothing thinking*. This style of thinking is when you look at a situation in absolute terms and believe that everything is either all one way or all the other way, but nothing is in the middle. For example, let's say a worker named Bill tried to do a really good job on something, and he put a lot of good effort into it, but there were still a few minor mistakes. If Bill believed that he was a failure because he didn't do a perfect job, that would be all-or-nothing thinking. How do you think Bill would feel if he put in all that effort but thought he was a failure because of a few minor mistakes?

Client: Pretty bad.

Therapist: That's right. So why would Bill's thinking that he's a failure in this situation be an example of all-or-nothing thinking? Why would that be inaccurate?

Client: Because he did a good job. Just because it wasn't perfect doesn't mean he didn't do a good job.

Therapist: Right. Doing a pretty good job, or even an excellent job with a few minor mistakes, is in between doing a perfect job and being a failure at the job. In this situation, what might be a more accurate way for Bill to think about how he did?

Client: He could say, "I did a pretty good job. Nobody's perfect."

Therapist: And if you were Bill and had that thought, how would you feel about your job performance?

Client: I think I'd feel pretty good about it.

Therapist: Good. So you can see that catching and changing these common styles of thinking can reduce upsetting feelings in situations that result from inaccurate thinking. Can you think of an example of when you engaged in all-or-nothing thinking?

Client: No, because I don't consider myself a failure, but I'm not perfect either.

Therapist: How about the thought you mentioned earlier, that "you can't trust men?" Could that be an example of all-or-nothing thinking?

Client: I don't know. I've been hurt by men. First by my brother. And then by my husband when we were married. I'm just trying to get rid of all my fear and hate. I think I would maybe like to be with a guy again, but then I'm afraid of men.

Therapist:	Right. So why might the thought "I can't trust men" not be completely accurate?
Client:	Because there might be some guys who are okay?
Therapist:	Yes. Can you think of any man you've ever known who could be trusted?
Client:	I think I can trust my minister. He seems like a good person.
Therapist:	Okay, so why is that thought all-or-nothing thinking?
Client:	It's an exaggeration. Some men probably can be trusted, like my minister.
Therapist:	Right, all-or-nothing thinking often involves exaggerations of the truth because the person doesn't recognize the in-betweens.

Okay, let's move on to another common style of thinking. This one is called *overgeneralization*, which is when you jump to conclusions by assuming that when something bad happens, it will happen again and again. Just because something has happened before, you're sure that it's going to happen again. For example, a person who was victimized as a child might believe that they'll continue to be victimized throughout their life because they might think, "I'm easy to take advantage of." Can you think of times when you have used overgeneralization? |

Homework

At the end of the session, the therapist develops an assignment with the client to practice recognizing and changing common styles of thinking related to negative feelings. The homework sheet provides separate columns for the client to briefly describe the situation, write the negative feeling he or she experienced, identify the common style of thinking related to that feeling, and describe a more accurate way of looking at the situation. The therapist explains that experiencing a negative or distressing feeling is a signal that the person may be engaging in a common style of thinking and that he or she should examine the thought underlying the feeling. Clients should be encouraged to practice identifying common styles of thinking even in situations in which they are experiencing only minor negative emotions.

After explaining the homework assignment, the therapist goes over the homework sheet (Common Styles of Thinking Worksheet: Handout #8; see Appendix) and completes at least one example with the client so it is clear the client understands how to complete it. The therapist and client should also discuss where the client can store the sheet and when it should be completed on a daily basis. For example:

Therapist: You've done a great job of coming up with examples of situations in which you used a common style of thinking. You can see how these common styles are often inaccurate and the distressing feelings that can be associated with them. You've also seen how challenging and correcting the common styles of thinking can reduce distress and improve mood. When you take a more balanced look at a situation, you usually don't feel as badly about it compared with when you have an inaccurate common style of thinking.

Let's come up with a plan for you to continue this work on your own and for you to get some practice identifying common styles of thinking in your day-to-day life.

FOLLOW-UP SESSION ON THE COMMON STYLES OF THINKING

The next session begins with a review of the homework assignment. Then, if all the common styles of thinking were not taught in the previous session, the remaining ones are taught. The bulk of the session is spent on additional teaching and practice recognizing and correcting these types of misperceptions. At the end of the session, a new homework assignment is agreed on for the following week.

Homework Review

For the homework review, any efforts by the client to recognize and correct common styles of thinking should be praised and discussed, even if the client did not compete any written homework sheets. If no homework sheets were completed, the therapist can supply the client with one at the beginning of the session and ask him or her to try to complete a few examples. The therapist should allow the client a few minutes to do this. If the client is unable to come up with any examples, the therapist should explore with him or her any recent situations in which the client felt distress and then evaluate the underlying thoughts, and possible common styles of thinking, related to those feelings.

When reviewing the client's attempts to recognize and change common styles of thinking, the therapist should avoid "correcting" the client if at least one common style was identified. The different common styles of thinking overlap with each other, and what is most important is that the client is able to recognize and change at least some of them and get the benefit of reduced distress. During this discussion, any success the client had with the exercise should be followed up by exploring whether recognizing and changing one of these thought patterns resulted in a reduction in distress. In most situations, replacing a common style of thinking with a more accurate thought leads to some alleviation in upsetting feelings. For example,

Therapist: I can see from your homework sheet that last Thursday you caught yourself using a common style of thinking when your daughter was late coming home from school.

Client: Yes, I remember that. She was really late, more than an hour, and I panicked. I was sure somebody had kidnapped her or something terrible had happened.

Therapist: That must have been pretty frightening.

Client: It was. I always think something has happened to her if she's late.

Therapist: So it sounds like you caught yourself using a common style of thinking. Did you catch yourself in the moment, or was it later that you recognized it?

Client: A little of both. At the moment, I was terrified, and all sorts of things started going through my head about what must have happened to her. I was getting more and more scared, when I suddenly said to myself, "Hold it! You're 'catastrophizing'!"

Therapist: That was it? You went from having those thoughts straight to recognizing that it was a common style of thinking?

Client: Well, as I was thinking about what might have happened to her, I remembered our session last week when we talked about the common styles. I knew from that discussion that I often jump to conclusions and panic or think the worst is going to happen, even when it usually doesn't.

Therapist: And that helped you make the connection. How did recognizing your thinking style affect your feelings?

Client: I felt a little relieved. And that helped me think more clearly.

Therapist: So what happened then?

Client: I thought of all the reasons my daughter's been late in the past and that made me feel a little more relieved. She ended up coming home at 5:00 p.m., almost 2 hours late. She'd gone home with a friend of hers, and boy did I let her have it for not calling me and telling me where she was.

Therapist: That's a really good example of how catching yourself using a common style of thinking can be helpful.

The therapist should explain that experiencing negative emotions is a sign that the person may be engaging in a common style of thinking but that not all unpleasant feelings are due to inaccurate thinking. Sometimes it is perfectly appropriate to have a negative feeling in a situation. For example, if someone is riding in a car with a reckless driver, it would make sense to feel anxious. Therefore, the therapist helps the client see that the goal of identifying common styles of thinking is to catch ourselves thinking inaccurate thoughts in situations that unnecessarily lead to high levels of distress.

Additional Teaching Strategies

A number of additional teaching strategies are useful for helping clients learn how to modify inaccurate thought patterns that lead to unpleasant feelings.

Reviewing the Common Styles of Thinking Together

If the client has difficulty determining whether an upsetting thought is the result of a common style of thinking, the therapist can simply go over the styles in the handout one at a time, prompting the client to consider whether the thought reflects that particular style. When the client identifies a possible style related to his or her thought, discussion can then focus on exploring whether the thought is accurate or not and on changing it if it is.

Client:	I feel depressed—like a failure—when I look back at my marriage. It was 25 years of just going through the motions. There weren't any happy times, and I feel like a fool for having stayed with it for so long.
Therapist:	It sounds like you have some pretty unhappy thoughts when you look back on your marriage.
Client:	I do. I feel like I've wasted half of my life.
Therapist:	Okay, let's examine your thought more closely, that "there were no happy times in your marriage and you were a fool to have stayed in it for so long." To make it easier, let's focus on the first part of that thought, "There were no happy times during my marriage." How about if we go over some of the common styles of thinking and see whether one or more of them apply here?
Client:	Sure, that thought really weighs on me.
Therapist:	Right. Let's begin with *catastrophizing,* which is when you jump to conclusions. That is, you assume the worst thing is going to happen before you really have enough evidence to reach that conclusion. Does your thought, "There was no happiness during my entire marriage" reflect catastrophizing?

Client: I don't think so. I'm not thinking about something terrible happening. I beat myself up when I think that I wasted my life married to someone I didn't really love.

Therapist: Okay, so it doesn't sound like this thought is an example of catastrophizing. Let's consider another one. *Overgeneralization* is when you see an event as part of a never-ending pattern of similar events, like "once a victim, always a victim." Is your thought, "There was no happiness during my entire marriage" an example of overgeneralization?

Client: I do tend to look at my marriage as an example of being a victim again, first when my brother sexually abused me, and then being in an unhappy marriage.

Therapist: Does that mean when you think of yourself as a victim because your marriage wasn't happy that you're overgeneralizing from your experiences in childhood?

Client: Well maybe. It certainly seems like it is a pattern in my life. And it makes me feel like a loser, like I'm a failure in life.

Therapist: And what makes your thought that your marriage had no happiness in it an overgeneralization from what happened to you in childhood? How was the sexual abuse you experienced in childhood different from that in your unhappy marriage?

Client: I really didn't have a choice about what happened to me in childhood. But I guess I could have gotten out of my marriage if I really wanted to.

Therapist: Okay, so when you think that "my marriage had no happy times," you might be overgeneralizing from what happened to you in childhood and from your belief that a lot of bad things have happened to you that are out of your control.

Client: Right.

Therapist: Before we explore that one further, let's consider another common style of thinking, *all-or-nothing thinking*. Do you remember this style?

Client: Yes. It's when everything is either one way or another.

Therapist: Right. For example, believing that you are either perfect or a miserable failure would be all-or-nothing thinking. Or someone might look back on something and tell themselves the experience was either totally horrible or truly wonderful, with nothing in between. Do you think that your thought that "my marriage was totally without any happiness" could be an example of that type of thinking?

Client:	Maybe so.
Therapist:	What about your thought makes you think that? Is it possible that your statement that you had "absolutely no happiness" in your marriage is an exaggeration?
Client:	I think so. It sounds kind of extreme.
Therapist:	Can you think of any times during your marriage when you laughed or had a good time together?
Client:	Well, I guess I could think of a few.
Therapist:	Can you give me an example?
Client:	I remember a few months after we were married we went to a neighborhood carnival together. We had a good time.
Therapist:	Okay. And that probably wasn't the only good time you had, right?
Client:	Right.
Therapist:	So it looks like the thought "my marriage was without any happiness" reflects the common style of thinking of all-or-nothing thinking because you acknowledge that you had at least a few good times together. Let's think of a way of looking back on your marriage that corrects this common style of thinking. What do you think would be a more accurate way of looking at your marriage?
Client:	I'm not sure. No matter how I think about it, I don't feel very good.
Therapist:	That's okay. Let's come up with a more accurate way of thinking about it, and then we'll see how you feel about that. The new thought should still be consistent with your experience but more accurate than your all-or-nothing thought. Let's think of a new, more accurate thought. Want to give it a try?
Client:	How about: "My marriage wasn't happy, but we had some good times?"
Therapist:	That sounds more accurate to me. How about you? Does that sound accurate to you?
Client:	Yes, it does.
Therapist:	And when you look back on your marriage and think, "My marriage wasn't happy, but we had some good times," how do you feel compared to before?
Client:	A little better. And I don't feel like such a fool either.

Shaping the Client's Ability to Identify More Accurate Thoughts

After a common style of thinking has been identified, and a new and more balanced thought is sought, it is critical that the client believe that this new thought is more accurate than the old one it is replacing. Clients often come up with new thoughts that are only slightly more accurate than the old ones but that still appear to the therapist to be inaccurate. Rather than having a lengthy debate about the accuracy of the new thought, the therapist should reinforce the client for modifying his or her thoughts and draw attention to the benefits of the change in terms of reduced distress related to the new thought. This shapes the ability of clients to identify and modify inaccurate thinking patterns through modest changes in the accuracy of their thinking and associated reductions in distress. Each time the client successfully corrects his or her thinking, and experiences some relief, the client is reinforced to use this skill again, with potentially greater gains down the line.

For example, the client in the vignette provided in the section above on "Homework Review" may have initially believed "my daughter has not come home from school because she has been kidnapped," and after some consideration she may have been able to recognize this thought as catastrophizing. However, even after recognizing that her initial thought was inaccurate, she might have believed that it was *likely* her daughter had been kidnapped, leading to the new, "more accurate" thought that "there is a good chance that my daughter has been kidnapped, but there *might* be some other reason she has not returned from school yet."

Focusing on, and reinforcing, small changes to more accurate thinking avoids problems that often occur when the therapist enters into a debate with the client aimed at producing more dramatic changes in thinking. For example, if the therapist is unsuccessful at convincing the client to make a major change in his or her beliefs (rather than a minor change), then an opportunity is lost to demonstrate the utility of the common styles of thinking because there is no reduction in distress. The chance of this occurring is minimized if the therapist is willing to settle for a more modest change in the client's thought. Helping clients making smaller corrections in their use of common styles of thinking, and taking responsibility themselves for the change, can support their self-efficacy for learning how to use this skill on their own.

TEACHING CLIENTS HOW TO RATE THEIR BELIEFS AND DISTRESS

As just discussed, learning how to recognize and change common styles of thinking often involves experiencing modest reductions in distress at first. It is important to reinforce these modest gains so that clients are encouraged

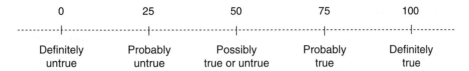

Figure 6.1. Belief scale.

to continue to hone their CR skills with the expectation of reaping greater benefits over time. To highlight small improvements in mood as a result of CR, it can be helpful to teach clients how to rate their belief in specific thoughts leading to upsetting feelings and how to rate the degree of distress experienced.

First, the client is taught how to use a belief scale, in which a rating is given between 0 and 100, corresponding to *definitely untrue* (0) in the accuracy of the thought to *definitely true* (100; see Figure 6.1). Then, after the client has provided a rating for a specific thought, he or she is taught how to rate the level of distress related to that thought on a distress scale, with 0 corresponding to *no distress at all* and 100 corresponding to *extreme distress* (see Figure 6.2).

After the upsetting thought and feeling have been rated on the belief and distress scales, the client examines the thought more closely to determine whether it reflects a common style of thinking and whether it is a completely accurate way of looking at the situation. When the thought has been thoroughly evaluated, and evidence for and against it has been weighed (including the common styles of thinking), the client provides another rating of conviction on the belief scale for the same thought. If the thought clearly reflects a common style of thinking or if new evidence against the accuracy of the thought has been considered, the client's second rating on the belief scale would be expected to drop by at least a few points, if not more. After a drop in conviction on the belief scale has been registered, regardless of how large, the therapist prompts the client to develop a more accurate thought about the situation. This new thought should be rated higher on the belief scale than the most recent rating given to the old thought. After the person has given a higher rating on the belief scale for the new and more accurate thought, the client provides a new rating on the distress scale for the new thought, which is usually lower than the original distress rating for the old thought.

Figure 6.2. Distress scale.

Clinical Example

Pam was extremely anxious because she had unwittingly smiled at a man she knew from her church. Although she liked this man, she was distrustful of men, avoided relationships, and did not want to encourage him to pursue her as a friend or any other kind of relationship. Since the incident at church, she had been very worried that he might try to get closer to her and would eventually end up victimizing her.

The therapist explained how to provide ratings on the beliefs and distress scales. After discussing her concern about the event, Pam articulated her initial thought about the situation as "he's going to pursue an intimate relationship with me, and take advantage of me, just like other men have in my life." She gave this thought a 95 on the belief scale and rated her distress as 90 on the distress scale.

After considering the thought in more detail, and reviewing the common styles of thinking, Pam decided that it was not completely accurate and that it reflected *overestimation of risk* (i.e., perceiving she was likely to be taken advantage of by the man) and *overgeneralization* (i.e., perceiving that because she had been victimized in the past she was likely to be victimized again). She gave a second rating on the belief scale for this thought as a 70. She then identified a more accurate thought for the situation: "He might try to get closer to me, which makes me feel nervous, but that doesn't mean he will necessarily try to take advantage of me." She gave this new thought a rating of 85 on the belief scale and a rating of 75 on the distress scale. By teaching Pam how to rate her level of conviction and distress before and after recognizing her thoughts related to common styles of thinking, the therapist was able to point to concrete evidence that catching and correcting inaccurate thoughts that lead to negative feelings can reduce the distress she experienced in everyday situations.

OBSTACLES TO COMPLETING HOMEWORK

Progress in the Cognitive Restructuring for Posttraumatic Stress Disorder (CR for PTSD) program depends on clients' ability and willingness to practice CR on their own, with homework assignments designed to facilitate this. However, clients do not always follow through on homework, especially early in treatment. Therefore, overcoming obstacles to follow-through on homework is critical to success in the program.

It is helpful to conceptualize *homework* as clients' attempt to use skills taught in session on their own, regardless of whether written assignments were completed. Thus, if a client reports successfully recognizing and challenging common styles of thinking related to negative feelings on several occasions over the past week but did not use the worksheet, the therapist should first provide him or her with reinforcement for following through on homework and using the skill. Then, the therapist can explore strategies for helping the client use the worksheet for the following week's homework assignment.

If no written homework was completed and the client did not try to recognize common styles of thinking related to distressful feelings, the therapist should problem-solve with the client about obstacles to completing homework before the next session. Common problems include forgetting, losing the homework sheet, not understanding the assignment, and feeling preoccupied or overwhelmed with other problems or crises.

When addressing lack of follow-through on homework, the therapist should first review with the client the role of homework in learning CR and then develop a plan to overcome any problems the client encountered during the past week. Going over and practicing with the client how to complete the homework sheet, prompting the client to set aside a time of the day and quiet place where the assignment can be completed, enlisting social support for the client to complete the assignment, and simplifying the assignment as needed (e.g., focusing the homework assignment on identifying and correcting the one or two common styles of thinking that are most frequently experienced by the client) are all useful strategies for overcoming obstacles. Clients who report feeling anxious about homework can make a plan to use breathing retraining before completing the assignment each day. All homework assignments should be collaboratively agreed on to ensure that the client understands the assignment and believes that he or she can complete it. Additional strategies for enhancing follow-through on homework are provided in Table 9.1.

CONTINUING WORK ON THE COMMON STYLES OF THINKING

Several issues are critical to further work on the common styles of thinking.

Focusing on Trauma-Related Thoughts

When teaching clients how to recognize the common styles of thinking, trauma-related thoughts and beliefs are sometimes readily apparent and can be easily explored. For example, thoughts such as "I can never trust anyone," "People will take advantage of you if given the opportunity," "I am a failure because I didn't get out of an abusive relationship and I should have," "Men can't be trusted," "I always feel vulnerable, like I am an easy target," and "My life has been ruined because of what happened to me," are all beliefs that incorporate a common style of thinking and can be explored and collaboratively disputed with the client. The Posttraumatic Cognitions Inventory (Foa, Ehlers, et al., 1999) can be useful for identifying such trauma-related beliefs.

However, many upsetting thoughts and feelings have no obvious relationship to the client's traumatic experiences. As a general rule, the therapist should help the client learn how to recognize and challenge common styles of thinking related to any distressing feelings, including those that appear to be unrelated to traumatic experiences. As clients become more skillful as identifying and challenging thoughts and beliefs that lead to negative feelings, the therapist can gradually shift the focus to trauma-related thoughts and beliefs that these do not automatically present themselves. Chapter 7 addresses this topic in more detail.

Dealing With Recurrent Trauma-Related Thoughts

Trauma-related schemas such as those described in the previous section, and the negative feelings associated with them, are sometimes repeatedly triggered despite previous success at disputing those beliefs. Clients may find this discouraging because their "old thinking" keeps reasserting itself again and again in their lives, and they may feel they are making no progress.

There are several strategies for helping clients overcoming trauma-related beliefs and thinking about things in a newer and more accurate way. First, the therapist should normalize the client's experience of an old thinking pattern returning, while at the same time providing encouragement that with practice at recognizing and correcting common styles of thinking, over time the client's beliefs and ways of thinking will in fact change. One useful analogy for conveying this is to describe thought patterns as similar to the path worn by a river, and that with many years of thinking a particular way, it is only natural for the water (thoughts) to flow down a particular path (way of thinking). However, with practice, clients can learn to shift their way of thinking and form new paths or ways of thinking that are more accurate and eventually feel more natural.

Second, clients may benefit from writing down and rehearsing the new and more accurate thought that is intended to replace an old thought based on a common style of thinking. Having the client practice catching the old thought, replacing it with the new one in the session, and writing it down and storing it somewhere accessible can help the person correct an old way of thinking with a new, more accurate one. It can also be useful to discuss the situations in which a trauma-related thought often occurs and to make a specific plan for the client to practice the new thought in those situations.

Third, for some clients, helping them simply recognize that an old trauma-related thought is a common style of thinking, and therefore is not accurate, can bring relief without strongly emphasizing the importance of replacing that thought with a more accurate one. For example, one client learned to say to himself when he recognized an inaccurate trauma-related thought, "There goes my stinking thinking!" This approach emphasizes that what is most critical is for people to recognize that their thoughts are not necessarily accurate, and while they cannot necessarily rid themselves of those thoughts, they need not pay them heed either—a central message reflected in mindfulness approaches to depression (Segal, Williams, & Teasdale, 2002) and therapies such as acceptance and commitment therapy (Hayes, Strosahl, & Wilson, 1999), dialectical behavior therapy (Linehan, 1993), and metacognitive therapy (Wells, 2009).

Moving on to Teaching the 5 Steps of CR

The therapist goes on to teaching the 5 Steps of CR when the client has shown some ability to recognize the common styles of thinking related to distressing feelings, usually after about two sessions of working on the identifying and correcting inaccurate thought patterns. If after two sessions the client still does not grasp the basic concept or is unable to use it to some extent on his or her own, a third session should be devoted to the common styles of thinking. After that session, regardless of the client's grasp of the concept, the therapist should move on to the 5 Steps of CR. Some clients find the general approach of the 5 Steps of CR easier to grasp than the common styles of thinking.

SUMMARY AND CONCLUSIONS

CR is the main skill taught to clients in the CR for PTSD program for managing upsetting feelings and for identifying and correcting trauma-related beliefs that underlie posttraumatic reactions. The introduction to CR involves teaching clients that thoughts and beliefs influence feelings, and that recognizing and changing inaccurate thoughts that lead to distress can reduce those upsetting feelings. The common styles of thinking are then described to normalize ways that people often distort information when they interpret different situations, which minimizes the chances that clients will feel bad about their own cognitive styles and how they misinterpret situations in their daily lives. In addition, discussing how traumatic events can influence people's beliefs about themselves and the world provides an impetus for clients to examine their thinking more closely in the context of their personal life experiences.

Teaching clients how to recognize and change common styles of thinking begins the active process of teaching CR as a skill for managing negative feelings. Helping clients practice the skill in sessions, and developing homework assignments to use the skill on their own, can begin to provide relief from the severe distress many trauma survivors experience. The most fundamental goal of introducing CR is for clients to begin recognizing that their thoughts underlie their feelings and that not all of those thoughts are completely accurate. Helping clients to understand these two points and to begin recognizing their own use of common styles of thinking is a crucial step toward clients being able to use CR as a self-management tool for dealing with common negative feelings related to PTSD symptoms.

7
COGNITIVE RESTRUCTURING II: THE 5 STEPS OF CR

KIM T. MUESER, STANLEY D. ROSENBERG, AND HARRIET J. ROSENBERG

Teaching clients how to recognize and challenge common styles of thinking (see chap. 6, this volume) provides them with a practical tool that can be used immediately to deal with upsetting feelings. Many clients experience some relief after just one or two sessions of learning how to use this skill, and they continue to benefit with further practice in later sessions and on their own. However, despite these advantages, the common styles of thinking approach to cognitive restructuring (CR) has two significant limitations.

First, although the ability to recognize and change common styles of thinking often reduces distress, simply knowing that one is thinking inaccurately does note enable one to pinpoint the trauma-related schemas or beliefs that are at the root of the problem. Thus, clients are less likely to alter core schemas and get long-term relief from their posttraumatic symptoms. Second, teaching clients how to identify and correct their common styles of thinking can reduce distress that arises from maladaptive thought processes, but it does not provide guidance for dealing with situations in which upset feelings do not appear to be the product of inaccurate thinking. This is an especially important consideration for preventing revictimization, a common problem in trauma survivors (Arata, 2002; Wilson, Calhoun, & Bernat, 1999) that can be addressed by helping clients develop better skills for responding to potentially threatening situations.

The 5 Steps of CR strategy builds on the common styles of thinking by teaching clients a step-by-step skill for identifying and examining the thoughts and beliefs underlying distressful feelings and either correcting those thoughts when they are inaccurate or making a plan to remedy the situation when the thoughts are accurate. The 5 Steps of CR (a) describe the situation, (b) identify the strongest negative feeling experienced in the situation, (c) identify the thought or belief most strongly related to that feeling, (d) evaluate the thought by considering all the evidence supporting it and all the evidence against it, and (e) take action by either changing an inaccurate or unhelpful thought to make it more accurate or more helpful or developing a plan for dealing with the situation that led to the upsetting but not inaccurate thought.

INTRODUCING THE 5 STEPS OF CR

The 5 Steps of CR are usually introduced one to three sessions after teaching clients how to recognize and challenge common styles of thinking (i.e., between the fifth and seventh sessions). The skill should be introduced toward the beginning of a session, following the review of homework on the common styles of thinking to allow enough time for therapist and client to work through an example of the steps together. This is important so that the client will experience some reduction in distress, thus demonstrating the potential utility of the skill.

Two versions of the 5 Steps of CR Worksheet are provided in the Appendix (Handouts #9 and #10), one that provides places for the client to record their ratings of distress and conviction for their thoughts (based on the scales described in chapter 6), and the other one that does not. Either version of the worksheet can be used to teach the 5 Steps of CR. The example provided next is based on the worksheet that does not prompt the client to give ratings.

> *Therapist:* Today, we're going to continue working on cognitive restructuring. For the last several sessions, we've talked about how your thoughts are connected to your feelings. We have also talked about how your life experiences, including traumatic ones, affect your thoughts and feelings. We have talked about the common styles of thinking, in which people tend to respond to events and experiences on the basis of on exaggerated or inaccurate ways of thinking. You have made a lot of progress in learning how to recognize and change your own common styles of thinking that lead to distress, so you know what it's like to get relief from examining your thinking when you feel upset.

Today, we are going to continue working on understanding how your thinking influences your feelings by focusing on a new skill for dealing with distressing feelings and the thoughts associated with them. This skill builds on the common styles of thinking and is called the 5 Steps of CR. [*therapist gives 5 Steps of CR Worksheet to client*] Let's go through the steps together, working on a recent situation in which you experienced some distress.

To demonstrate the 5 Steps of CR, the therapist should use a situation in which the client experienced strong negative feelings that are clearly out of proportion, suggesting the presence of inaccurate thoughts or beliefs that can be readily disputed and changed in the session. Although the 5 Steps of CR can be used to help clients deal with other distressful feelings, focusing initially on feelings that are related to inaccurate thoughts makes it easier for clients to grasp all the steps of the skill and is more likely to lead to rapid relief of negative feelings in the session. Helping clients use the 5 Steps of CR to get immediate relief from distress reinforces their use of the skill, increasing the chances that they will use it on their own.

The therapist has several options for selecting an example. If the client completed homework for the common styles of thinking, the therapist can select an example from the homework and use it to demonstrate the 5 Steps of CR, knowing in advance that the client does not believe his or her thought in that situation was accurate. For example, if the client indicated on her homework sheet that she felt anxious when her boss said he wanted to talk with her, but she was then relieved to recognize that her feelings were due to a catastrophizing thought, the therapist illustrates the 5 Steps of CR with that situation.

Alternatively, the therapist can focus on a recent experience in which the client described upsetting feelings that appear to be out of proportion to the situation, suggesting the presence of inaccurate thoughts that may be corrected when demonstrating the 5 Steps of CR. If the therapist has recently had the client complete the posttraumatic stress disorder (PTSD) and depression monitoring assessments, distressing thoughts, feelings, or situations can be identified by reviewing these and selecting an example to demonstrate the 5 Steps of CR.

When teaching and working through the 5 Steps of CR with the client, the core thought or belief that is examined should be expressed in the strongest possible manner and as specifically as possible. The more extreme and specific the thought, the easier it is to weigh the evidence for and against it and to effectively dispute it. For example,

- Instead of challenging the thought "I'm a terrible student," try challenging the thought "I'm a terrible student because I did poorly on this test and I'll probably flunk my class."

- Instead of challenging the thought "I'm a bad person," try challenging the thought "I'm a bad person because I allowed myself to be sexually abused as a child when I could have put a stop to it."

When selecting a situation to demonstrate the 5 Steps of CR, it is also preferable to work on one in which the client reports feeling anxiety, depression, or guilt rather than anger. Clients are usually more open to considering evidence against thoughts underlying anxiety, depression, or guilt than against those underlying anger. Working on these feelings initially maximizes the chances that the 5 Steps of CR will result in changing the underlying thoughts, leading to relief from the distressing feeling. Guidelines for using CR to address anger are provided in chapter 8 of this volume.

We provide an example of introducing the 5 Steps of CR next.

Step 1: Identify the Upsetting Situation

Therapist: The first step is to keep track of the situations in which you feel upset. In Step 1, you write down the upsetting situation, just like you did on the Common Styles of Thinking Worksheet. This worksheet can be used to help you first identify upsetting situations and then to identify the thoughts that lead to your upsetting feelings. Let's use a distressing situation you recently experienced to work through an example of the 5 Steps of CR. You described in your homework for last week that you felt anxious when you had to go shopping for groceries in the middle of the day. How about if we work on that example?

Client: Okay.

Therapist: Good. So, in Step 1 you write down the upsetting situation. For this situation, how about if I write down "going to the grocery store"?

Client: Sounds good to me.

Step 2: Identify the Upsetting Feeling

Therapist: Now, in Step 2 you want to identify the upsetting feeling that you had in this situation. Try to focus on one of the four major feelings listed on this sheet: anxiety/fear, depression, guilt/shame, or anger. Sometimes a person feels more than one emotion in a situation. That's okay. We want to focus on the strongest or most upsetting feeling. What was your strongest feeling when you had to go shopping the other day?

Client: Afraid. I was feeling very anxious.

Therapist: Okay, let's go with anxiety for this example.

Encourage the client to stick with one of the "big four" feelings in learning the 5 Steps of CR. These are common feelings associated with PTSD that can lead to high levels of distress. When the client reports several different feelings in a situation, it can be helpful to explore these feelings before deciding which one to focus on. Encourage the client to talk a bit about each feeling and what it was like. Then, ask the client to consider which of the feelings was most distressing and to focus on completing the 5 Steps of CR to address that feeling. Alternatively, the client can select more than one upsetting feeling and then, after identifying upsetting thoughts related to those feelings (in Step 3), return to Step 2 and choose the feeling related to the most distressing thought.

Because different thoughts are associated with different feelings, the 5 Steps of CR can be used to address only one thought and related feeling at a time. If the client chooses, after completing the 5 Steps of CR for one thought, a separate worksheet can be completed to address another thought and feeling that he or she experienced in the same situation. However, this is rarely necessary.

Step 3: Identify the Thoughts Underlying the Feeling

Therapist: In Step 3, you want to identify your thoughts about the situation. To deal with upsetting emotions, we need to pinpoint the thoughts or beliefs that resulted in the upsetting feeling. One clue to what you are thinking about is the nature of the upsetting feeling. This sheet [*i.e., the Guide to Thoughts and Feelings: Handout #12*] summarizes the thoughts associated with common distressing feelings. [*therapist gives handout to client*] For example, feelings of anxiety or fear are related to thoughts of being threatened. Feelings of guilt and shame are related to thoughts or beliefs of having done something wrong. Depression or sadness is related to thoughts of having lost something. Feeling angry is related to thoughts of having been wronged by someone else.

When reviewing the Guide to Thoughts and Feelings, prompt the client to give a brief example of each feeling and the thought underlying it. The therapist can help by drawing on examples of feelings and associated thoughts based on previous sessions in which the client has practiced recognizing and changing common styles of thinking. The therapist can continue explaining Step 3 along the following lines:

Therapist: Okay, let's go back to this situation. You were in the grocery store and you felt afraid. What kinds of thoughts were going through your mind at the store that could have led to your feelings of anxiety?

Client:	I'm not sure. I think I was afraid that something bad might happen.
Therapist:	Like what?
Client:	I sometimes worry that someone might try to follow me home. Or that one of the men in the store might try to pick me up or come on to me.
Therapist:	And your concern that someone might follow you home— would that be to try to hurt you in some way?
Client:	Yes, to rape me, or attack or rob me.
Therapist:	I see. Do any other thoughts come to mind when you recall how you were feeling in the grocery store?
Client:	When I'm in public I often think that people are looking at me or talking about me.
Therapist:	I see. You've done a good job of identifying several possible thoughts that might have led you to feel anxious in that situation. Let's write each of these thoughts down for now. [*therapist writes*] It's common to have more than one thought in a situation that is related to the feeling you are having. Sometimes, identifying one thought can lead to another even more important thought related to the situation. When this happens, the best thing to do is to write down all the different thoughts you are having, just as we have written down all the thoughts you had in the grocery store. Once you have done that, you can go through those thoughts and choose the one that is associated with the strongest negative feeling. Examining this thought more closely is the best way of dealing with your distress in this situation and getting some relief.
	In this situation, you identified several thoughts you had in the grocery store: that something bad might happen, that someone might follow you home and hurt you, that a man might try to pick you up, and that other people might be looking at you or talking about you. When you consider each of these thoughts, which one is most distressing?
Client:	They all worry me. But I'm most afraid that someone will follow me home.
Therapist:	Okay, so that's the thought we'll work on. [*therapist circles that thought on worksheet*]

If the client has difficulty articulating thoughts related to fear and anxiety, the therapist can refer the client to refer to the Guide to Thoughts and Feelings: Handout #12 (see Appendix):

> *Therapist:* Sometimes it's hard to know what thoughts you are having. Let's look at your Guide to Thoughts and Feelings and consider the questions next to the feelings of anxiety/fear. Did you think that harm might come to you? [*therapist points to the handout and reads from it*] Did you think that you were going to be embarrassed? Okay, so the main thought that led to feeling anxious was thinking that something bad was going to happen. What did you think might happen?

Clients sometimes mix up thoughts and feelings. When this happens, help the client distinguish between feelings (e.g., anxiety, guilt, depression) and thoughts (e.g., "I'm no good"). Encourage the client to use the words "I feel . . ." when talking about feelings and "I think . . ." when talking about thoughts. Normalize the fact that it takes practice to separate thoughts and feelings but that learning how to do so will pay off in terms of overcoming distressing feelings.

When a specific thought or belief has been identified and written down, the client is prompted to make a preliminary evaluation of whether that thought reflects a common style of thinking. If so, the client circles the particular style on the worksheet. If the thought does not appear to reflect a common style of thinking, the therapist moves onto Step 4.

> *Therapist:* Before we begin with Step 4, let's look at the thought you are working on to see whether it might reflect a common style of thinking. If you think that the thought is related to any common styles of thinking, you can circle on the worksheet which specific ones. That means that you think the thought you are working on may not be completely accurate. When you consider the thought, "Someone might follow me home and hurt me," do you think that it might reflect a common style of thinking?
>
> *Client:* Overgeneralization?
>
> *Therapist:* Why overgeneralization? What about this thought might be overgeneralizing from your past experiences?
>
> *Client:* I've had some bad things happen to me, and I'm afraid they're going to happen again.
>
> *Therapist:* I understand. That's a good point. So let's circle *overgeneralization* on the worksheet. Are there any other common styles of thinking that your thought might reflect?
>
> *Client:* Emotional reasoning?
>
> *Therapist:* Why might your thought reflect emotional reasoning?
>
> *Client:* I'm often afraid when I'm around a lot of people.

Therapist:	And when you feel that way, does that then make you think something bad is going to happen?
Client:	Yes.
Therapist:	That's a good example of emotional reasoning. So let's circle that style on the worksheet. Are there any other common styles of thinking that this thought might reflect?
Client:	Not that I can think of.
Therapist:	Okay, then let's go onto the next step of evaluating the evidence.

Step 4: Examine the Evidence for the Thought

| Therapist: | Once you have identified the thought most strongly related to your upsetting feeling, the fourth step is to closely examine the evidence supporting it. This includes evaluating the evidence supporting beliefs that you may have had for a long time and have never questioned. If you decide that your thought is not accurate, then you can change it, just like you have been changing inaccurate thoughts that you recognize as common styles of thinking. And as you already know, changing inaccurate and unhelpful thoughts usually makes you feel better.

In this step, the goal is to think of all the evidence you can that supports your thought, as well as all the evidence that doesn't support it. The way that we do this is to pretend that we are scientists or jurors in a court of law and to gather evidence for and against the thought. What do you think is so special about how scientists evaluate evidence when they're trying to understand the results of an experiment or when jurors examine the evidence in a court case to determine whether someone is innocent or guilty of a crime? |
|---|---|
| Client: | They try to look at all the evidence? |
| Therapist: | That's right. Scientists and jurors look at all the available evidence, not just some of the evidence. And when they examine the evidence, do they look at all of it the same way, or do they look some evidence more closely than other types of evidence? |
| Client: | Some evidence is more important than other evidence. |
| Therapist: | And what type of evidence is most important and most helpful when determining whether something is true? |
| Client: | Evidence that is clear and straightforward. |

Therapist:	That's right. The most important evidence to focus on when evaluating the accuracy of a thought is evidence that is objective. By *objective*, I mean evidence that is based on facts and not just what someone thinks, feels, or believes is true. Why do you think it's important to focus on objective evidence when evaluating an upsetting thought?
Client:	So you can really know whether the thought is accurate?
Therapist:	Exactly. By acting like a scientist or a member of a jury, and by focusing on the most objective evidence available, we can be confident that our judgments about the truth of a thought are as accurate as possible. And that's important because sometimes we believe that something is true because we've believed it for so long, even though there is little objective evidence to support it, and the belief is actually dead wrong. During this step, we'll work hard together to come up with as much evidence for the thought as we can and as much evidence against the thought as possible. We'll first consider all the evidence we can think of, including both good and bad evidence. Next, we'll examine the evidence closely, focusing on the most objective evidence, to determine whether the thought is accurate and helpful. How's that sound?
Client:	Okay.
Therapist:	Now that we've talked about generating evidence for and against the upsetting thought, let's go back to the grocery store situation. So you are in the grocery store and you feel anxious. Your anxiety is related to thoughts that something bad could happen to you in the store. In particular, you're worried that someone might follow you home and assault you. Let's first think of all the evidence we can that might support your concern. What evidence can you think of that supports the thought that someone might try follow you home from the grocery store and hurt you?
Client:	Well, I was raped once.
Therapist:	Okay, that's a good start. Let's write that down on the worksheet in the section under "things that do support my thought." What other evidence can you think of that could support your thought that somebody might follow you home from the store?
Client:	I just don't think you can trust anybody.
Therapist:	I understand. When coming up with evidence for and against a specific thought, it can be helpful to be as specific as possible. Can you be more specific about why you don't think you can trust anybody?

Client:	When I was 11 years old and my mother remarried, my step-father began abusing me.
Therapist:	I see. You should have been able to trust your stepfather to be someone who wouldn't hurt you. Is that right?
Client:	Yes, no one should do that do a child, especially someone close like that.
Therapist:	Okay. So let's write that down too on the worksheet as evidence for the thought. How about if we write "my stepfather abused me when I was a child"?
Client:	Okay.
Therapist:	What other evidence can you think of in this situation that supports the thought that someone might follow you home and hurt you?
Client:	My first husband abused me.
Therapist:	Can you tell me a little more about that and how it supports the thought?
Client:	He would yell at me, call me names. Sometimes when he was drunk he would hit me.
Therapist:	So, was that situation a little like the situation with your stepfather? Your husband was an important person in your life and you should have been able to trust him, but he hurt you and wasn't trustworthy?
Client:	Yes, that's right.
Therapist:	Okay, so let's also note that under the heading of "evidence that supports the thought." Can you think of any more evidence supporting the thought that someone might follow you home from the grocery store?
Client:	I feel scared when I am in the store. That makes me think something bad will happen.
Therapist:	Okay, we'll write that down too—that you feel scared.

Prompt the client to come up with evidence supporting the thought, using other questions if needed, recording all examples, including nonobjective evidence. Once the evidence for the thought has been generated, the therapist summarizes it and then elicits evidence against the thought. In general, people have more difficulty coming up with evidence against their thoughts due to *confirmation bias*, a normal human tendency to selectively attend to evidence supporting one's thinking and to ignore evidence that does not (Stanovich, 2001; Wason, 1960). The therapist may be tempted to directly provide evidence to refute the client's thought. However, this can backfire when the client minimizes, discounts, or counters the therapist's evidence instead of accepting it. Rather than directly providing counterevidence, the therapist should help the client explore the evidence against the thought in a collaborative fashion by asking questions using the Socratic method, without appearing to be invested in proving that the thought is wrong.

There are several ways of helping clients to consider evidence against a thought. The client can be asked to think of whether there is any evidence that might indicate that the thought is not completely accurate. For example, if the thought or belief is very strongly worded in categorical terms (e.g., "No man can be trusted," "I'm a complete failure as a mother"), any exceptions to it can serve as evidence against the thought (e.g., a single trustworthy man, an example of good parenting). If the client has identified a common style of thinking that the thought might reflect, and therefore recognizes that it may not be accurate, discussing why it might be a common style of thinking can lead to evidence against the thought. Evidence against a thought can also be generated by asking questions such as whether there is another way of looking at the situation, what someone else might think if the same thing happened, and whether the thought is helpful.

> *Therapist:* Okay, let's summarize the evidence so far. One piece of evidence that someone might follow you home is that some bad things have happened to you before, namely, that you were raped once, you were physically abused as a child, and your husband also abused you. Another piece of evidence is that you believed that something bad was going to happen because you felt afraid. One more piece of evidence was that you noticed a man looking at you in the store. Right?
>
> *Client:* Yes.
>
> *Therapist:* Good. Now that we have identified evidence supporting the thought that someone might follow you home from the grocery store, let's think of all the evidence we can that doesn't support that thought. In other words, what evidence can you think of that someone *won't* follow you home from the store and try to hurt you?
>
> *Client:* I don't know. I just feel so scared in those situations that I freeze up.
>
> *Therapist:* I understand; it can be scary to be around people you don't know, especially when you've tried to avoid those situations as hard as you have. Let me help you by asking a few questions. You mentioned that you had been raped before. Was that by a stranger, someone you had never met before?

Client: No, that was someone I had met a few times. We were out together once and he forced himself on me.

Therapist: Sexually?

Client: Yes.

Therapist: Okay, so you weren't assaulted by a stranger, but by someone you knew a little. Have you ever been followed home by a stranger from a public place, such as the grocery store?

Client: No.

Therapist: Okay, so let's note that under the column of evidence not supporting the thought. Let's think of some more evidence that doesn't support the thought. You mentioned that because of your experiences with your stepfather and your first husband you don't believe that anyone can be trusted. We can examine that thought together at a different time. But let me ask—it sounds like your belief that people can't be trusted has mostly to do with people you know, not total strangers. Have you ever been attacked in any situation by someone you didn't know?

Client: When I think of it that way, no.

Therapist: Okay, let's also put that down as evidence against the thought that someone might follow you home and hurt you—that "I've never been attacked by a stranger before." Does that sound accurate to you?

Client: Yes.

Therapist: Let's see if there is any more evidence you can think of against that thought. Even though you feel uncomfortable going to the grocery store, you have to do it once in a while. Has anything seriously bad ever happened to you at the grocery store, like being threatened or someone trying to hurt you?

Client: Not that I can think of.

Therapist: Good, let's also make note of that on the worksheet. Here's another question: You mentioned that you feel afraid in the grocery store. Have you ever been afraid in a situation, but nothing bad happened?

Client: All the time. I'm almost always anxious when I'm around other people, but bad things usually don't happen.

Therapist: Good, that's another piece of evidence against the thought that something bad might happen when you are in the grocery store. In other words, just because you feel anxious, it doesn't mean something bad is going to happen.

Step 5: Take Action

The last step of CR involves evaluating the evidence for the thought and then taking action on the basis of whether the thought is accurate. If the evidence does not support the thought, then an alternative, more accurate one is identified. This is often the case in people with posttraumatic reactions, who frequently overestimate the probability that a low-occurrence event will happen again (e.g., being raped or assaulted by a stranger, being in an accident or disaster; Foa & Rothbaum, 1998) or who believe that because they experienced traumatic events early in their lives (e.g., childhood sexual or physical abuse), they will always be vulnerable to victimization throughout their adult lives (Briere, 1992). Similarly, individuals with PTSD often experience guilt and shame about not stopping or somehow being complicit in their victimization when they look back with the full knowledge of what they now know much later in their lives (Street, Gibson, & Holohan, 2005).

Although many thoughts associated with distressing feelings are inaccurate, not all are, and it is important to help people develop concrete steps toward resolving situations that lead to valid negative feelings. To take an extreme example, if someone smelled smoke from the next room and opened the door to find a fire there, they would probably be afraid and think, "I'm in danger!" Instead of altering this thought, one would want to come up with a practical action plan, such as calling the fire department or throwing water on the flames. Thus, after reviewing the evidence for and against the thought, if the client concludes that the evidence supports the thought, then an action plan is formulated. Specific strategies for developing action plans to address these types of situations are provided in the section "Developing Effective Action Plans."

Continuing with the example, the therapist uses the Socratic method to prompt the client to consider the evidence for and against her thought:

Therapist: The last step of cognitive restructuring involves weighing the evidence and taking action. Once you have gathered all the evidence for and against your thought, you have to look at the evidence closely and make a decision about whether the thought is accurate or not. When looking at the evidence, it is important to focus on the strongest and most objective evidence, or evidence that is concrete, specific, and not just based on feelings or impressions. Why do you think that evidence based on facts is better, and more convincing, than evidence based on feelings?

Client: Because anyone can see the facts, but only I can feel my feelings?

Therapist: Right. And we know that thoughts we have related to our feelings aren't always accurate. For example, do you remember which common style of thinking is associated with the thought "I feel afraid, and therefore I must be in danger"?

Client: Emotional reasoning?

Therapist: That's right. Just because you feel afraid doesn't mean you're in danger. That's why evidence based on feelings is not as strong as evidence based on facts. Another way of determining whether evidence is strong and objective is to ask, "Could I could convince someone else that this thought is true based on the evidence?" Why do you think asking whether someone else could be convinced by the evidence is a good way of determining how strong the evidence is?

Client: Because another person can be more objective?

Therapist: Right! It's easier for people to see the facts of a situation that they aren't directly involved in and don't have strong feelings about.

After briefly discussing how to weigh the evidence, the therapist finishes the introduction to the last step of CR:

Therapist: After examining all of the evidence and focusing on the strongest and most objective evidence, it's time to decide overall whether the evidence supports your thought or not. As we have discussed, the thoughts behind negative feelings are often inaccurate and are not supported by the evidence. When the evidence does not support your thinking, it's time to develop a new, more accurate thought to replace the old one. This new thought should be supported by the evidence you have. Even if some of the evidence supports your thought, but there is good evidence against it, and the thought is not completely accurate, and it is important to come up with a new, even more accurate thought to replace the old one.

If the evidence *does* support your thinking, then it's time to develop an action plan for dealing with the situation. Why do you think it's important to come up with a plan for dealing with an upsetting situation in which your concerns are supported by the facts?

Client: So that the situation doesn't continue to be a problem?

Therapist: Right, that way you can try to resolve the distressing situation. In some situations, you may also decide that you don't have enough information, or evidence, to determine whether your thought is accurate. In these situations, you can make a plan to get more information to decide whether your concerns are realistic or not.

After the last step of CR has been described, the therapist returns to the example, as described next.

Therapist: Let's continue with the situation in which you felt afraid in the grocery store. Before going over the specific evidence, it is helpful to note that when you considered whether your thought might reflect a common style of thinking, you indicated two common styles, overgeneralization and emotional reasoning. [therapist points to where these are circled on the 5 Steps of CR Worksheet] This means that even before you looked at all the evidence, you were thinking that your thought might not be completely accurate.

Client: Right.

Therapist: Good. Now we'll go over the specific evidence for and against your thought that someone might follow you home from the store and hurt you. Let's consider the evidence about bad things having happened to you in the past—the fact that you were abused by your stepfather as a child, and then later as an adult you were raped. Is that specific evidence about what might happen in the grocery store?

Client: It's specific, but not about the grocery store.

Therapist: Right. So would you consider it strong evidence, or not?

Client: I guess not.

Therapist: How about the evidence that "nobody can be trusted"? Is that strong?

Client: It makes me anxious, but I guess it's not very specific.

Therapist: Right, you may have a general belief that people can't be trusted, but that doesn't provide very strong evidence that somebody's going to hurt you when you go into a grocery store. Would you agree with that?

Client: Yes.

Therapist: The last piece of evidence for the thought was "I feel anxious, so I must be in danger." You've already identified that as a common style of thinking—emotional reasoning—so we know that's not very strong evidence because it's based on feelings and not facts. Right?

Client: Right.

Therapist: Okay, now let's look at the evidence against the thought. How about the evidence that "I've never been assaulted by a stranger before." Is that objective?

Client:	Well, it's true, and it's specific.
Therapist:	Right, so that is good evidence. And how about the evidence that "nothing really bad has ever really happened to me in the grocery store?" How's that?
Client:	That's also true.
Therapist:	And how about the evidence that you have felt anxious in lots of situations and bad things have not happened?
Client:	I know that's true, but it doesn't stop me from feeling anxious around strangers.
Therapist:	Right, just because you feel anxious doesn't mean something bad is going to happen. Okay, so now let's look at all of the evidence together and decide: Is your thought in the grocery store that "someone is will follow me home and hurt me" supported by the evidence?
Client:	No.
Therapist:	Okay. So let's check off on the worksheet that the thought is not supported by the evidence. Now let's try to come up with a more accurate thought for that situation. Considering all of the evidence against the thought that someone might follow you home, what's a more accurate thought in that situation?
Client:	That nothing is going to happen to me?
Therapist:	Okay. Now when you look at that situation and you feel anxious because you think someone might follow you home, how accurate and believable does it seem after looking at the evidence to tell yourself, "No one is going to hurt me"?
Client:	Well, I know it's accurate, but it doesn't quite seem realistic because I still feel anxious.
Therapist:	I understand. So maybe we can come up with a more accurate thought that also acknowledges that you feel uncomfortable. How about the thought "Even though I feel somewhat anxious, I am safe in this store"?
Client:	That sounds better to me.
Therapist:	Okay, let's write that new thought down. This is a good example of a new, more accurate, and more balanced thought for that situation. Let's compare your feelings related to your old, upsetting thought in this situation with your new, more accurate thought. How did you feel when you thought, "Someone is going to follow me home from the store and hurt me"?

Client: Very anxious. I have those feelings all the time.

Therapist: Okay. Now that we have challenged the thought and come up with a more accurate one, how do you feel when you think in that situation, "I feel somewhat anxious, but I know that I'm safe in this store"?

Client: Better, because I no longer feel as vulnerable.

Therapist: That's good. This shows how using the 5 Steps of CR can help you carefully examine the evidence supporting upsetting thoughts, and by changing these thoughts to more accurate ones, your upsetting feelings can also be reduced.

Additional Practice in the Introductory Session

If time permits (e.g., 15–20 minutes), the therapist may be able to work through another example of the 5 Steps of CR with the client. If another example is done, the therapist should try to help the client get through all five steps within that session rather than beginning the steps and then finishing them the following week. This prevents an unresolved, distressing problem situation from lingering between sessions.

Homework

At the end of the session, the therapist develops a homework assignment with the client to practice the 5 Steps of CR, using the worksheet to record efforts.

Therapist: For homework, I would like us to make a plan for you to practice the 5 Steps of CR on your own over the next week. The 5 Steps of CR can be used to address any situation that is upsetting or distressing. That's your cue to use the five steps—feeling bad in some way. When you feel that way, you can use the 5 Steps of CR to evaluate and change your thoughts, or take action, based on the evidence supporting them. If you have trouble identifying the thought that is underlying your negative feeling, you can use the Guide to Thoughts and Feelings handout to help you figure it out.

The goal is for you to get as much practice as possible using the 5 Steps of CR. To do this, it helps to make a homework plan. For example, you could have the plan of using the 5 Steps of CR to deal with at least one upsetting situation and feeling each day and to record your work on the worksheet. Even if you get stuck on one of the steps, that's okay. Do your best, and when we get together again next week we can work together on any steps you got stuck on. How's that sound?

Review

As with each session, the introductory session for the 5 Steps of CR should conclude with a review. It can also be helpful to elicit any comments or observations the client has about the session, such as what was interesting or helpful. An example of concluding the session follows.

> *Therapist:* Okay, let's review what we have covered today. You learned a new CR skill: the 5 Steps of CR. These steps include describing the situation; identifying the upsetting feeling; identifying the thought underlying that feeling; examining the evidence for and against the thought; and then taking action, either by coming up with a new, more accurate thought or by developing an plan to deal with the situation. You saw how carefully examining the evidence related to upsetting thoughts can lead to more accurate thoughts and less distressing feelings. Learning how to use the 5 Steps of CR can be especially helpful when people have had upsetting, traumatic events in their lives because these experiences have often shaped their thoughts and beliefs, which on close examination are often not accurate or helpful. CR is a skill that takes practice to get better at, and you are already on your way!

TEACHING THE 5 STEPS OF CR IN SUBSEQUENT SESSIONS

After the introduction to the 5 Steps of CR, the remaining sessions are devoted to helping clients learn how to use the skill to deal with their negative feelings, and to addressing trauma-related beliefs and schemas that underlie their PTSD symptoms. Each session begins with homework review, with the therapist reviewing the client's efforts to use the 5 Steps of CR and helping the client with steps on which he or she got stuck. When the client reports using the 5 Steps of CR on his or her own, the therapist should explore whether he or she experienced relief from using the skill. Any reduction in distress, however small, should be highlighted. If the client describes using the 5 Steps of CR but is not experiencing any relief, the therapist should praise the client for trying the skill and then review the situation to determine whether additional work together may lead to a reduction in distress. The rest of the session is spent using the 5 Steps of CR to address other negative feelings the client may have experienced during the week, including feelings related to PTSD or depressive symptoms, or other trauma-related thoughts and beliefs that can be identified.

After the client has been introduced to the 5 Steps of CR and the therapist has walked him or her through one or two examples in the first session, the focus shifts to teaching clients how to use the skill on their own, rather than continuing to lead them through the steps. This involves handing over the role of completing the worksheet to the client, asking questions to prompt the identification of each step and its purpose (e.g., "Okay, so what's the first step of CR? Why is it important to describe the situation?" "Now that you've identified your upset feeling, what's next?"), and assuming the role of a coach rather a leader in helping the client learn how to use the skill. It is also important to reinforce the client for using the steps correctly, both by providing positive feedback and drawing attention to reductions in distress that usually occur when the 5 Steps of CR are completed. The more involved clients are in keeping track of the 5 Steps of CR, providing evidence for and against their thoughts and developing new thoughts or action plans based on the evidence, the more they will be able to use the skill on their own to deal with upsetting feelings.

Strategies for Teaching Specific Steps of Cognitive Restructuring

The therapist may encounter a variety of challenges when teaching the 5 Steps of CR. In this section, we describe specific strategies for teaching each of the five steps.

Step 1: Describe the Situation

The cue for the client to use the 5 Steps of CR is experiencing an upsetting feeling. Clients are sometimes confused about what to write under "Situation" on the 5 Steps of CR Worksheet when a distressing feeling seems to come out of nowhere. The therapist can explain that a brief description should be given about what the client was doing or the circumstance in which the upsetting feeling occurred (e.g., "I was eating breakfast when I had a memory of my stepfather abusing me").

Upsetting situations to address with the 5 Steps of CR in session can be identified in a variety of ways. The brief discussion of the past week at the beginning of the session may identify possible situations to address with the 5 Steps of CR, as may a review of the client's homework assignment. Distressing situations can also be identified through the regular monitoring of PTSD and depressive symptoms that is conducted every third session. The therapist may also be aware of distressing beliefs the client has previously talked about, but that have not been resolved, and raising those beliefs as a focus of CR is another way of identifying a situation to address with the 5 Steps of CR.

Sometimes clients make rapid progress and report experiencing minimal distress to address with the 5 Steps of CR. When this fortunate situation occurs, the therapist can explore with the client steps that need to be taken toward the goals of treatment established earlier in the program (e.g., closer relationships, work, school). This can help them move forward in their lives and identify perceived obstacles to achieving the goals that can then be addressed with the 5 Steps of CR.

Step 2: Identify the Strongest Emotion

Although the 5 Steps of CR can be completed for only one feeling and one thought at a time, it is often preferable for the therapist to not make the client choose just one feeling in Step 2 before identifying the underlying thoughts in Step 3. Instead, the client can be encouraged to note on the worksheet which distressing feelings he or she is having and then to go onto Step 3 and identify the thoughts underlying each of those feelings. Some upsetting thoughts may even be identified that are related to feelings that the client did not initially describe in Step 2 (e.g., client reports feeling angry but exploration of thoughts leads to ones also related to fear). These thoughts should be recorded and the feelings associated with them noted in Step 2. Once several thoughts have been identified related to the feelings, the client should identify the one that is most distressing and circle it. The client then goes back to Step 2 and circles the feeling associated with this upsetting thought. The feeling and thought should always correspond with one another.

The reason for not limiting the client to one feeling in Step 2 before going on to Step 3 is that the exploration of thoughts underlying upsetting feelings can lead to identifying other thoughts or beliefs, previously not articulated, that are even more distressing to the person. These core thoughts or beliefs often tap trauma-related schemas that are important to challenge in CR. For example, a client whose child got into a fight in school became angry when asked about the incident by a friend because she perceived it to be an insult to her competence as a mother. Exploration of the thought underlying the anger led to thoughts of inadequacy as a mother (anxiety), which then led to the thought that she was "damaged goods" because she had been sexually abused as a child, which was accompanied by a feeling of depression. The client identified her thought of being damaged goods as the most distressing thought in Step 3, so she went back to Step 2 and circled *depression* as the strongest feeling.

Step 3: Identify the Most Distressing Thought

When the client has difficulty identifying thoughts underlying the upsetting feeling, the therapist can prompt him or her to consult the Guide to Your Thoughts and Feelings handout, using the probe questions related to the feelings in question to pinpoint the thought. Once a distressing thought has been identified, the therapist can teach the client how to explore the thought to see if it has a deeper meaning. One method, called the *downward arrow technique* (Burns, 1999), is to teach clients to ask about each upsetting thought, "If this thought were true, what would it mean or say about me?" Additional questions such as "If this belief were true, what does this mean to me?" "If this happened, what would happen then?" and "What would be so bad about that?" can get at the deeper meaning and beliefs underlying strong emotional reactions to often minor events (D. M. Clark, 1989).

For example, a woman who wanted a close relationship with a man but who was also afraid of such a relationship responded with fear when a man casually initiated a conversation with her. Her initial thought underlying her anxious feeling was, "He wants to have a relationship with me." Exploration of the thought and its meaning led to other thoughts, including, "I don't know if I can handle a relationship," "If he gets to know me better he won't like me," "Nobody would like me if they knew me better," "People would think I'm sick if they knew what my brother did to me," and "I'm bad because I sometimes had sexual feelings when my father abused me and I didn't try to stop it." This last thought was most distressing because it was related to the client's underlying schema that she was a shameful person because she had allowed herself to be abused and even had enjoyed aspects of it.

Step 4: Examine the Evidence

Teaching clients how to critically examine their upsetting thoughts is a crucial step in CR. When clients have previously identified their thought as reflecting a common style of thinking (end of Step 3), they can be taught to consider the specific reasons why their thought is inaccurate. The evidence is most effectively evaluated by the therapist initially asking the client questions to generate all the evidence supporting the thought (including weak evidence), then asking questions for evidence against the thought, and then carefully examining all of the evidence together while focusing on that which is most objective (i.e., most scientific or most compelling in a court of law). This avoids the problem of debating the quality of each piece of evidence when it is generated, while emphasizing the importance of giving greatest weight to the strongest types of evidence.

Teaching clients how to ask specific questions can help them learn how to generate evidence against their thoughts. Some useful questions include the following:

- "Are there any examples that would suggest this thought isn't completely true?"
- "What is another way of looking at the situation?"
- "What is another possible explanation for what happened?"
- "What would someone else think about the situation?"
- "Is this thought helpful to me?"

- "Is my thought based on how I feel rather than what happened?"
- "Am I setting for myself an unrealistic and unobtainable standard?"

Step 5: Make a Decision and Take Action

When the client concludes that the evidence does not support the upsetting thought, the last step involves coming up with a more accurate and more believable thought for the situation. Clients can sometimes come up with more accurate thoughts, but still find these new thoughts not very "believable." The therapist should encourage the client to talk about the evidence against the thought to prompt a more realistic appraisal of the situation and to ensure that the new thought is believed more strongly than the old one. Sometimes the new thought may not feel believable, even though the client knows it to be true. In this case, the therapist can point out that this odd feeling reflects the newness of the client's thought but does not challenge its validity. The strange feeling people sometimes experience when they first challenge and change long-held beliefs can be normalized by explaining that their old thoughts and beliefs have been reinforced over many years and that it takes time and practice to replace them with new and more accurate thoughts, which will eventually feel just as believable. The therapist can also help the client devise a way of reminding him- or herself of the new thought when the old one keeps cropping up (e.g., write it on a note card and carry it around, review it daily, post it somewhere prominently where the client will see it).

Another strategy for developing highly believable new thoughts is to teach the client to incorporate some of the evidence against the old thought into the new thought. For example, a client was plagued by feelings of guilt and shame when memories of her childhood sexual abuse by her father were triggered. These feelings appeared to stem from the fact that as a young child, when her father first initiated sexual contact with her, she had not resisted him and had even welcomed his attention. She used the 5 Steps of CR to evaluate the thought underlying these feelings that "the sexual abuse was my fault" and concluded that it was not accurate. The client identified a new, more accurate thought that "the sexual abuse was not my fault." Although she found this thought more accurate and believable than her former thought, she still did not find it highly believable. The therapist explored with the client how the new thought could be made more believable; they ended up strengthening the new thought by incorporating some of the evidence against the old thought into it: "The sexual abuse was not my fault because as a child I could not make a true decision about engaging in sex."

A related strategy is to teach the client to incorporate some of the evidence supporting the old thought into the new one to make it more balanced. For example, Robert was raped by another man after they went out drinking together and he passed out. He felt ashamed because he believed that "the assault was my own fault and I could have prevented it." After reviewing the evidence, Robert concluded that it was not his fault and identified a new thought: "The assault wasn't my fault." However, he found that this new thought was only slightly more believable than the old one. The client believed that the rape was his fault because his drinking put him at risk for his victimization. With the therapist's help, he modified his new thought to "Although my drinking put me at risk for this assault, it wasn't my fault because he was a friend whom I trusted." The client found this new thought much more believable and helpful in reducing his distressing feelings. Table 7.1 is the 5 Steps of CR Worksheet completed by Robert for this situation.

In some situations, developing both a more accurate thought and an action plan may be appropriate. In other words, the client may conclude that the evidence does not support the distressing thought but he or she still experiences significant distress after coming up with a new and more accurate thought, and an action plan can be made to address the situation. For example, a client who had been in a bad car accident rarely drove and was unable to attend her son's sports events. She was afraid to drive because she was convinced that "driving is a very dangerous activity." She evaluated the evidence supporting the belief and concluded that the evidence did not support the belief. She identified a new belief that was more in line with the evidence, but she also acknowledged some of the apprehension she felt about driving: "Even though I feel anxious about driving because I don't drive very much, driving is quite safe." The client reported a significant reduction in her distress related to the new thought but nevertheless continued to feel anxious about driving. The therapist then worked with the client to identify an action plan for dealing with the client's anxiety about driving. The plan included the client practicing breathing retraining before driving, mentally preparing herself for a trip by going through it in her mind before actually going out, and planning several short excursions to familiarize her with driving in easy, uncrowded conditions. The steps of this plan were developed by the client in consultation with the therapist, who was able to implement them successfully and overcome her fear of driving.

DEVELOPING EFFECTIVE ACTION PLANS

Everyone experiences problems in their lives, and negative feelings are often an important clue that something is wrong and that corrective action is necessary. People with a trauma history often need help learning how to attend to their negative feelings and deal with upsetting situations. Anxiety, avoidance, and denial are common responses in trauma survivors to threatening situations that can contribute to revictimization (Arata, 2002). Teaching clients how to take decisive action when faced with real-life problems can

TABLE 7.1
Example of Five Steps of Cognitive Restructuring Worksheet Completed by Robert Addressing Trauma-Related Belief

Step	Response on worksheet
1. Situation	
Ask yourself, "What happened that made me upset?" Write down a brief description of the situation.	Thinking about being sexually assaulted.
2. Feeling	
Circle your strongest feeling (if more than one, use a separate sheet for each feeling): Fear/anxiety Sadness/depression Guilt/shame Anger	[Robert circles "Guilt/shame"]
3. Thought	
Ask yourself, "What am I thinking that is leading me to feel this way?" Use your Guide to Thoughts and Feelings handout to identify thoughts related to the feeling circled above. You may identify more than one thought related to the feeling. Write down your thoughts below, and circle the thought most strongly related to the feeling.	1. I am responsible for the sexual assault. 2. I am a sick, twisted person who acted against his own principles. 3. I am disgusting because I willingly engaged in a sexual relationship with another man. [Robert circles "I am responsible for the sexual assault."]
Is this thought a common style of thinking? If yes, circle the one: All-or-nothing Overgeneralizing Must/should/never Catastrophizing Emotional reasoning Overestimation of risk Self-blame Mental filter	[Robert circles "All-or-nothing"]
4. Evaluate your thought	
Now ask yourself, "What evidence do I have for this thought?" "Is there an alternative way to look at this situation?" "How would someone else think about the situation?" Write down the answers that *do* support your thought and the answers that *do not* support your thought.	

(continues)

TABLE 7.1

Example of Five Steps of Cognitive Restructuring Worksheet Completed by Robert Addressing Trauma-Related Belief   *(Continued)*

Step	Response on worksheet
Things that *do* support my thought.	I was drinking that night and passed out. I engaged in a consensual relationship with him after the assault. I should have known better. He was a friend. I should not have been hanging out with him, but he had been helpful to me.
Things that *do not* support my thought.	It was against my will. I was raped by one man and held down by another. I did not want to be raped. I was unable to protect myself. I was in a compromised situation (i.e. I needed him to provide me with shelter). I had no reason to suspect that a "friend" would rape me.

5. Take action!	
Next, ask yourself, "Do things mostly support my thought or do things mostly *not* support my thought?" If the evidence does *not* support your thought, come up with a new thought that is supported by the evidence. These thoughts are usually more balanced and helpful. Write your new, more helpful thought in the space below. And remember, when you think of this upsetting situation in the future; replace your unhelpful automatic thought with the new, more accurate thought. If the evidence DOES support your thought, decide what you need to do next in order to deal with the situation, and complete an Action Plan.	[Robert chooses "**NO,** the evidence does *not* support my thought."] New thought: "While drinking and other circumstances may have put me at risk, I was not responsible for being assaulted."

provide them with a useful skill for overcoming challenges and taking control over their lives. Therapists should make a point of helping every client work through at least one action plan in the program.

Effective action plans generally include the following four features: a clear goal, a list of possible strategies for achieving the goal, a step-by-step plan for implementing the selected strategies, and a date to follow up on the plan. The Action Plan Worksheet (Handout #11; see Appendix) can be used to facilitate planning on how to deal with the problem situation.

The purpose of the goal statement is to specify the aim of the action plan. For example, if the client felt anxious about an impending move to a new apartment and concluded that the evidence supported her thought, "I'm going to have trouble adjusting to my new apartment," some possible goals of the action plan would include "to learn more about my new neighborhood," "to feel more comfortable about moving into my new apartment," or "to prepare for my move so I'll be ready when it comes."

It can be helpful to start by brainstorming strategies for achieving the goal before evaluating each one. This can lead to identifying several possible solutions to choose from, including some unusual and creative ones. Next, each solution is evaluated and the best ones selected for implementation. Potentially effective strategies for dealing with the problem situation can come from any source (e.g., client, therapist, significant other, books); the client may have past experiences using some strategies to handle similar challenges that can be applied to the problem situation at hand.

Planning how to implement the strategies involves determining the steps necessary to achieve the desired goal. Effective implementation plans should take into consideration several questions, including the following: "Do I need to get more information about what to do?" "Do I need help?" "When will I implement the plan?" and "How could I prevent or deal with possible obstacles?" Once the core elements of the plan have been determined, the steps for implementing it can be established.

The final component of the action plan is to specify a time to follow up on the plan. This facilitates troubleshooting problems implementing the plan or developing additional strategies for achieving the goal, if needed. The therapist should be active in following up on the plan by checking on it with the client at the beginning of the next session. In addition to setting a follow-up time, when the plan involves interactions with people that the client feels anxious about or lacks experience with, it can be helpful to engage the client in some role-plays to practice handling the situation, providing positive feedback and suggestions for improvement after each role play.

An example of teaching the client how to develop an action plan follows:

Therapist: You've finished evaluating whether the evidence does or does not support your thought "I'm going to have trouble adjusting to my new apartment," and you've decided that, on balance, the evidence does support your concern.

Client: Right.

Therapist: Okay. As you know, when the available evidence supports a particular thought or belief, then the fifth step of CR is to develop an action plan to deal with that situation. Developing an action plan means figuring out how to deal with the situation and, we hope, determining how to solve the problem.

	What happens to most problems or upsetting feelings when you just try and ignore them?
Client:	They come back?
Therapist:	Right. Or they get worse. Developing an action plan is like, as the expression goes, "taking the bull by the horns." It means tackling the problem directly and either trying to get rid of it or reducing it so it's not so much of a problem anymore. How does that sound?
Client:	Good.
Therapist:	Good. I have a worksheet that can help you in developing an action plan. [*therapist gives Action Plan Worksheet to client*] The first step is to define the goal of the plan. In other words, what would you like to accomplish in terms of dealing with the problem situation? You concluded that the evidence supports your thought that you're going to have trouble adjusting to your new apartment, which is in a new part of town. What would you like to accomplish in your action plan to address this problem?
Client:	I'd like to stop worrying about it so much.
Therapist:	Okay. So one possible way of defining the goal of the action plan would be "to stop worrying about moving into my new apartment." If you were to stop worrying about your move, but not forget about the fact that you are moving, how would you feel about the move?
Client:	Comfortable, I guess.
Therapist:	All right, so another way you could define your goal would be "to feel comfortable about my upcoming move." Right?
Client:	Yes.
Therapist:	When you feel anxious and worry about your move, what do you worry about? What gets in the way of feeling comfortable about it?
Client:	There's just so much I don't know.
Therapist:	Like what?
Client:	Like where I'll shop for food. The closest pharmacy.
Therapist:	Anything else?
Client:	How to get to the mental health center. How to get to visit my mother.
Therapist:	I see. Do you think if you figured out the answers to some of these concerns that you'd feel more comfortable about the move?

Client:	Yes, I think so.
Therapist:	Okay. So, another way of defining the goal of the action plan would be for you "to learn more about my new neighborhood." Would you agree?
Client:	Yes.
Therapist:	Good. We've come up with three possible goals: "to stop worrying about moving into my new apartment," "to feel comfortable about my upcoming move," and "to learn more about my new neighborhood." Of those three goals, which one best describes what you'd like to accomplish with your action plan?
Client:	I think learning more about the new neighborhood would be helpful.
Therapist:	Okay. Let's write that down and go onto the next step of the plan.

Action plans need to be developed to address a broad range of different situations, as described next.

Need for More Information

Sometimes insufficient evidence is available to permit drawing a definitive conclusion about the accuracy of a thought. In these circumstances, an action plan may be made to obtain more information about the situation, with the additional evidence used later to reevaluate the thought and either modify it or plan a course of action.

Clinical Example

With the help of a vocational rehabilitation program at his community mental health center, Jose recently obtained a part-time job working in the kitchen of a local restaurant. Two days before his weekly CR for PTSD session, he received a letter that his Social Security disability income (SSDI) would be reduced because of his new job. Jose was very distraught over this because he had met with a benefits counselor before taking the job who had informed him that his SSDI would not change as a result of his new job. Jose was concerned because he now believed that he would not be able to move to a better apartment, which had been his primary motivation for getting the job.

Jose went through the 5 Steps of CR, evaluating the thought "I'll never be able to afford a larger apartment," which was accompanied by strong feelings of depression due to the perceived loss. He concluded that the evidence did not fully support the thought, which was changed to "I'm concerned that my SSDI check will be reduced and I won't be able to move to a new apartment." Because Jose's new thought was still associated with distress, he developed an action plan to deal with the situation. Jose decided that the goal of this plan was to "find out more information about whether my SSDI check will be reduced." After brainstorming several possible options for accomplishing this goal, Jose decided to set up meetings the following week with his vocational counselor and his case manager but to wait until after these meetings to find out whether he would also need to contact his local Social Security office. Jose learned from his meeting with his vocational counselor that the letter was a mistake. This counselor helped Jose contact his representative at the Social Security office, and in 2 weeks the problem was sorted out.

Distressing Posttraumatic and Other Symptoms

Action plans can be developed to help people manage PTSD and other distressing symptoms that are not just the result of inaccurate thinking. For example, overarousal (e.g., difficulty sleeping, constantly feeling "on edge") and reexperiencing symptoms (e.g., intrusive memories, nightmares) can be distressing, even in the absence of inaccurate thinking. Similarly, while CR may help overcome avoidance of safe situations that are reminiscent of traumatic events, clients may still feel anxious when first confronted with these situations.

Symptoms may be identified through routine monitoring of PTSD symptoms and depression, review of homework, or discussion with the client about the past week. Action plans that address distressing symptoms are generally aimed at bolstering coping efforts designed to either reduce symptoms or minimize their effects on functioning. Possible coping strategies for symptoms can be elicited from the client, the therapist, treatment manuals for posttraumatic disorders (Cloitre et al., 2006; Kubany & Ralston, 2008; Najavits, 2002; Zayfert & Becker, 2007), or self-help books (Allen, 2005; Copeland & Harris, 2000; Follette & Pistorello, 2007; Matsakis, 1996, 2003; D. Miller, 2003; Naparstek, 2005; Pennebaker, 2004; Schiraldi, 2000; Solinsky, 2002; M. B. Williams & Poijula, 2002). Examples of coping strategies are provided in Table 7.2.

Clinical Example

During a review of Sandra's PTSD symptoms at the beginning of a session, her therapist noted that she reported feeling very distressed by her problems in sleeping. After confirming that Sandra wanted to work on this, the therapist helped her use the 5 Steps of CR to evaluate the upsetting thought, "I can't get a good night's sleep," which she perceived as supported by the available

TABLE 7.2
Coping Strategies for Common Posttraumatic Stress Disorder Symptoms

Symptom	Coping strategies
Reexperiencing the trauma (e.g., intrusive memories, flashbacks)	■ Practice breathing retraining. ■ Spend time with soothing pets. ■ Use positive self-talk (e.g., "I can handle this"). ■ Use thought stopping. ■ Practice acceptance (e.g., just acknowledging memories without giving undue attention). ■ Use grounding (shift awareness to present, such as feeling of body against chair). ■ Don't watch TV news. ■ Stay active during the day. ■ Use prayer.
Overarousal (e.g., hypervigilance, increased heart rate and breathing)	■ Practice breathing retraining. ■ Get physical exercise. ■ Practice meditation or prayer. ■ Recognize triggers and increase awareness (e.g., negative thoughts, sounds, smells). ■ Maintain a sense of humor. ■ Find your own space, such as a room or corner that is safe, and make it soothing.
Difficulty sleeping (i.e., improving sleep hygiene)	■ Avoid caffeine 5 hours before bedtime. ■ Set a bedtime and waking time and stick to them. ■ Don't nap, even if you get a poor night's sleep. ■ Do something relaxing before going to bed (e.g., warm bath, reading, watching TV). ■ Get regular exercise. ■ Don't stay in bed trying to sleep more than an hour.
Nightmares	■ Distinguish between dream and reality. ■ Use soothing objects (e.g., blanket, photos) or pets. ■ Positive self-talk, reassurance. ■ Write down or draw nightmare. ■ Get out of bed to interrupt leftover feeling. ■ Create a different end to the nightmare. ■ Put feet on ground, look in mirror, splash cold water on face to ground self. ■ Keep lights on or use a night light.
Problems with concentration	■ Remove distractions when trying to concentrate. ■ Use underlining, highlighting, or note taking when reading. ■ Schedule rest breaks after concentrating for set. ■ Play computer games to improve concentration.
Avoidance of safe, trauma-related stimuli	■ Use grounding (for numbing or detached feelings). ■ Set gradual goals and take small steps. ■ Get someone to accompany you at first. ■ Use breathing retraining or self-talk when in previously avoided situation. ■ Use distraction when you're in a previously avoided situation (e.g., looking at magazines in store).

evidence. They then began to formulate an action plan and established the goal as "to get a better night's sleep."

Therapist:	Now that you've set the goal, we can go onto the next step. The second step of developing an action plan is to think of different strategies for achieving your goal. At this point it can be helpful to brainstorm as many strategies as possible. Then you can decide which strategies are best and make a plan to put them into action. Let's think of some ways of helping you get a better night's sleep. Do any ideas come to mind?
Client:	Not that I can think of.
Therapist:	Sometimes people find it helpful to relax before they go to bed. What do you think of that?
Client:	That's a good idea.
Therapist:	So, what are some relaxing things you could do before going to bed?
Client:	Read?
Therapist:	Okay, let's note that. What else?
Client:	Taking a bath sometimes relaxes me.
Therapist:	Okay, let's note that too on the worksheet. Are there any things you've found help you calm down when you feel anxious during the day?
Client:	The breathing retraining helps sometimes.
Therapist:	Let's write that down too. Difficulty getting a good night's sleep is a pretty common problem. One approach to getting a better night's sleep is to change one's habits related to sleeping, or what is called *sleep hygiene*. For example, not drinking beverages with caffeine after 3:00 p.m. can help. Should we write that down?
Client:	Sounds like a good idea.
Therapist:	Good. Let's consider some other habits. [*Therapist helps client expand list of coping strategies by exploring other sleep hygiene skills, such as setting a fixed bedtime and rising time, not napping during the day, and getting regular exercise. When the list is complete, the different strategies are evaluated, the best ones identified, and a plan is made to implement them.*]

Current Problem Situations

Having a rewarding life involves being able to rise and meet everyday challenges, including handling difficult situations that anyone would find upsetting. Learning how to recognize and deal with such situations, including potentially threatening ones, may reduce the vulnerability of trauma survivors to revictimization.

Clinical Example

Darlene had a history of childhood sexual abuse as well as involvement in several relationships with men who were physically abusive to her. She had been going out with a new boyfriend, Jim, for the past several months, when on their last date, he shoved her in the midst of an argument. She was shocked and frightened by his behavior because this was the first time he had showed any physical aggression toward her. At the same time, she was ambivalent about confronting Jim with her concerns because she really liked him and was afraid he would break off their relationship.

Darlene completed a 5 Steps of CR worksheet, examining the thought, "I'm going to get into another abusive relationship." She concluded that there was sufficient evidence to support her concern, and with her therapist's help she formulated an action plan, which is presented in Table 7.3.

After developing the action plan, the therapist explored with Darlene her comfort in implementing it:

Therapist: I think you did a really nice job of coming up with good plan for dealing with this situation with Jim.

Client: Thanks.

Therapist: We've talked about how in the past you've had some abusive relationships with men. I'm wondering whether this plan is a different way of handling these situations for you.

Client: Oh yes, it's totally different!

Therapist: In what way?

Client: Standing up for myself, instead of just taking it. That's new.

Therapist: So, when you think of standing up for yourself with Jim, and letting him know how you really feel about his behavior, how does that make you feel?

Client: Nervous.

Therapist: I understand. Being assertive in close relationships, and standing up in this way, is kind of new for you, isn't it?

Client: Yes, it is.

Therapist: Sure. And it's very natural to feel a bit nervous when you are trying something new. Sometimes it can be helpful to practice

TABLE 7.3
Example of an Action Plan Completed by Darlene

General plan	Specific plan
1. Define the goal. Consider what change you would like to see as a result of your action plan. Be as specific as possible.	To prevent my relationship with "Jim" from becoming physically abusive.
2. Brainstorm possible strategies. Think of all the possible ways of achieving your goal. Then, when you have identified a variety of different strategies, evaluate each one and place an asterisk (*) next to the best ones.	Break up with Jim now. Tell Jim that he may not push, hit, or threaten me again.* Tell Jim that if he pushes, hits, or threatens me again that our relationship is over.* Encourage Jim to get into counseling.
3. Plan on how to implement the strategies you selected. Consider these questions: Do I need to get more information about what to do? Do I need to get some help? When will I implement the plan? What obstacles could interfere with the plan? How could I prevent or deal with these obstacles? Then, write down the plan.	Find a quiet, public place where I can meet with Jim to explain my concerns— this week. Tell Jim I was upset when he pushed me last week. Tell Jim that he must respect me, and that he may not push, hit, or threaten me. Tell Jim that I will break up with him if he does any of these things again.
4. Set a date to follow up your plan.	One week from today [date].

Note. Instructions: "Follow the steps below to develop a detailed Action Plan."

what you are going to say before you say it to someone. How about if I play the role of Jim, and you can practice saying to him what you plan to say later this week when you get together?

Client: Okay.

Unresolved Feelings About Past Situations

People with posttraumatic symptoms often have persistent, unresolved distress about prior traumatic events. These feelings may surface when recent events trigger relevant memories or when clients are preoccupied or ruminate about their traumatic experiences. Clients are often able to benefit from using the 5 Steps of CR to identify and change maladaptive beliefs about their traumatic experiences. However, some clients continue to experience distress related to thoughts about past events. For example, some clients may have strong feelings of guilt or rage about events that occurred many years ago, and the feelings may persist even after examining the thoughts underlying them.

Action plans can be developed that have the potential for reducing negative, unresolved feelings about past events. For example, clients with strong, angry feelings about prior abusive experiences may benefit from action plans that explore the value of forgiveness (Freedman & Enright, 1996; Reed & Enright, 2006). Forgiveness involves willfully abandoning resentment against someone who has wronged one and adopting a position of beneficence characterized by qualities such as compassion and generosity (J. North, 1987). Forgiveness is a personally transformative process that needs to be distinguished from condoning or justifying the actions of the other person, forgetting, or reconciliation (Enright & Fitzgibbons, 2000). There are many different ways to forgive, and useful guidance for exploring the benefits of forgiveness is available to clinicians and clients (Enright & Fitzgibbons, 2000).

Similarly, clients with persistent feelings of guilt or shame about prior events may benefit from action plans that incorporate compassion or forgiveness for oneself, as in the *compassionate mind* approach (Gilbert, 2005; Gilbert & Irons, 2005). This approach assumes that the ability to feel compassion for oneself, like compassion for another person, is an attribute that can be learned through practice addressing self-attacking cognitive styles with strategies such as empathic (self)-understanding, considering alternative perspectives, and the use of positive imagery (Gilbert & Irons, 2005; Lee, 2005).

Aside from attempting to reduce distress related to unresolved feelings, action plans can focus on minimizing the negative effects of those feelings on functioning or personal goals. For example, a client who experiences persistent feelings of rage related to a past abuser with whom she has no contact could develop an action plan designed to minimize the effect of those feelings on her current relationships.

Clinical Example

Nicholas was sexually abused between the ages of 12 and 14 by an uncle, and during this period he began abusing a younger boy in his neighborhood. Both Nicholas's uncle's abuse and his own abuse of the younger boy stopped when the boy told his mother what had been happening and a police investigation ensued. During the CR for PTSD program that occurred many years later, when Nicholas was an adult, he described strong feelings of guilt over his abuse of the younger boy in the neighborhood. When applying the 5 Steps of CR, he was able to understand that his actions toward this boy were a direct result of his own abuse at the hands of his uncle. However, this realization only led to minimal reduction in his distress, and Nicholas continued to blame himself for what he had done and to think that he was a "bad person."

When talking about the goal of his action plan, Nicholas said he did not think it would be possible for him to be free of guilt about his abuse of the neighborhood boy. However, he thought it might be easier to bear those feelings if he had a better opinion of himself, so he defined the goal of his action plan as "to feel better about myself." Before brainstorming strategies about how Nicholas could feel better about himself, his therapist prompted him to talk about the qualities he admired in other people whom he considered "good," which of those qualities he had, and which ones he might strive to achieve. One personal quality Nicholas admired was the inclination to help other people or try to make the world a better place. Nicholas admitted that he did not do much in his life along these lines and that he would feel better about himself if he were helping others in some way. This led to brainstorming strategies about how Nicholas could help others, with a particular focus on volunteer jobs. After considering a range of options, Nicholas decided to look into volunteering at the local hospital and made a plan to explore this possibility.

ADDRESSING TRAUMA-RELATED THOUGHTS AND BELIEFS

Helping clients identify and change trauma-related thoughts and beliefs that lead to distress is a fundamental goal of the CR for PTSD program. When and how these thoughts and beliefs are identified and addressed vary from one client to the next. For some clients, the questions previously described (see "Strategies for Teaching Specific Steps of CR," section, Step 3) for identifying the most distressing thought quickly lead to upsetting trauma-related beliefs and schemas, which can then be addressed with CR. For other clients, the relationship of traumatic experiences to current feelings and functioning is less clear, and CR focuses primarily on helping them deal with their distressed feelings. When teaching the 5 Steps of CR, the initial focus is on helping the client learn how to use the skill to deal with negative feelings, whether they appear to be related to traumatic events or not. Over time, as clients become more adept at using CR, the relationship between those feelings and their traumatic experiences often becomes more apparent to the client and therapist and naturally becomes a focus of CR.

Sometimes the relationship between distressful feelings and trauma-related beliefs may seem apparent to the therapist but not to the client, who may even actively avoid making the connection. With still other clients, the impact of trauma-related beliefs on negative feelings may continue to be unclear to both the client and therapist. In both of these situations, the therapist has a number of options for bringing trauma-related thoughts and beliefs into focus and for addressing their effects on negative feelings and PTSD symptoms, as described next.

Exploring the Link Between Distressing Thoughts and Traumatic Experiences

One strategy for helping people make the connection between distressing feelings and prior trauma is to simply inquire whether a particular upsetting thought may be related to the client's traumatic experiences. The therapist can ask a general question, inviting the client to consider this possibility. For example:

Therapist: Let's review for a minute where we are in the 5 Steps of CR. In Step 1, you identified the upsetting situation was when you found out that you didn't get the job you had applied for. In Step 2, you said that your strongest negative feeling was depression. Then, in Step 3, you identified the thought "I'm no good" as the most upsetting thought contributing to your depression. Right?

Client: That's right.

Therapist: Do you think that your thought that you are "no good" could be related to your experiences growing up in your family as a child?

Client: I guess so.

Therapist: Let's talk about how they might be related. As a child, you experienced a lot of physical abuse and not very much loving. How do you think that getting beaten a lot when growing up could affect the way you think about yourself?

Client: That's what they were always telling me: That I'm no good.

Therapist: Could you explain a little more? Who was telling you that?

Client: My parents. I've always had self-esteem problems because my parents told me I was no good. I don't know why I believed them, but I did.

Therapist: Did they actually say that, or was that the impression you got from how they treated you?

Client: Both. When my father used to punish me, he sometimes said it, literally. But mostly I think it's because my parents never treated me like I was worth anything.

Therapist: I see. It sounds like when you told yourself "I'm no good" because you didn't get the job, you were repeating something that you've believed about yourself for a long time and that's related to how your parents treated you. Is that true?

Client: Yes, that's right.

Therapist:	Maybe we could look at that more closely. Let's examine the evidence supporting your belief that "I am no good because my parents beat me as a child."
Client:	Okay.

Identifying Trauma-Related Themes Across Multiple Cognitive Restructuring Exercises

Sometimes a theme emerges across multiple uses of CR and the relationship between this theme and the client's traumatic experiences can be explored. The therapist can use questions to help the client identify and explore the theme. For example:

Therapist:	Let's spend a few more minutes talking about the situation you described in your homework that happened last Sunday when you went to church.
Client:	Okay, I remember that I felt really nervous because this guy I don't know came up to me after the service and tried to start a conversation.
Therapist:	Yes, and I can see from the worksheet that you identified your strongest feeling at the time was anxiety.
Client:	Yes, that's right.
Therapist:	And when you considered what you were thinking that made you feel this way, you identified the thought that concerned you most was "I don't know if I can trust this man."
Client:	That's right, I felt really uncomfortable.
Therapist:	Something that I've noticed over the past few weeks of working together is that in several of the situations in which you felt uncomfortable, the underlying thought you identified had to do with the question of trust.
Client:	That's true. I don't know if I can trust anybody.
Therapist:	Do you think that this concern could be related to some of the traumatic experiences that you have had in your life?
Client:	I think so.
Therapist:	How? In what way?
Client:	Being sexually abused as a child has made it hard to trust people. And then I was raped by my boyfriend—that also makes me feel that I can't trust anybody.

Therapist:	I see, so the fact that your stepfather sexually abused you and you were then later raped by your boyfriend makes it hard for you to feel that you can trust anyone?
Client:	Yes.
Therapist:	I understand. It sounds like that belief is a really important one to examine because it's having a major effect on your daily life, including just casual interactions with other people. Shall we examine this belief more carefully?
Client:	Okay.

Explore Trauma-Related Beliefs Directly

There are several ways the therapist can directly identify the client's trauma-related beliefs. One strategy is to return to the handout How Trauma Affects Thoughts and Feelings (Handout #6; see Appendix) and to examine distressing thoughts that the client identified were due to traumatic experiences or to related thoughts. Although the client may recognize that some of the trauma-related thoughts are not accurate (i.e., reflect common styles of thinking), the client may nevertheless continue to endorse the overall belief, and the therapist could prompt a closer examination of the belief using the 5 Steps of CR. Alternatively, discussion of a thought noted on this handout could lead to identifying another upsetting trauma-related thought, which could then be the focus of the 5 Steps of CR. For example:

Therapist:	Let's return to the handout How Trauma Affects Thoughts and Feelings and look at some of the thoughts you previously described as related to your abuse experiences. I can see that when you completed this you indicated that you thought "the world is an unsafe place." When you look back on that thought now, overall, do you still believe it's true?
Client:	Yes, I think so.
Therapist:	How do you think some of your traumatic experiences may have contributed to that belief?
Client:	I was abused as a child. And then in my first marriage my husband used to beat me. I never knew when something bad was going to happen. There was no such thing as being "safe."
Therapist:	Okay, so you had some really difficult experiences of not being able to feel safe, even in your own home. And that makes it hard for you to feel safe anywhere right now?

Client:	Right.
Therapist:	How does not feeling safe interfere with your day-to-day life?
Client:	I'm always nervous that something's going to happen. I have trouble sleeping, and I jump at the slightest sound. It's even hard for me to go out of my house.
Therapist:	Okay, so feeling unsafe and that the world is a dangerous place is a belief related to your traumatic experiences earlier in your life. And this belief seems to contribute to a lot of the anxiety you experience in your daily life. Shall we examine this belief more closely together?
Client:	Okay.

Another strategy for directly identifying and addressing trauma-related beliefs is to use a standardized measure, such as the Posttraumatic Cognitions Inventory (Foa, Ehlers, et al., 1999). Table 7.4 includes common trauma-related thoughts and beliefs endorsed by clients with PTSD. Because these thoughts and beliefs may change over the course of treatment, the therapist may choose to track changes over time by repeatedly administering a trauma-related beliefs questionnaire (e.g., in conjunction with regular monitoring of PTSD symptoms and depression severity). Once the client has endorsed a particular thought or belief, it is relatively straightforward to establish a connection between that cognition and the person's traumatic experience and to use CR to examine the evidence supporting the thought.

TABLE 7.4

Ten Most Commonly Endorsed Thoughts or Beliefs on the Posttraumatic Cognitions Inventory in 108 Persons With Severe Mental Illness and Posttraumatic Stress Disorder

Thought or belief	Belief rating
1. You never know when something terrible will happen.	4.93
2. I feel isolated and set apart from others	4.79
3. You can never know who will harm you.	4.76
4. I have to be especially careful because you never know what can happen next.	4.73
5. The world is a dangerous place.	4.62
6. I have to be on guard all the time.	4.59
7. People are not what they seem.	4.46
8. My life has been destroyed by the trauma.	4.40
9. People can't be trusted.	4.36
10. I can't rely on other people.	4.13

Note. Belief rating scale: 1 = totally disagree; 7 = totally agree (Posttraumatic Cognitions Inventory; Foa, Ehlers, Clark, Tolin, & Orsillo 1999). Data from Mueser et al. (2008).

TIPS FOR TEACHING THE 5 STEPS OF CR

The following tips are useful for teaching and honing clients' ability to use the 5 Steps of CR on their own.

1. *Teach CR to clients as a self-management skill for dealing with negative feelings rather than using it as a tool for changing their thoughts and feelings.* Teaching clients the 5 Steps of CR as a skill fosters self-reliance and self-efficacy and avoids creating unnecessary dependency on the therapist for challenging and correcting thinking patterns that lead to distress. This is especially important when it comes to evaluating the evidence for and against the client's distressing thought. Prompting clients to generate their own evidence, rather than directly providing it for them, engages and invests them more in the task, leading to more convincing conclusions, including new and more accurate thoughts. In addition, focusing on skill development instead of changing the client's mind avoids the problem of *psychological reactance* (i.e., strongly resisting others' attempts to control one's behavior; Brehm, 1966) during the evaluation of evidence, which can paradoxically increase the client's conviction in a thought or belief rather than decrease it.

2. *Prompt the client to begin using the 5 Steps of CR as soon as possible after a negative feeling or problem situation has been identified.* The more help and practice a client gets using the 5 Steps of CR, both in session with the therapist and out of session on his or her own, the better the learning and outcomes. To maximize the time devoted to teaching CR, the therapist should initiate it soon after an unpleasant feeling or problem situation has been identified. For example, if at the beginning of a session the client indicates feeling upset about a recent fight she had with her boyfriend, the therapist should empathize with the client, explore whether she would like to work on the problem, and then begin the 5 Steps of CR by taking out a worksheet rather than just talking about the problem for the next 15 to 30 minutes.

3. *Avoid getting bogged down during the 5 Steps of CR and failing to get through the exercise in a single session.* To ensure that clients are encouraged and reinforced for using CR when they feel upset, they must repeatedly experience relief as a result of using the skill in sessions with the therapist. This can only occur if the therapist strives to get through all 5 Steps of CR within a session and avoids working on one situation over multiple sessions. Working through all the steps at one time also makes the over-

all skill easier for clients to comprehend and eventually to use on their own.

4. *When teaching the 5 Steps of CR, pause frequently to review what has been discussed so far.* Pausing frequently to review progress when working on the 5 Steps of CR is a powerful teaching technique because it helps clients to grasp the overall flow and logic of the approach. Frequently reviewing what has been covered can also help correct any misunderstandings that may have occurred along the way. For example, after completing the second step of CR with the client:

Therapist: Let's pause for a moment to review what we have done so far in the 5 Steps of CR. You first indicated that the situation in which you felt upset was when you went into the grocery store and saw how crowded it was. Then, in the second step you identified several distressing feelings you had, including feeling embarrassed, nervous, anxious, afraid, and confused. Of all of these feelings, you said that your feeling of fear was most intense. Now let's begin the third step of CR, which involves identifying the thought underlying that feeling.

5. *Reinforce small gains in the client's ability to use CR.* It takes time and effort to learn CR, and gains often occur slowly over time and with much practice. The therapist should generously reinforce all efforts by the client to learn CR and provide specific reinforcement for incremental improvements in the client's skill. The therapist needs to be attuned to small but significant gains in the client's ability to use the 5 Steps of CR and to provide positive feedback accordingly (e.g., "You did a great job in generating a lot of evidence for and against your thought"). Similarly, clients may experience only modest reductions in distress from CR at first, but these improvements should be highlighted and used to encourage them that their relief will grow with continued practice of the skill.

6. *Encourage the client to take ownership of CR as soon as possible.* Because the goal of teaching the 5 Steps of CR is for clients to use the skill in their day-to-day lives, the therapist should be on the alert for opportunities to encourage the client to take responsibility for using the skill. In addition to having the client complete the 5 Steps of CR worksheets after the first demonstration, the therapist can also use language when referring to CR that promotes a sense of ownership over the skill by the client. For example, the therapist can ask, "How is your cognitive

restructuring working for you?" or state, "I'm interested in finding out from you in what ways you find the cognitive restructuring skill most helpful." The therapist should encourage the client to make whatever adaptations they want to make the 5 Steps of CR work most effectively for them.

SUMMARY AND CONCLUSIONS

Teaching clients how to use the 5 Steps of CR builds on the common styles of thinking in three unique ways. First, clients are taught strategies for identifying core thoughts related to their upsetting feelings, including trauma-related beliefs about oneself, other people, and the world. Modifying these beliefs or schemas about traumatic experiences may be critical to effective treatment and long-term relief from posttraumatic symptoms and distress. Second, clients are taught how to systematically evaluate evidence for and against those thoughts and how to weigh evidence based on its objectivity. Teaching clients how to distinguish between strong and weak evidence when evaluating the accuracy of their beliefs enables them to more critically examine the truthfulness and helpfulness of their thoughts and ultimately to change long-held and previously unchallenged trauma-related cognitions. Third, clients are taught to either change their thought (if the weight of evidence is against it) or to make an action plan for dealing with the upsetting situation (if the weight of evidence supports the thought). This final part of the 5 Steps of CR is crucial because it recognizes that not all distressed feelings arise from inaccurate thought processes and it prompts clients to formulate a plan for dealing with situations in which those thoughts occur.

8

COGNITIVE RESTRUCTURING III: SOLUTIONS TO COMMON PROBLEMS

KIM T. MUESER, STANLEY D. ROSENBERG,
AND HARRIET J. ROSENBERG

Therapists may encounter a variety of obstacles when teaching cognitive restructuring (CR). For example, clients may have difficulty using CR in the moment when they are upset, or they may cling to beliefs despite overwhelming evidence against them. In addition, specific symptoms of posttraumatic stress disorder (PTSD) may pose a particular challenge for therapists using CR, such as nightmares, anger, or dissociation. This chapter addresses strategies for overcoming these challenges.

PROBLEMS TEACHING COGNITIVE RESTRUCTURING

A variety of useful texts are available that describe a wide range of strategies for teaching CR and overcoming common problems (J. S. Beck, 1995, 2005; Leahy, 2003a, 2003b). Strategies for dealing with challenges in teaching CR to people with posttraumatic reactions are described in the following subsections.

Difficulty Using Cognitive Restructuring in Distressing Situations

Clients are often able to use CR on their own to deal with a recently upsetting experience, but they may have difficulty using the skill in the moment when they are feeling distressed. It takes time for most people to be able to use the 5 Steps of CR when they are upset, even after they have mastered the basic steps. Therefore, the therapist should foremost normalize the challenge of learning how to use CR when feeling distressed and provide encouragement that with continued practice the person will eventually be able to use the skill in these situations.

Anxiety can interfere with remembering how to use the 5 Steps of CR, especially evaluating evidence for and against thoughts. One option is to encourage the client to first use breathing retraining to calm down and then to use the steps. Another option is to explore whether the client is able to identify a common style of thinking in distressing situations. If the client can recognize when a thought reflects a common style of thinking, the formal evaluation of evidence can be skipped, and the person can be taught to simply identify a thought or belief that corrects that erroneous thought pattern.

People with posttraumatic symptoms may spontaneously recoil in fright, withdraw into depression, or become angry or hostile without being able to clearly identify their feelings at the time. These clients may benefit from teaching that focuses on recognizing upsetting feelings as a cue for initiating CR. The steps for accomplishing this are outlined in Exhibit 8.1.

Reducing Dependence on Written Worksheets

The ultimate goal of teaching clients cognitive restructuring is for them to be able to use the skill when they are feeling upset. However, some clients have difficulty transitioning from the 5 Steps of CR worksheet to using the skill "in the moment" of distress. In this situation, it can be very useful to offer the client a small, pocket-sized card summarizing the 5 Steps of CR and to coach the client how to use the card as a prompt when faced with the kinds of real-life situations in which they are likely to become upset. A brief description of each step is sufficient for this card. For example,

1. What is the *situation*?
2. What is my upsetting *feeling*?
3. What is my upsetting *thought*?
4. *Evaluate the thought.*
5. *Take action!*
   - Does the evidence support the thought?
   - Yes: Come up with a *more accurate thought.*
   - No: Make an *Action Plan* to deal with the situation.

EXHIBIT 8.1
Steps of Teaching Clients How to Recognize Distressing Feelings as a Cue for Initiating Cognitive Restructuring

1. Describe four broad types of negative feelings:
   - Anxiety/fear
   - Depression/sadness
   - Shame/guilt
   - Anger

2. Talk about common situations in which different negative feelings are experienced, supplemented by review of the Guide to Thoughts and Feelings handout:

Feelings	Situations
Anxiety/fear	Potential threat to oneself or other people, concern about meeting one's own or others' expectations, worry about how one will be perceived or evaluated by others
Depression/sadness	Losing something valuable that cannot be easily replaced, such as family, a loved one, a close r elationship, a job, a home, independence, health, specific hopes and opportunities for the future, the respect of others, one's own self-respect and self-confidence, one's "innocence"
Shame/guilt	Having done something that oneself and others believe is inappropriate, distasteful, reprehensible, or morally wrong; not living up to one's own, others', or society's expectations or obligations
Anger	Being harmed, threatened, or taken advantage of by another person, such as being physically injured, sexually abused or assaulted, being robbed of money or possessions, having something else valuable taken away (e.g., family, friends, trusting relationships, opportunities, independence, respect)

   - Provide generic examples of situations for each type of negative feeling (e.g., "How would someone feel if they were alone, in a bad part of town, walking on a street late at night when they heard someone rapidly coming up behind them?").
   - Elicit from client personal examples of situations in which he/she has experienced each type of negative feeling.

3. Review with client his/her own signs of each feeling, including associated thoughts, sensations, and behaviors:

Feelings	Thoughts	Sensations and behaviors
Anxiety/fear	Racing thoughts, such as "I am unsafe," "I'm being threatened"	Muscular tension, pounding heart, rapid breathing, perspiration, hypervigilance, panicky feelings, agitation, numbness, avoidance

(continues)

EXHIBIT 8.1
Steps of Teaching Clients How to Recognize Distressing Feelings
as a Cue for Initiating Cognitive Restructuring   *(Continued)*

Feelings	Thoughts	Sensations and behaviors
Depression/ sadness	Slower thinking, thoughts about lack of self worth or death, such as "I have lost something," "I am missing something," "I want to give up"	Loss of energy, lethargy, heaviness, disengagement from situation, feeling helpless or hopeless, feeling trapped or suffocated, withdrawing from others
Shame/guilt	Thoughts about not being moral or lacking self-worth because of perceived misdeeds, such as "I've done something wrong," "I'm a bad person"	Hot or prickly sensations, wanting to "hide" or "escape from" oneself, avoiding looking at other people, agitation
Anger	Strong thoughts about others' wrong-doing or being offended, such as "He/she has hurt me," "I've been robbed of something important"	Muscular tension, increased heart rate and breathing, feeling pressure in one's head, staring at or confronting others, agitation

4. Identify what situations and which negative feelings the client most often experiences:
   ■ Review situations identified in homework.
   ■ Discuss situations that are avoided or that trigger trauma-related memories and distress based on PTSD Symptoms handout and worksheet (Handout #4; see Appendix).
   ■ Discuss most prominent upsetting feelings based on the Associated Problems handout and worksheet.

5. Engage client in role plays to practice recognizing and labeling feelings based on those situations:
   ■ Work on one or two recently experienced situations that could happen again.
   ■ After identifying the situation, model for the client how to respond to it by talking out loud, first noting the signs of the feeling, and then labeling that feeling (e.g., "I'm feeling tense right now and my heart is pounding. I'm thinking I might be hurt. I'm feeling anxious, afraid.").
   ■ Engage client in one or two role plays of same situation, at first talking out loud, and then to oneself.
   ■ Provide feedback and encouragement after each role-play.

6. Add the initiation of cognitive restructuring to the role plays described above:
   ■ When client is comfortable with role plays of identifying negative feelings, review how negative feelings are a cue for using cognitive restructuring.
   ■ Model the same situation(s) out loud again for the client, adding the initiation of cognitive restructuring at the end of the role play (e.g., conclude the role play with "I'm feeling anxious. This is a time to use the 5 Steps of CR.").
   ■ Engage the client in one or two more role plays as before, providing feedback and encouragement.

EXHIBIT 8.1
Steps of Teaching Clients How to Recognize Distressing Feelings
as a Cue for Initiating Cognitive Restructuring   *(Continued)*

7. Develop homework assignment to practice recognizing negative feelings and initiating cognitive restructuring:
   - Plan assignment to practice in situations that client expects to encounter in future.
   - Explore whether client can deliberately seek out a safe situation that produces a moderate amount of distress in which to practice recognizing negative feelings and initiating cognitive restructuring (e.g., going to a store, reminding oneself about an trauma-related thought).
   - Talk about the nature of any inaccurate thoughts that might occur in the planned situations, and how cognitive restructuring may correct them and lead to reduced distress.

The card can be introduced during a session with the client as a strategy for learning how to use the 5 Steps of CR without the worksheet. After giving the client the card and reading through the steps together, the therapist can explain how the card can be consulted when the client feels upset and wants to use CR. The therapist can then suggest practicing the 5 Steps of CR in the session with the card as a prompt, using a distressing situation the client has recently experienced. Instead of doing this passively, as part of a discussion, it may be helpful to stand up and actually role-play the situation with the client as if it were an actual social situation, not a treatment setting. When the client is familiar with the card, a homework assignment can be agreed on for the client to practice the 5 Steps of CR using just the card or to practice with the card on some days while continuing to use the worksheets on other days. Part of this homework plan should address where the client can keep a copy (or copies) of the card so that it will be convenient during times of distress (e.g., in a pocket or purse) and times when he or she is away from home and around other people. As the client becomes more skilled at using the card to facilitate the 5 Steps of CR, or at cognitive restructuring without any prompts, the therapist can tailor the homework assignments accordingly to reduce or eliminate the use of the written worksheets.

Minimal Reduction in Distress Associated With New and More Accurate Thoughts

Sometimes, using the 5 Steps of CR leads to new, more accurate, and more believable thoughts that are associated with only modest reductions in distress. In these situations, it is important to reinforce the client's use of CR by pointing out the decrease in distress, which may grow over time as the client becomes more familiar with the new and more accurate thought.

However, additional work may be required to address the continued distress the client experiences.

As described in chapter 7, when significant distress persists after identifying a new and more accurate thought, it can be helpful to develop an action plan to deal with that distress. Sometimes the need for and potential utility of an action plan may be readily apparent to both the client and therapist. For example, Jose was upset when his case manager cancelled an appointment with him, which he believed was because he judged him and did not like him. When reviewing the evidence for and against his thought, Jose noted that his case manager had cancelled several other appointments with him recently, even though Jose had seen him around on at least one of those days and he had met with other clients. After closely examining the evidence, Jose concluded that he did not have strong evidence that his case manager's cancellation of appointments was due to his negative opinion of Jose, and he changed his thought accordingly. However, he still felt upset about the situation; he was unsure why his case manager had cancelled their appointments, and he still felt it was possible that he disapproved of him in some way. To address this lingering distress, Jose and his therapist developed an action plan for Jose to talk about his concerns with the case manager at their next meeting. After formulating the plan, Jose and the therapist role played how Jose would broach the subject at his next meeting with his case manager.

Sometimes significant distress persists after a new and more accurate thought has been identified, although the reason for the continued distress is unclear. This often occurs when there are several overlapping thoughts or beliefs related to traumatic experiences that lead to similar upset feelings. Successfully challenging and changing one particular thought or belief leads to only a small reduction in distress because other, potentially more central beliefs have not yet been identified and examined. However, it is through the evaluation of these more peripheral upsetting thoughts that the core distressing beliefs can eventually be identified and challenged. Thus, the use of CR can be viewed as similar to peeling an onion in which the exterior layers (or thoughts) are gradually peeled away (i.e., challenged by repeated use of the 5 Steps of CR) before one gets to the more central beliefs at the core of the distress.

Clinical Example

Lisa felt guilty and shameful about her sexual abuse by her father. She used the 5 Steps of CR to address her belief that she had been responsible for the abuse because she had not stopped it. Although she concluded that the evidence did not support this belief, and changed her thought accordingly, she reported that she still felt strong feelings of shame when she was reminded of the events. Subsequent exploration of Lisa's feelings related to her abuse indicated that she had felt sexual arousal during some of her experiences with her father, which she thought meant that she was a "sick person with no morality." The 5 Steps of CR were then used to address this belief. When examining the evidence, the therapist explained to Lisa that sexual response is a normal physiological reaction to sexual stimulation that is not a matter of choice and does not reflect the individual's preferences or morality. Lisa was relieved to learn this, and she concluded that the evidence did not support her belief, which resulted in a dramatic reduction in her feelings of shame.

Persistent Overestimation of Danger

People with posttraumatic reactions often have exaggerated perceptions of danger that interfere with their lives, prevent them from achieving their goals, and result in chronic anxiety. Repeated use of the 5 Steps of CR is often effective at reducing these appraisals of risk and vulnerability and the anxiety associated with them. However, some clients experience only minimal reductions in anxiety after reviewing the evidence and concluding that their initial perceptions of risk were exaggerated and continue to report high levels of distress associated with any risk, no matter how small. An action plan then needs to be developed to help the client deal with this distress.

For clients who are preoccupied by excessive concerns over relatively low-risk situations, when developing an action plan it is first useful to have a discussion about the risks inherent in life and to explore whether the client is willing to accept those risks. That is, a certain amount of risk in life is inescapable and to get on with life people need to decide whether they accept the risks they face on a day-to-day basis and are likely to face in the future. This discussion can be initiated by the therapist pointing out that all of life involves risks and that an unforeseen event (e.g., natural disaster) could happen to anyone, despite their best efforts to minimize their vulnerability. After talking about how no one's life can be completely free of risk, the therapist can then shift the conversation to the risks that the client faces in his or her life and whether the client is willing to accept those risks.

The goal of the action plan is then determined by the client's decision regarding the acceptability of the risks he or she faces in life. For clients who accept the degree of risk inherent in their current lives, the goal of the action plan is to reduce the distress associated with those risks (e.g., use of breathing retraining, reminding oneself that risks are low, thinking of positive outcomes associated with the acceptable risks). For clients who do not accept the risks associated with their current lives, the goal of the action plan is to help them explore how to make changes in their lives that could further reduce their risk to an acceptable level. Such changes could involve modifying one's habits (e.g., stopping substance use to reduce chances of victimization) or living situation (e.g., making long-term plans to move to a safer neighborhood).

Clinging to Excessive Self-Blame or Perfectionist Expectations

People with PTSD often blame themselves for their own victimization or for not being stronger in coping better with their traumatic experiences. One common strategy for helping clients evaluate evidence for and against this self-blame is to ask them to consider how they would judge another person in the same situation. Clients frequently respond by saying that they would not blame another person in the same situation, which then leads to a reappraisal of their own beliefs of responsibility and a reduction or the elimination of associated feelings of guilt or low self-worth. Similarly, clients may anguish over not meeting unduly high expectations of themselves, such as being a perfect mother, student, or worker, which therapist can modify by encouraging them to consider what they would expect of other people in the same situation.

However, on some occasions clients stick to unrealistic beliefs about their responsibility for bad events or their need to be perfect while frankly acknowledging that they would not hold others to the same standards. In these situations it is useful to explore why the client has higher expectations for him- or herself than others. An implicit assumption in holding oneself to a higher standard is the belief that the person is either better than other people or is capable of being better. Most people will not admit to thinking they are better than others but will acknowledge believing that they are capable of being better and that setting such high standards for themselves is a reasonable expectation they should be able to live up to. The therapist can help the client evaluate these beliefs, with the goal of supporting the person in trying to be better while not engaging in excessive self-blame when their efforts are not always successful. An example is provided next.

Therapist: So, let me summarize our discussion so far. You said that when your son told another boy that he was a gang member, his behavior reflected poorly on you, which meant that you were a bad mother.

Client: Right.

Therapist: But then you also said that if the same thing happened to someone else, you wouldn't blame them or think they were a bad mother.

Client: That's right.

Therapist:	What makes you so special? Why is it that you have such a high standard for yourself but you don't expect the same of others?
Client:	I expect more of myself. I really think I can be better, and I try to hold myself to those higher expectations.
Therapist:	I understand. So you strive to be better mother than other people. Does that mean that you also think that you are a better person than other people?
Client:	I don't think I am necessarily better than others, but I try to be.
Therapist:	I see. So you're human. As the saying goes, "To err is human"—you make mistakes, just like everyone else.
Client:	I guess so.
Therapist:	So, would it be fair to say that you expect a lot of yourself, that you strive to be a better mother, but that you're human and therefore not perfect?
Client:	Yes, I think so.
Therapist:	Do you think it's possible to try to be a better mother and try to be a better person but not to beat up on yourself when you're not perfect because you're human, just like everyone else?
Client:	I suppose it is possible . . .

Sometimes beliefs about excessive responsibility or perfectionism are related to learning experiences when growing up, whether traumatic or not. For example, one client was beaten severely by her parents whenever her performance in school was less than stellar, whereas another client was forced to be responsible for the behavior of her younger siblings at the young age of 12 and was punished when they misbehaved. The therapist can help the client identify such events that may have led to unrealistic expectations of perfection or personal responsibility and examine whether these early experiences were accurate and helpful lessons on life.

Difficulty Letting Go of Beliefs Despite Evidence Against Them

Sometimes clients to cling to a belief even after concluding that the evidence does not support it and after identifying a new thought they consider more believable. This often occurs without the client appearing obstinate or coming up with more evidence to support the old belief. Clients may also continue to hold on to old beliefs despite understanding that just because a belief feels true it doesn't mean it is true (i.e., the emotional reasoning common style of thinking). For example, the client may say, "I know the thought isn't true, but I keep coming back to it again and again" or "I know the evidence doesn't support this thought, but I still think it's true."

Two different approaches can be useful when clients hold on to old beliefs despite the preponderance of evidence favoring alternative thoughts. First, the therapist can address the fact that newer and more accurate thoughts often feel foreign to an individual at first, whereas older and less accurate beliefs may be familiar and feel more comfortable. The therapist should normalize this by reminding the client that their old beliefs have been reinforced over many years to the extent that they have been accepted as unquestioned truths. It takes time and practice to replace old thoughts with new ones, but eventually those new ones will feel just as true as the old ones. The therapist can help clients develop a strategy for reminding them to think the new and more accurate thought in situations in which the old and familiar one keeps cropping up (e.g., writing the new thought down, carrying it around, and reviewing it periodically).

Second, the therapist can explore with the client the perceived value and costs of holding onto the belief versus letting it go in favor of a more accurate one. One strategy for facilitating this comparison is to construct a *payoff matrix* with the client aimed at understanding what they have to gain by continuing to hold the belief and the costs of giving it up (see Handout #15 in Appendix). Constructing a payoff matrix (also known as *conducting a functional analysis*) assumes that adhering to a belief that is not supported by available evidence is not irrational but rather serves an important purpose for the person. Once the perceived costs and benefits of holding onto an inaccurate belief have been identified, those perceptions can be the focus of further attention.

A payoff matrix is a 2×2 table with the horizontal axis split into two halves for the belief in question and the alternative belief, and the vertical axis split into two halves for the advantages and disadvantages of each belief, yielding a total of four quadrants. The therapist works with the client to identify all of the advantages of holding onto the belief in question (upper left quadrant), all of the disadvantages of holding onto that belief (lower left quadrant), the advantages of accepting the alternative belief (upper right quadrant), and the disadvantages of giving up the old belief and adopting the new one (bottom right quadrant). Similar to generating evidence for and against a thought when teaching the 5 Steps of CR, the therapist first helps the client write down all of the perceived advantages and disadvantages of the old belief and new one, regardless of how accurate they appear to be. Sometimes just becoming more aware of the high cost that the individual is paying to hold onto an old belief can help to shift the balance to a greater readiness to endorse the new belief. Often, however, it is also useful to more closely examine some of these perceptions, such as why the client sees holding onto the belief is beneficial or the perceived costs of giving up that belief in favor of a more accurate one.

Clinical Example

Juanita continued to have strong feelings of guilt related to her belief that she was responsible for her childhood sexual abuse by her uncle, despite abundant evidence identified during the 5 Steps of CR that she had done nothing to invite the abuse and had felt powerless to stop it at the time. The therapist helped Juanita complete a payoff matrix (see Exhibit 8.2) to better understand why she continued to hold on to her belief of responsibility. When completing this, it became clear that by assuming responsibility for her own sexual abuse, Juanita was able to feel a sense of control over her life and the world and that the prospect of accepting the alternative (i.e., the abuse was not her fault) made the world seem scarier, less predictable, and much less controllable. On the basis of this discussion, the therapist suggested they examine Juanita's belief "If I am not responsible for my abuse, then the world must be a dangerous, unpredictable place" together. As they evaluated the evidence for and against this belief, the therapist prompted Juanita to consider her experiences with victimization as a child compared with these experiences as an adult. Juanita reported that she had been more able to fend for herself as an adult than a child and began to realize that her anxiety about the world being a dangerous place was more strongly based on her experiences in childhood than in adulthood. Juanita concluded that even if she accepted the fact that her sexual abuse was not her fault, it would not mean that the world was an extremely unsafe place. This made it easier for her to give up her belief that she was responsible for her abuse, resulting in relief from her feelings of shame and guilt.

Difficulty Mastering the 5 Steps of CR

Some clients have difficulty learning how to use the 5 Steps of CR on their own It is not critical that the client master this specific method to learn the essence of how to use CR as a skill. There are several alternative approaches that clients may find easier to learn. For clients who have trouble using the 5 Steps method, the therapist should focus several sessions on selecting and teaching one of these CR strategies and developing homework assignments to practice them.

Exhibit 8.3 summarizes several alternatives to the 5 Steps of CR. All of the approaches begin with the recognition that distressful feelings reflect underlying thoughts that may not be accurate or helpful. The first two methods (recognizing the common styles of thinking and the 3 Cs: Catch it, Check it,

EXHIBIT 8.2
Example of a Completed Payoff Matrix for Juanita

Thought or belief: I am responsible for my own sexual abuse.

Alternative thought or belief: I did not cause my uncle to abuse me.

Instructions: Please be as specific as possible about what you believe are the advantages and disadvantages of keeping your thought or belief, despite the evidence against it, versus changing the thought or belief to a more accurate one.

Advantages of keeping thought or belief	Advantages of changing thought or belief
In what ways does holding onto your thought or belief make your life seem more manageable, safer, or easier to handle? Does the thought or belief provide you with a sense of control, security, or predictability about the future?	How could changing your thought or belief improve your life? Consider whether changing your thought or belief would reduce distressing feelings and free you up from concerns about past events.
■ If I was responsible for my own abuse, then the world seems safer since I can prevent such things from happening again.	■ I would feel better about myself if I accepted that the abuse was not my fault. ■ I might be able to enjoy sexual relations more if it didn't make me feel ashamed about what happened with my uncle.

Disadvantages of keeping thought or belief	Disadvantages of changing thought or belief
In what ways does holding onto your thought or belief make your life more difficult? Consider the role of the thought or belief in creating upsetting feelings for you and in restricting you from doing things you would like to do.	What are the possible disadvantages or costs of changing your thought or belief? Would changing the thought or belief lead to your feeling less control, security, or ability to predict the future?
■ I feel bad about myself and ashamed when I have memories of my uncle abusing me. ■ It's hard to me to enjoy sexual relations because it reminds me of what happened and I feel ashamed.	■ If I accept that the abuse wasn't my fault, then the world seems scary and unpredictable; if an adult can abuse an innocent child, then anything could happen.

Change it) are similar in that they focus on recognizing when an upsetting thought is inaccurate and then changing it. Clients who are able to recognize when they are engaging in a common style of thinking, but are not able to master the 5 Steps of CR, may benefit from using this skill as their main approach to CR. Some clients find the common styles of thinking too abstract and benefit more from the simplified 3 Cs approach.

EXHIBIT 8.3
Alternative Cognitive Restructuring Skills to the
5 Steps of CR

Recognizing the Common Styles of Thinking
- "What thought is upsetting me?"
- "Is this thought a Common Style of Thinking?"
- "What would be a more accurate way of looking at the situation?"

The 3 C's: Catch it, Check it, Change it (Granholm et al., 2005)
- Catch it: "What am I thinking that is upsetting me?"
- Check it: "Is this thought accurate? Does the evidence support my thought?"
- Change it: "What new thought would be more accurate?"

Brainstorming Multiple Perspectives for Upsetting Situations
- "What am I thinking that is upsetting me?"
- "What is another way I could think of this situation?" (generate at least two or three alternative thoughts)
- "Which way of thinking about this situation is most helpful to me?"

Recognizing But Not "Buying Into" Negative Thinking
- "What am I thinking that is upsetting me?"
- "There goes my stinking thinking!"

For some individuals, the ability to think of several different perspectives or interpretations of a situation in which they are feeling upset is more crucial to alleviating distress than trying to determine the "correctness" of any single interpretation. Brainstorming multiple perspectives on an upsetting situation can in and of itself reduce distress (Suarez, Mills, & Stewart, 1987). Some clients benefit from just the process of generating different interpretations for an upsetting situation, while others benefit more from also choosing which perspective is most helpful to them.

The fourth approach of recognizing but not "buying into" upsetting thoughts differs from the other three methods in that it does not focus on changing the thoughts themselves but rather on lessening the importance the person attaches to them and their psychological impact on the individual. It may be impossible to completely replace old, inaccurate, and upsetting thinking styles that have been reinforced over many years with new, more accurate, and less distressing thoughts. Instead of actively disputing these familiar and upsetting thoughts, the person is taught to acknowledge the thought while at the same time recognizing that it reflects one's old thinking style and is not necessarily true. For example, one client learned to respond minimally to his upsetting thoughts by jokingly saying, "Thank you, brain, for that wonderful insight!" This method is frequently used in mindfulness-based approaches to coping with distress (Hayes et al., 1999; Linehan, 1993; Segal et al., 2002; Wells, 2009).

COGNITIVE RESTRUCTURING FOR PROBLEMATIC SYMPTOMS OF POSTTRAUMATIC STRESS DISORDER

In chapter 7, we briefly described the use of CR to address symptoms of PTSD and depression. However, CR for some PTSD symptoms, including nightmares, anger, and dissociation may pose special challenges.

Nightmares

Nightmares, a common symptom of PTSD, frequently involve dreams that are thematically related to the individual's traumatic experiences but are not a simple repetition of those events. Sometimes there is no apparent relationship between the nightmares and the person's trauma history. Regardless of the nature of the nightmares, they are often a major source of distress that interfere with sleep both by abruptly waking the person up and by creating anxiety about going to sleep. A consequence of this anxiety is that people often postpone going to sleep until long after they are exhausted and are prone to using alcohol and drugs to cope with their sleep problems, increasing their vulnerability to substance abuse and dependence.

CR can be used to help clients cope more effectively with nightmares and often to overcome them. To implement this approach, the therapist should explain to the client that nightmares can be due to unresolved concerns or problematic beliefs related their traumatic experiences and that the first step to addressing them is to begin keeping a journal of the nightmares they experience. The journal can be kept by the person's bed and when the person is awakened by a nightmare (or the next morning) he or she can write down what happened in the nightmare. The therapist should ask the client to bring the journal to each session. After reviewing the homework assignment, each journal entry should be read out loud, either by the client or the therapist, and then briefly discussed. Sometimes there is an obvious relationship between a particular nightmare and the client's traumatic events. At other times a common theme may emerge across several nightmares, or even after several weeks of journal review, that appears to be related to the person's traumatic experience. After a particular issue or theme related to trauma has been identified, the therapist can help the client identify the feelings and beliefs related to it and then use the 5 Steps of CR examine those beliefs more closely. Addressing and resolving trauma-related issues that underlie nightmares can reduce both the frequency of the nightmares and the distress associated with them.

CR can also be used to help clients deal with anxiety or other negative feelings they have about trying to get back to sleep after a nightmare. Under these circumstances, CR can be used to help clients address common styles of thinking that may interfere with coping with the nightmares, such as catastrophizing (e.g., "I can't stand it if I have another nightmare tonight; I won't be able to go through the day tomorrow if I don't get at least 6 hours of sleep"), all-or-nothing thinking (e.g., "I'm a basket case because I keep having nightmares"), or jumping to conclusions (e.g., "I'm always going to be beset with nightmares") and develop more adaptive self-statements for coping with these experiences. In addition, CR may help clients develop action plans for dealing with nightmares. Such action plans can involve journaling the content of nightmares (as previously described); challenging beliefs concerning the beneficial effects of alcohol and drugs as a coping strategy for nightmares; and taking steps to improve poor sleep habits (i.e., sleep hygiene; see coping strategies for difficulty sleeping in Table 7.2). Although improved sleep hygiene may not have a direct impact on nightmares, it may improve the quality of sleep when the person is able to sleep and decrease some of the disruptive effects of the nightmares on sleep.

Clinical Example

Vanessa had a history of severe physical and emotional abuse by her mother, who held her responsible as a child for her siblings' behavior and for running the household. When Vanessa was invariably unable to live up to her mother's expectations, her mother would repeatedly tell her that she was "no good" and beat her. Vanessa experienced frequent nightmares, which caused high levels of distress and led her to avoid sleep as much as possible and to abuse alcohol to get to sleep and attempt to suppress her nightmares. Vanessa began to write down her nightmares, and a review of her journal entries with her therapist indicated that they usually involved a theme of her being unable to control someone or a situation and yet somehow being expected or responsible for doing just that. Identifying this theme led to a discussion of Vanessa's experiences as a child and her mother's unreasonable demands on her. This then led to talking about Vanessa's own beliefs, based on these experiences, that when things go wrong they are always her fault, that she should be more responsible, and that she is an unfit mother because she is not perfect. These beliefs were then examined with CR. As Vanessa became more adept at using the 5 Steps of CR to deal with themes that appeared in her nightmares, she also began to use the skill when she was awakened by a nightmare and had difficulty going back to sleep. Gradually, Vanessa's nightmares began to decrease in frequency, and eventually she was able to sleep normally and restfully.

Anger

Anger is generally viewed as a "negative" emotion, but there are some important distinctions between anger and other distressing feelings. Anxiety, depression, and guilt are invariably unpleasant feelings, and most people want them to go away for those reasons alone. Anger, in contrast, is associated with thoughts of having been wronged, and this externalization of blame can be energizing and contribute to feelings of righteousness and injustice. Thus, while people are readily motivated to use CR to reduce distress associated with anxiety, depression, and guilt, they are often less motivated to use it to reduce their anger. However, strong angry feelings can be disruptive and interfere with functioning, including relationships, school or work performance, and feelings of well-being.

Several strategies can be useful when helping clients use CR to address anger. When clients describe angry feelings, the therapist should not automatically assume that they find these feelings unpleasant or unwelcome. Care must be taken to first explore the situation with the client, including the associated thoughts and feelings, to determine whether anger or some other emotion should be the focus of CR. It is normal for people to feel either angry, anxious, or both when they perceive threat (i.e., the "fight–flight" response). Strong fear can be paralyzing, leaving the person feeling vulnerable and defenseless and contributing to avoidance and hypervigilance. Similarly, feelings of depression or shame can be immobilizing due to beliefs of helplessness and low self-worth. Anger can serve as a defense against any these vulnerable feelings, replacing them with a sense of empowerment and activation. One strategy for addressing situations involving anger is to help the client understand and identify other negative emotions underlying his or her anger and to make these feelings (e.g., anxiety, shame) the focus of CR. Recognizing the link between anger and other negative emotions involves exposing one's vulnerability, and thus it requires a good therapeutic relationship between the client and therapist. However, if clients are able to use CR to address these other emotions, their angry feelings often dissipate.

Helping clients recognize that feelings of vulnerability may underlie anger takes time, and there is often a need for other CR strategies to address anger. When deciding how to respond to anger described by a client, the therapist first needs to determine how prominent and important it is to address at that time. Sometimes anger is only one of a host of different negative feelings the person has in response to a situation and is not necessarily even the strongest feeling. Bearing in mind that the client may be less motivated to work on angry feelings compared with other negative feelings, the therapist can often help the client use CR to address one of those other feelings. Similarly, the client may describe several upsetting situations involving a variety of different feelings, and it may be more productive to first focus on situations that do not evoke strong feelings of anger, at least until CR skills are well developed. The primary decision as to whether to work on anger or another negative feeling is determined by how strong the anger is. If it is stronger than the other negative feelings, then it needs to be addressed.

Clients sometimes reject the use of CR to address their angry feelings. They may see CR as an attempt to invalidate or make their anger go away, when in truth they feel that their anger is justified. The therapist should assure the client that the purpose of CR is to help him or her deal with the upsetting situation, whether that means correcting inaccurate or unhelpful thoughts or developing plans for responding to realistic concerns. Clients often accept this, but if the client does not want to work on the situation, the therapist can let him or her vent briefly before moving on to other concerns.

When addressing angry feelings with the 5 Steps of CR, the therapist should be extra careful to avoid directly disputing evidence provided by the client supporting his or her thought or providing any evidence against the thought and instead rely on the Socratic method of asking questions. Direct argumentation is almost always counterproductive. If the client firmly believes that the evidence supports the thought after a review of all the available evidence, the therapist should accept this and move on to developing an action plan to address the situation. This is true even if the therapist believes the evidence does not support the thought. It is the client's perception that is important.

Developing an effective action plan depends on the nature of the situation and how the client has handled it up to that point. Different action plans are required to address anger related to three types of upsetting situations: (a) a recent situation that the client is angry about, (b) events that occurred long ago that the client is still angry about, and (c) a pattern of maladaptive angry responses to a variety of situations.

Action Plans for Anger About a Recent Situation

When developing an action plan for dealing with a recent upsetting situation, the therapist should begin by prompting the client to establish a goal of the plan. This goal should not only resolve the situation or prevent it from happening again but also do so in a way that is consistent with the person's long-term personal goals. Thus, if the client is angry with a partner, relative, employer, or teacher, it might be important for the action plan to take into consideration the importance of preserving that relationship.

After establishing the goal of the plan, the therapist should adopt a problem-solving approach with the client, encouraging him or her to brainstorm possible solutions and posing questions to prompt consideration of additional ones. Although clients may be convinced that the preponderance of evidence supports their thought, sometimes obtaining additional information about the situation is crucial to establishing an effective action plan.

For example, Francis was angry when his case manager, who had previously cancelled several meetings with him, cancelled yet another meeting. On the basis of some comments the case manager had made in one of their meetings, Francis believed that the cancellations were due to the case manager not liking him and judging him. After reviewing the different options for dealing with the situation, Francis decided that checking out his concerns with his case manager would be the best next step for the action plan. After talking about how to do this, Francis role played with the therapist how to initiate the conversation with his case manager.

Sometimes an action plan is needed to address an ongoing situation that is frustrating and annoying to the client, such as dealing with a landlord who has not responded to the client's requests to fix a leak in the bathroom. Other times an action plan is needed after an upsetting incident with someone the client has a relationship with to prevent a recurrence of it in the future. For example, Janice was angry when her boyfriend borrowed her car without asking. Still other times an action plan may be needed to address a recent situation that involved someone who is not familiar to the client. For example, the client could report feeling angry over an incident involving a rude clerk at a store or encountering someone driving unsafely on the highway. In the first case, the action plan might include strategies for addressing the concern (e.g., talking to the store manager); in the second case, the plan might address ways of coping with the angry feelings the situation aroused (e.g., talking over frustration with someone). Regardless of the nature of the action plan, the therapist should follow up with the client in the next session to see how it went and do additional troubleshooting as needed.

Residual Anger Over Events That Occurred Long Ago

Anger can persist long after an event is over, particularly a traumatic one. When the 5 Steps of CR are used to examine the evidence supporting the client's thought of having been wronged in such an event, clients typically conclude that their thought is supported and that they need to develop an action plan. In this circumstance, it can be helpful to formulate the goal of the action plan with clients as either reducing the persistent anger they feel about what happened or minimizing any disruptive effects those feelings have on their functioning or well-being. To facilitate developing a goal for the action plan, it may be useful to explore with clients how their anger has affected their life and whether it interferes with their enjoyment of life or attainment of goals (e.g., developing a close relationship with someone). Several possibilities may be considered when helping a client develop an action plan to deal with persistent anger.

First, many clients benefit from discussing the fact that letting go of anger over past victimization is not the same as forgetting what happened or its wrongfulness (i.e., "letting the person off the hook"). Letting go of anger means accepting what happened as a part of the past and retaining a memory of the events in the form of personal narrative or story, rather than strong feelings (anger) about what happened, thereby freeing oneself to experience the present emotions of the here and now. This discussion may also benefit from exploring and challenging absolutist and idealistic beliefs the client may have about how the world "should" be that are at variance with how the world really is. Some clients report that they feel that letting go is like allowing their victimizer to "win." The therapist can reframe this concern by posing the question of whether continuing to be preoccupied with anger over what happened cedes power to the victimizer that can be taken back by the client choosing to move forward in his or her life.

Second, some clients are reluctant to let go of their anger over past events because they are afraid of "letting their guard down" and increasing their vulnerability to future retraumatization. Holding on to anger for these individuals is tantamount to maintaining control—as long as they are angry, they are energized, alert, and ready to respond to any new threat. When beliefs about maintaining control underlie persistent anger, the fear of imminent threat can be examined with CR. For example, the therapist can help the client examine how controllable and predictable their traumatic events were and what is different now about the client's life. In many cases, the actually predictability and controllability over the events were low or the person did not know better how to extricate themselves from the situation (e.g., an abused spouse), whereas now the person now has more control over his or her life.

Third, for some clients, the possibility of forgiving another person for his or her transgressions deserves serious consideration. For the forgiver, forgiveness can be a powerful medicine, for a number of reasons. For religious people especially, the act of forgiveness may be imbued with a positive, spiritual significance in part because the ability to forgive others means that one may also be forgiven for one's acts. There are many examples in religious texts, especially Christian ones, of forgiveness that can be used to support this decision. People who are able to forgive others are often more at peace with themselves and their lives.

Fourth, clients may benefit from completing a payoff matrix to evaluate what they are gaining from holding on to anger and what this holding on is costing them (see Handout #15 in Appendix). Systematically examining the benefits and costs of holding on to anger can make it clearer to the client the price he or she is paying for holding onto anger and can challenge the perceived costs of giving the anger up. For example, clients may perceive that holding onto anger protects them from future victimization by maintaining a high level of vigilance (as described in the preceding paragraphs). The accuracy and helpfulness of this belief can be examined by asking questions such as: How effective is the anger at protecting the person? Is it possible to protect oneself without remaining angry? Has the anger ever caused bad things to happen that would otherwise not have occurred? What has been given up to maintain the high level of alertness? Is it worth it? Thus, completing a payoff matrix can facilitate weighing the pros and cons of holding onto versus letting go of anger and identifying core beliefs related to the function of anger that can be examined with CR.

Maladaptive Behavior in Response to Anger

If the client's response to anger reflects a maladaptive behavioral pattern (e.g., verbal outbursts, aggression), the action plan should identify a better way of handling those situations. When developing a plan for dealing with situations in which the client feels he or she is justifiably angry, it is important for the therapist to first guide a discussion of how the client dealt with the situation and to then evaluate together the effectiveness of the responses. It is common for people to feel justifiably angered by a particular situation but to still acknowledge the negative consequences of their behavior and to be open to exploring alternative ways of dealing with similar situations. This is especially common when the client's behavior has threatened relationships or role functioning. In these circumstances, the action plan should focus on developing strategies for responding more effectively in anger-provoking situations.

Three strategies may be useful for developing action plans for situations that lead to maladaptive behavior. Depending on the situation, more than one strategy can be used. First, the client may benefit from talking about similar situations that have provoked anger in the past and the thoughts associated with them. This discussion can help clients be more prepared for future situations in which they may feel angry and in dealing with these events more effectively. For example, if the client felt angry because he or she was challenged by an authority figure who did not show him or her sufficient respect, other situations involving authority figures could be identified. Knowing the specific signs associated with angry feelings can also be important, such as thoughts about the unfairness of the situation and increased muscular tension and heart rate.

Second, clients may benefit from identifying and practicing positive self-statements for coping more effectively with anger-provoking situations. Such self-statements generally acknowledge the nature of the angry feelings while simultaneously conveying that the person can manage those feelings without acting on them.

Third, the client may benefit from learning more effective social skills for handling the conflict situation. Effective skills may include appropriate self-assertiveness, making efforts to compromise, or asking for a break from the interaction and expressing a willingness to talk about it later. Specific skills can be most effectively taught by first discussing their importance with the client, then breaking the skill down into specific steps; modeling the skills in a role play; engaging the client in one or two role plays of the skill; and finally providing positive and specific feedback about what the client did effectively. Suggestions for more effective performance should be given in an upbeat, helpful manner. Specific steps for skills and more information about social skills training can be found in Bellack et al. (2004) and Monti et al. (2002).

Clinical Example

Leo, a high school student, tended to have anger outbursts in situations involving arguments with authority figures, including teachers and the principal. After a recent outburst at his principal resulted in a 3-day suspension, Leo and his therapist completed a 5 Steps of CR Worksheet. In the situation, the principal had told Leo to go back to his class when he saw him in the hallway between classes, even though Leo had permission to be out. Leo felt disrespected and refused to go back. After reviewing the evidence, Leo concluded that his thought, "Mr. Smith doesn't respect me," was supported, so he and his therapist developed an action plan. Because completing school was important to Leo's goal of becoming a veterinarian, they agreed to develop a plan that included self-statements that he could use in similar situations at school. They came up with the self-statement "Okay, I can handle it. I don't like having to listen to the crap this guy dishes out, but I don't have to let him get my goat either." After developing this self-statement, the therapist demonstrated it in a role play (speaking out loud the self-statement). Then she engaged Leo in practicing it in a few role plays, with Leo first saying the self-statement out loud and then saying it covertly to himself.

Dissociation

Dissociative symptoms are a common posttraumatic reaction in which the individual experiences a break in the usual connections between thoughts, feelings, and behaviors. Common dissociative symptoms include flashbacks, numbing, depersonalization, and derealization. These symptoms are frequently distressing because they can interfere with the person's ability to relate to others and the integration of experiences into his or her sense of self. CR can be used to reduce distress associated with these symptoms as well as the symptoms themselves.

Flashbacks of traumatic experiences involve the momentary reexperiencing of an event in which the person loses his or her connection with the present and feels as though the event is actually happening again. Flashbacks tend to be brief, but they can be extremely upsetting to the individual. CR can be used to address flashbacks in two ways. First, because flashbacks involve the reexperiencing of upsetting events, CR can be used to examine distressing thoughts the client has about those events (e.g., "I'm tarnished because of what happened") as well as concerns about the flashbacks themselves (e.g., "I'm never going to be able to live a normal life").

Second, flashbacks may be triggered by specific stimuli, including feelings. Teaching clients how to recognize distressing feelings that precede flashbacks can facilitate their ability to use CR to cope with those feelings, thus preventing flashbacks from occurring. Clients can be taught to keep a log of their flashbacks, including when the flashback occurred, the situation, possible trauma-related stimuli, and any thoughts or feelings that preceded it. The therapist can review this log with the client to identify possible precipitants of flashbacks (e.g., thoughts of being trapped, feelings of anxiety and panic, a trauma-related stimulus) and then engage the client in practicing how to recognize those thoughts, feelings, or stimuli and to initiate CR as soon as they are detected. Ehlers and her colleagues have described a method for treating intrusive posttraumatic symptoms, including flashbacks, that involves learning how to discriminate triggers of memories and then how to break the link between the trigger and associated memory (Clark & Ehlers, 2005; Ehlers et al., 2005; Ehlers, Hackmann, & Michael, 2004).

Numbing, depersonalization, and derealization symptoms are disturbing because they interfere with people's connection with others and with the world around them. CR can be used to help clients cope with these symptoms based on the assumption that historically they have served a protective function in shielding the person from extremely distressing thoughts and feelings. Because the client has developed new skills for dealing directly with negative feelings (i.e., CR), there is no longer a need for these symptoms to protect the person from those feelings. However, because numbing and related symptoms are a learned response to distress that has been reinforced over many years, practice is needed to preempt this response with CR. Practice using CR to address distressing feelings that precede numbing and related symptoms can be facilitated by helping clients increase their awareness of those situations and associated feelings. This can be accomplished by teaching clients to maintain a log of when these experiences occur, as described in the preceding paragraph, when addressing flashbacks.

SUMMARY AND CONCLUSIONS

A wide range of strategies can be used to overcome common obstacles encountered when teaching CR to clients, such as difficulty using the skill in the moment when the person feels distressed, persistence of beliefs despite the evidence against them, and only minor reductions in distress associated with replacing inaccurate thoughts or beliefs with new and more accurate ones. Similarly, CR can be used creatively to deal with a variety of posttraumatic symptoms that can interfere with functioning and enjoyment of life, including nightmares, anger, and dissociation. This chapter has described some strategies for addressing these obstacles and challenges, and therapists are encouraged to use their ingenuity in developing additional strategies when the need arises.

9

GENERALIZATION TRAINING AND TERMINATION

KIM T. MUESER, STANLEY D. ROSENBERG,
AND HARRIET J. ROSENBERG

The effectiveness of the skills taught in the Cognitive Restructuring for Posttraumatic Stress Disorder (CR for PTSD) program depends on the extent to which clients are able to use and transfer these skills from the therapy sessions to their daily lives. Special populations of trauma survivors may face particular obstacles in learning how to use the skills in their personal lives because of problems such as severe symptoms (e.g., psychosis), cognitive impairment, interpersonal conflict, or multiple stresses. This chapter describes strategies for overcoming barriers to the generalization of skills taught in the therapy sessions to clients' daily lives, with an emphasis on cognitive restructuring (CR), the most critical skill for overcoming PTSD.

Although clients usually experience a significant reduction in their PTSD symptoms over the course of treatment, and many no longer meet diagnostic criteria for PTSD, some continue to have symptoms. Strategies for addressing persistent PTSD symptoms are also described in this chapter. Finally, the termination of therapy is discussed. The CR for PTSD program is a time-limited intervention, and clients are prepared for the ending of therapy from the beginning of the program. Planning for termination, reviewing progress, and identifying needs the client has or may develop in the future can maximize the long-term benefits of participation.

GENERALIZATION TRAINING

There are two broad approaches to maximizing the generalization of skills taught in therapy to clients' daily lives: increasing the client's competence in the skills and increasing environmental supports for using them. *Competence* resides within an individual and is the ability to use a skill effectively, in appropriate situations. *Environmental supports* reside outside the person and are facilitators of the individual's use of a skill in day-to-day situations. Attention to both approaches is critical for clients to get the maximal benefit from the CR for PTSD program.

Increasing Competence

The more competence clients develop at CR over the course of treatment, the more likely it is that they will continue to be able to use the skill after the program ends. The ability of clients to use CR independently can be improved by strengthening their skills within treatment sessions and promoting their use of the skills in natural settings.

Strengthening Skills Within the Session

CR is a complex skill that is taught in sessions by focusing on the specific components of the skill and gradually building the client's competence through repeated practice and reinforcement of those components. Central to teaching clients how to use CR is the therapist's systematic use of *shaping,* or the successive reinforcement of approximations to a desired goal or skill.

To shape the client's competence at using CR, the therapist needs to actively engage him or her in repeatedly practicing the skill during treatment sessions and to provide feedback and guidance to hone the skill over multiple efforts. This requires more than just talking about the 5 Steps of CR or leading the client through the steps of the skill; the client must be involved in actually trying to use CR in the session. Shaping the specific components of the CR skill involves explaining and demonstrating the steps (with the therapist taking the lead), prompting the client to use the steps of the skill (with the client taking the lead), reinforcing the client for steps that were performed well, providing additional prompts or instructions to teach other steps, and then gradually fading the instructions and prompts as the client becomes more able to perform the skill independently. Once clients are able to use the overall skill, their competence is reinforced by the natural effects of CR on reducing negative feelings (i.e., *negative reinforcement*), and they no longer depend on the therapist for reinforcement.

Promoting Use of Skills in Natural Settings

Homework practice between therapy sessions gives clients the opportunity to see whether they can use the skills taught in session on their own. Independent use of skills is naturally reinforced, increasing the chances that clients will use the skills again in the future. Difficulties using skills independently provide valuable information to the therapist, who can focus on teaching those aspects of the skill the client has not mastered.

Once clients begin trying to use skills on their own, the therapist modifies homework assignments to shape the skills and to make them both as effective as possible and likely to be maintained after completing treatment. Strategies for increasing follow-through on homework assignments are summarized in Exhibit 9.1.

Tailoring the skills to the individual client and maximizing the effectiveness of homework assignments have been addressed in previous chapters. In chapter 4, options were described for modifying breathing retraining to adapt it to client's needs, with homework assignments first focusing on practicing the skill in comfortable, nonstressful situations before trying them in more challenging ones. Similarly, the majority of sessions devoted to CR focus on teaching a specific approach to the skill (the 5 Steps of CR) and to using

EXHIBIT 9.1
Strategies for Enhancing Adherence to Homework

Routinely use the following techniques to encourage adherence:
- Conceptualize "homework" broadly as efforts to practice or use targeted skills outside of session, not just completion of written materials.
- Develop assignments collaboratively with client to ensure buy-in and feasibility.
- Individualize assignments for the client (e.g., be specific, plan when and where assignment will be done, anticipate and problem solve possible obstacles).
- Follow up on homework assignments toward the beginning of each session.
- Provide ample reinforcement for any efforts to practice or use skills outside of session, regardless of their success.
- Elicit whether the client's use of a skill outside of session was associated with a reduction in distress.
- Develop a plan for homework at the end of each session, addressing any obstacles the client previously encountered to completing assignments.

If problems occur with follow-through on homework, try the following approaches:
- Review the rationale for homework as trying skills learned in program to see how they work and where there are problems.
- Have the client practice completing part of homework at the end of the session, addressing problems or misunderstandings as needed.
- Simplify the assignment, reinforce efforts to follow through, and gradually increase difficulty as the client succeeds with easier assignments.
- Have the client complete part of homework assignment at the beginning of the session, and then review it together and address any difficulties.
- Engage significant other(s) in helping the client follow through on assignments.

worksheets to help the client keep track of the steps. In later sessions, when attention shifts to the generalization and maintenance of skills, consideration must be given to how the client can continue to use CR after the program has ended. Two strategies can be used to facilitate this.

First, if the client has difficulty mastering the 5 Steps of CR, the skill can be simplified to make it easier. For example, as discussed in chapter 8 of this volume, the client might find it easier to rely on recognizing and challenging the common styles of thinking to deal with distress, with homework assignments in the generalization phase of the program focusing on practicing this skill rather than the 5 Steps of CR.

The second method for facilitating the maintenance of CR is to reduce or eliminate the client's reliance on worksheets and handouts. Although these materials are an important aid to teaching CR, reliance on them for the day-to-day handling negative feelings is impractical, and most clients do not continue to use them after the program has ended. Teaching clients how to use CR without relying on the worksheet can foster skill generalization and maintenance. Competence at using the 5 Steps of CR without the worksheet can be shaped through a combination of in-session work and homework assignments. For example, after a distressing situation has been identified in session, the therapist could say,

> *Therapist:* Over the past several sessions you've done a really good job of learning how to use the 5 Steps of CR to deal with upsetting feelings. Up until now you've used a worksheet to go through the steps. However, to be able to use the five steps at any time and in any situation, it might be helpful to be able to use the skill without the worksheets. How about if we try working on this problem today without the worksheet?
>
> *Client:* Okay.
>
> *Therapist:* Good. So, what's the first step of CR?

After practicing the 5 Steps of CR in the session without the worksheet, a homework assignment can be developed for clients to practice it that way on their own. In collaboration with the client, homework assignments can be graded in difficulty to shape the ability to use the skill without the worksheet. For example, the client might begin practicing the 5 Steps of CR without the worksheet for 2 or 3 days of the following week, while continuing to use the worksheet on the remaining days. Success at using the skill without the worksheet can be followed up with assignments to decrease or altogether eliminate the worksheets. Alternatively, an assignment can be developed for the client to try to do the first two or three steps of CR without the worksheet and then to use the worksheet for the remaining steps. In subsequent assignments the client can practice doing more steps of the skill without the worksheet.

Some clients lack confidence that they will be able to use the 5 Steps of CR without the worksheet. The therapist can acknowledge the client's concern while suggesting that he or she try it, and pointing it that if it does not work he or she can resume using the worksheet. Some clients may find that a combination of using worksheets for the most upsetting problems, but not using them for less distressing problems, is optimal. Therapists should discuss with clients how to ensure they have an ample supply of CR worksheets after the program has ended.

Increasing Environmental Supports for Skills

Environmental supports can play an important role for helping clients learn, use, and maintain skills taught in the CR for PTSD program. Environmental supports include people with regular contact with the client who can prompt or help them to use the targeted skills (e.g., professionals and significant others).

Professional Supports

Some clients have a long-standing relationship with a professional but a time-limited relationship with their CR for PTSD therapist. For example, people with a severe mental illness may have a case manager, individuals with an addiction may have a long-standing relationship with an addiction counselor, adolescents may have a working relationship with a school counselor, and people with chronic medical conditions may have such a relationship with a nurse or doctor. Any of these professionals can be a valuable resource for supporting clients' use of CR in their daily lives.

As described in chapter 3 of this volume, it is important for the therapist providing the CR for PTSD program to have regular contact with supportive professionals. Brief updates every few weeks (and more often if needed) can inform the professional about the client's progress and any stresses or challenges he or she is experiencing. These contacts can also serve to get input from other professionals about how they think the client is doing. Toward the end of the program, the therapist should explain to the client that they will work together to develop a plan with the professional aimed at helping him or her continue to use their skills after the program is over. This plan will include a joint session with the professional. The last section of this chapter describes how to prepare the client for this joint session.

Supports From Significant Others

Significant others such as family members and friends can also play an important role in helping clients maintain their skills. The decision to involve significant others in treatment is based on three considerations: (a) Is the significant other crucial to delivering the CR for PTSD program to the client, (b) is there strong conflict between the client and significant other that could undermine the client's ability to use the skills taught in the program, and (c) does the client have marked cognitive impairment that could limit his or her ability to follow through on homework assignments and use the skills in their daily lives? The first two considerations are discussed next, and the topic of cognitive impairment is addressed in the following section.

Engaging Significant Others Is Crucial to Delivering the Program. Some clients depend on a significant other for transportation. For example, an adolescent may have to rely on a parent for transportation to therapy sessions. A variety of stresses (e.g., poverty, health problems), multiple demands on the parent (e.g., constraints due to work), and family chaos can all jeopardize the parent's ability to get the adolescent to treatment sessions. In situations in which the client depends on another person for getting to therapy, it is crucial for the therapist to solicit that person's understanding and support for the client's participation in the program.

Facilitating the support of a significant other should be done in close collaboration with the client and in a manner respectful of the person's preferences (e.g., not talking about details of his or her trauma history). One approach is to arrange to have the significant other attend part of a session with the client on a regular basis to inform the significant other about the program and the client's progress. For example, the significant other can be invited to join the client and therapist for the last 15 minutes of the first session and then to join again every third or fourth session. During these joint meetings, the therapist can encourage the client to take the lead in explaining the program, describing skills he or she has learned and the nature of homework assignments, summarizing progress made, and answering questions. Depending on the relationship between the client and significant other, and the client's need for support, these discussions can also address ways that the significant other can facilitate the client's homework practice and use skills on his or her own.

Addressing Conflict Between the Client and Significant Other. Posttraumatic symptoms frequently lead to friction in close interpersonal relationships (Cloitre, Miranda, Stovall-McClough, & Han, 2005; Kuhn, Blanchard, & Hickling, 2003; Mueser, Essock, Haines, Wolfe, & Xie, 2004; Zlotnick, Bruce, et al., 2003). Sleep problems, hypervigilance, pervasive mistrust, anger outbursts, numbing of feelings, and avoidance (e.g., social situations, sex) can all take a heavy toll on people who have a close relationship with the client. These difficulties are often compounded by related problems, such as inability to work, substance abuse, and chronic depression. So that clients can practice skills such as breathing retraining and the 5 Steps of CR on their own, a modicum of peace and quiet is required in their home environment. Conflict in close relationships can result in a tense environment that is not conducive to the client's practicing these skills. Addressing this conflict may be crucial to maintaining the client's involvement in, and benefit from, the program.

One approach to minimizing the effects of interpersonal conflict is for the therapist to enlist the support of the significant other for the client's participation. This can be accomplished by including the significant other in some joint sessions, as described previously. Depending on the degree of conflict, the therapist will need to take the lead in structuring and running these joint meetings and in setting limits to minimize tension. In addition to helping the significant other understand PTSD, how the program works, and the skills taught, the therapist can use these meetings to validate concerns or complaints they may have, while also trying to make a link between these problems and the client's PTSD. Helping significant others understand how the client's traumas and PTSD have contributed to their present problems can both normalize the client's behavior and provide hope to everyone that they can be overcome through participation in the program.

Managing Cognitive Impairment

There is a complex interplay between cognitive functioning (i.e., attention, memory, planning, abstract reasoning) and PTSD. People with cognitive impairment are more vulnerable to developing PTSD following a traumatic event (Bustamante, Mellman, David, & Fins, 2001; Gilbertson et al., 2006; McNally & Shin, 1995). Once PTSD has developed, problems with memory and other cognitive functions are common (Brandes et al., 2002; Brewin, Kleiner, Vasterling, & Field, 2007; Yehuda, Golier, Halligan, & Harvey, 2004). Furthermore, cognitive impairment is common in some populations with a high prevalence of PTSD, such as people with schizophrenia (Heinrichs, 2001). Cognitive impairment can interfere with learning and retaining skills taught in the CR for PTSD program. However, if therapists are aware of the client's cognitive limitations, steps can be taken to minimize their effects on outcome. Strategies for compensating for the effects of cognitive impairment can be divided into two broad types: teaching methods and capitalizing on environmental supports.

Teaching Methods

Individuals with cognitive impairment require more practice to acquire the information and skills taught in the CR program. The most important strategies for teaching skills to these clients include providing new information in small amounts, breaking skills down into small steps, frequent practice and repetition, and abundant reinforcement for all efforts.

When working with clients who have cognitive impairment, the therapist needs to give greatest priority to teaching the two skills most critical to reducing

PTSD symptoms: breathing retraining and CR. Because more time may be needed to teach these skills, the therapist should limit the amount of time spent teaching basic facts about PTSD and associated problems to the recommended two sessions. This may require selectively teaching only the most important points about PTSD, such as the specific symptoms the client has and the fact that it is a treatable disorder.

Parts of the CR for PTSD program involve providing information to the client, such as the orientation to the program, psychoeducation about PTSD, and the introduction to CR. Teaching this information is most effective when the therapist keeps it as simple as possible, provides information in small chunks to avoiding overloading the client, frequently pauses to review what has been discussed, and regularly stops to ask the client to describe his or her understanding of the material.

The introduction and rationale for breathing retraining should be provided as briefly as possible to reserve the most time for actually teaching and practicing the skill. The therapist may need to model breathing retraining several times, each time followed by the client practicing the skill, until he or she masters it. Repeated in-session practice may be necessary to consolidate the skill.

Similarly, the introduction and rationale for CR should be kept to a minimum to reserve time for practicing the skill. When providing an example of how thinking affects feelings, the therapist should stick to the simplest possible example (e.g., a scratching sound outside of one's window at night—is it a burglar or the cat?) and move on when the point has been made. If the client clearly understands just one or two of the common styles of thinking and can recognize examples of them in his or her life, the therapist should focus on those styles and not try to teach recognition of the other ones.

Teaching the 5 Steps of CR is most effective when working through specific examples with the worksheet and spending a minimum of time just talking about the skill. After a brief explanation, the therapist begins by leading the client through the 5 Steps of CR and then shifts to the client going through the steps, with the therapist prompting him or her as needed. Before beginning each step, the name of that step should be clearly stated or elicited (e.g., "The third step is identifying the thoughts that led to the distressing feeling"). The therapist should avoid spending too much time on any one step so that the whole sequence of five steps can be understood by the client as a single skill. In addition, the therapist should frequently pause to review what was accomplished in the previous steps or to elicit the review from the client (e.g., when beginning Step 3, briefly review what was done in Steps 1–2; then, when beginning Step 4, briefly review Steps 1–3). As described in chapter 8 of this volume, if the client has difficulty mastering the 5 Steps of CR, alternative approaches to CR should be taught.

Homework assignments should be as easy and specific as possible early in the program to maximize follow-through. Demonstrating and having the client practice a new homework assignment at the end of the session ensures that the client understands how to do it. After an assignment has been agreed on, asking the client to summarize it is a useful check. Making plans with clients to arrange for environmental prompts (e.g., posting a sign on the refrigerator or putting a worksheet by the bedside table) to do their homework can also facilitate adherence. As discussed in the next section, professionals and significant others can be important environmental supports for facilitating follow-through on homework.

Capitalizing on Environmental Supports

The greater the extent of the client's cognitive impairment, the more important the role of environmental supports in acquiring the skills. Supportive persons or significant others can help clients learn and generalize skills by facilitating their completion of homework assignments. For clients who have a basic understanding of the skill but who forget to practice it for their homework, the support person can prompt them. For clients who do not yet have a basic grasp of the skill from their work in the session with the therapist, the support person can help them follow through on their homework assignment by providing supplementary prompting and coaching.

Clearly, the greater the role of the support person in helping the client practice the skills and follow through on homework, the more closely treatment needs to be coordinated between the therapist and that person. At a minimum, if the client needs to be prompted to do homework by the support person, that person needs to know what the assignment is. This can be arranged by having a brief meeting at the end of the session with the client and support person or through a phone call. If the client needs or would benefit from assistance from the support person in practicing the skill as their homework assignment, additional time should be spent with that person, either as part of the therapy session or outside of the session. Involving a support person in helping the client practice CR outside of therapy sessions is the most powerful strategy for developing competence at the skill because teaching the skill is not limited to the restricted time and place of the therapy hour, thus fostering generalization.

The maintenance of clients' CR skills after the CR for PTSD program has ended depends on the level of competence the client has achieved at the end of the program. Clients who have basic competence at the skill, but forget to use it during times of stress, may benefit from the prompting of support persons to use it at appropriate times. However, some clients with significant cognitive impairment do not achieve independent competence at CR by the end of the program, although they benefit from assistance in using the skill provided by the therapist and support person. The support person can play a more integral role in helping these clients continue to use CR after the program has ended. Plans for involving the support person in this way can be made during the last several sessions, when the need for such an arrangement has been clearly established.

ADDRESSING PERSISTENT POSTTRAUMATIC STRESS DISORDER SYMPTOMS

PTSD symptoms sometimes persist despite clients' ability to learn CR and generalize its use to their everyday lives. Three approaches can be used when working with clients whose PTSD symptoms persist later in the program. For most clients, a combination of all three strategies is optimal.

Encourage Continued Practice of Cognitive Restructuring

Clients are often relieved to learn that it is common for some PTSD symptoms to persist over time but to gradually improve with continued practice at CR, even after the end of treatment. Normalizing the slowness at which some symptoms improve, and pointing out that when a client has been thinking a certain way for many years it will take time to learn new ways of thinking, helps a person understand the long-term process of overcoming the effects of trauma and PTSD and encourages him or her to stick to CR as a crucial tool to aid in recovery. Any improvements in symptoms over the course of the program can be used as evidence to support its value and the importance of continuing to use CR after the program has ended.

Target Posttraumatic Stress Disorder Symptoms

When PTSD symptoms persist throughout the course of the program, the therapist should focus CR directly on the most distressing of those symptoms. A number of strategies for using CR to address PTSD symptoms have been described in chapters 6, 7, and 8 of this volume. We briefly describe here the application of CR to the three main PTSD symptom clusters of reexperiencing, avoidance, and overarousal.

The common theme across the symptoms of reexperiencing is that clients feel upset when they think about what happened to them. When clients continue to have high levels of distress related to thoughts or memories of traumatic events, the therapist should take this as a cue that an underlying (and unaddressed) schema may exist that perpetuates the distress. The therapist's task then is to identify the critical trauma-related beliefs that compose the schema and to help the client use CR to correct them. Beliefs can be identified by examining themes associated with thoughts related to distressing situations previously tackled with CR (see chap. 7, this volume), previously stated thoughts by the client about the trauma, or questionnaires such as the Posttraumatic Cognitions Inventory (Foa, Ehlers, et al., 1999). The therapist should be mindful that the distress related to memories of traumatic events may have little to do with the events themselves but rather with how clients reacted to an event at the time, how others reacted, or how clients coped with the experiences over the long term (Ehlers & Clark, 2000). If the client continues to experience distress related to reexperiencing symptoms, whether or not trauma-related schemas have been successfully identified and corrected, the therapist should help the client use CR to develop action plans (see Table 7.1).

Similar to reexperiencing symptoms, persistent avoidance symptoms may reflect the presence of an underlying trauma-related schema that has not yet been fully resolved through CR. The therapist can engage similar strategies to help the client use CR to identify and challenge trauma-related beliefs that perpetuate fear and avoidance of particular situations. Sometimes clients continue to avoid trauma-related stimuli despite having successfully challenged and changed beliefs that originally led to the avoidance in the first place. For example, a man who was in a car accident may avoid driving or being in cars because of his belief that driving is extremely dangerous; a woman who was sexually abused as a child may avoid physical intimacy because of her belief that no man can be trusted. In both cases, avoidance of those situations (driving, intimacy) could persist, even after CR has successfully modified the core beliefs underlying their avoidance. In these situations, avoidance occurs not because of a belief about the situation but because the anxiety has become classically conditioned through repeated avoidance of the situation over many years. When this occurs, the therapist can explain that the client's experience of anxiety in these situations is a normal response to many years of avoidance and that with gradual exposure and familiarity with the situations the person's anxiety will eventually go away. If the client wants to overcome his or her avoidance of a safe but anxiety-provoking situation, the therapist can then help the client to develop an action plan as part of CR to promote comfortable, graded exposure to the situation, potentially in combination with breathing retraining.

People with chronic PTSD often continue to experience distressing symptoms of overarousal, such as racing heart and exaggerated startle response, even after trauma-related beliefs and schemas have been successfully corrected. For many clients with persistent overarousal, the best option is to use CR to develop action plans for coping with these symptoms (e.g., exercise, sleep hygiene), such as those summarized in Table 7.1. Strategies for addressing anger problems, which are part of the overarousal cluster of symptoms, have been described in chapter 8 of this volume.

Shift Focus to Personal Goals

Clients with PTSD often assume that reducing or eliminating their PTSD symptoms is a prerequisite to pursuing and achieving personally important goals such having as a meaningful relationship or returning to school or work. These individuals may erroneously conclude that the persistence of their PTSD symptoms is a barrier to living a "normal" and rewarding life. When significant PTSD symptoms persist into the later stages of the program, the therapist should shift attention away from symptoms and toward the client's goals, using CR to address any perceived or real barriers to achieving them.

The therapist should be familiar with the client's goals from the second psychoeducation session, based on their discussion of what changes the client would most like to see happen in his or her life (see chap. 5, this volume). The client may already be working toward these goals with the therapist's help, but if not, the therapist should explore what steps the client can begin taking to achieve them. With encouragement, some clients begin working toward their goals immediately. Others may be skeptical that important life changes can be made as long as they have PTSD symptoms.

There are several options for addressing this common skepticism. First, the therapist can normalize the client's persistent symptoms by explaining that sometimes PTSD symptoms do not completely go away with treatment, while also informing them that it is possible to live a happy and rewarding life despite having symptoms. The notion that one can live a fulfilling life while still having PTSD may be surprising to the client but is generally received as good news. Second, the therapist can note that PTSD symptoms sometimes improve as a result of pursuing personal goals. For example, people with PTSD are often more prone to reexperiencing symptoms during unstructured than structured time; pursuing meaningful activities such as work, school, or being a more involved parent can decrease unstructured time and hence decrease reexperiencing symptoms. For another example, people are often willing to confront and overcome their PTSD avoidance symptoms when doing so is important to achieving their personal goals.

Third, the therapist can prompt the use of CR to examine the belief that the client cannot make progress toward his or her goals as long as he or she continues to have PTSD symptoms. Fourth, the therapist can positively challenge some clients who harbor deep anger toward the person who abused or assaulted them by asking them if they want to allow that person or those events to continue to control their lives or whether they want to seize that power and run their own lives. This message reframes the client's helplessness as a way of letting the perpetuator win, which can evoke the counterresponse of not wanting to let that happen, which can result in the client's making a decision to take charge of his or her own life.

The actual process of helping clients work toward personal goals is relatively straightforward. The therapist helps the client to determine the steps necessary to achieve the goal and supports any efforts the client makes in taking those steps. If the client perceives significant obstacles to the next step (i.e., is frustrated or anxious that the step cannot be accomplished), CR is used to evaluate the validity of the concerns, which either result in altering the client's perception (e.g., "I really can take the step") and developing an action plan to deal with the obstacle. Action plans may need to address obstacles to achieving a goal that are either within the person (e.g., anxiety) or external to the person (e.g., need for money or more information). When used in this way, CR is a tool the client can use to work toward achieving personal goals by removing perceived but unrealistic obstacles and by developing plans for addressing and overcoming realistic challenges to achieving those goals.

TERMINATION

Clients are prepared for termination from the CR for PTSD program from the beginning of their participation by the therapist clearly communicating that the program is time limited. Such communication is critical to shaping clients' expectations for the program, motivating them to take an active role in learning during the therapy sessions, and preparing them for moving on after the program has ended.

The date of termination from treatment should be jointly determined by the therapist and client on the basis of the client's progress during the program, with 12 to 16 sessions recommended as the usual program duration. An earlier termination date can be agreed on with clients who show rapid improvement over the first four to seven sessions. Between Sessions 8 and 10, the therapist should discuss the client's progress in treatment and additional treatment needs to estimate the number of sessions until treatment completion. Additional input from another professional involved in the client's treatment, such as the case manager or addiction counselor, may also inform this decision. Most clients who continue to experience some PTSD symptoms at this stage of the program benefit from completing the full 16 sessions.

Around the 10th session, the therapist should remind the client again of the time-limited nature of the program and state the number of sessions remaining. The therapist should also discuss the option of meeting every 2 weeks instead of every week toward the end of the program to give clients more practice using the skills on their own. The therapist and client can set a date for when they will begin meeting every other week.

During this session the therapist should get input from the client about his or her perception of progress during the program, possible concerns about termination, and what he or she would like to focus on in the remaining sessions, including remaining PTSD symptoms and the client's personal goals. Therapists can reassure clients that the therapist will help them develop a plan to continue using the skills they have learned to manage distress after the program has ended.

The organization of the final termination sessions depends on whether the client has a long-standing relationship with another professional (e.g., case manager, therapist) who will continue to help and support the client after the program has ended. In circumstances in which a significant other has been an active supporter of the client's treatment, and continued support after the program ends may be critical, this person may play a role similar to that of a professional with a long-term relationship. The next section describes the general approach to termination. Following that section, modifications are described for coordinating termination with another professional who is involved in the client's long-term care.

General Approach to Termination

At the beginning of the second-to-last session, the therapist should remind the client that the next session will be the last. Toward the end of the session, the therapist should explain that the last session will be devoted to reviewing the progress that the client has made in the program, identifying any specific needs he or she has or anticipates having, and discussing plans for getting those needs met. For some clients, such as those with cognitive difficulties, multiple stressors, or a low educational level, the activities involved in the termination session can be accomplished in two sessions rather than a single session. As preparation for the final session, the therapist gives the client two worksheets that review their experiences in the program (My Most Distressing PTSD Symptoms and Summing Up; Handouts #13 and #14; See Appendix) and asks the client to complete them as homework. Some clients may find it helpful to begin filling out the worksheets during the session itself to ensure they understand how to complete them and then to complete the rest at home.

After greetings and a brief discussion of how things have been going since the previous session, the therapist begins the last session by setting the agenda:

> *Therapist:* We have spent the last few months working together to help you learn about, understand, and manage upsetting emotions related to your past traumatic experiences. You've worked really hard and have done well. I'd like to talk about the progress you've made and the skills you've learned and how you can continue to use them after we stop meeting. I'd also like to take a few minutes to tell you how much I've enjoyed working with you.

After addressing any questions that arise, the therapist can initiate a discussion about the client's participation in the program and what he or she has found helpful. What follows is an example of how to initiate this conversation:

Therapist: Some clients feel a little anxious at the prospect of ending treatment and wonder whether they will be able to manage on their own. Let's talk about that for a moment. The major focus of the CR for PTSD program has been on helping you to develop the skills necessary to cope with posttraumatic issues, other distressing emotions, and to help you get on with your life and pursue goals that are important to you. Let's see where you have come toward achieving these goals.

Client: Okay.

Therapist: Let's review some of the information and skills you've learned in this program. First, we spent some time talking about the common effects of trauma, such as symptoms of PTSD, feelings of depression and guilt, and interpersonal difficulties. As we have talked about these problems, you have learned that your reactions to your traumatic experiences are normal and are similar to those of others with similar experiences. In what ways did you find learning about the symptoms of PTSD helpful?

Client: It was good to know that I wasn't crazy or anything like that. I never realized that other people have these same symptoms. Like the memories, the feelings, and everything that goes with it.

Therapist: That's right. It's good to know you aren't alone in how traumatic experiences affected you. Second, early in treatment you learned an important skill for dealing with tension and anxiety—breathing retraining. Over the course of the program I've been pleased to hear about how you have practiced this skill and your ability to use it in a variety of situations where you have felt anxious. How has the breathing retraining been helpful? In what situations have you found it useful?

Client: Lots of times. Sometimes I feel really tense when I'm out in public, like in a store, and I use it to relax.

Therapist: Any other situations?

Client: I still sometimes have those memories of being abused. I use the breathing retraining then and it helps me calm down.

Therapist: Good, I'm glad to hear that. The third thing that you learned in the program is the skill of cognitive restructuring. This skill has helped you see that unpleasant feelings are related to unhelpful and inaccurate thoughts and that some of those thoughts are related to your traumatic experiences. By identifying the thoughts associated with unpleasant feelings and evaluating the evidence supporting them, you have learned that you can change your thinking and that these changes can improve your mood. You've also learned that sometimes the thoughts associated with negative feelings are accurate, and when that happens, how to take action to address the problem rather than avoiding it or pretending it doesn't exist. As we've worked together, I've been really impressed with the progress you've made in learning the 5 Steps of CR, including your ability to identify upsetting thoughts and to challenge your own thinking. What stands out for you as having been the most helpful part of cognitive restructuring?

Client: I used to be so afraid of everything and everyone. I still get anxious sometimes, but the 5 Steps of CR help me figure out when I'm overreacting to a situation or when there really is a problem.

Therapist: And have you found that your overreactions are sometimes related to your traumatic experiences?

Client: Yes. I used to react like I was still a child and couldn't protect myself. Now I know that things are different—I'm not vulnerable the way I was as a child.

Therapist: That's really good to hear. I think you've done a great job of learning these skills in the program. And just like any other skill, such as bowling or tennis, you'll get better and better with more practice over time. I have found that many clients continue to improve after they have finished this program. For this reason, it's important for you to keep practicing the skills that you've learned here, so that you get even better than you are now.

After this discussion, the therapist reviews the worksheets completed by the client for homework (My Most Distressing PTSD Symptoms and Summing Up). If the client did not do the worksheets or only partially completed them, they can be completed together at this point. The first worksheet focuses specifically on PTSD symptoms and other related problems and is designed to highlight either trauma-related beliefs that the client corrected through CR or effective action plans for coping with symptoms. For some clients, these symptoms may no longer be present and the worksheet summarizes what worked, whereas for others the symptoms may persist and the worksheet serves to remind them how to cope with them most effectively.

The Summing Up worksheet pulls together the client's experience in the program by summarizing what has improved, what still needs to be worked on (e.g., client goals), what skills will be most helpful, and how the client can remember to use them. If the client has significant others who have supported his or her participation in the program, their role in helping the client continue to use the skills should be discussed. If specific stresses are known to have triggered or worsened PTSD symptoms in the past (e.g., anniversary dates of losses, family gatherings), these can be discussed along with the skills the client can use to cope with them.

The therapist concludes the session by providing positive feedback and encouragement to the client, pointing out the gains he or she has made. For clients who continue to have symptoms, the therapist should emphasize that the benefits of the program continue to accrue after treatment has ended, as clients continue to use and sharpen the skills they have learned. Providing specific examples of improvements clients have made in symptoms, behaviors, or functioning can reinforce this point.

Coordinating Termination When Another Professional Is Involved

When another professional has a long-standing relationship with the client, coordinating termination from the program can maximize the chances that the client will have support for continuing to use the skills he or she has learned. This coordination can be accomplished by planning for a joint session with the client and professional to be conducted toward the end of the program. The therapist can prepare the client for this meeting one to three sessions before the last session. If two sessions are planned to accomplish all the tasks of termination, the joint session can be conducted as either the last or second-to-last session. An example of how to introduce this plan to a client (Mike) with a case manager (Lisa) is provided next.

Therapist: Our work together will be ending shortly, Mike. You will continue receiving services from your case manager, who can also help you work on some of the skills we have been working on together. I want to make sure that you feel like you are able to continue using the skills that you learned in this program, including the breathing retraining and cognitive restructuring, after we finish. One way that might help you is for us to meet with your case manager, Lisa, during our last session so that the three of us can talk about the skills you've learned and how she can help you continue using them.

One strategy for reinforcing the client's self-efficacy at CR is for him or her to take the role of the "expert" in explaining what CR is to the professional and to describe how it helps one deal with upsetting feelings. To prepare the client for this meeting, the therapist can role play with the client how to talk with the professional about CR. Several role plays may be helpful, each accompanied by positive feedback and suggestions for improvement, for the client to feel comfortable with the plan. It may also be useful for the therapist to model how to talk to the professional. The therapist should assure the client that the therapist will be there to help as needed. Continuing with the previous example, this suggestion can be introduced as follows:

> *Therapist:* I wonder if you would be comfortable taking the lead in a role play where you act the part of the coach and practice teaching Lisa the 5 Steps of CR?
>
> *Client:* Okay, I'll give it a shot.
>
> *Therapist:* Great. Let's practice how you are going to coach Lisa on how to do cognitive restructuring.

After agreeing to do a role play, the therapist works with the client to identify an upsetting situation that he or she can use as an example of how CR works, such as a specific situation they have already worked on before (e.g., going to a large family gathering or reunion) or a generic frustrating situation (e.g., getting stuck in traffic). Once a situation is selected, the therapist can initiate the role play as described next.

> *Therapist:* Okay, let's get a clean copy of the 5 Steps of CR Worksheet and practice by you coaching me on how to go through the steps.
>   [*Following the role play*] That was great, Mike. You really seem to have that down now. Do you feel ready to help Lisa learn to be your cognitive restructuring coach? After we help Lisa learn the basics of the 5 Steps of CR, we also will discuss with her a plan that you could follow in case you have difficulties with your PTSD symptoms after we stop meeting. How does that sound?

Before the joint final session, the therapist should discuss the terms of the meeting with the professional, with an emphasis on disclosure/privacy issues that have been agreed on with the client. For example, many clients prefer not to discuss any details about their traumatic experiences with the professional, and this desire should be respected. The general structure and plan of the meeting should also be described to the professional.

The final session begins with just the therapist and client in attendance, with the therapist setting the agenda and then briefly reviewing with the client the skills he or she has learned in the program, as described earlier. Then the therapist checks whether the client completed the worksheets, and if so, whether the client would like to review them later in the session with the professional or with just the therapist before the professional joins them. Some clients like to get input from the professional about benefits they may have seen, whereas others prefer to keep the details of their participation in the program more private.

The other professional is then invited to join the session. If the client has agreed to play the role of the expert in CR, the therapist provides a brief introduction, and the role play of the client teaching the professional commences. Continuing with the previous example of Mike (the client) and Lisa (the case manager), the therapist can begin as follows:

Therapist: Thanks for joining us, Lisa. As you know, the CR for PTSD program that Mike has been participating in involves learning and practicing skills for dealing with upsetting feelings, including some that are related to traumatic experiences. One of the most important skills Mike has been learning is cognitive restructuring. Because Mike has developed some real expertise in this skill, we thought it might be helpful for him to teach you in a role play how it works. When we've finished that, we can talk together about how Mike has benefited from the program and ways that you can support him and the skills he has learned after the program has ended.

When the role play is over, the therapist prompts the client to describe how he or she has found CR helpful in coping with negative feelings and stressful situations, and to discuss ways that the professional can support the client in using the skill in the future. This is then followed up by reviewing (or completing) the two worksheets with input from the professional (for clients who agree to this), and a final wrap-up, as previously described in the termination section.

As previously noted, the therapist may elect to cover all the activities of termination in two sessions rather than in one. The specific logistics of what is covered in the two sessions may vary across clients, depending on the client's preferences and what seems most practical to the therapist. For example, clients who do not want to talk about the details of their traumatic experiences might prefer to complete the My Most Distressing PTSD Symptoms and Summing Up worksheets in the second-to-last session with the therapist and to leave the final session to the joint meeting with the professional and final wrapping up. Alternatively, some clients might prefer to have the final session alone with the therapist and arrange for the joint session with the professional to be held as the second-to-last session.

SUMMARY AND CONCLUSIONS

From the outset of the CR for PTSD program, the therapist aims at helping clients generalize the skills taught in session to their daily lives, especially CR, which is the core of the program. Generalization is fostered through a combination of strengthening the client's competence at skills within the session, tailoring skills as needed to the individual client, assigning homework so clients can practice skills outside of sessions, and facilitating environmental supports for using the skills in day-to-day living. Attention to the generalization of skills taught in sessions over the course of the program also facilitates the maintenance of skills over time after the program has ended.

PTSD symptoms may persist in some clients despite their mastery of the skills taught in the program. When faced with such symptoms, the therapist has the combined task of treating them as clues to possible underlying trauma-related schemas that can be challenged with CR, encouraging the client to continue using the skills taught in the program with the expectation of long-term benefits in symptom reduction, and shifting the emphasis of treatment away from immediate symptom reduction and toward helping the client achieve personal goals. As clients approach the later stages of treatment, regardless of whether they still experience PTSD symptoms, the therapist helps them conceptualize CR and other skills taught in the program as personal life skills applicable to dealing with unpleasant feelings and useful for addressing obstacles to personal goals. This shift in emphasis away from symptoms and toward desired life changes, along with the focus on teaching skills that promote coping and self-reliance, serves to empower trauma survivors by helping them see themselves not as helpless victims of circumstances beyond their control but as the masters of their own destiny.

Termination plays a vital role in the CR for PTSD program because it is crucial in genuinely empowering clients to take control over their lives and in avoiding dependency on the therapist. Clients are prepared for termination from the outset of the program, with specific plans based on the client's needs drawn up as they near the end. Central to these plans is addressing the issue of how clients can continue to use and hone their skills as they pursue their personal life goals and the role of available supports in assisting them in their efforts. By reinforcing the client's skills and responsibility for change throughout their work together and working with the client to plan for life after program has ended, the therapist ensures that graduation from the program is not experienced as a loss by the client but instead as another step forward in his or her life.

III
SPECIAL POPULATIONS

10
PSYCHOSIS

RACHAEL A. FITE

Cognitive–behavioral treatments for posttraumatic stress disorder (PTSD) have been shown to be effective in the general population, but treating clients who also have psychotic disorders such as schizophrenia and schizoaffective disorder poses special challenges. This chapter describes how to use and adapt the Cognitive Restructuring for PTSD (CR for PTSD) program for these clients, including strategies for managing hallucinations and delusions and for minimizing the effects of cognitive impairments, a common problem in clients with psychotic symptoms. By understanding the nature of the special challenges posed by people with psychotic disorders and by using flexibility and creativity in applying the CR for PTSD model, therapists can be effective at helping these clients cope with and overcome their PTSD.

UNDERSTANDING THE POPULATION WITH PSYCHOSIS

Psychotic disorders present a wide array of significant challenges. Disorders such as schizophrenia typically have a profound negative impact not only on cognition and perception but also on mood, language, behavior, and basic functioning (e.g., work, self-care, relationships). People with psychotic disorders are also far more likely to have many other problems, such as substance use disorders, medical illnesses, housing instability, and poverty. All of these factors can have a devastating impact on the individual's life, and collectively, can keep the person in a state of ongoing crisis and personal misery.

Schizophrenia-spectrum disorders, including schizophrenia, schizoaffective disorder, schizophreniform disorder, and schizotypal personality disorder, have a prevalence of approximately 1% to 2% (Jablensky, 1997). Because these disorders have a similar course and are treated with the same methods, we refer to them in this chapter collectively as *schizophrenia*.

TRAUMA AND POSTTRAUMATIC STRESS DISORDER IN PSYCHOTIC DISORDERS

Individuals with psychotic disorders are at increased risk of victimization and trauma compared with the general population. Most surveys of trauma in persons with psychotic disorders and other severe mental illnesses report high rates of trauma exposure (Bebbington et al., 2004; Goodman, Rosenberg, Mueser, & Drake, 1997). For example, one study of 275 clients with severe mental illness reported that 98% had been exposed to at least one traumatic event (Mueser et al., 1998). Furthermore, the traumas experienced by these clients are often interpersonal in nature, such as physical and sexual abuse and assault, sexual assault, physical abuse, and physical assault (Cascardi, Mueser, DeGiralomo, & Murrin, 1996; Goodman, Dutton, & Harris, 1995; Mueser, Salyers, et al., 2004). In fact, victimization and trauma are so common in this population that they can be considered normative events.

The high rate of trauma in persons with severe mental illness is reflected in a high prevalence of PTSD. The incidence of current PTSD in the general population is about 1.2% for men and 2.7% for women (Stein, Walker, Hazen, & Forde, 1997). By comparison, as illustrated in Figure 1.1, most estimates of current PTSD in people with psychosis range between 28% and 48%.

IMPACT OF TRAUMA AND POSTTRAUMATIC STRESS DISORDER ON PSYCHOTIC DISORDERS

In addition to increased vulnerability to PTSD in people with psychotic disorders, there are other important clinical implications of the high rate of victimization in this population. Exposure to interpersonal violence is related to increased severity of psychiatric symptoms, including psychotic symptoms, depression, and anxiety, as well as increased frequency of hospitalizations

(Briere, Woo, McRae, Foltz, & Sitzman, 1997; Craine, Henson, Colliver, & MacLean, 1988; Figueroa et al., 1997). Trauma exposure has also been linked to worse psychosocial functioning (Lysaker, Meyer, Evans, Clements, & Marks, 2001), lengthier hospital stays, and more contacts with emergency rooms (Briere et al., 1997; Carmen, Rieker, & Mills, 1984; Goodman et al., 2001).

CHALLENGES IN TREATING POSTTRAUMATIC DISORDERS IN PERSONS WITH PSYCHOSIS

Therapists will be far more effective with clients experiencing psychotic symptoms if they have a clear understanding of the many and varied barriers to treatment that are particularly problematic and ubiquitous within this population. Poor motivation, mistrust of others, overwhelming stress levels, cognitive impairments, and the psychotic symptoms themselves are examples of significant challenges that need not derail the CR for PTSD treatment for these highly vulnerable clients.

Engaging the Client in Treatment

The first challenge with this population is in engaging and maintaining clients in consistent and continuous treatment. There are many reasons why this is particularly difficult. Motivation to follow through with PTSD treatment can wax and wane for these individuals, just as it does for people without psychotic disorders. Poor motivation can be due to chronic and episodic life stressors, a reluctance to address the issues central to PTSD, or a sense of overwhelming resignation due to multiple personal setbacks. The negative symptoms of schizophrenia also affect motivation. Anhedonia and apathy can result in poor motivation for treatment and a weak therapeutic alliance. This can be reflected in problems such as not completing homework assignments, missing or canceling appointments, and prematurely terminating treatment. It is important for clinicians to provide support, optimism, and encouragement to their clients and to reinforce any efforts they make to overcome the barriers to getting treatment.

The second major issue impeding the engagement of clients is that of mistrust. As previously discussed, prior interpersonal victimization is common in people with severe mental illness, both in childhood and adulthood, which can naturally lead to feelings of mistrust, including toward clinicians who are trying to help them. In addition, clients may have frank symptoms of paranoia or delusional thinking, which again, can act as a major barrier to establishing and maintaining a trusting relationship with a therapist. Just as with all clients, it takes time and patience to develop trust with clients with severe mental illness.

Psychotic Symptoms

Psychotic symptoms can complicate treatment of PTSD substantially. By their nature, they are frightening and confusing for the individual experiencing them. They can destroy the most basic security people take for granted, namely, the ability to trust one's own senses and thoughts. For those individuals whose psychotic symptoms are based on elaborations of past traumatic experiences, the delusions and hallucinations can be even more frightening.

Superficially, psychotic symptoms often appear to be unrelated to life experiences. However, by trying to understand the thoughts and beliefs that underlie specific hallucinations and delusions, the therapist can often discover themes rooted in central concerns related to traumatic experiences. Distilling the thoughts behind the psychotic symptoms allows a clinician to isolate and effectively challenge the cognitive distortions and trauma-related beliefs that fuel delusional elaborations of traumatic experiences. This use of CR can substantially decrease the severity and distress associated with these symptoms.

Hypersensitivity to Stress

Clients with severe mental illness experience high levels of stress in their daily lives because of low employment and poverty, social marginalization and discrimination, and limited social support compounded by frequently dysfunctional relationships. Helping clients deal with the chaos and stress in their lives is made more challenging by their high sensitivity to stress. This can lead to more frequent cancellations or no-shows for treatment appointments, as a result of clients' feeling overwhelmed or discouraged, and greater sensitivity to stress within the therapy session. This combination of actual stress and heightened sensitivity to stress can make it more difficult for clients to learn the information and skills taught in the CR for PTSD program. Therapists can minimize the effects of stress on clients' engagement and learning skills for managing posttraumatic symptoms by being aware of the stress experienced by the individual, coordinating treatment with other providers (e.g., the case manager) who can address stressful life circumstances (e.g., housing problems), using relaxation strategies to reduce stress in the session, and adopting a slow, gradual, and comfortable pace for teaching the requisite skills.

Cognitive Impairments

Cognitive impairment is another common problem for individuals with psychotic symptoms, particularly those with schizophrenia (Gold & Harvey, 1993; Heaton et al., 1994). Typically, problems with attention, memory, abstract reasoning, and concentration need to be accommodated when providing the CR for PTSD program to clients with psychotic disorders. Problems caused by these types of cognitive impairments include difficulty attending to, understanding, and learning the basic material taught in the treatment. Additionally, individuals with cognitive impairments have more difficulty generalizing the skills learned in sessions to their home life.

STRATEGIES TO ADDRESS SPECIAL CHALLENGES

Therapists providing the CR for PTSD program can use a wide range of different strategies to deal with the challenges described above and to maximize the benefits clients can reap from participating in the program. Guidelines for managing in treatment the two most significant challenges of this population, psychotic symptoms and cognitive impairments, are outlined in the following subsections.

Psychotic Symptoms

Although it can be difficult, it is important to try to distinguish between trauma-related and non-trauma-related psychotic symptoms. The importance of this distinction is that for trauma-related psychotic symptoms, the clinician needs to develop an understanding of the nature of the symptoms and the thoughts behind them within a broader trauma-related schema that can eventually be the focus of CR. For example, for an individual whose paranoid delusions are based on a history of physical assaults, one core belief may be "I will never be safe." Once the individual's delusions can be understood and distilled into a singular core belief of this kind, that belief can be the focus of CR. This, in turn, can have ameliorating ripple effects, reducing the negative emotional impact of all of the cognitive distortions and delusions based on this core belief.

It is very important to address trauma-related delusions and hallucinations in the same manner as other trauma-related thoughts and beliefs, namely, by using CR to challenge thoughts and beliefs underlying distressing feelings. For example, for a client who describes a hallucination of a voice repeatedly belittling or demeaning her because she was sexually abused as a child (e.g., "You wanted it, you are dirty and damaged"), the clinician should directly address the content of that hallucination by helping her identify the negative emotions related to hearing the voice (e.g., shame, guilt), articulating the thoughts underlying those feelings (e.g., "It was my fault that I was molested by my stepfather," "Now that I've been molested, I'll never be okay again," "I'm bad"), and then challenging the most distressing of those thoughts.

Just as distress related to trauma-related psychotic symptoms can be reduced by CR, so too can upsetting psychotic symptoms that are not clearly related to traumatic experiences. Clients are taught that the cue for initiating CR is the experience of stressful feelings, regardless of their origins, and the therapist should look for every opportunity to teach clients how to use these skills within sessions and to practice them outside of sessions. There is ample evidence from controlled research that CR is effective at reducing distress and severity of psychotic symptoms in schizophrenia (Zimmermann, Favrod, Trieu, & Pomini, 2005). It can be particularly useful to teach clients CR on less emotionally charged symptoms and to then shift the focus to more upsetting trauma-related symptoms when they have more competence with the skill.

Cognitive Impairment

Several strategies can be used to help individuals with cognitive challenges learn the skills taught in the CR for PSTD program. Information should be presented more slowly and reviewed more frequently, pausing often to check on the client's understanding. The absorption and development of skills should be bolstered by more frequent modeling by the clinician and role play practice by the client.

People with cognitive impairments often conceal the fact that they do not understand what is being said to them. The clinician should avoid assuming that the client understands what is being taught and instead verify comprehension through direct questioning. The clinician should use abundant praise and encouragement to reinforce the client's efforts and small, incremental improvements in understanding and skill. In this manner, through the reinforcement of successive gains in the breathing retraining and CR skills, the clinician can slowly shape the client's ability to use these skills to address his or her PTSD.

Another useful method for working with individuals with cognitive impairments is to involve family and others who are supportive of the client and also perhaps available to the client in his or her daily life. This allows for skills initially taught in session to be prompted, practiced, and reinforced in clients' day-to-day lives. A useful strategy for minimizing the effects of cognitive impairment is to reduce the amount of information and the complexity of skills taught to the client in the CR for PTSD program. For example, the therapist could choose to focus on teaching just two or three common styles of thinking, rather than all eight styles. In addition, breaking down information and skills into smaller chunks can facilitate learning and retention.

Clients with cognitive impairment may also have more difficulty following verbal instructions and grasping homework assignments. Although it is recommended that clinicians briefly demonstrate and practice completing homework assignments in sessions with all clients, additional time and practice are often needed with cognitively impaired clients. In addition, homework assignments can be presented in a graduated manner, each of them being clear, specific, and involving skills that the client has already demonstrated an ability to perform in session. Again, ample encouragement and praise should be provided to all of the efforts made by clients to complete the homework, regardless of whether they followed the directions correctly. Over time, the clinician can shape and expand the client's behavior and skills without the client having had a failure experience in session.

The clinician should help the client identify cues in the home living environment that will serve as a signal to use and practice skills taught during the sessions. Individuals with cognitive impairments have often stable routines that they can rely on, and the clinician can make use of these routines to establish connections between the new skills that need to be practiced and these previously established habits. For example, establishing an association between the practice of breathing retraining and a client's habit of taking daily medicine or brushing teeth can be a very effective memory aid.

For individuals with limited reading and writing proficiency, the therapist should devise alternatives to written homework materials. For example, when teaching the 5 Steps of CR, the clinician can develop one-word cues with the client and write them down on a card numbered 1 through 5. By repeatedly going over these five steps in session and using the card with the one-word cues, the client can learn to recognize a single word as meaning an entire step of CR. The client may be given the card to take home to prompt practicing the 5 Steps of CR, and new cards can be made together with the client during subsequent sessions.

Clinicians working with cognitively impaired clients should anticipate that more of the work will have to be done in session, particularly for those individuals unable to utilize the written materials, unless reliable supportive persons can be found who can help clients practice the skills between sessions. Similarly, when teaching more information-dense material, such as the symptoms of PTSD, the clinician should simplify the material and if necessary to conserve time, focus on only the most critical facts.

Other Clinical Considerations

It is important that the clinician not attempt to directly challenge or refute the client's thoughts or evidence used to support the thought, as confrontation can inadvertently strengthen conviction in thoughts, especially delusional beliefs (Milton, Patwa, & Hafner, 1978). Instead, the clinician should maintain a stance of neutrality and guidance through the process of evaluating the various thoughts and evidence for those thoughts, without a strong preconceived determination of what the client's thoughts "should" be.

The easiest way to do this is for the clinician to view teaching CR as a skill clients can learn to manage their negative feelings, rather than a process of changing the way they think, and to focus on achieving small, incremental improvements in negative thoughts and associated distress.

People with psychotic disorders often have a sense of not being in control of their own lives. Some of these beliefs are grounded in reality, such as when clients have experienced uncontrollable symptoms, involuntary hospitalizations, or loss of control over their own finances. But these beliefs often go far beyond reality, to the point where people feel they have no control whatsoever, which can hinder them from taking steps to improve the quality of their lives. The clinician can foster empowerment and self-efficacy by using every opportunity to communicate to clients that they can develop skills, attitudes, and behaviors that will allow them to regain control over their lives and by making sure that the client, rather than the therapist, takes credit for gains made over the course of treatment.

For example, when teaching CR, the therapist emphasizes that it is a skill that is always available to clients and that will allow them to better manage their internal, emotional life. Clients can learn to think through situations, logically and methodically, and then decide how they want to interpret and respond to them. Similarly, when teaching clients how to complete their crisis plans, the therapist can present it as a strategy for taking more control over their mental health. One strategy for promoting empowerment is to use the analogy of the relationship between the therapist and client as similar to one between a coach and athlete. The coach's role is to provide support, guidance, and expertise, although the athlete is responsible for the actual performance in the sport and deserves the lion's share of credit for any success. In the CR for PTSD program, the therapist provides the client with helpful information, skills, and encouragement, although it is the client who actually does the hard work of using those skills and changing his or her life.

Individuals who struggle with PTSD often inadvertently merge their traumatic experiences with the memory of those events, a process described as *fusion* (Hayes et al., 1999). That inevitably leads to the memory of the trauma becoming as frightening and upsetting as the trauma itself. When the client shows strong emotional reactions to memories of traumatic experiences, distinguishing between the two and explaining that "the memory can't hurt you" can be surprisingly helpful. Helping clients make this distinction can be combined with teaching healthy self-talk aimed at reminding individuals that what happened in the past cannot affect them now.

Often the process of helping a client change thoughts from extremely distressing ones to slightly less distressing ones is long and arduous. The clinician must be satisfied with progress that is measured in tiny increments and not push for the client to suddenly switch over to an entirely different manner of thinking. The latter is not a reasonable expectation, and it is a damaging one to inadvertently communicate to a client. Even small changes in a client's interpretation will result in a corresponding decrease in the negative emotional consequence and represents progress.

One of the clinician's most effective tools is the installation of hope. Clients often want to believe that they can get better and look to the clinician for hope and signs that they will. Even clients who lack hope can benefit from and be inspired by the hope of others (Deegan, 1996). Therapists need to believe in the inherent ability of every client to recover from PTSD and to live a worthwhile and rewarding life.

Expectancies can play an important role on the outcome of treatments, just as they are important in the outcome of other human interactions. There is strong evidence that people with psychotic disorders who participate in the CR for PTSD program do improve significantly (Mueser et al., 2008). Therapists can explicitly inform clients about this and repeatedly convey their belief in the client and his or her ability to recover. Believing in the client and instilling hope that learning the skills taught in the program will improve their symptoms and help achieve their personal goals, can stimulate and maintain the client's effort and motivation, thereby maximizing the gains realized in the program.

CLINICAL EXAMPLE

Mary was a 31-year-old woman with schizoaffective disorder and a history of extensive abuse. She was physically and emotionally abused by her mother and stepfather from the age of 2 until she was 19, when she ran away from home. She was sexually abused by her stepfather and uncle from the age of 6 until 13, when she became pregnant by one of them and had to have an abortion. Mary had been receiving treatment for schizoaffective disorder in a community mental health clinic for many years when she was identified as needing additional treatment to address posttraumatic symptoms of nightmares, intrusive memories, and flashbacks. The therapist at the community clinic sought specialized help for Mary and referred her for treatment to the CR for PTSD program.

Mary was seen for 16 weeks for the treatment of PTSD while continuing to see her regular clinician at the community clinic. One important key to engaging Mary early in treatment was the success of teaching her breathing retraining. She experienced multiple panic attacks on a daily basis, brought on by intrusive memories and flashbacks of one or more of her abuse experiences. The therapist found it helpful to regularly practice the breathing retraining together with Mary in sessions when discussions related to her traumatic experiences would trigger intense anxiety. She became quite adept at preventing panic attacks and calming herself through the breathing, which she described as her first experience of having any control over her life.

A second major key to engaging Mary in treatment was her learning about PTSD. Mary had come to believe that many of her PTSD symptoms were not symptoms but instead were components of her personality. For example, Mary believed that her inability to concentrate, her irritability, and her avoidance of many places and activities were just parts of who she was and would always be. The psychoeducational sessions were eye-opening experiences for Mary, as she learned that the symptoms were part of a disorder that she could work toward recovering from.

These early successes were important because midway into treatment Mary experienced a rapid increase in her psychotic symptoms. On the sixth session, she came in looking tired and distracted and reported trouble sleeping. "Trouble sleeping" was on Mary's crisis plan as a warning sign of relapse of her psychotic symptoms.

The therapist asked her about some of the other warning signs and learned that several had been occurring over the previous week, including increased isolation, paranoia, and auditory hallucinations. The therapist asked whether Mary had realized that she was exhibiting a number of the warning signs of a relapse. Mary appeared to become more anxious and had difficulty expressing her thoughts coherently. To reduce her anxiety and avert a panic attack, the therapist practiced breathing retraining with Mary.

> *Therapist:* Mary, that was really, really good. You were breathing nice and calmly again, like we've done in the past few weeks, and it was working. You were regaining control over the panic. Let's keep going for another minute and then we can talk.
>
> *Client:* No, no, I don't want to talk. Too much talking, talking, tattletale talking.
>
> *Therapist:* Mary, we were just talking about your crisis plan. Do you remember when we made this plan together so you could prevent a relapse and another hospitalization? Mary, try to look at me and focus. Remember, you were going to stop the relapse this time, when you saw the early warning signs. Please sit with me again, and let's breathe together and calm ourselves. Come on, try it with me . . .

When Mary appeared calmer, the therapist praised her for using the breathing retraining so effectively. They talked about the crisis plan helping her to take some control over her mental health and about the voices being a symptom of her schizoaffective disorder.

> *Therapist:* Mary, you know those voices that are demeaning you are a symptom. We've talked about this before. The voices are a warning sign that we need to reach out for help *right now*

before you begin feeling even worse. Let's look at what we wrote on your plan, so we can see what might help. You wrote that if you experienced these warning signs, you would first contact your psychiatrist and request an increase in your medication. Now, Mary, do you think that's a good idea, to let your psychiatrist know that you're having a temporary increase in symptoms?

Client: Yes. Okay, I'll call him.

Mary and the therapist went through the remaining steps and made a plan for her to follow in the subsequent days, including making an appointment the following day with her regular therapist and with the psychiatrist. Mary left the session feeling calmer.

Mary came in the following week for her regular PTSD appointment and was more emotionally stable. She reported very upsetting voices yelling at her and putting her down, and she appeared as if she was currently hearing them as she winced and physically reacted. Despite Mary's very limited experience with CR, the therapist decided to use CR to address the content of the auditory hallucinations in order to alleviate Mary's intense distress.

Therapist: Mary, this is our chance to put to the test what we've been learning in sessions together. Do you remember that CR is the key to recovering from PTSD? We did the CR together a few times during that session and you learned that you don't have to believe every thought that comes into your mind. Do you remember us talking about that? In fact, sometimes thoughts should *not* be believed. CR involves identifying the thoughts underlying your upsetting feelings and then determining whether or not they're really true. Do you remember doing that together a couple of weeks ago?

Client: Yeah, but I can't think right now. No, I never did that. [*responding to voices*]

Therapist: Mary, stay with me. I know you're hearing voices, but remember, they are a symptom, and we can get through this so you can feel better. But I need you to stay with me, Mary. Please try to ignore them while we talk. Can you try to do that?

Client: Yeah, yeah, okay. No more voices, no more voices, no more voices. [*to herself, looking off, still grimacing*]

Therapist: Good job, Mary. Okay, tell me one thing that the voices have said that is really upsetting you.

Client: I'm a bad, bad girl. I ripped the whole family apart. She says I did it on purpose, Uncle Jim never got back with the family, but the other one did it too and he never got in trouble. My mother said it was my fault, "can't keep your hands to yourself, you're a dirty nasty girl." She says I liked it and I tried to steal her husband away, but I didn't, it was sickening . . . nasty, nasty, dirty girl.

Therapist: Okay, Mary, help me understand. I can't tell which things are voices and which things were really said to you.

Client: She knew all along and acted so angry when I got pregnant. "Dirty, nasty," she said, "you're dirty," but she's the one who knew and she never stopped him, "you're a dirty, nasty girl, you did it on purpose." But she never protected me. "No *you* did it."

Therapist: Mary, let's talk about one of the things you keep saying, "You're a dirty, nasty girl." Clear your mind, focus with me now. When you think "you're a dirty, nasty girl," what emotion does that make you feel? Are you angry? Sad?

Client: I'm embarrassed; I don't want to be dirty. I didn't want to do it, he was so awful. I'm disgusted. How could I have done that over and over . . . I did do it, I am dirty . . . I'm ashamed, it's all disgusting. I'm disgusting . . .

Therapist: Okay, so you think the thought "I'm a dirty, nasty girl" and then the emotion that follows is shame and embarrassment, is that right?

Client: Yes, I'm disgusted with myself. I let it go on and on. I'm just disgusting.

Therapist: So you believe this thought, that you are dirty and nasty? Do you believe that your thought is 100% true?

Client: Yes . . . [becoming quieter and looking sad]

Therapist: Okay, Mary, let's get to the bottom of this thought. It is such a painful, awful thought to think about yourself, let's make sure it deserves to be there and to be causing you all that suffering, okay?

Client: How do we get to the bottom of it?

Therapist: Good question. What I mean by getting to the bottom of it is finding out together whether it's really true. Now, if it *is* really true, we'll have to deal with that, and we can deal with that together. But maybe it's *not* true, or maybe only partially true, and if that's the case, we need to know that. All of us think thoughts that are upsetting, and when we discover that there's a thought that is causing us a lot of

	pain, it's worthwhile taking the time and effort to determine if it really is true. Do you agree?
Client:	Yes.
Therapist:	Okay, let's write the thought down, just like we did before. So, let's write down the thought "I'm a dirty, nasty girl." Now the emotion you described that this thought causes is shame and embarrassment. Let's write that down on the sheet too. You're with me so far, right? [*she nods*] Let's go on to Step 4 of CR. Just like we did before, let's make a list of the evidence. Let's think of evidence that supports the thought and evidence that goes against it. We'll do both sides, so that at the end we can make an accurate decision about whether the thought is correct or not. I'm not trying to convince you to think about this differently. I'm trying to help you evaluate whether your thought is accurate and deserves to make you feel as awful as it does. Maybe it does. And maybe it doesn't. Let's find out. Shall we do this together?
Client:	Yes.
Therapist:	We can pretend like we did before, that we're presenting this evidence to scientists. We want to try to stick to the facts. We want to try to stay reasonable. Okay? Let's start with evidence that supports the thought "I'm a dirty, nasty girl." First, tell me, what makes a girl nasty? What makes a girl dirty?
Client:	She screws people. It doesn't matter who, she screws men, any man will do. She does what they want, and no one respects her. She sleeps with everyone. She likes it. She wants it like that, she wants it all the time; she's nasty, nasty . . .
Therapist:	Okay, I got it. Let's bring this back to you. We're trying to decide whether there is evidence that *you* are a dirty nasty girl. So, did you sleep with everyone? Did you want sex all the time?
Client:	Oh, no, God no! He was disgusting, with his hands all over me, he was awful. No, I'm disgusted when anyone touches me. I don't sleep with anyone. I haven't since the abortion. Men make me sick.
Therapist:	Okay, you've just come up with some good evidence against the thought that you're a nasty girl. That is, you did *not* want to have sex with everyone and you didn't want to have sex all the time and that's what dirty, nasty girls want, right?
Client:	Right.

Therapist:	So let's write down those two pieces of evidence. All right, let's come up with some more evidence. You also said a dirty, nasty girl likes to sleep with everyone and "she likes it like that." Does that describe how it was for you? Did you like it like that?
Client:	Oh, God, no, [starts to cry] I hated it, I hated them both. Men are pigs. How could they have done that?
Therapist:	Mary, I'm so sorry this happened to you. I don't know how they could have done that to you, it was awful, I agree. You described dirty, nasty girls as liking it, liking and wanting all the sex, but that's not true for you. You didn't want it, you hated it, you said. So, Mary, this is more evidence that goes in the "against the thought that you're a nasty girl" column. So far, the description you gave me of a dirty, nasty girl is not at all the way you were. Let's try again to see if there is any evidence that supports this thought.

Mary and the therapist continued to evaluate the evidence. As she slowly realized that the evidence did not support the thought, she became very upset and agitated and reverted back to the fact that she feels dirty and nasty. To remind Mary that feeling something does not necessarily make it true, the therapist took out the Common Styles of Thinking Worksheet and pointed out emotional reasoning. The therapist reviewed with Mary why feeling something is true does not mean it is true. Mary calmed down a little and was relieved that her thought might not be accurate, even if it felt that way.

Mary generated only one piece of evidence that supported the thought—that she did engage in sex throughout her childhood and adolescence, with considerable frequency. This was noted, along with the fact that this sex was not of a voluntary nature. The therapist was careful to avoid directly challenge this evidence to remain focused on helping her use CR to deal with her upset feelings.

After more tears and another temporary lapse back into the voices speaking to her, the therapist was able to move with Mary on to the last of the 5 Steps of CR: weighing the evidence and taking action. After reviewing the evidence for and against the thought, Mary concluded that the thought was not supported and began to explore alternative, more accurate thoughts. This was difficult and required continuing Socratic questioning and redirection from voices, by the therapist. Eventually Mary was able to generate a new thought that was less shame-inducing, namely, "I did do dirty things but I'm not a dirty girl." When the therapist then asked her whether she believed the new thought, she said she did not. "I really am a dirty, nasty girl," she said. When asked why she believed this, she simply responded "I did do all those things, all the sex with him. I *am* dirty."

Over the next two sessions, with each use of CR to address Mary's distressing belief that she was dirty, there were small but consistent changes in the thought. In each case, when Mary arrived at a new thought, if she believed it, there was also a small parallel reduction of her distress associated with it. The therapist continued in this manner for several additional sessions.

As the severity of Mary's psychotic symptoms decreased, she became more able to recognize and challenge her thinking, and she succeeded in achieving more significant and lasting reductions in her negative feelings. However, as Mary's auditory hallucinations subsided, she experienced more difficulty identifying her thoughts because her voices were no longer shouting them out to her. To address this, the therapist reviewed the Guide to Your Thoughts and Feelings handout to help her articulate the thoughts underlying her negative feelings.

Mary continued to display occasional illogical speech patterns and disorganized thinking, which were stable features of her schizoaffective disorder. The therapist redirected her as needed to help her focus on specific tasks and to use the breathing retraining. The therapist continued to use other techniques described in this chapter, including providing generous positive reinforcement, warmth, and support for Mary's efforts; frequently reviewing important points; paraphrasing what her said to confirm understanding of her perspective; asking questions to assess her understanding of the material; and role-playing to practice skills.

Toward the end of the CR for PTSD program, the therapist initiated a discussion with Mary about who could support her in continuing to use her skills when the program was over. Mary thought her regular therapist from the community clinic would be most helpful, as well as her long-term friend and roommate. Both individuals were invited into separate sessions with Mary and the therapist. Mary explained that when she becomes upset, sometimes she just needs "a reminder to stop the roller coaster and think." She asked each of them to remind her of this and to intervene when she becomes lost in her emotions. Both of Mary's support people praised her for all her hard work and readily agreed to help her in any way they could.

At the end of the program, Mary reported that she felt very supported and was in much greater control over her life. She also described feeling better about her future and being more comfortable in her own skin. Functionally, Mary had stabilized sufficiently to be interested in work, which she followed up on by enrolling in the clinic's supported employment program. The assessment measures used throughout treatment indicated that Mary no longer met the criteria for the diagnosis of PTSD. In addition, her depression scores, although still elevated, were significantly reduced compared with her scores at the beginning of the program.

SUMMARY AND CONCLUSIONS

Treating PTSD in people with severe mental illness can be challenging because of psychotic distortions, cognitive impairments, and the high sensitivity of these individuals to stress. However, with a strong therapeutic alliance, flexibility, and sensitivity to the special needs of these clients, therapists can successfully engage them in the CR for PTSD program and teach them the skills that will help them overcome their posttraumatic reactions. Helping people with psychotic disorders cope with and recover from their traumatic experiences can not only reduce their distressing PTSD symptoms but other psychiatric symptoms as well, including psychotic ones. Of equal or greater importance, treating PTSD in these individuals can improve psychosocial functioning, including increasing self-reliance, role functioning, quality of relationships, and enjoyment of life.

11
BORDERLINE PERSONALITY DISORDER

ELISA E. BOLTON AND KIM T. MUESER

Individuals with a diagnosis of borderline personality disorder (BPD) typically report intense feelings of anger, anxiety, sadness, emptiness, and intense fear of real or imagined abandonment. Additional hallmark behaviors are deliberate self-harm (e.g., cutting, burning), history of suicide attempts, numerous hospitalizations, poor interpersonal relationships often characterized by extremes of idealization and devaluation, and impulsivity (e.g., reckless spending, binge drinking, overeating). There are a few authors who argue that BPD and severe posttraumatic stress disorder (PTSD) stemming from early childhood sexual abuse (CSA) are the same entity or at least that CSA is a necessary and sufficient cause of BPD (Gunderson & Sabo, 1993; Herman, 1992b). Yet most researchers and clinicians simply acknowledge the strong relationship between the two diagnoses and agree that they are separate diagnoses with unique predictors and trajectories (Golier et al., 2003).

We begin this chapter with a review of research on the prevalence of trauma and PTSD in people with BPD, problems associated with PTSD in this population, and a brief examination of relevant treatment studies. We then consider special problems and challenges that may occur when treating PTSD in individuals with a comorbid diagnosis of BPD and follow this with a discussion of additional strategies to complement the treatment protocol. Finally, we present a sample dialogue.

PREVALENCE OF TRAUMA AND POSTTRAUMATIC STRESS DISORDER IN BORDERLINE PERSONALITY DISORDER

People with BPD are more likely to have experienced trauma in their lives than those in the general population (71% vs. 22%; comparison group individuals with major depression [Ogata et al., 1990]; 92% vs. 79%, comparison group individuals with major depression [Yen et al., 2002]). In general, high rates of exposure to traumatic events are documented in individuals with personality disorders. However, individuals with BPD report even higher rates of trauma compared with those with other personality disorders, such as avoidant and obsessive–compulsive personality disorder (Yen et al., 2002). Moreover, Yen et al. (2002) found that more severe trauma exposure in people with personality disorder was associated with greater distress and worse symptoms.

The rate of current PTSD in individuals with BPD is high, ranging between 25% and 56% (Golier et al., 2003; Mueser et al., 1998; Zanarini et al., 1998), compared with the lifetime rate of PTSD in the general population of about 8% (Kessler et al., 1995). BPD is also one of the most common comorbid Axis II diagnoses in individuals with PTSD (66% BPD and PTSD vs. 22% other personality disorders and PTSD [Zanarini et al., 1998]). Moreover, among people diagnosed with a personality disorder who have a history of traumatic exposure, individuals with BPD report the highest rates of PTSD (51%), in contrast to all other groups of individuals with personality disorders (i.e., schizotypal, avoidant, and obsessive–compulsive) combined (33%; Yen et al., 2002).

Problems Associated With Posttraumatic Stress Disorder in Clients With Borderline Personality Disorder

People with co-occurring BPD and PTSD experience greater interpersonal and functional problems than do individuals meeting criteria for only one of these diagnoses (Bolton, Mueser, & Rosenberg, 2006; Heffernan & Cloitre, 2000; Zlotnick, Franklin, & Zimmerman, 2002). They may also experience more severe overall symptoms. For example, Bolton, Mueser, and Rosenberg (2006) found that clients with PTSD and BPD reported significantly higher levels of general distress, physical illness, anxiety, and depression than those with BPD alone. Zlotnick and colleagues found that the additional diagnosis of PTSD in clients with BPD was not associated with more severe BPD symptoms than in clients with BPD alone but that a diagnosis of BPD was associated with additional interpersonal difficulties and use of more services compared with PTSD alone (Zlotnick et al., 2002; Zlotnick, Johnson, et al., 2003).

Furthermore, Heffernan and Cloitre (2000) examined the additional impact of BPD on individuals with PTSD. They found that although the two groups did not differ in terms of PTSD symptomatology, individuals with both disorders had more severe difficulties with anger, dissociation, anxiety, and interpersonal problems than did those with PTSD only. In addition, Connor et al. (2002) reported that individuals in their community sample who had a combined diagnosis of PTSD and BPD had greater health status impairment, higher utilization of mental health services, and more severe impairments in social and occupational functioning than did individuals with PTSD alone.

Review of Relevant Treatment Studies

A few published studies have assessed the efficacy of treatment for PTSD in individuals with BPD. These early studies demonstrated that individuals with BPD are able to tolerate and benefit from treatment for PTSD (Feeny, Zoellner, & Foa, 2002; Harned & Linehan, 2008; Hembree, Cahill, & Foa, 2004; Mueser et al., 2008; Wagner, Rizvi, & Harned, 2007). However, of the studies that have included a comparison group, two found that the end-state functioning of individuals with a comorbid diagnosis of BPD and PTSD was not as high as that of individuals meeting criteria for PTSD alone (Feeny et al., 2002; Hembree et al., 2004).

In addition, as noted previously, individuals who meet criteria for both diagnoses tend to report more intense feelings of anger, depression, and distress than those individuals meeting criteria for one disorder or the other. These feelings, especially anger, have been correlated with poor response to treatment in studies targeting PTSD, especially those that are based on an exposure paradigm (Chemtob, Tomas, Law, & Cremniter, 1997; Foa et al., 1995; Forbes, Creamer, Hawthorne, Allen, & McHugh, 2003; Ford, Fisher, & Arson, 1997; Ford & Kidd, 1998). However, complementary research indicates that for anxiety disorders in general, personality disorders do not negatively affect treatment outcome (Dreessen & Arntz, 1998; van Minnen, Arntz, & Keijsers, 2002). The apparent contradiction in these findings may simply be a result of the fact that the presence of significant feelings of anger may interfere with the efficacy of exposure-based therapies because exposure does not necessarily have the same extinguishing effect on anger as it does on anxiety. Regardless, more evidence is needed before it can be determined whether the presence of BPD symptomatology makes the provision of cognitive–behavioral treatment (CBT) for PTSD, be it cognitive restructuring (CR) or exposure, less successful.

CHALLENGES IN TREATING POSTTRAUMATIC STRESS DISORDER IN PERSONS WITH BORDERLINE PERSONALITY DISORDER

Among the unique challenges clinicians face when treating individuals for PTSD who also have BPD are difficulties that arise when engaging and retaining clients in treatment and coordinating treatment with other providers. Clinicians working with these clients must also help them to manage multiple crises and chaotic lives, intense emotional distress, impulsive and destructive behaviors (e.g., self-injurious behavior, binge eating, substance abuse), poor interpersonal skills, and instability in relationships. Each of these challenges is discussed in the sections that follow.

Engaging and Retaining Clients in Treatment

People with BPD are frequently suspicious or distrustful of others, low in their tolerance of emotional distress, poor at regulating their own emotions, and not skilled in maintaining constructive relationships. People with PTSD are also often distrustful of others and avoid therapy because it requires dealing with memories, thoughts, and feelings of distressful events. Not surprisingly then, engaging and retaining clients with both disorders in treatment can be very challenging (Zlotnick, Bruce, et al., 2003).

In addition, approximately 97% of individuals with BPD have been in treatment with an average of six different therapists (Lieb, Zanarini, Schmahl, Linehan, & Bohus, 2004). This statistic likely reflects, to some extent, the effects of the characteristically poor interpersonal skills of individuals with BPD, which may make maintaining the therapeutic relationship difficult for the therapist as well as for the client. Another logical consequence of these numerous therapeutic relationships is that these clients may hold little confidence in the efficacy of treatment as a whole and they may have expectations for treatment that are at variance with the practice of CBT (e.g., believing that therapy is a place to simply talk about distressing events of the past week, focusing solely on the crisis of the week and not skill building).

Coordinating Treatment With Other Providers

As the treatment of BPD is often multimodal, it often encompasses psychopharmacology, individual or group therapy, and day treatment, which results in multiple providers involved in ongoing treatment. Although the coordination of the CR for PTSD program with other services is important for all clients with posttraumatic symptoms, it is especially crucial for individuals with BPD, whose propensity for unstable and vacillating relationships can lead to conflict among treatment providers, thereby undermining the effects of treatment. Therefore, the coordination of treatment with all providers is important to the success of the CR for PTSD program to ensure support for working on trauma-related issues and to avoid clients' receiving conflicting advice or guidance from different providers.

Multiple Crises and Chaotic Lives

The lives of individuals with BPD are often chaotic and filled with numerous crises. These crises may interfere with teaching of skills, monitoring of change, and identifying of core maladaptive or unhelpful thoughts. It can be a challenge to maintain the focus on the trauma work within a session and across sessions when new problems appear and dominate the client's attention. The dilemma facing the therapist is to acknowledge the distressing situation in order to validate the client's experience while not allowing the focus of the treatment program to be derailed.

Intense Distress and Difficulty Tolerating Emotions

Individuals with BPD tend to experience their emotions very intensely and may become overwhelmed by even relatively minor levels of negative affect. These two characteristics coupled together may make it a challenge in the beginning of treatment to shift a client from a simple rehashing of the upsetting or traumatic situation to a conversation focused on skills acquisition, despite the fact that the application of the skills will lead to a more enduring relief.

Self-Harm, Suicidal Thoughts, and Potentially Lethal Actions

Clients with BPD may present with a variety of other pressing problems, such as significant substance abuse, binge eating, serious thoughts of suicide, and self-injurious behavior, such as cutting. The challenge that such behaviors pose to the well-being of clients and the course of treatment are clear.

Poor Interpersonal Skills, Instability in Relationships, and Family Conflict

Poor interpersonal skills are another characteristic of individuals with a BPD diagnosis. Demonstrations of this lack of skill may include the use of threats when negotiating with others (e.g., "Stay or I'll kill myself"), aligning with someone at another's expense, and strong fluctuations in feelings about others (e.g., from "I love you" to "I hate you"). All of these means of relating may manifest themselves in the individual's life, creating conflict with family, friends, and coworkers and resulting in instability in relationships. Again, this may distract from focusing on the impact of the traumatic events and is likely to have an effect on the therapeutic relationship.

The families of origin for individuals with a comorbid diagnosis of BPD and PTSD may pose specific difficulties over the course of treatment above and beyond those created by interpersonal problems with friends and coworkers. Specifically, these families may not be willing or able to provide support during treatment. In fact, they may actively undermine treatment by not acknowledging the trauma or by portraying the client as too fragile to actively participate in treatment. Even more fundamentally important to the etiology and maintenance of distress in these individuals is the fact that the majority of individuals with BPD report childhood sexual abuse by a male noncaretaker, emotional denial from a male caretaker, or inconsistent treatment by a female caretaker (Zanarini et al., 1997). These family dynamics clearly placed many of these individuals at risk as children and, as a result, may often expose individuals as adults to people and situations that serve to trigger reminders of past traumatic events. Furthermore, there is some evidence suggesting higher rates of substance abuse, antisocial personality disorder, and possibly BPD in family members of individuals with BPD (White, Gunderson, Zanarini, & Hudson, 2003), all of which make establishing supportive healthy relationships with family members much more challenging for clients.

STRATEGIES FOR ADDRESSING COMMON PROBLEMS

A number of different strategies can be used to overcome common challenges to treating posttraumatic disorders in persons with BPD. Although few modifications to the CR for PTSD program are necessary, the following suggestions may facilitate treatment.

Engaging and Retaining Clients in Treatment

When introducing the program, it is helpful to clarify that it is a skills-based therapy. The therapist serves as consultant to the client, and the client retains control. For example, clients can elect to not discuss certain topics in a session, keep their eyes open during breathing retraining, and so on. In addition, although the therapist should present the program with confidence, the client should not be asked to accept its efficacy without question. Instead, he or she should be encouraged to keep an open mind that the treatment may be helpful with the understanding that the client will collect his or her own evidence for or against the effectiveness of the therapy.

In keeping with the therapist as consultant model, it can be helpful to review the client's primary motivation for participating in the program (i.e., what areas of living the client most wants to improve, such as relationships, parenting, work, school, self-care) so that the therapist is working with client to use the CR for PTSD program to ultimately improve functioning in those areas. By creating an agreement between the client and the clinician for the goals of treatment, the client is much more likely to be engaged and to remain in treatment, even when the work is challenging.

It is also important to point out to the client that he or she is more likely to benefit from the treatment by actively participating and by completing homework assignments. This point should not be understated given the growing body of evidence that documents that the success of treatment is highly correlated with clients' timely homework completion (Coon & Thompson, 2003; Edelman & Chambless, 1995; Mueser et al., 2008).

Coordinating Treatment With Other Providers

Strong treatment coordination between providers and treatment settings (i.e., inpatient and outpatient) is essential so that support for the treatment can be as consistent as possible. Ideally, each clinician involved can reinforce the skills and the treatment expectations can be kept constant (e.g., individuals should be hospitalized when they are unable to keep themselves safe; medication as needed may be helpful, but with practice, the skills can be as effective if not more effective than medication). To ensure coordination, it may be useful to have the client sign a release so that the clinicians can communicate with each other to dispel any misunderstandings that may arise as a result of the client's potentially poor interpersonal skills. It may also be helpful to schedule case conferences among the various providers.

Multiple Crises and Chaotic Lives

It is not uncommon for these clients to arrive at each session with a new crisis. It is important that the clinician acknowledge the crisis and convey empathy, but then gently and firmly focus on a review of homework. When appropriate, and when time permits, the clinician can then initiate a discussion of the crisis and point out when and how the skills of breathing retraining, and CR can be implemented.

Intense Distress and Difficulty Tolerating Emotions

Several skills covered in the program can be helpful for individuals struggling with intensely distressing emotions. During peak times of distress, breathing retraining, possibly with the addition of a mantra, can be helpful as the client works to move through intense waves of emotion. Once the intensity of the feeling has begun to subside or the client has become well practiced, he or she may be able to use the skill of CR either in the moment or somewhat after the event. Eventually, the client can also use CR to tackle relevant thoughts, such as "I will not be able to tolerate this feeling or this pain," "This feeling will never end," or "If I relapse (i.e., drink, binge, self-harm) I have failed at treatment again."

It is important to emphasize that the acquisition of skills takes practice and that in the beginning the client may be able to apply the skills only after the event has passed or in situations in which the resulting distress is not overwhelming. As the client becomes more skilled, the therapist can encourage him or her to use the skills closer to the timing of the distressing event, with events that are increasingly more distressful, and ultimately in the moment as the event is unfolding.

If an individual reports feeling intensely distressed and unable to complete a CR, it can be helpful to remind him or her that there may be more than one way to interpret a situation. Inserting a glimmer of doubt in a catastrophic thought may be sufficient to allow the client to complete a CR or, at the least, to remain in control until the strong emotional distress that might otherwise have prompted self-harm (e.g., cutting, burning, binging) subsides.

Self-Harm, Suicidal Thoughts, and Potentially Lethal Actions

The therapist can use several strategies to help the client reduce or eliminate self-destructive and potentially life-threatening behaviors. Clinicians must first acknowledge the behavior and assess for lethality of thoughts or actions and respond to life threat appropriately. It is also often helpful to develop a crisis plan with the client at the onset of treatment. The plan should outline how the client will respond to an emergency or to a significant increase in frequency or intensity of self-injurious behavior. In addition, it is important to monitor such behavior over time so that progress or pitfalls can be noted and discussed without too much attention being drawn to them. Keeping a log also makes it possible to develop an awareness of the patterns in the behavior and, using CR, to address negative feelings that precede self-injurious actions. It is beneficial to discuss the pattern in a neutral or scientific manner so that the individual has the opportunity to evaluate the short-term gain of self-harm behavior (e.g., reduces emotional pain in the moment) and compare it with the long-term consequence (e.g., nothing changes, result may be a worse outcome).

Further, self-injurious behavior can be triggered by a number of stimuli, including negative feelings, trauma-related thoughts, images, and trauma-related stimuli. The implicit assumption is that self-injurious behavior is mediated by negative feelings, even if the client is not aware of those feelings or triggers. The goal of CR is to help clients become aware of these feelings and triggers and to arm them with skills that defuse much of the intensity of the emotion.

Finally, adjunct treatment or support, such as a dialectical behavior therapy (DBT) skills group (Linehan, 1993) or Alcoholics Anonymous, can be helpful, especially for clients whose self-harm is potentially life threatening, whose suicidality necessitates frequent hospitalization, or whose substance use significantly impairs their functioning. Although there are no studies directly addressing the integration of CR and DBT, some data suggest that combining exposure treatment for PTSD with stress inoculation and social skills training (Mueser & Taylor, 1997) or with standard DBT can be effective (Harned & Linehan, 2008; Wagner et al., 2007).

Poor Interpersonal Skills, Instability in Relationships, and Family Conflict

Clients' difficulty with maintaining positive working relationships may affect the therapeutic relationship as well. The therapist can help to reduce the likelihood that this will interfere with treatment by validating the client's efforts and by staying neutral. In addition, CR should not be presented as a skill to correct cognitive errors or maladaptive thoughts but as simply a useful tool that the client can use to figure out when a thought is not helpful, contributes needlessly to his or her emotional distress, or simply not supported by the evidence. Finally, if the client becomes upset with the therapist, it is important that the therapist encourage the client to use the skills of CR as he or she would in any upsetting situation; the therapist should then respond in an open, nondefensive manner.

CLINICAL EXAMPLE

Nell was a 34-year-old woman with a significant history of childhood sexual abuse and physical and sexual assaults as an adult. Since her early 20s she had been hospitalized approximately three to four times per year prior to beginning the CR for PTSD program. She had a history of alcohol abuse, self-injurious behavior (e.g., cutting), and anorexia. At the time of her participation in the CR for PTSD program, her diagnoses included PTSD, BPD, anorexia in partial remission, major depression, and alcohol abuse in remission.

When she presented for treatment, she had also just been assigned to a new case manager at the community mental health center. She was in a fairly stable relationship with a man. When she began the CR for PTSD program, she had not been hospitalized for 4 months, her cutting was fairly well controlled, and she was not drinking. Halfway through treatment, she decided on her own to start attending Alcoholics Anonymous. However, as an example of the fact that she continued to be out of control at times, her fiancé would still occasionally hide all the knives in the house when he thought she was "losing control." In addition, she was unable to work, and she was overexercising (e.g., she was working out at the gym 3 to 4 hours a day).

Nell's parents divorced when she was 11. After her father left the house, her care became inconsistent. At times her mother was abusive, and at other times she was simply neglectful. When Nell was 15 years old, her uncle moved in with them. Over the course of the next 3 years, he sexually abused Nell, but he also took care of her (e.g., he would sneak food to her when her mother was out of the house). During these years, she ran away often and started drinking. Although she reported being close with her father, she never disclosed the abuse to him or anybody else.

When she was 18 years old, Nell moved out of the house to attend college. While away at school she functioned fairly well, but she developed posttraumatic symptoms after being reminded about her trauma history while serving as a volunteer on a university hotline. Shortly thereafter, she left school. In the years that followed, she began to drink heavily and to be involved with many different men. During this time, she experienced several additional traumas, including a violent date rape, numerous physical assaults, and the death of a child days after giving birth. She began to cycle in and out of the hospital for suicide attempts and for treatment of anorexia.

There were a variety of challenges encountered over the course of treatment. On occasion, her case manager unintentionally undermined the CR for PTSD program by presenting CR as simply the "power of positive thinking" devoid of the evaluation of the accuracy of the thought. Nell also started and lost a job, which triggered strong feelings of distress and thoughts of failure for her. Several other stressors also developed in her relationship with her fiancé. In addition, her father, who had been very supportive of her, decided to move to a different state.

Nell and the therapist used the 5 Steps of CR with little variation. In the beginning, Nell found them to be very difficult because she often experienced several strong emotions at once. During such practices, Nell and her therapist would carefully work through CR sheets for each separate emotion that occurred during the upsetting situation. Over time, the skill of CR became easier for her, and she was able to use it in response to core thoughts (e.g., "The abuse was my fault," "This pain is unbearable and will never end").

The accommodations made to the standard treatment were simply to address common problems associated with Nell's additional diagnosis of BPD. The therapist was clear from the beginning of treatment that the therapist's role was one of consultant. In keeping with this model, the treatment focus was determined by Nell. She chose to focus on relationships, specifically her relationship with her boyfriend. The treatment also included an emphasis on evaluating her thoughts without judgment and validating her distress. It placed a strong emphasis on the breathing retraining with elements of meditation, which Nell suggested because she had found it helpful in the past. Furthermore, because Nell had been in a DBT skills group before, the therapist reminded her of several relevant skills when her urges to self-harm were particularly strong.

Sample Dialogue

Client: I almost didn't come today. I completely lost it on Sunday and I haven't left the house since then.

Therapist: What happened?

Client: After dinner on Sunday, as my dad was leaving, he announced that he had decided to move in with Mary, his girlfriend. It takes at least 12 hours by car to get to her house from here. I am so furious with him. He waited until the last minute to tell me because he knows that I can't deal without him. I can't believe he would do this to me. My boyfriend had to pry me off of my dad just so that he could leave. Afterward, I ran into the bathroom and wouldn't come out for hours. After a bit, I was able to pull it together. I lit some candles and then started trying to use some relaxed breathing and meditation. I tried to use one of those CR worksheets, but I got nowhere.

Therapist: Sounds really rough. Let's see what we can do using the 5 Steps of CR Worksheet. Please describe the situation in your own words.

Client: I completely lost it when my father announced that he is moving away.

Therapist: How did you feel?

Client: Hmmm, anger, sadness, guilt, and fear.

Therapist: Can you tell me more?

Client: Well, I will definitely miss him, and I feel bad about causing such a scene. It is just that I can't face life without him. And I am scared. During all the bad stuff I experienced as a kid and as an adult, I could always count on him. He has always been there for me.

Therapist:	Which feeling would you like to work on first? What is your strongest feeling?
Client:	Fear.
Therapist:	How strong is your feeling of fear on a scale of 1 to 10?
Client:	Right now, a 9.
Therapist:	Let's write that down. What about your father moving scares you?
Client:	I am terrified. I am terrified that I won't be able to cope with his leaving.
Therapist:	What is it you are afraid will happen? Remember, usually when people become so upset they can't stand it, it is because the thought behind the feeling is disastrous.
Client:	I am terrified that I won't be able to cope and the pain will be unbearable.
Therapist:	Okay. The situation is your dad's announcement that he is planning on moving. The feeling is intense fear. Your thought is . . .
Client:	He will move away. I will never see him. I will become so upset that I won't be able to stand it.
Therapist:	What evidence do you have that supports that idea?
Client:	Look what happened when he just mentioned the idea that he was moving. And when things have gotten bad in the past, I could always go to him. He would always let me crash at his house when I needed to.
Therapist:	Anything else? Any other evidence to support the idea?
Client:	Not really. I guess this means that I am an idiot.
Therapist:	Definitely not. Now, what evidence do you have that doesn't support your thought?
Client:	There have been times, plenty of times, when we have been out of touch. I am an adult. I have had bad times when you, Jim, or other friends have helped me through.
Therapist:	Anything else?
Client:	I guess that I can still call him. And he said he would send me a plane ticket if I need him to.
Therapist:	Anything else?
Client:	No.

Therapist:	And have you ever had the experience before when you believed the pain was unbearable, but then as time passed the pain became bearable?
Client:	Well, yeah, of course.
Therapist:	So then, is it fair to say that even if the pain seems unbearable right now that it is possible that over time and with some work you will be able to manage it?
Client:	Yes, I guess so.
Therapist:	Okay, so let's look at the evidence you have written down here for and against the thought. You said the thought was supported by your reaction to his news. Then you noted the thought was not supported by the fact that you have been out of touch with him in the past and you did all right and that other people have helped you through crises. You also added that you could call or visit him and that you have survived other times in which you initially thought the pain would be unbearable. What do you think? Does the evidence mostly support your thought or not?
Client:	Mostly not.
Therapist:	So, what is the next step?
Client:	Come up with an alternative thought?
Therapist:	Right. Give it a try.
Client:	I am scared now, but I can cope. He is not gone forever. I also have other people in my life I can count on.
Therapist:	Great. So, you can get help when you feel overwhelmed and you can cope. How strong is your feeling of fear on a scale of 1 to 10 now?
Client:	Five.
Therapist:	More manageable now?
Client:	Yes.

Outcome

By the end of 16 sessions, Nell had made a lot of progress. The number and severity of the PTSD and depression symptoms she had endorsed at the beginning of treatment dropped significantly. She had not been hospitalized in close to a year. Her cutting had ceased. She had decided to return to school and to get married. Over the course of the program, she became better able to inhibit the urge to self-harm (i.e., cut) by adopting the adaptive self-soothing skills of breathing retraining and scheduling of positive events. She also became more skilled at maintaining a perspective on her distress as she built on her success experiences of managing her distress more judiciously. Moreover, through her practice with the 5 Steps of CR she was less likely to catastrophize and to see things dichotomously, as either black or white. She did continue to experience some days during which she felt unable to cope with her feelings, but she was able to see those days as "brief vacations" from her otherwise more functional life and not as a sign of treatment failure.

SUMMARY AND CONCLUSIONS

Research has established that trauma and PTSD are a significant problem for individuals with BPD. Individuals who carry a diagnosis of BPD and PTSD tend to endorse greater levels of distress, interpersonal troubles, health problems, and functional concerns than people who meet criteria for only one of these diagnoses. However, preliminary research suggests that the CR for PTSD program is tolerated, feasible, and effective for people with BPD.

Clinicians face a variety of challenges when treating individuals carrying both diagnoses. These include engaging and maintaining clients in treatment and coordinating with other treatment providers. Clinicians may also need to manage treatment for clients who report intense feelings of distress and strong urges to self-harm. Yet, a variety of strategies that can be incorporated into CR can make focused treatment for PTSD for individuals with BPD possible and effective.

12

CO-OCCURRING POSTTRAUMATIC STRESS DISORDER AND SUBSTANCE USE DISORDER IN ADDICTION TREATMENT SETTINGS

MARK P. MCGOVERN, ARTHUR I. ALTERMAN,
KEITH M. DRAKE, AND AMANDA P. DAUTEN

Substance use disorders are common in people with posttraumatic stress disorder (PTSD) and present an array of challenges to clinicians who treat both disorders. In this chapter, we review co-occurring PTSD and substance use disorders, the clinical implications of comorbidity, common challenges of treating PTSD in people with addictions, and different treatment models for the two disorders. We then describe our adaptation of the Cognitive Restructuring (CR) for PTSD program for people with substance use disorders and trauma histories in addiction treatment settings and discuss initial feasibility testing of the model and provide a clinical vignette.

PREVALENCE AND CORRELATES OF CO-OCCURRING POSTTRAUMATIC STRESS DISORDER AND SUBSTANCE USE DISORDERS

In epidemiological studies of the general population, the lifetime rate of substance use disorders is about double in people with PTSD (43%) compared with those without PTSD (22%; Breslau, Davis, Peterson, & Schultz, 1997;

Cottler, Compton, Mager, Spitznagel, & Janca, 1992; Kessler et al., 1995; Kulka et al., 1990). Among men with PTSD, substance use disorders are the most common co-occurring disorders; for women with PTSD, only depression and anxiety are more frequent. Two different pathways may explain the high comorbidity of PTSD and substance use disorders. First, trauma and PTSD may lead to substance abuse or dependence in an effort to cope with distressing symptoms. For example, a recent 15-year longitudinal study found that childhood PTSD was associated with the development of drug use disorder (J. P. Read, Brown, & Kahler, 2004). In the second pathway, substance use problems may contribute to poor judgment and risk appraisal ability, leading to traumatic experiences and development of PTSD. Of course, independent or parallel etiological pathways are also possible (Chilcoat & Breslau, 1998; Jelinek & Williams, 1984; Simpson & Miller, 2002).

Posttraumatic Stress Disorder in Addiction Treatment Programs

Significant proportions of patients in addiction treatment have PTSD. Approximately 35% to 50% of people in addiction treatment programs have a lifetime diagnosis of PTSD, and 25% to 42% currently have PTSD (Back et al., 2000; K. T. Brady, Back, & Coffey, 2004; P. J. Brown, Recupero, & Stout, 1995; Cacciola, Alterman, McKay, & Rutherford, 2001; Dansky et al., 1996; Jacobson, Southwick, & Kosten, 2001; Mills, Lynskey, Teesson, Ross, & Darke, 2005; Ouimette, Ahrens, Moos, & Finney, 1997).

Patients with PTSD in addiction treatment programs manifest more problems than those without PTSD, including more severe depression and other psychiatric symptoms, greater substance use problems, more medical problems, and poorer functioning in areas such as social relationships and employment (Back et al., 2000; K. T. Brady, Killeen, Saladin, & Dansky, 1994; Najavits, Weiss, Shaw, & Muenz, 1998; Ouimette, Goodwin, & Brown, 2006; J. P. Read et al., 2004; Trafton, Minkel, & Humphreys, 2006). The multitude of problems associated with comorbid PTSD in people with addiction has important treatment implications for routine community addiction treatment programs. Indeed, most of the studies conducted have shown that patients with PTSD respond less favorably to routine treatments than those without PTSD. Patients with PTSD use more treatment services over their lifetime, are more likely to drop out of intensive outpatient addiction treatment and to require readmission, and are less likely to follow through on aftercare treatment. They also show worse outcomes following addiction treatment in substance use, subjective distress and psychiatric symptoms, psychosocial functioning, and health (K. T. Brady et al., 1994; P. J. Brown et al., 1995; P. J. Brown, Stout, & Mueller, 1999; Hein, Nunes, Levin, & Fraser, 2000; Koppenhaver et al., 2007; McGovern, Drake, & Weiss, 2005; Mills et al., 2005; Ouimette et al., 1997; Ouimette, Finney, & Moos, 1999; Trafton et al., 2006).

Challenges in Treating Posttraumatic Stress Disorder in Addiction Treatment Settings

Historically, addiction treatment programs have operated with the overriding assumption that their primary focus should be the treatment of the substance use disorder and that only after a period of stable abstinence or remission might the "underlying" psychiatric condition be addressed. This approach may be effective for many patients with less severe psychiatric problems, in particular those who have substance-induced mood and anxiety disorders (Flynn & Brown, 2008).

However, delaying psychiatric treatment has been less than optimal for patients with addiction and PTSD. Addiction counselor textbooks have recommended against raising trauma-related issues with a patient during the initiation of abstinence or early recovery phases. The conventional clinical wisdom, much like with the proverbial Pandora's box, was not to open up these matters until the person had at least 2 years of stable sobriety. Clinicians were warned about triggering trauma-related memories and feelings, which could disrupt the primary focus on recovery from addiction (S. Brown, 1985). Nevertheless, many patients were obviously experiencing severe PTSD symptoms, particularly those associated with reexperiencing and hyperarousal during their early phases of addiction treatment. In fact, considering that many patients with PTSD use substances to manage or anesthetize their trauma-related symptoms, the shaky abstinence achieved during the early phases of addiction treatment was often accompanied by terror when their usual coping strategies were removed, precipitating dropouts from treatment and relapses.

Over the past decade, two movements have caused addiction treatment providers to question the wisdom of this conventional clinical approach. The first was precipitated by the recognition that many principles of addiction treatment were developed by men and for men. Research and awareness about the need to improve access, retention, and treatment relevance for women with substance use disorders proliferated. Gender-sensitive treatment programs were developed to respond to the needs of women and their children. Related to the appropriate design of services for these programs was the concern about the particularly high rates of co-occurring psychiatric disorders in women with addiction (Kushner & Mueser, 1993) and the strong associations between PTSD symptoms and childhood sexual trauma, domestic violence history, and present living situation (e.g., living with others who drink or use drugs). The treatment community began to seek programs and interventions to respond to the broad needs of these women, including the comorbid substance use disorder.

The second movement was precipitated by the growing awareness of the high rates of psychiatric and substance use disorders in clinical populations.

In mental health and addiction treatment programs, the negative outcomes for patients who had both sets of problems were also remarkable. National efforts were launched to create a "no wrong door" to treatment and to provide integrated or at least highly collaborated services to address both mental health and addiction problems (Institute of Medicine, 2006; Substance Abuse and Mental Health Services Administration, 2002). Addiction treatment providers have now arrived at an "action" stage of readiness and motivation to address co-occurring PTSD within the context of their treatment programs. They now view PTSD as an important disorder to address early in addiction treatment and indicate favorable attitudes toward using cognitive–behavioral approaches in their work (McGovern, Fox, Xie, & Drake, 2004).

TREATMENT DEVELOPMENT FOR CO-OCCURRING POSTTRAUMATIC STRESS DISORDER AND SUBSTANCE USE DISORDERS

Several standardized interventions have been developed and are summarized in Table 12.1. These interventions vary along a number dimensions, including approach, format, duration, setting, integration with addiction treatment, gender composition, retention rate, and whether there is an active research program continuing to test and refine the therapy.

Inspection of the different characteristics of the programs reveals several important points when considering their utility for treating PTSD in patients with addiction. First, with the exception of Transcend, which is a residential program that treats both addiction and PTSD, all of the other programs were designed to be implemented in community settings and not necessarily in addiction treatment centers. Community-based programs focus on the treatment of PTSD, with minimal or no considerations of integrating services with an addiction treatment program, raising a question about the viability of delivering these programs in the context of addiction treatment.

Second, the limited data on retention in treatment for the community-based programs indicate problems with dropout. The two published studies on Seeking Safety reported retention rates of 63% (Najavits et al., 1998) and 61% (Hein, Cohen, Miele, Litt, & Capstick, 2004), and the one study of Concurrent Treatment of PTSD and Cocaine Dependence reported only a 38% retention rate (K. T. Brady et al., 2001). These relatively low rates of retention in PTSD treatment are troubling considering the previously reviewed research documenting that PTSD contributes to dropout from addiction treatment and poor follow-through on aftercare.

Third, only one intervention, Seeking Safety, used a randomized controlled trial design. Although one study found that Seeking Safety resulted in greater improvement than treatment as usual (Najavits et al., 1998), two

TABLE 12.1
Characteristics of Psychosocial Treatments for Co-Occurring Posttraumatic
Stress Disorder (PTSD) and Substance Use Disorders

Characteristic	Seeking Safety	Treatment program		
		Concurrent Treatment of PTSD and Cocaine Dependence	Substance Dependence PTSD Therapy	Transcend
Theoretical orientation	Eclectic	Cognitive–behavioral	Eclectic	Eclectic
Exposure based	No	Yes	Yes	No
Format	Group + individual	Individual	Individual	Group (residential program)
Integrated with addiction treatment	No	No	No	Yes
Duration	12 or 24+ sessions (depending on study)	16 sessions	40 sessions	60 sessions
Retention criteria	25% of sessions	10 sessions	NA	NA
Retention rate	61%–63%	38%	NA	91%
Gender	Women	Women and men	Women and men	Men
Setting	Community	Community	Community	VA addiction treatment program
Therapist education	All at least MA/MS/MSW	All at least MA/MS/MSW	All at least MA/MS/MSW	PhD
Active research program	Yes	No	No	No

trials found that the program led to similar improvements in PTSD compared with a relapse prevention program (Hein et al., 2004) or a women's health education program (L. R. Cohen & Hein, 2006).

Given the significant limitations of the programs designed to treat PTSD in people with co-occurring substance use disorders, there is still a need for an effective treatment program for PTSD that can be delivered in the context of addiction treatment. The CR for PTSD program described in this book has been shown in controlled research to be effective with another at-risk comorbid disorder group—persons with severe mental illness (Mueser et al., 2008). There are several reasons why the CR for PTSD program may be especially well suited for persons with addiction. The program is relatively brief (12–16 sessions), coinciding with the duration of addiction treatment in many settings (3–4 months). The CR for PTSD program has been implemented with low dropout rates (under 20% in one pilot study and one controlled trial; Mueser et al., 2008; Rosenberg et al., 2004) in persons with severe mental illness, possibly because of its reliance on CR rather than exposure therapy, suggesting that it may be readily tolerated in the vulnerable population of people in addiction treatment. In addition, the program has also been successfully used to treat PTSD in a variety of other challenging patient populations, as described in the other chapters in this part of the volume.

STRATEGIES AND ADAPTATIONS OF THE COGNITIVE RESTRUCTURING FOR POSTTRAUMATIC STRESS DISORDER PROGRAM

In this section, we describe the modifications of the CR for PTSD program that were made prior to conducting a safety and practicality application of the intervention with several patients in an addiction treatment program. CR for PTSD in addiction treatment is being adapted, refined, and evaluated with a grant from the National Institute on Drug Abuse. We began by conducting the therapy using the adapted manual with a small number of cases. Although not described in this chapter, CR for PTSD has since successfully progressed and demonstrated excellent outcomes (PTSD, substance use, and retention) in a sample of 11 cases (McGovern et al., in press). In this phase, research therapists delivered the CR to patients in three community intensive outpatient addiction treatment programs. At present, the intervention is being studied in a randomized controlled pilot trial, and community therapists are learning, being trained in, and delivering the program.

Providing Cognitive Restructuring for Posttraumatic Stress Disorder in Addiction Treatment Programs

The CR for PTSD in Addiction Treatment therapist manual was modified from the manual developed for use with persons with severe mental illness receiving treatment in community mental health centers. The programs serving both severe mental illness and substance use disorder populations adapt to address the highly variable cognitive and emotional capacity of patients with comorbid psychiatric and substance use disorders. This flexibility enables therapists to use their clinical judgment to determine the appropriate pace of treatment, need for repetition, and need for integration with other treatments. With respect to motivation, it is important for the therapist to assess not only the stage of readiness to address substance use but also the stage of motivation to address PTSD (and other psychiatric problems).

Because the CR for PTSD program is focused on PTSD, it is important that the patient be actively involved in treatment for substance use disorder and "in good standing" while in the addiction treatment program. In intensive outpatient programs, this may mean that patients are abstinent from substances or at least report a level of use that can be addressed at this level of care. Also, in intensive outpatient programs, addiction treatment may occur in stages. The initial stage may involve attending treatment sessions two to four times per week, for 3 to 4 hours per session. The second stage, sometimes called *aftercare* or *continuing care*, may last for 2 to 3 or more months beyond the more intensive phase, and typically involves once per week group sessions (60–90 minutes in duration). Patients in these stages of intensive outpatient programming may be regularly monitored for substance use via toxicological methods, receive family sessions as needed, but primarily obtain services in group formats focused on motivation to abstain, education about addiction and recovery, relapse prevention, and peer support group facilitation. Patient status in these programs may be determined by substance use, attendance, and behavior in groups. Other abstinence-based programs (e.g., residential, outpatient) may have similar considerations to determine patient status, but the key is that for patients to benefit from the CR for PTSD program, the other problems they have, particularly those that are addiction related, should be addressed by a program or clinician other than the therapist providing CR for PTSD. This enables treatment to be focused, brief, and target only the PTSD symptoms.

Medication-assisted recovery programs, such as methadone maintenance, often operate more on harm reduction and public health principles. Good standing in these clinics may be determined by use of substances such as opiates or benzodiazepines and also by compliance with methadone dosage and other clinic policy. Because methadone is a Food and Drug Administration-approved medication for the treatment of opioid dependence, it is important that the patient be receiving services at the clinic to target problems other than opioids. These services could include group and individual counseling for use of all mood-altering substances, as well as services geared to medical, social, work, and legal problems. The patient needs to have these concerns attended to; otherwise there will be a strong pull to use the CR for PTSD therapy to handle all other life problems.

There are several other important factors that a CR for PTSD therapist must consider before initiating the treatment and while determining the context within which the treatment will occur.

Chart and Assessment Review

Before meeting the patient, the therapist should review the addiction program chart, along with any PTSD assessment information. It is essential to have information regarding trauma history and current PTSD symptoms. Standardized clinical interview or assessment information is recommended, such as the Clinician Administered PTSD Scale (CAPS; Blake et al., 1995) or the Posttraumatic Stress Disorder Checklist (PCL; Blanchard, Jones-Alexander, Buckley, & Forneris, 1996). Knowledge of this information may be useful to communicate to the patient during the first session to potentially relieve his or her anxiety, tendency to avoid, and burden of retelling. Also, during the patient education Modules 4 and 5 (see "Modifications of the Treatment Program" section), patients identify symptoms of PTSD that apply to them. Comparing this information with data obtained during the assessment, including clarifying discrepancies, is important as patients address their symptoms. Reviewing the chart is also useful with respect to the history of substance use and relapse precipitants. Other clinical data may also be useful, such as level of functioning, symptoms, treatment participation, social supports, and involvement in peer recovery support groups.

Communication With the Addiction Treatment Program

The smooth integration of CR for PTSD and the current addiction treatment is important. The counselor and treatment team should understand the role of the CR for PTSD program therapist, and both the therapist and the team should be clear about the nature of communication among them. Involvement during and after the PTSD intervention, and amount and format of contact, should be specified in advance. Good rapport should be established and concerns about the treatment, either related to addiction or PTSD, should be discussed.

The patient's substance relapse and crisis plan, compliance issues, and patient progress, particularly outside of therapy (e.g., "Have there been times when therapy skills have helped?") should also be reviewed. Details about the PTSD treatment, specifically regarding the traumatic events, need not be divulged to addiction staff unless there is clearly a risk associated with not exchanging this information. Patients in addiction treatment may also want to know the procedures if they reveal substance use within the context of the CR for PTSD program but would rather withhold this information from the addiction treatment program. To avoid collusion and splitting among treatment staff and to promote a unified treatment approach, patients are informed at the beginning of the program that information about substance use will be shared with all treatment providers.

Therapeutic Relationship

It is well established that any treatment is only effective to the degree there is a positive relationship between patient and therapist (Luborsky,

Crits-Christoph, Alexander, Margolis, & Cohen, 1983). The two main ingredients are the therapeutic alliance and the therapeutic frame. The term *therapeutic alliance* refers to the relationship between the therapist and patient that fosters an atmosphere conducive to achieving therapy goals. Competent and skilled CR for PTSD therapists establish an emotionally contained yet active interchange with patients. If the patient is inhibited, the therapist attempts to engage with open-ended questions; if the patient discloses readily with associated increased emotional arousal, the therapist focuses on containment with supportive empathy, close-ended questions, and gentle redirection. It is important to the patient's progress toward therapy goals for the therapist to establish him- or herself as empathic and supportive yet task-focused and to establish the therapy as a place where trauma work will be contained and safe.

The term *therapeutic frame* refers to the structure and boundaries of the therapy within which the therapy and therapeutic relationship take place. Of particular importance are the following: the therapist's ability to start sessions punctually and hold them to a consistent duration, to provide sufficient notice for missed sessions, to manage the therapist's own feelings, to clearly communicate what and when material is discussed with the addiction treatment program staff, and to negotiate contacts between sessions. Consistency and reliability are essential aspects of managing the therapeutic frame.

Practitioners familiar with addiction treatment program culture may have observed that individual treatment often takes a "back seat" to group formats (in traditional residential, intensive outpatient, and outpatient levels of care) and medication administration (in medication-assisted recovery programs). Individual treatment is often squeezed in between or around structured group sessions, adjusted on the basis of the urgent situation of the day, or arranged, postponed, or cancelled by fiat.

If likewise acculturated, the CR for PTSD therapist will be vulnerable to this loose format, which could undermine the therapeutic alliance with the patient and compromise effectiveness. This would likely lead to poor follow-through between session practice assignments and ultimately to negative outcomes. The therapist needs to be attentive to these potential violations of the therapeutic frame and to take steps to prevent them and their disruptive effects.

MODIFICATIONS OF THE TREATMENT PROGRAM

The basic framework of the CR for PTSD program for persons with severe mental illness was adapted for use with persons with substance use disorders in addiction treatment programs. The similarities outnumber the differences, and are summarized in Table 12.2.

TABLE 12.2
Comparison Between Cognitive Restructuring for Posttraumatic Stress Disorder (CR for PTSD) Therapist Manuals

Module	Topic	CR for PTSD for Persons With Severe Mental Illness Therapist Manual	CR for PTSD in Addiction Treatment Therapist Manual
1	Introduction	■ Engage patient in treatment. ■ Provide treatment overview.	■ Discuss relationship between therapy and addiction treatment program, substance use.
2	Crisis and Relapse Plan Review	■ Decide on a crisis plan with patient. ■ Clarify with patient's treatment team plan for managing any crises, slips, or relapses.	■ Develop and discuss written list of substance relapse triggers, early warning signs, alternative coping tactics, pre– and post–slip/relapse contact persons and numbers.
3	Breathing Retraining	■ Improve patient's ability to manage physical tension and anxiety associated with PTSD.	■ Improve skill to reduce tension and anxiety as specific relapse antecedent.
4	Psychoeducation Part I: Core symptoms of PTSD	■ Help patient to understand nature of PTSD. Make education relevant to patient's own experience of symptoms.	■ Examine relationship among trauma, PTSD symptoms, and substance use, by historical and current coping strategies.
5	Psychoeducation Part II: Associated Symptoms of PTSD	■ Help patient understand how other problems and symptoms are related to PTSD and trauma.	■ Educate on specific relationships between substance use, addiction treatment compliance, use of peer recovery support groups, and associated symptoms.
6	Cognitive Restructuring Part I: The Common Styles of Thinking	■ Clarify relationship between thoughts and feelings. ■ Teach common styles of inaccurate thinking.	■ Special focus on identifying feelings previously influenced by substances (three steps).
7	Cognitive Restructuring Part II: The 5 Steps of CR	■ Help patient understand how trauma influences thinking. ■ Facilitate changing maladaptive thoughts through weighing evidence and challenging irrational beliefs. ■ Instruct patient in how and when to take appropriate action when needed.	■ Use cognitive restructuring techniques with enhanced focus on PTSD avoidance and numbing and hyper arousal symptoms and their impact on these specific behaviors: substance use, treatment compliance, and use of peer recovery support groups (five steps).
8	Generalization Training and Termination	■ Bring treatment to closure. ■ Ease transition from specialized PTSD treatment to care as usual with treatment team.	■ Focus on generalization of skill acquisition, integration with addiction treatment and peer recovery support groups, and minimizing retraumatization potential.

The primary modifications involve formally integrating discussion and work that address the relationship between PTSD and addiction. Module 1 makes clear the nature of the relationship between the addiction treatment program and the CR for PTSD therapist, including the requirement for the patient to be in "good status" in the addiction program for the PTSD treatment to continue, and the type of information that might be shared (e.g., substance use) or not shared (e.g., details of trauma) by the CR therapist. Module 2 focuses on relapse to substances and not relapses of psychiatric symptoms. Module 3, breathing retraining, is essentially unchanged. Modules 4 and 5 more thoroughly establish the relationship between PTSD and substance use, such as use of substances to cope with reexperiencing and hyperarousal symptoms and as the primary manifestation of avoidance symptoms. When reviewing the associated symptoms of PTSD, it is important to make distinctions between the effects of the PTSD symptoms and those of the patient's downward spiraling addiction problems.

Module 6 is broken down into three steps: (a) identifying the situation, (b) identifying the thought and feeling, and (c) recognizing the common style of thinking. The language of "steps" is familiar to persons in addiction treatment, and beginning with the first three steps is also an approach consistent with this phase of their recovery. Module 7 completes the tasks of CR (evaluating the evidence, changing the thought, and taking action) and is called the 5 Steps of CR. Again, consistent with 12-step recovery programs, Steps 4 and 5 are considered the "action" or "change" steps, so building this language into the CR for PTSD program manual fits with what is currently being addressed in their addiction recovery program.

Because addiction can be conceptualized as a chronic condition, most people either remain in treatment (e.g., medication-assisted recovery program) or transition to a less intensive level of care (e.g., continuing care, aftercare). Also, many are encouraged to attend peer recovery support group meetings in the community for the foreseeable future. Module 8 on generalization training and termination addresses the weaving of skills learned in the CR for PTSD program into these treatments (and how PTSD affects participation). As a companion to the CR for PTSD Therapist Manual, a Patient Workbook has also been developed based on the handouts and worksheets of the original program.

CLINICAL EXAMPLE

Lara was a 46-year-old divorced woman who was admitted to a hospital-based outpatient addiction-treatment program. Lara had never received either addiction or mental health treatment prior to this episode. Her employer referred her to the program after noticing that Lara was frequently absent and sometimes came to work intoxicated or hung over. Lara accepted this recommendation mostly to save her job but also because she felt her drinking was out of control.

Lara began the intensive outpatient program with considerable apprehension because she was fearful in social situations, and all treatment was to be conducted in groups. The program staff was sensitive to this fact and did not push her beyond her comfort level, affirming any participation as she eased into the program. A trauma history revealed that she had been sexually abused in early adolescence by an uncle, who had forced sexual intercourse with her on at least three occasions. She had never reported these events to anyone because she felt that no one would understand and she would probably be blamed for it.

Lara had her first child, a son, when she was 16 years old, and she married the man who was the father. He was insecure and possessive of her and would accuse her of having affairs and of being interested in other men. He would tie her up and beat her, trying to get her to confess to infidelity or interest in other men, sometimes leaving her tied up for hours at a time. She was married to this man for 23 years, with these abusive episodes interspersed throughout the relationship. They had another child, a daughter, who was born 7 years into the marriage. Lara divorced at the age of 40 after considerable pressure from her son and daughter as well as from her mother.

Lara had used alcohol episodically, sometimes drinking to the point of intoxication but other times controlling her use. After the divorce, she took a second job as a bartender at a local biker bar, where she began to drink more because she did not want to offend the patrons who wanted to buy her drinks. By the time she entered the treatment program, Lara was using alcohol (beer and whiskey) on a daily basis, drinking both alone and at her bartending job. Her primary care physician had warned her about some new health problems, although she never mentioned her increased use of alcohol to him. Lara said she felt it was a "blessing" when she entered the addiction program, and she appeared motivated to follow any recommendations concerning the treatment of her alcohol problems.

Trauma and Posttraumatic Stress Disorder Assessment

Lara had never been previously diagnosed with PTSD, but she screened positive for it during the addiction program's routine self-report assessment process. A subsequent clinical interview using the CAPS confirmed that she met criteria for PSTD related to her childhood sexual abuse. Her PTSD was chronic and involved thoughts of self-blame and weakness.

Following the identification of Lara's PTSD, she was offered the opportunity to receive the CR for PTSD program but declined, stating that between her attendance at the addiction program, her bartender job, and her regular job she had no time for anything else. Lara was committed to not using alcohol and began to notice that she was remembering more things from her past and was having a hard time "shaking" these thoughts away. In addition, there were some men in the group, and men at the Alcoholics Anonymous (AA) meetings she was asked to attend, who were making her feel increasingly uncomfortable. She was surprised by this because she worked in a bar and frequently came into contact with men but had not experienced this problem before. At the same time, she also recognized that her drinking may have reduced her anxiety around men, which became apparent when she became abstinent during the addiction program.

Lara commented on a few of these issues in passing to her counselor, who reminded her that the CR for PTSD program was still available to her if she was ready. Lara thought a bit more about it and decided that because it was individual-based treatment (and not group based) that she might be willing to try it.

Treatment Progress

At the first session, Lara was surprised and somewhat relieved to learn that she had a diagnosis of PTSD. The diagnosis, by labeling many of her more negative experiences, helped to frame her problem and to feel as though she was not alone. As Lara learned about the primary and associated symptoms of PTSD, and connected her experiences to them, she became increasingly agitated and anxious and reported increased memories of her traumatic events. At this juncture, Lara said that her desire to drink was more intense than after her 1st week of abstinence in the addiction program. She wondered whether the CR for PTSD program was too difficult for her and whether she should "stop being such a weakling" and "just get on with my life."

The therapist approached this issue with a two-part strategy. First, she validated that Lara's feelings were normal for a person with PTSD, reminding her that avoidance was a common symptom and pointing out that it took great courage for her to experience feelings that anyone would be naturally inclined to avoid. Second, the therapist began to teach CR to help Lara examine the feelings of anxiety, guilt, and shame that her memories evoked and how she responded to her traumatic experiences. Lara felt relieved as she began to learn how to challenge her negative thinking, such as her common style of thinking that she "should" have been able to get over her traumatic experiences by now.

Lara stayed in the CR for PTSD program and began to apply the CR skills to her reexperiencing symptoms (gradually recognizing that she was safe in the here and now and that events regarding her uncle and her ex-husband were in her past), her anxiety (feeling fearful in social situations, particularly where men were present), and avoidance (not wanting to experience feelings because they represented weakness). A particular challenge was the paradox of Lara trying to engage in a life of recovery and her part-time job as a bartender. She revealed that this was a matchless source of income for the hours, and that as much as there were parts of it she did not like, she did find the attention from men appealing. At the same time, Lara did not find it easy to affiliate with the local peer support group community, such as AA. She described feeling vulnerable and anxious at meetings and thought that the men were "all looking at me."

An additional unexpected challenge was the difficulty Lara had in positively connecting with women. During the course of her addiction treatment and in efforts to help her go to AA meetings and find a sponsor, it became clear that she had problems feeling comfortable with women. As her less obvious avoidance of women became apparent, the therapist began to help examine her thoughts about women with whom she came in contact (e.g., "They are judging me," "They think I am a floozy"). Lara was able to use CR to reevaluate and conclude that the evidence did not support these assumptions. This had a major effect on her comfort around women and led not only to her finding a female AA sponsor but also to attending women's AA meetings in the community.

Outcome

Lara was able to complete the CR for PTSD Program in 10 sessions. She benefited from the breathing retraining to reduce anxiety symptoms; she experienced significant relief in learning about PTSD and that she was not alone in having it; and she learned how to use CR to deal with her reexperiencing, avoidance, and hyperarousal symptoms. A particularly important gain was Lara's ability to use CR to manage and reduce these symptoms without using alcohol. Finally, she learned how to approach relationships with women in a more open-minded and rewarding way.

Lara's data on the CAPS and days of alcohol use are summarized in Figures 12.1 and 12.2, along with data from the two other patients treated in the Stage I, Phase I safety and practicality study of CR for PTSD in addiction treatment programs. Figure 12.1 shows that Lara's CAPS score declined from 60 at baseline to 25 (well below PTSD diagnostic threshold) at posttreatment. Her score increased somewhat, to 34 at 3 months, which she reported was probably related to the wedding of her son, where she saw her ex-husband. Even though she was exposed to one of her abusers, her symptoms remained well below diagnostic threshold for PTSD. As can be seen on Figure 12.2, Lara maintained abstinence from alcohol at both post-

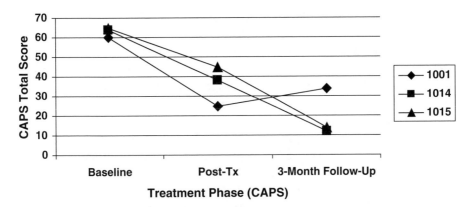

Figure 12.1. Stage I, Phase I, Cognitive Restructuring for Posttraumatic Stress Disorder (PTSD) in addiction treatment: Clinician-Administered PTSD Scale (CAPS) scores at baseline, posttreatment, and 3-month follow-up. 1001, 1014, and 1015 are patient identification numbers.

treatment assessment periods. She maintained her positive affiliation with women AA members, despite continuing to work as a bartender, against the treatment program's recommendation.

The data on the other two patients treated were similarly positive with respect to PTSD and substance use outcomes. All patients scored below PTSD threshold at both follow-up periods, two were abstinent from all substances, and one had reduced alcohol use by 50%.

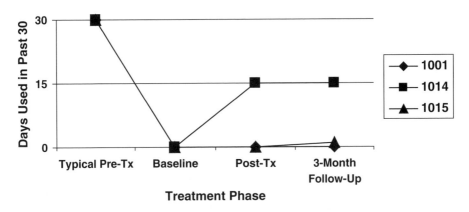

Figure 12.2. Stage I, Phase I, Cognitive Restructuring for Posttraumatic Stress Disorder in addiction treatment: Time line follow-back interview about alcohol or drug use for typical month before treatment, baseline, posttreatment, and 3-month follow-up. 1001, 1014, and 1015 are patient identification numbers.

SUMMARY AND CONCLUSIONS

Co-occurring substance use and PTSD are common in the community and even more so in treatment settings. In addiction treatment programs, although providers have historically been reluctant to address PTSD, there is now willingness to implement interventions that can be integrated into routine treatment. Although at least four other treatments have been studied for co-occurring PTSD and substance use disorders, the CR for PTSD program may hold particular promise for implementation and sustainability. This program has been adapted for persons with PTSD in addiction treatment programs, and safety and practicality studies suggest that it is feasible to implement and associated with favorable outcomes in terms of both PTSD and addiction (McGovern et al., in press). Further work is currently under way to more rigorously evaluate the effectiveness of the CR for PTSD Program in addiction treatment settings.

13

ADOLESCENTS

HARRIET J. ROSENBERG AND M. KAY JANKOWSKI

Over the past 2 decades, recognition of trauma exposure and its effects in children and adolescents has been growing steadily. Rates of exposure to trauma in general population studies of adolescents range from a low of 16% (Cuffe et al., 1998) to a high of more than 80% (Elklit, 2002), with a number of studies reporting rates of approximately 40% of youth reporting exposure to a traumatic event (Boney-McCoy & Finkelhor, 1995; Breslau, Davis, Andreski, & Peterson, 1991; Giaconia et al., 1995; Schwab-Stone et al., 1995). In a national representative survey of adolescents (12–17 years old), 5 million reported serious physical assault, 1.8 million reported sexual assault, and 8.8 million witnessed interpersonal violence (Kilpatrick et al., 2000). Adolescents, in particular, are the victims of violence at greater rates than any other age group (Klaus & Rennison, 2002).

Trauma exposure is distributed unevenly in the child and adolescent population. Gender, living situation, socioeconomic status, geographic place of residence, and service sector all are factors impacting risk level. For example, children living in chronic poverty, those in the juvenile justice system, and those living in and out of home placement or hospitalized for mental or behavioral problems have a higher risk of being traumatized. In a representative population sample (1,420 children, ages 9–16) in a rural community in North Carolina, 67.8% experienced at least one traumatic event by age 16, and 37% were afflicted by multiple or repeated trauma (W. E. Copeland, Keeler, Angold, & Costello, 2007). In a study of youths in urban settings, with interviews at baseline of 6 years and follow-up at 20–22 years, 82.5% endorsed one or more lifetime traumatic events, and exposure to violent assault peaked at 16–17 years (Breslau, Peterson, Poisson, Schultz, & Lucia, 2004). Rates of trauma exposure in service system samples generally exceed general population rates (Abram et al., 2004; Seng, Graham-Bermann, Clark, McCarthy, & Ronis, 2005).

Although adult samples indicate that males are more likely to be traumatized than females, this is a less consistent finding with adolescents, with some studies finding higher rates for girls (Cuffe et al., 1998), others for boys (Breslau et al., 1991), and others finding no difference between genders (Elklit, 2002; Giaconia et al., 1995). There is also some discrepancy as to rates of exposure by race, with findings ranging from no differences (Costello, Erkanli, Fairbank, & Angold, 2002) to higher rates of exposure among ethnic minorities (Buka, Stichick, Birdthistle, & Earls, 2001; Cuffe et al., 1998).

Trauma exposure is also associated with many high-risk health behaviors during adolescence that pose significant public health concerns, including substance abuse, delinquent behaviors, and engaging in self-injurious behaviors (Downs & Harrison, 1998; Roberts & Klein, 2003; Wright, Friedrich, Cinq-Mars, Cyr, & McDuff, 2004). W. E. Copeland et al. (2007) showed that by age 16 increasing trauma exposure affects the cumulative rates of psychiatric comorbidities (e.g., depression, anxiety). In an interdisciplinary review article, Mulvihill (2005) concluded that childhood trauma has both short- and long-term impacts on physical as well as psychological health, citing such illnesses as immune system disorders, ischemic heart disease, liver and lung disease, and fibromyalgia.

PREVALENCE OF POSTTRAUMATIC STRESS DISORDER IN ADOLESCENTS

The high rates of trauma in the adolescent population have led to increased examination of mental health problems related to traumatization, particularly posttraumatic stress disorder (PTSD). The National Survey of Adolescents found rates for current PTSD related to victimization of 6.3% for girls and 3.7% for boys (Kilpatrick et al., 2003). Other general population surveys have found lifetime estimates of about 9%, with a higher prevalence in girls than in boys (Breslau et al., 1991; Elklit, 2002). PTSD, like trauma exposure, is unevenly distributed in the population, and rates of PTSD among specific populations of adolescents are even higher than shown in general population studies. Figure 1.3 in this volume shows the high rates of PTSD in homeless adolescents, substance abusing teens, delinquent and incarcerated youth, and psychiatric inpatients and adolescents with severe emotional disturbance. The rates of PTSD among children and adolescents exposed to physical or sexual abuse range between 14.5% and 48% (Deblinger, McLeer, Atkins, Ralphe, & Foa, 1989; McLeer, Callaghan, Henry, & Wallen, 1994; McLeer, Deblinger, Henry, & Orvaschel, 1992; Seedat, Nyamai, Njenga, Vythilingum, & Stein, 2004).

Adolescents with PTSD also commonly meet criteria for other psychiatric disorders, including depressive disorders, externalizing disorders, and substance use disorders (Donnelly & Amaya-Jackson, 2002; Kilpatrick et al., 2003). In the largest, most representative sample of adolescents to date, three fourths of PTSD cases had at least one comorbid diagnosis (Kilpatrick et al., 2003). There is also evidence that PTSD mediates the relationship between victimization and risk of current substance use disorder and delinquent behavior (Breslau, Davis, & Schultz, 2003; Kilpatrick & Saunders, 1999). Therefore, effective treatments for PTSD potentially could not only ameliorate troublesome symptoms of PTSD but also could help to deter adolescents' engagement in risky behaviors that result in increased morbidity and mortality.

According to PTSD treatment guidelines from the International Society for Traumatic Stress Studies (Foa, Keane, & Friedman, 2000), the best-supported interventions for PTSD symptoms, and those with the largest treatment effects, are well delineated, theoretically based cognitive–behavioral approaches. Cognitive–behavioral treatments are also recommended for treatment of PTSD in children and adolescents, according to the American Academy of Child and Adolescent Psychiatry's (1998) treatment guidelines. However, the empirical support for these treatments in child and adolescent populations is more limited (J. A. Cohen, Berliner, & March, 2000). Only 10 randomized controlled trials have been conducted with traumatized child and adolescent populations, and only 1 of these included adolescents over the age of 14. In this study, King et al. (2002) compared child alone cognitive–behavioral therapy (CBT), family CBT, and wait-list controls. They found that children who received treatment were less symptomatic than controls at posttreatment with respect to PTSD symptoms and self-reports of fear and anxiety. Improvement was maintained at a 3-month follow-up. However, the additional involvement of parents did not improve clinical outcomes. No treatments for PTSD in older adolescents, to our knowledge, have been tested using a rigorous controlled design.

SPECIAL PROBLEMS AND CHALLENGES
IN TREATING ADOLESCENTS

Adolescence is a developmental stage that includes normative turmoil and anxiety about sexuality, identity issues, peer relationships. and strivings toward independence and separation from family (Erikson, 1968). Trauma can further exacerbate and disrupt the developmental process. Oppositionality and resistance toward rules and demands imposed by adults are prevalent dynamics in adolescence, and conflicts can lead to high-risk behaviors such as heavy substance use, violence, cutting and suicidality, antisocial behaviors, and risky sexual behaviors. These same behaviors can also be adverse consequences of trauma and correlates of PTSD. The maturational pressures of this period of life can create special challenges in trauma treatment, especially in regard to engagement in therapy, possibility of retraumatization, and treatment retention.

Trauma history is underidentified and posttraumatic symptoms are underdiagnosed in adolescents. Adolescents as a group, whether traumatized or not, typically are reluctant to seek mental health treatment. If they do present for treatment, they frequently present with symptoms nonspecific to trauma, such as behavioral problems and aggression, school failure, family conflict, or substance abuse. Many adolescents who present in these ways also have been traumatized and have posttraumatic reactions, but their reactions are often overlooked because they are not causing as great concern or upset to others (e.g., parents, school personnel). Standardized, routine screening for trauma exposure and posttraumatic symptoms at intake could help to more efficiently and accurately identify those adolescents who have been traumatized, have posttraumatic reactions as a result, and could potentially benefit from time-limited PTSD treatment.

As identified previously, traumatized adolescents, more so than other populations, are more likely to engage in dangerous, high-risk behaviors, such as self-injurious behaviors, substance abuse, and sexual risk taking. These are behaviors that can co-occur with more classic posttraumatic symptoms (i.e., reexperiencing symptoms, avoidance of reminders, difficulty sleeping). They can present at the outset of treatment, or they can develop or become exacerbated during the course of treatment. If not addressed and understood within a trauma framework, they can significantly interfere with treatment.

Effective approaches to engaging and retaining adolescents in mental health treatment are important discussion topics for clinicians attempting to maximize therapeutic effects. However, research findings about factors influencing positive outcomes are inconclusive, possibly because of definitional issues (e.g., definition of *dropout*), lack of standard assessment measures, and lack of consensus about pathways (Armbruster & Kazdin, 1994; Harpaz-Rotem, Leslie, & Rosenheck, 2004; Morrissey-Kane & Prinz, 1999). Few studies specifically focus on engagement and retention of adolescents in trauma treatment. A number of variables have been related generally to engagement and retention of adolescents in psychotherapy. These include referral source, geographic distance to treatment, income, gender, race or ethnicity, and the quality of therapeutic relationships and alliances. Characteristics of either the parent (e.g., emotional instability, previous psychiatric treatment, history of personal trauma) or the child (e.g., suicidality, comorbid psychopathology, externalizing disorders) may also impact completion of treatment. Parental factors and the quality of the therapeutic relationship are most consistently seen to impact treatment adherence. Parental factors are more consistently predictive than child factors. See Armbruster and Kazdin (1994), Harpaz-Rotem et al. (2004), and Morrissey-Kane and Prinz (1999).

For clinicians engaged in trauma treatment of adolescents, therapeutic alliances with both parent and child, and parental characteristics per se, may particularly impact dropout rates and success or failure of treatment. Most adolescents presenting for trauma treatment live with their family or are under the care of a guardian (in some kind of a family-like setting). Family can have a strong influence on an adolescent's treatment, even if the direct involvement of family members is minimal. Although the support of family can be important for any treatment population, it deserves particular attention for the adolescent population. To maximize the potential support of caretakers as much as possible, clinicians need to attend to family issues that either help or hinder an adolescent's participation and success in treatment. A chaotic family environment, a high level of stress due to adolescent risk behaviors, and parental depression (often seen in families of traumatized children) can all be predictive of treatment attrition. Parents are more likely to seek treatment for their traumatized adolescents because of unwelcome acting-out behaviors rather than severity of trauma-related symptoms.

In a practical sense, parental motivation becomes a crucial factor when an adolescent cannot transport him- or herself to therapy. Even if the disruptive behaviors motivate treatment-seeking by parents, there can be some resistance (conscious or unconscious) or barriers to obtaining help for the child from parents with personal trauma histories, PTSD symptoms (especially if untreated), and/or some involvement in the traumatization of their child. Past treatment failures (either parental or child) often predict lower parental expectations. Poor therapeutic relationships have been found to predict dropout more than the child's need for treatment or improvement. In regard to the clinician–child relationship, in general, female–female gender-matched patient–therapist dyads seem to yield the highest retention rates, and racially mismatched therapist–patient dyads can have a negative impact on retention. Unfortunately, there are large numbers of traumatized boys and girls from multiethnic and minority racial backgrounds and a dearth of culturally sensitive "matched" therapists trained in evidence-based trauma treatment.

THE COGNITIVE RESTRUCTURING
FOR POSTTRAUMATIC STRESS DISORDER
PROGRAM FOR ADOLESCENTS

We have done a small pilot study as an initial step to determine the feasibility and efficacy of the adult CR for PTSD treatment program (Mueser, Rosenberg, et al., 2004), described in this volume, for use with adolescents. Our treatment program follows our adult model in incorporating cognitive restructuring (CR) as the primary therapeutic component. The best-known evidence-based cognitive–behavioral treatment for PTSD in children and adolescents (J. A. Cohen, Mannarino, & Deblinger, 2006) includes an exposure component (creating a trauma narrative). Although proven efficacious for those who complete treatment, researchers have remarked that use of exposure increases the difficulty in recruiting and retaining clients in treatment. In light of the particular challenge that adolescents pose with regard to these issues, we believe that emphasizing CR rather than exposure has been an important variable in our success in achieving treatment compliance. Using a skill-based approach is especially important with multitraumatized adolescents who, while in treatment, might be living in situations in which they are in continuing danger of experiencing new traumas and retraumatization.

Modifications to the Program

Most other PTSD treatments provide guidelines for information needing to be covered in sessions but do not include specific components central to our approach (i.e., scripts, a safety plan), detailed handouts, and a troubleshooting guide for conducting CR. We have made the model as user-friendly as possible for clinicians as well as adolescent clients because there are few clinicians at this point who have expertise in cognitive–behavioral approaches to adolescent trauma treatment.

In adapting the intervention for adolescents, we did not change the basic modular components of the CR for PTSD treatment program for adults. We did use assessment measures more appropriate for adolescents, and we modified the manual and handouts, simplifying language and concepts and increasing flexibility to allow for considerable variability in cognitive maturation. For example, we changed the term *breathing retraining* to *relaxation breathing* and described it as "learning how to use your breathing to relax the tension in your body and feel calmer." The revised manual for adolescents titled *Cognitive Behavioral Therapy for PTSD in Adolescents* (Jankowski, Rosenberg, Mueser, Rosenberg, & Hamblen, 2005) has been printed, and the handouts and worksheets have been shortened and printed in the format of a softcover workbook, titled *The Coping With Stress Handbook* (Dartmouth Trauma Interventions Research Center, 2006). The adolescent model also emphasizes the teaching of CR as a skill that adolescents can own, which has the benefit of empowering them with tools for self-management. The approach focuses on the use of the therapist as "coach" and emphasizes transferability of coping skills to outside the therapy session and into the daily lives of adolescents. Adolescents are asked to practice their new skills to help reinforce learning. There is strong emphasis on helping adolescents generate their own evidence and counterevidence to challenge their thoughts. Similarly, therapists help adolescents to identify solutions to their problems themselves and think through the pros and cons of certain behaviors (e.g., in the action plan phase) rather than providing advice (e.g., being in some potentially dangerous situation). The literature on recruitment, retention, and efficacy of adolescent treatment supports these therapeutic elements (Kendall, 2000; Oetzel & Scherer, 2003).

Description of the Study

We recruited 9 adolescents through a community mental health center and 3 through a tertiary medical center clinic. We enrolled 9 girls and 3 boys with a mean age of 16 years (range: 14–18) in the study. Ten of the enrollees were Caucasian, 1 was Native American, and 1 was Hispanic. Once identified, they were evaluated for study eligibility with the assessment instruments identified in the following paragraphs. Inclusion and exclusion criteria for participation in the study were the following: (a) current *Diagnostic and Statistical Manual of Mental Disorders* (4th ed.; *DSM–IV*; American Psychiatric Association, 1994) diagnosis of PTSD, (b) no active suicidality or homicidality, (c) no psychiatric hospitalization within the past 3 months, (d) no substance dependence, and (e) parent willing to give consent and adolescent willing to provide assent for the study. Clients were paid for their participation in each assessment. Assessments were conducted pre- and posttreatment and at 3-month follow-up by an independent evaluator. Either PhD psychologists or master's level clinicians who were experienced in both CBT and treatment of PTSD conducted the therapy. Sessions were reviewed in weekly group supervision meetings. All of the clients enrolled were receiving other clinical services in addition to the present treatment, including medication management, case management, or other non-trauma-focused therapy.

Assessment Measures

Exposure to traumatic life events was assessed using a modified version of the Traumatic Life Events Questionnaire (Kubany et al., 2000). We shortened the measure and simplified the wording to better meet the needs of adolescents. The trauma exposure measure was administered only at pretreatment and assessed 16 different types of trauma. PTSD was measured with the Child Posttraumatic Symptom Scale (CPSS; Foa, Johnson, Feeny, &

Treadwell, 2001). The scale has shown good reliability and validity with a child and adolescent sample. It was administered in interview format, as recommended by the AACAP Practice Parameters (American Academy of Child and Adolescent Psychiatry, 1998) at pre- and posttreatment and at 3-month follow-up. The CPSS assesses both Criteria A1 and A2, the 17 diagnostic criteria, and impairment in different dimensions of life functioning. Depressive symptoms were measured with the Beck Depression Inventory—II (BDI; A. T. Beck et al., 1996), a 21-item self-report measure designed to assess degree of depressive symptomatology. Although it has been tested primarily with adult populations, it is also widely used clinically with adolescent populations. The Buss–Perry Physical Aggression Scale (Buss & Perry, 1992) was used to measure self-report of physical aggression. We slightly modified the wording of the scale to make it more relevant to younger populations. The Buss–Perry scale was shown to have good internal consistency, test–retest reliability, and construct validity.

Results of the Pilot Study

Of the 12 total adolescents who consented, 9 completed the program. Of the 3 noncompleters, 1 was never able to even begin treatment because of transportation barriers. One dropped out for unknown reasons. The third dropout was a 15-year-old boy who, in addition to PTSD, was also experiencing psychotic symptoms, was unable to be managed in the public schools, and was dealing with multiple stressors including medical problems. He completed five sessions with inconsistent attendance until he finally decided not to continue, reportedly because the treatment was too stressful. It is interesting, however, that his school counselor recontacted the therapist several months after he dropped out to say that the boy was interested in reengaging in PTSD treatment.

The number of types of trauma reported (out of a possible 16) ranged from 1 to 13, with a mean of 6.14. The most common types of trauma were sudden death of a close friend or loved one; someone threatening to kill or hurt them; being badly hurt by a parent, teacher, or caretaker; seeing or hearing family fighting; being beaten up by a friend or acquaintance; and being the victim of child sexual abuse. Paired sample t tests were used to test pre–post change for PTSD symptoms, depression, and aggression for the 9 completers. We had hypothesized that the treatment would result in improvements in PTSD symptoms and secondarily that improvements would occur in comorbid conditions, including depressive symptoms and aggression. There were statistically significant improvements in both PTSD symptoms and depression from baseline to posttreatment but no change in aggression from pre- to posttreatment.

Treatment gains were maintained at the 3-month follow-up for both PTSD symptoms and depression. BDI scores moved from the severe depression range at baseline to the mild depression range at posttreatment and to the minimal range at follow-up. These reductions in depressive symptoms are consistent with other studies examining use of CBT for PTSD in both adult and younger child populations (J. A. Cohen, Deblinger, Mannarino, & Steer, 2004; Resick et al., 2002). Although differences between posttreatment and 3-month follow-up for both depression and PTSD were not statistically significant, there was even greater improvement at the 3-month follow-up than at posttreatment (i.e., mean PTSD symptoms of 12.25 at posttreatment vs. 9.00 at the 3-month follow-up). Furthermore, examination of individual PTSD severity scores for the 9 adolescents completing treatment showed that everyone improved to varying degrees; not one participant got worse from pre- to posttreatment.

The results for change in PTSD diagnosis from baseline to posttreatment and follow-up showed a slightly different pattern. Four of the 9 completers (44%) no longer met criteria for PTSD at posttreatment, whereas at the 3-month follow-up, 6 of the 8 completers (75%) for whom we had 3-month follow-up data no longer met criteria for PTSD. Taken together, these findings suggest that the severity of PTSD symptoms from baseline to posttreatment decreased, but adolescents did not necessarily achieve a remission of their PTSD diagnosis immediately following treatment. Approximately 3 months later, however, they became even less symptomatic, to the point that the majority no longer met diagnostic criteria for PTSD.

Our pilot study is ongoing, and the results to date show the feasibility of implementing the CR for PTSD program in urban and multiethnic populations. Among the participants currently enrolled or having completed treatment, feedback is extremely positive. Every participant rated him- or herself as improved and as very satisfied with treatment at both posttreatment and follow-up. Feedback about the program from the referring clinicians has also been very encouraging.

CLINICAL EXAMPLE

At time of treatment, Doug was a 17-year-old boy who was living with a foster family, where he had been placed for approximately 2 years. He was a junior in high school, did fairly well academically, and played soccer and basketball for his school. He was referred for treatment for PTSD by his psychiatrist and therapist at a local community mental health center.

Trauma History and Background

Until about age 8, Doug was raised by his biological parents. They were both substance abusers and, at times, neglectful of Doug and his younger sister. Doug experienced physical abuse (by his father) and witnessed considerable violence by his father against his younger sister and mother. At the age of 8, Doug and his sister were taken into state custody because of the neglect and abuse charges against their parents. He was placed in a series of foster families until his grandparents assumed custody when he was about 12. While living with his grandparents, he experienced considerable conflict with his grandfather. The conflict escalated until it became physical, and Doug was taken out of his grandparents' home when he was in 9th grade. He was placed in a foster family with whom he was living at onset of treatment. Doug reported that his current situation was the best living arrangement he had ever had. He had not had any contact with his biological mother for many years but did have intermittent contact with his father.

Psychiatric History

Doug endorsed episodes of suicidal ideation, intent, and plan but had no history of psychiatric hospitalization. He had been diagnosed with major depressive disorder, recurrent, with depressive episodes being precipitated by various life stressors, including a breakup with a girlfriend, escalation of conflict with grandfather, and contact with father. He had been in treatment for 2 years prior to the initiation of the CR for PTSD program, on prescribed antidepressant medication and was receiving supportive therapy for depression, suicidality, anger, and maladaptive coping with various life stressors. He was referred for the program because his PTSD symptoms persisted and his earlier history of trauma had not been fully addressed in prior treatment. Prior treatment had been helpful in relieving his depressive symptoms and in helping him cope more effectively in other domains.

Posttraumatic Stress Disorder Symptoms at Treatment Initiation

Doug endorsed a moderate level of PTSD symptoms. Reexperiencing symptoms included intrusive memories, emotional and physical upset when reminded of the trauma, and occasional nightmares. Active avoidance included a desire to avoid thinking about and talking with others about his traumatic past, in part because it raised difficult feelings for him and also because he was very concerned about being the target of others' disdain for him due to his past. It was very important to Doug to "rise above my past" and "do something with myself, unlike my parents." His primary hyperarousal symptom was anger. He experienced being out of control when he would get angry and acknowledged that his anger caused him considerable problems and made him fear that "I would end up just like my father." He also had difficulty sleeping and concentrating and endorsed some hypervigilance.

Response to Treatment

Doug was easy to engage in treatment. He clearly understood that he had PTSD and acknowledged ways that it interfered in his life, with the primary problem being what he perceived as out-of-control anger that interfered in his relationships and subsequently led to guilty, unpleasant feelings about himself. He quickly connected with the therapist and attended sessions on a regular basis.

He responded well to the psychoeducation modules. Even though he had learned about PTSD from prior clinicians, he appreciated an in-depth discussion of the specific symptoms and gained a better understanding of his own reactions and problems as related to his past traumatic experiences. Doug learned breathing retraining and recognized its potential as a helpful tool to calm himself down when angry.

Doug also readily learned CR and quickly identified examples of maladaptive thinking patterns from his own life. He appeared to benefit from the stepwise process of identifying thoughts and feelings in upsetting situations (i.e., the 5 Steps of CR), coming up with evidence for and against the thoughts, challenging the thoughts when necessary, and coming up with alternative thoughts or action plans depending on the situation. He learned the skill quickly, and the therapist was therefore able to spend much of treatment addressing trauma-related thoughts and beliefs. Some of these included sayings such as "I am just like my father," "I'm never going to amount to anything because of my past," "It's not fair that I have suffered (been deprived of) so much more than most people," and "No one will like me because of all my problems." Each of these beliefs was challenged at some point during the treatment but reoccurred in multiple situations in which Doug felt threatened or rejected.

During treatment there were episodes in which Doug became extremely angry in response to different stressors in his life. These provided opportunities to use the breathing retraining and CR skills to better manage his anger. For example, about halfway through the treatment, Doug became extremely angry with a girl who declined his request to go to the prom with him. He became so upset that he verbally threatened her. The therapist spent the next session applying the 5 Steps of CR to this situation. His feeling was anger (and shame about his behavior following the anger), and his primary thought was this: "It's unfair that she's not interested in me. I deserve to have a girlfriend." The evidence used to support the thought was the following series of thoughts: "I've had so many bad things happen to me, I deserve to have something good happen. I really want a girlfriend. And, I'm a really nice guy, I treat girls well, and I'd be a great boyfriend to her." His counterevidence included this thought process: "This girl is not responsible for making up for my past. And, just because I want a girlfriend doesn't mean that I can demand it."

After weighing the evidence he came up with an alternative thought, which was "I had a lousy childhood, but this girl has a right to choose whether or not she wants to go to the prom with me. I can't make her like me." Doug also identified another thought as well, that "I'm just like my father anyway, so why not threaten her?" This thought proved to be important to challenge because it served to rationalize his threatening behavior (which he later regretted and felt shameful about).

Doug no longer met criteria for PTSD at the end of treatment or at 3-month follow-up. He showed a greater ability to cope with significant stressors during and immediately following completion of the program.

SUMMARY AND CONCLUSIONS

Trauma and posttraumatic reactions are common problems for adolescents, with PTSD frequently comorbid with other psychiatric disorders, substance use disorders, and other problems (e.g., runaway-homelessness, involvement in the juvenile justice system). Adolescents present a number of challenges to treatment providers because of their intermediate developmental stage between childhood and adulthood, the importance of establishing dual relationships with the youth and guardians, and the often chaotic family lives and multiple stresses they face. However, despite the high rate of PTSD in adolescents and their vulnerability to forces beyond their control, limited work has been done to develop treatments tailored to their special needs, with extant programs most commonly relying on exposure therapy techniques.

Relatively minor adaptations were made to the CR for PTSD program for adolescents. A pilot study with 12 adolescents was conducted. The results of the pilot indicated a high rate of retention and completion of the program. Furthermore, the adolescents demonstrated significant improvement in PTSD symptoms and depression, with 44% no longer meeting diagnostic criteria for PTSD at posttreatment, and 75% not meeting criteria at the 3-month follow-up. The results support the feasibility of the CR for PTSD program in adolescents and suggest that it may be a viable non-exposure-based intervention for PTSD in this vulnerable population.

14

DISASTER, TERRORISM, AND OTHER MASS VIOLENCE

JESSICA L. HAMBLEN, FRAN H. NORRIS, AND KIM T. MUESER

Interest in the treatment of the psychological impact of disasters and other mass traumatic experiences peaks following major events, such as the September 11, 2001, terrorist attacks; the tsunami in Southeast Asia in December 2004; and Hurricane Katrina in August 2005. The collective and acute nature of disaster creates a unique public and mental health challenge, as thousands of individuals can be affected simultaneously and in need of services. This chapter discusses some of the unique aspects of disaster and describes how we adapted our Cognitive Restructuring for Posttraumatic Stress Disorder (CR for PTSD) model to create a 10-session program designed to treat a range of psychological problems that may persist after exposure to disaster or mass violence.

DEFINING DISASTERS AND THEIR EFFECTS

Disasters are typically divided into two types, natural and human-caused. Natural disasters are events such as hurricanes, earthquakes, and fires. Human-caused events are further classified as either technological accidents involving technological or human failure, such as chemical spills and transportation accidents, or mass violence involving human intent, such as a terrorist attack. Disasters have a sudden onset and an identifiable end point, which distinguishes them from other ongoing collective traumas such as war and community violence.

Disasters are relatively common events. According to the Web site of the Federal Emergency Management Agency (http://www.fema.gov), on average 31 disasters occur annually in the United States. Estimating the number of people affected by disasters is more complicated. In the National Comorbidity Survey (NCS), 18.9% of men and 15.2% of women reported experiencing a natural disaster sometime in their lifetime (Kessler et al., 1995). The International Federation of Red Cross and Red Crescent Societies (2000) reported that in a typical year over 300,000 residents of the United States are affected by disasters and over 500 are killed.

PREVALENCE OF TRAUMA AND POSTTRAUMATIC STRESS DISORDER IN DISASTERS

The mental health impact of disasters on individuals is particularly important given that one event can affect so many people. In a comprehensive review on the effects of disaster, Norris and colleagues (Norris, 1992; Norris & Elrod, 2006) found that PTSD was the condition most often studied and observed in disaster samples, followed by depression and anxiety, respectively. Other common problems included somatic concerns and chronic problems in living. In an extensive review of PTSD prevalence following disaster, Galea, Nandi, and Vlahov (2005) concluded that the postdisaster prevalence of PTSD is 30% to 40% among direct victims, 10% to 20% among rescue workers, and 5% to 10% among the general population, including but not limited to those people in the community who suffer personal losses.

From the general literature on trauma and PTSD, we know that PTSD can have detrimental effects on people's ability to function. In the NCS, PTSD was associated with increased academic failure, marital problems, and current unemployment (Kessler, 2000). Findings are similar in disaster studies; survivors of the Oklahoma City bombing with PTSD reported significantly more impairment in occupational and social functioning than those without a disorder (North et al., 1999). In the case of disaster, these effects create a further burden because many disaster survivors are also faced with making important, pressing decisions regarding housing and resource loss. At the same time, because of the collective nature of disasters, they may also be faced with helping family members recover or may be coping with the loss of a loved one.

The effect of PTSD on disaster survivors is further exacerbated by frequent comorbidity. In the NCS, 79% of women and 88% of men with lifetime PTSD also met criteria for at least one other disorder (Kessler et al., 1995). In a study of adult survivors of the Oklahoma City bombing, 63% of survivors with PTSD related to the bombing also had a comorbid psychiatric condition, most typically depression (North et al., 1999). This is somewhat lower than epidemiological studies looking at comorbidity in individuals with lifetime PTSD from any event.

Risk and protective factors for mental health problems following disaster are generally consistent with those in the trauma field at large. Norris and colleagues (Norris, 1992; Norris & Elrod, 2006) provided a comprehensive review of these factors. Briefly, severity of exposure is consistently related to distress, with those most directly impacted or having the greatest level of exposure faring worse than those less directly or minimally exposed. Being female, middle-aged, or a member of an ethnic minority group also puts one at risk of worse outcomes. Disaster survivors who come from lower socio-economic backgrounds also have poorer mental health functioning, as do those with predisaster mental health problems. One of the most important factors to consider is social support, which has been shown to buffer the negative effects of disaster. Disaster survivors with high perceived social support function better relative to those with low perceived social support (Norris, 1992; Norris & Elrod, 2006).

SPECIAL PROBLEMS AND CHALLENGES IN TREATING DISASTER SURVIVORS

By definition, a disaster affects many people simultaneously, often resulting in a sudden need for mental health services that may surpass what local providers can manage. Even if providers could absorb the need, many lack the expertise to provide state-of-the-art trauma services to survivors. There are several immediate challenges, two of which are identifying the evidence-based trauma treatments for disaster survivors and determining how best to train therapists in these practices. A third challenge is reducing barriers to treatment acceptance for survivors. Finally, unlike treatment for individual trauma, treatment for disaster is typically delivered through a community response, which poses unique systems issues around implementation and referral.

Identifying Evidence-Based Treatments for Prolonged Disaster Distress

Limited research has examined treatment for prolonged disaster-related distress. This may be due in part to the difficulty conducting research in the conditions that accompany disasters, but it may also be because few treatments have been developed for postdisaster distress. A few uncontrolled studies have evaluated treatment for disaster survivors with PTSD (Basoglu, Livanou, & Salcioglu, 2003; Basoglu, Livanou, Salcioglu, & Kalender, 2003; Gillespie, Duffy, Hackman, & Clark, 2002). Gillespie et al. (2002) studied the effectiveness of cognitive–behavioral therapy in 91 survivors of a bombing in Northern Ireland 10 months postbombing. All survivors had PTSD related to the bombing. After treatment, the survivors had significant improvement in PTSD, depression, and general health.

Only two randomized controlled trials have evaluated treatments for disaster survivors with PTSD. Basoglu and colleagues conducted two separate investigations of earthquake survivors with PTSD more than 2 years after an earthquake. In the first study, participants were randomly assigned to either a single session of behavioral treatment that included instructions for self-exposure, or to a wait-list control (Basoglu, Salcioglu, Livanou, & Acar, 2005). In the second study, the single session behavioral treatment was enhanced by the addition of an earthquake simulator, with survivors randomly assigned to the behavioral treatment or to repeated assessment (Basoglu, Salcioglu, & Livanou, 2007). In both studies, behavioral treatment was superior on all measures at posttreatment and 1- to 2-year follow-up, with effect sizes for PTSD remarkably high: 1.7 and 2.6, respectively.

The most effective evidence-based psychological treatment for PTSD is CBT, including both exposure therapy and cognitive restructuring (CR; Bisson & Andrew, 2007; Bradley et al., 2005). CBT is also effective for disorders commonly comorbid with PTSD, including depression (Gloaguen, Cottraux, Cucherat, & Blackburn, 1998), generalized anxiety disorder (Borkovec & Whisman, 1996), and panic disorder (Barlow & Craske, 1994). Thus, there is strong support for applying cognitive–behavioral interventions for the most common postdisaster diagnoses.

Training Community-Based Clinicians to Deliver Evidence-Based Treatments

A few studies have evaluated whether community based clinicians can be trained to effectively deliver evidence-based psychosocial treatments. Rape crisis counselors, community mental health clinicians, and school-based counselors have been shown to be able to learn specific cognitive–behavioral interventions and to provide them with good outcome (Foa et al., 2005; Gillespie et al., 2002; B. Stein et al., 2003).

There are several important differences in the training that would be required to respond to a major disaster. The first is therapist selection; in each of these studies researchers worked with clinicians from a single agency. A second difference is number of therapists; in each of these studies there were relatively few therapists to train and supervise. Although considerable time was spent in training and supervision in the Foa study, this would not be feasible following a major disaster. Effective response to a disaster could require the training of more clinicians from different agencies in less time and with less intensive supervision.

Following the September 11, 2001, terrorist attacks, researchers at Columbia University in New York trained 104 frontline clinicians, from many different agencies, to deliver an evidence-based treatment for PTSD (Marshall, Amsel, Neria, & Jung Suh, 2006). The clinicians received a 2-day training in prolonged exposure for PTSD. Results from the pretraining assessment indicated that therapists assessed exposure therapy favorably, but they felt that they lacked the skill to adequately deliver the exposure treatment. No posttraining data were available.

We conducted a 2-day training on our adapted CR for PTSD manual for postdisaster with 104 therapists following Hurricane Katrina. Results indicate that the training was effective, and therapists showed significant improvements in their ratings of the importance of various elements of the program, their knowledge and understanding of those elements, and their confidence that they could use them effectively.

Although data are preliminary, these studies indicate that it may be possible to train community-based clinicians in manualized interventions for postdisaster psychological distress. Both in New York and Baton Rouge, a substantial number of therapists were recruited for the trainings, suggesting that they were open to and interested in learning and delivering the interventions. Data from the Baton Rouge training further suggest that the training prepared therapists to implement the interventions as well.

Implementation and Referral

Treatments for postdisaster distress are developed not merely for the purpose of helping individuals in need but also for fostering the recovery of whole communities. One of the key challenges, then, is developing mechanisms for delivering and disseminating new treatments rapidly and on a large scale. Numerous problems interfere with the timely or effective delivery of disaster mental health services. Well-meaning volunteers and experts can actually add to the chaos in disaster-stricken settings (Lanou, 1993; Norris et al., 2006; Sitterle & Gurwich, 1998). A variety of professionals aggressively market treatments and interventions, and local planners may not have the experience or background to know whom to trust or believe. Evidence-based approaches, such as CBT, compete with other approaches for the attention of service planners. Postdisaster service delivery is predictably impaired by turf boundaries, failure of organizations to work together, communication gaps, confusion, the emotionally stressful nature of disaster work, ambivalence and suspicions regarding outsiders, funding gaps, limited resources, and survivor stigma (Canterbury & Yule, 1999; Lanou, 1993; Norris, Watson, Hamblen,

& Pfefferbaum, 2005). Ideally, the delivery of treatments should be embedded in a mental health system that has the capacity to find and reach out to people in need and make credible services accessible to them (Hodgkinson & Stewart, 1998).

The need for effective mechanisms for outreach, screening, and referral is especially important for implementing new treatment programs after disasters (National Institute of Mental Health, 2002; Pfammatter, Junghan, & Brenner, 2006). Without them, good treatments and good providers will be underutilized. Screening and referral tools have to be short, easy to use, and simple to score, yet sensitive to treatment need. An example of this is the SPRINT-E (Norris et al., 2006), which was developed to identify people in crisis counseling who might benefit from more intensive services. The SPRINT-E was used in New York and in Baton Rouge as a screen for post-disaster treatment need.

Barriers to Treatment Acceptance

In many cases, disaster survivors may not be aware of services. Following the September 11, 2001, terrorist attacks, Project Liberty launched an extensive $9 million media campaign to inform residents of New York State about available services. Even then, just over half of New Yorkers said they were aware of the Project Liberty (Stuber & Galea, 2005). In most cases media advertising is unaffordable, and therefore getting the word out is even more difficult.

Even if survivors are aware and in need of services, many choose not to access services. Data from Project Liberty indicate that 71% of crisis counseling recipients who were determined to need treatment accepted a referral (Norris et al., 2006). No data were available to determine how many of these individuals went on to access these services. Referral acceptance was substantially lower for a group of male utility disaster workers referred for symptoms related to the September 11 attacks. Only 48% chose to accept referral (Jayasinghe, Giosan, Difende, Spielman, & Robin, 2006), and of those, less than half attended the first session, despite the fact that the treatment was confidential, free, and could be accessed during or after work hours. In both studies individuals with more severe symptoms were more likely to accept a referral.

Stuber and Galea (2005) evaluated barriers to care in a general sample of over 2,700 adults from the Greater New York Metropolitan area, conducted 6 months after September 11. Sixty-four percent of people with probable PTSD or depression did not seek mental health services. Of those who did seek help, the vast majority (86%) had a previous connection to mental health, having received mental health services in the prior 6 months. The most common reason for not seeking services was that other people needed the services more than themselves (58%), but 42% said they did not have time, and 39% indicated they lacked the money. Stigma, typically considered a major barrier to help seeking overall, was reported by 27% of individuals as a barrier. Only 17% of people said they lacked the knowledge about how to get help.

Overall, there appear to be both systems-level and individual-level barriers to the delivery of disaster mental health services. Systems need to work together to create a feasible delivery mechanism. Even services that are free, confidential, and easy to access are underutilized. Finding ways to increase the acceptability of these services will be critical for any postdisaster intervention.

STRATEGIES AND ADAPTATIONS OF COGNITIVE–BEHAVIORAL THERAPY IN THE POSTDISASTER CONTEXT

As discussed previously, following the September 11 terrorist attacks, New York received a federally funded Crisis Counseling Grant and established Project Liberty to address short-term mental health needs of communities affected by disasters through public education, outreach, and crisis counseling. Project Liberty recognized the constraints of the model and advocated for a continuum of care in which a subset of individuals experiencing more severe reactions could receive longer term, evidenced-informed interventions. Hamblen, Gibson, Mueser, and Norris (2006) developed CBT for Postdisaster Distress (originally called the Brief Intervention for Continuing Postdisaster Distress) to meet this need. Subsequently the intervention was used in Florida after the 2004 hurricanes and in Baton Rouge following Hurricane Katrina. Evaluation was minimal in the first pilots of the approach, but preliminary results were promising (Donahue et al., 2006; Hamblen & Norris, 2007). More recent data from the Katrina evaluation suggest the intervention resulted in a clinically significant reduction in postdisaster distress (Hamblen et al., in press).

Development of the Intervention

Several major considerations went into the development of the intervention. The intervention had to be informed by the evidence, consistent with the crisis counseling program guidelines, feasible to deliver, and acceptable to those individuals accessing the service.

As reviewed previously, CBT is an effective treatment for a range of disorders common after disaster. Several studies have compared the effects of CR with those of exposure, with most finding comparable benefit (Marks et al., 1998; Resick et al., 2002). One possible explanation for the robust outcomes associated with CR is that they emphasize the teaching of skills that can be used across a range of settings or problems. The identification of problematic thinking patterns and modification of those patterns can have a positive impact on a range of negative feelings and behaviors. This skill can just as easily be used to challenge catastrophic thoughts as to challenge depressed or angry thoughts. If individuals can be taught to use these skills for a variety of difficult emotions in a variety of settings, it may help them learn to generalize the skills and integrate them still further. Thus, we decided to rely on CR, which can then applied to a range of postdisaster distress symptoms, including PTSD, depression, anxiety, anger, and guilt.

Although many different cognitive–behavioral interventions are available, the CR for PTSD program described in this book was especially well-suited to this purpose. Because this program was originally developed for people with severe mental illness and PTSD, considerable effort had been applied to determining how to make an intellectually challenging concept as basic and understandable as possible.

We elected to gear CBT for Postdisaster Distress toward distress, rather than PTSD or another specific psychiatric disorder for several reasons. First, we believe that the focus on distress increases acceptability. Although disaster survivors with PTSD or another disorder could certainly benefit from the intervention, focusing on distress could make the program more broadly accessible to survivors who do not meet criteria for a disorder or who would be less inclined to participate in psychiatric treatment but willing to try a skills-based intervention. Second, no formal diagnostic assessment was necessary, only the ascertainment of psychological distress. Third, the intervention was consistent with crisis counseling guidelines so that individuals could be referred from the crisis counseling program into the intervention. Finally, focusing on one intervention provided to anyone in distress substantially decreased the training needs of providers.

Modifications to the Model

In adapting the program to the disaster context, several modifications were necessary. For example, we needed to significantly expand the psychoeducation module. In addition to providing information about PTSD and common negative feelings associated with trauma exposure, we included information on depression, anxiety, alcohol and substance use, grief and bereavement, sleep problems, and functioning difficulties. We also added a behavioral activation component (i.e., pleasant activities scheduling) to target the high rates of depression. Both breathing retraining and activities scheduling were taught as coping skills for immediate use to target symptoms of anxiety and depression. No major changes were made to the CR component of the intervention. Table 14.1 provides a summary of the session num-

TABLE 14.1
Outline of Cognitive–Behavioral Therapy for Postdisaster Distress
Program Modules, Estimated Time, and Session Numbers

Component	Approximate time (minutes)	Session no.
Orientation to program	10	1
Education on postdisaster distress	25–55	1
Breathing retraining	10	2
Pleasant activity scheduling	25	2
Rationale for cognitive restructuring	15	3
Identification of thoughts and feelings	20	3
Problematic thinking styles	15	4
Five steps of cognitive restructuring	20	4
Cognitive restructuring practice	300 (i.e., 5 hours)	5–9
Progress and treatment review	25	10
Aftercare plan/termination	20	10

bers in which the different components of the program are covered. In addition to these core modifications, other changes were made to improve feasibility and implementation in postdisaster settings. The maximum number of sessions was dropped from 16 to 10.

A client workbook was also developed that contains session summaries and practice exercises, written at a seventh-grade reading level. The workbook is organized similarly to a self-help guidebook so that survivors can refer back to information at a later time. Completed practice exercises serve as further support as survivors can often work through new upsetting situations by applying strategies that they have used to successfully challenge past situations.

Strategies for Dealing With Postdisaster Circumstances

Real world client crises such a housing, employment, or interpersonal problems can easily derail manualized interventions. If therapists allow crises to become the focus of the sessions, they can take considerable time away from the necessary teaching and practicing of core skills. Typically when using a structured intervention the goal is to either address these issues within the context of the manual or to address them briefly at the beginning or end of a session. When the CR for PTSD Program was developed for persons with severe mental illness, all clients had case managers who could assist clients with real world crises (Mueser, Rosenberg, et al., 2004).

In the disaster context, the therapist may be the sole provider and the likelihood of housing- or employment-related crises may be exacerbated by the property loss that can be a byproduct of a disaster. Many survivors are focused on pressing issues such as where they are going to live, how they are going to support themselves, and how to make insurance claims. In some circumstances these issues are better addressed in advance of the program, and therapists may want to consider delaying therapy. In cases where therapy is initiated, as part of the consent process therapists may want to be specific about which services they will be able to deliver and which go beyond their scope of work. We recommend having this discussion in advance so that if a crisis does arise therapists can remind survivors that their role is to teach the skills that will help them tolerate the problems, rather than to solve the immediate crisis. In many situations, specific agencies provide case management after the disaster and therapists may want to make a referral early in the process to prevent these issues from taking away from the therapy.

A second issue that is unique to the delivery of this intervention in the disaster context is that the therapists delivering it have typically experienced the disaster themselves. In traditional PTSD treatment, therapists may have experienced similar past traumatic events as their clients, such as physical or sexual abuse. However, there are clear distinctions between the two events. In disaster treatments, therapists are typically from the community where the disaster took place and therefore have recently experienced the exact same event. In conducting trainings and providing case consultation to therapists in CBT for Postdisaster Distress, it is evident that this collective experience has an impact on the therapist and also on the therapy.

In training role plays and in discussing cases, therapists often remark that survivors bring up accurate rather than maladaptive thoughts. For example, typical client thoughts such as "tall building, subways, or airplanes are unsafe" were often considered by therapists to be accurate beliefs after the September 11 attacks. In Florida after the hurricane, many therapists believed that the thoughts "A Category 4 hurricane will hit in Florida this year and I won't be able to handle it" and "My home will never be repaired" were accurate thoughts. And, in Baton Rouge, some therapists believed the thoughts "The levee breach was deliberate," "I can't provide for my family," and "I will never be a part of the community" were accurate after Hurricane Katrina.

There are several problems that arise when therapists' own beliefs interfere with teaching CR process. First, therapists are more likely to skip going through the steps of CR and may move straight to developing a plan for handling the situation. For example, rather than challenging the thought that a storm is coming, they may help survivors prepare for the storm. Second, even if they work through the steps it is more difficult for them to use Socratic questioning to elicit evidence against the thought because they themselves struggle to identify such evidence. Third, therapists have more difficulty moving from the specific (and potentially accurate thought) to the deeper, core belief that may be maladaptive. For example, therapists may be so convinced that the thought "Another storm is coming" is accurate that they miss the chance to explore the situation and discover the core belief "I cannot protect my family," or "It's my fault we were stranded, I should have evacuated sooner." In each of these cases, therapists miss the opportunity to successfully challenge maladaptive thoughts and replace them with more accurate ones, thereby reducing distress. Through training and supervision, therapists can learn to identify when their own beliefs may be hindering the process and can learn to allow the teaching of CR to unfold in steps.

CLINICAL EXAMPLE

Client Background and Presenting Problems

Shawna was a 46-year-old woman who evacuated her home following Hurricane Katrina. She and her husband permanently relocated several hours away from where they had been living. Prior to the hurricane, Shawna and her husband lived close to her elderly parents who still resided in the home she grew up in. She had two grown children who lived independently and was employed as a nurse.

Shawna and her husband chose to evacuate their home early on in the disaster response. She called her parents, explained the situation, and encouraged them to evacuate as well. Shawna's father said that her mother was too sick to move and that they planned on remaining in the house. She offered many times to help with her mother, but her father refused because he did not want to "abandon" his home and his belongings. He stated, "We'll be fine. We have always been fine before. Your mother is comfortable here."

Shawna's home and belongings were destroyed. Her parents' home flooded and her father was not strong enough to physically move her mother to the second floor above the water line. Her mother drowned in the house. Shawna's father was air-lifted out a few days later. Shawna stated that she had not been back to her parents' home since her mother's death. The house was going to be torn down, and Shawna believed that she should go back to the house to see if anything was salvageable but was afraid to go because she would "lose it."

Shawna reported feeling "sad and hopeless" about the future, "like nothing will ever be okay again." She experienced overwhelming feelings of shame and guilt that she had not made her parents evacuate and that she was responsible for the death of her mother. Shawna reported that she could not stop imagining what it was like for her mother to drown. Although she was able to focus her attention at work, when she came home she could not stop thinking about her mother. Shawna was not sleeping well and had frequent nightmares about the drowning.

Challenges Encountered During Treatment

Because Shawna had been forced to relocate, she lacked the social support from her community that other trauma survivors are more typically able to access. With her mother gone, Shawna had no one other than her husband for support. She no longer lived close to her friends or church, which had been her main sources of support before the hurricane.

Other challenges that faced Shawna were secondary stressors related to the disaster. As with many disaster survivors, Shawna faced financial difficulties, getting used to a new environment, finding a new job, and coping with the loss of a loved one. She had to deal with funeral arrangements for her mother and with finding her father an appropriate place to live.

A central treatment challenge for Shawna was helping her to evaluate the thought that it was her fault that her mother had died. In many cases, guilt serves a protective function. At times it can be easier to hold oneself responsible than to accept that an event was either someone else's fault or, worse, just an accident. This was the case with Shawna, who would rather blame herself than her parents and who could not accept that it was just an unforeseen accident. As a result, it was difficult to challenge the thought that she was responsible for her mother's death.

Protocol Adaptations Used to Deal With Problems

The pleasant activity scheduling introduced into CBT for Postdisaster Distress is one way to address the lack of social support common after disaster. Therapists can help clients select activities designed to improve social connectedness. For example, Shawna made a plan to find a new church and attended a different service each week until she found a church she wanted to join. Because her tendency to stay home and isolate was beginning to have a negative impact on her marriage, another pleasant activity that Shawna scheduled was one dinner out each week with her husband.

Many of the secondary stressors that Shawna experienced were resolved prior to the initiation of therapy. Specifically, she had already relocated and found new employment. An important unresolved issue was the pressure Shawna felt to return to her parents' home. This issue was addressed through the CR in several stages. First, the therapist helped Shawna to challenge the thought "I have to go to my parents' home right away" and replace it with the more accurate thought "I would like to go to my parents' home when I am ready." Next the therapist helped Shawna carefully examine her thought "I will lose it if I go to my parents' home," which she concluded was not supported by the evidence, and replaced it with the new thought "If I go to my parents' home and become overwhelmed, I can always leave and come back another day." Last, the therapist helped Shawna challenge her thought "I need to be strong at my parents' house," which she ended up replacing with "However I respond at my parents' house is okay. It is normal to be upset."

The third challenge addressed in the therapy was Shawna's core belief that she was responsible for the death of her mother. This belief was resistant to change as the guilt was in some ways protective against other emotions including anger and anxiety. The sample dialogue below illustrates how the self-blame was challenged in the treatment process, and how the associated guilt was lessened. What follows is a segment of Shawna's CR to the thought "It's my fault my mother died."

Therapist: So the situation you say is most upsetting for you is thinking about the death of your mother. You said that when you think about her you feel guilty and the thought is that it's your fault your mother died.

Client: Yes, I mean I know I did not physically kill her, but it is because of me that she died. It's my fault. I should have done more to make my parents leave.

Therapist: Okay, so the upsetting situation is thinking about your mother. The feeling is guilt and the thought is that it is your fault that your mother died. Let's look for evidence for and against the thought. Let's start with the things that support the thought. What makes you think that?

Client: Well, like I said, I should have done more to prevent it. I could have gone over there and demanded that they come with us.

Therapist: Okay. What else could you have done?

Client: I could have refused to go without them.

Therapist: Okay, anything else?

Client: I don't know. [*pause*] I should have made them understand how important it was to leave. I should have told them that the house is not more important than they are. I really should have forced them to leave.

Therapist: It sounds like you really felt responsible for them.

Client: Yes. They couldn't take care of themselves. I bought their groceries, took them on errands. How could I think they could stay?

Therapist: So, there are lots of reasons why you think it was your fault.

Client: Yes.

Therapist: Now what about evidence against the thought? What things can you think of to show that it was not your fault?

Client:	Well, my husband always tells me to remember that it was the hurricane that was responsible—not me.
Therapist:	Okay. What else?
Client:	I should have gone over there and demanded that they come with us.
Therapist:	Do you think that would have done any good?
Client:	I don't know. My parents can be very stubborn. They are very set in their ways and hated to change their routines. Once my father makes up his mind about something, he hates to back down. Still and all, I might have been able to convince them.
Therapist:	As you think about all the things you just told me about your parents, do you believe it's likely that he would have agreed to go with you if you had gone to their house?
Client:	Not really likely, but not impossible. But maybe I would have stayed there with them. If my husband and I had stayed we could have moved my mother upstairs. She would still be alive.
Therapist:	Why didn't you stay?
Client:	Because he insisted that we leave and because I did not think it was going to turn out like this. We left because we figured we might lose power or that the house could be damaged. Our house seemed to be more likely to be damaged than my parents' from all the warnings on the radio and TV. And really, we never thought anyone would be killed, more like inconvenienced.
Therapist:	So you would not have left them if you knew what you know now.
Client:	Of course not!
Therapist:	Could you have known? Did other people you spoke to know?
Client:	I really don't think so. It was really hard to know what to believe then, and most people didn't take it really seriously until it was too late.
Therapist:	Do you ever think about what happened to your mother in other ways, besides blaming yourself for what happened to her during the storm?
Client:	Usually not. I just feel that I am to blame.
Therapist:	How about right now? Who or what else do you think could have changed the final outcome?

Client:	A lot of people really could have. My dad could have listened and believed me. Their neighbors could have checked on them. The police could have gone from house to house sooner.
Therapist:	What about your husband? Did he know about leaving your parents?
Client:	Yes. He thought they should come with us, but he could not talk any sense into them either.
Therapist:	So, is it his fault?
Client:	Of course not. They aren't his parents. It was my responsibility.
Therapist:	What makes it your responsibility?
Client:	Well, since my brother and sister left, I have been their primary caregiver.
Therapist:	Did your parents run their own lives before the storm? Did they get easily confused or not understand things?
Client:	No. They were both sharp. It's just that my mother could not get around and my father did not like to do the shopping. So, I would get their groceries, run errands, sometimes I would cook.
Therapist:	But they understood what was going on when Katrina hit and they chose to stay anyway?
Client:	Yeah, I guess they did.
Therapist:	So, do you think your parents should share the responsibility?
Client:	Of course not. They would never have chosen to stay if they knew what was going to happen.
Therapist:	And we already discussed that neither you, nor your husband, nor most anyone really understood what was going to happen. Isn't that true?
Client:	Yes, that is true.
Therapist:	So let me ask you again, to what extent was your mother's death your fault? When you look at the evidence you came up with for and against the thought, do you think the evidence supports the thought that it is your fault or does not support the thought? Or, let me put it another way, how much do you think that you are to blame for what happened?
Client:	[crying slightly] I guess I'm not completely to blame, but I do have some guilt that I did not do more.

Therapist:	Okay. Now, can you come up with a thought that is more supported by the evidence than the thought that it's your fault that your mother died?
Client:	I still feel somewhat to blame, but I think that really a lot of people could have helped. A lot of people could have acted differently and she would still be alive. And a lot of what happened was just plain bad luck.
Therapist:	Okay, so it seems to you now that it is not completely your fault?
Client:	Yes.
Therapist:	So what alternative thoughts do you have now?
Client:	That I would not have left my mother to die if I had known. That many other people have some responsibility, but no one made this happen. The storm overwhelmed and confused us all until it was too late to help some people.
Therapist:	Okay, let's imagine that you start thinking about your mother and feeling guilty. Instead of telling yourself that it is your fault, do you think that you might replace that idea with these other thoughts and explanations?
Client:	I think so. I'll have to try and see what happens when I'm feeling bad.

Outcome

Over the next few weeks Shawna was able to make progress replacing her old thought with the new, more accurate one. She was then able to think about her mother without feeling overwhelmingly guilty. As part of an action plan, she decided to return to her parents' house with a friend. She did get emotional while there but did not "lose it" as she had feared. Shawna looked around, saved a few things, and then said good-bye to the house.

Shawna's mood improved significantly. She reported feeling happier and more connected with her friends and family. Her involvement in her church expanded as well. At the end of treatment Shawna reported was that she was now able to remember some of the happy times she had with her mother instead of being so focused on her mother's last moments.

SUMMARY AND CONCLUSIONS

CBT for Postdisaster Distress extends the CR for PTSD Program to individuals experiencing distress resulting from disaster. By adding treatment components suitable for common postdisaster disorders, the program could be adapted to disaster survivors who may not have identified themselves as being in need of treatment, but who would acknowledge a need for support. CR remains at the core of the intervention as disaster survivors identify upsetting situations and learn to modify inaccurate beliefs or develop plans for managing the situation.

The modified program has important advantages for the postdisaster context. Because the intervention targets a range of clinical problems, a single training in CBT for Postdisaster Distress can serve as initial preparation for clinicians who will be seeing survivors with varying symptoms and experiences. In addition, the nonclinical, skills-based focus may reduce the stigma surrounding mental health treatment. The improved acceptability of the intervention should also increase the likelihood that disaster survivors will access the intervention.

15

MINORITY AND REFUGEE CLIENTS

LISA R. FORTUNA

This chapter focuses on considerations for the delivery of the Cognitive Restructuring for Posttraumatic Stress Disorder (CR for PTSD) program to culturally diverse clients, including minority and refugee communities. Given the multiple cultures and the diversity of social contexts that a clinician can encounter, this chapter cannot provide an exhaustive review of all possible recommendations. We present some insights and approaches from clinical practice and research with minority populations of diverse backgrounds and with a variety of traumatic circumstances (Lu et al., 2009). The topics considered in this chapter for the delivery of the CR for PTSD program in multicultural populations include the following: engagement in treatment, language barriers, variations in PTSD symptom expression, clinical and psychosocial assessment, transportability and outreach to underserved communities, and training issues.

Large nationally representative epidemiological studies have reported lifetime PTSD prevalence rates in the United States ranging from 7% to 12% (Alim et al., 2006; Kessler & Zhao, 1999). However, none of these studies has included rates specifically for African American, Latino, Asian, or other major minority groups in the United States. Recent studies suggest that there may be noteworthy differences in the rates of PTSD in the United States by race and ethnicity, with socioeconomic status and the types and frequency of related traumatic experiences affecting these rates (Alim et al., 2006; Fortuna, Porche, & Alegria, 2008). Although exposure to traumatic events is ubiquitous in the United States, different ethnic or racial groups may vary in the most common types of experienced traumas. For example, many immigrant groups have experienced political violence (Bauer, Rodriguez, Quiroga, & Flores-Ortiz, 2000; Fortuna et al., 2008; Hjern, Angel, & Jeppson, 1998; Jaycox et al., 2002; Martin-Baro & Canas, 1989), although African Americans in the United States report high rates of witnessed and experienced community violence and personal assaults compared with the rates reported by their non-Latino White counterparts (Alim et al., 2006). Similar to patterns in the general population (Kessler et al., 1995), age and gender also play a role in rates of PTSD among minority populations, with women and younger age groups (youth and young adults) demonstrating higher rates of PTSD than men or older age groups (Breslau et al., 1997).

Understanding potential variations by race and ethnicity in trauma exposure and risk of PSTD may provide important insights into specific vulnerabilities and expressions of illness that could inform treatment delivery. For example, research has found that the nature of the trauma (e.g., chronic vs. disaster vs. personal assault), severity, frequency, and feelings of helplessness associated with traumatic experiences can all have an impact on the development of PTSD (Fox, Burns, Popovich, & Ilg, 2001; Montoya et al., 1995). Some research has shown an association between risk of developing PTSD and social position, socioeconomic status, and race. For example, Loo (1994) found that adverse race-related events during military service, including experienced discrimination, were a risk factor for PTSD in Asian American Vietnam veterans. Rheingold et al. (2004) also found an effect of cumulative loss and low social support in the context of traumatic experiences as related to the development of PTSD in minority youth. Similarly, Stevens et al. (2005) found that psychosocial variables such as low family support, substance abuse, and other risk behaviors differentiated singly and multiply victimized minority youth. These studies point to the importance of considering multiple and chronic stressors in assessing posttraumatic responses. Ethnic racial minorities and refugees meet the criteria as vulnerable populations in this regard, as evidenced by potentially additive risk factors such as immigration, racism, poverty, and chronic community violence, especially in urban settings where a large concentration of minority individuals live.

CHALLENGES ASSOCIATED WITH POSTTRAUMATIC STRESS DISORDER DIAGNOSIS AND TREATMENT IN DIVERSE POPULATIONS

Studies have suggested that psychological responses to trauma, such as fear; numbing; arousal; intrusive memories; and avoidance of people, places, or things that are reminders of the traumatic event, tend to be present in individuals across race and ethnicity (Charney & Keane, 2007; Clear, Vincent, & Harris, 2006). However, social stressors tied to race and ethnicities are important for understanding illness presentation and for facilitating the engagement of clients in treatment. For example, the therapist needs to consider that experiences of everyday racism and discrimination may be among the client's most salient psychosocial stressors, adding meaningfully to his or her psychological distress. Assessment and psychoeducation go hand in hand in that therapists need to be open to considering the stressful experiences of minorities and immigrants in the United States and prepared to be supportive and explore with clients how these stressors may be related to their experiences of trauma and PTSD.

As described in other chapters, tailoring therapy to the client's own circumstances is an integral part of implementing the CR for PTSD program. For racial and ethnic minorities, the therapist may need to consider things like the impact of immigration-related separations and losses on clients' distress. Some clients may find it critical to include family members in some of the treatment sessions if they are members of a cultural group that is traditionally more collectivist or family oriented. Other clients may initially present with physical complaints as the primary means of expressing psychological distress, as somatic presentations have been found to be higher among some racial and ethnic minorities, including Latinos and Asians (Dansky et al., 1996; Fox et al., 2001). To accommodate these differences, the therapist should consider possible adaptations to the CR for PTSD program, such as paying particular attention and monitoring to somatic complaints and including family members in some or all sessions.

SPECIAL NEEDS OF IMMIGRANT POPULATIONS

It is worth considering the potential needs of immigrant and refugee populations more specifically, including the added effects of immigration exit circumstances and their potential mental health consequences in terms of lost social supports and status, acculturative stress, and displacement. For example, guilt and shame about leaving others behind or the added fear of legal status and discrimination can all add anxiety and fear that interact with core

PTSD symptoms and related cognitions. One male client of Latino ancestry with a history of sexual abuse initiated his treatment for traumatic stress with complaints of chronic headaches and poor digestion. He was also distressed by his fatigue, which had affected his functioning as a husband and provider, both important social roles for him. Further discussion resulted in the client sharing that he felt discriminated against by employers because he was a Mexican immigrant. He had developed panic attacks and other symptoms of hyperarousal whenever he went to work. Even though he had legal papers to be in the United States, he began to fear he would be deported and separated from his children because he thought his employers would falsely report him to immigration officials. These were all meaningful difficulties and stressors in their own right but were also an entry to understanding the client's distress and for discussing PTSD-related symptoms and cognitions and how they were related to his everyday experiences. With the help of the therapist he was able to understand how thoughts like "I will never be safe" were related to his traumatic experiences, were often triggered by current stressors, and contributed to his emotional and physical symptoms but could be effectively challenged and replaced with more helpful thoughts and actions.

When providing treatment, the therapist needs to listen for themes relevant to trauma and immigration, which may underlie strong feelings ranging from pervasive anxiety or depression to guilt and despair. Types of political and other violence exposure also vary and have a differential impact on mental health needs and services use among specific immigrant subgroups. For individuals with exposure to political violence, PTSD symptoms and cognitions may vary depending on the client's level of exposure and the nature of the traumatic event (e.g., witnessing vs. experiencing violence or torture; Alim et al., 2006; Norris, 1992). Similarly, differences in experiences in the United States (e.g., socioeconomic, social status, structure of social supports) may influence or present additive stressors for certain groups.

Eisenman et al. (2003) found that up to 54% of immigrants in clinical samples have a history of political violence. In turn, political violence exposure is associated with psychiatric disorders, especially PTSD, other anxiety disorders, and depression (Eisenman et al., 2003; Fox et al., 2001; Jaycox et al., 2002; Martin-Baro & Canas, 1989; McCloskey, Southwick, Fernandez-Esquer, & Locke, 1995; Pedersen, 2002; Rousseau & Drapeau, 2004; Sabin, Cardozo, Nackerud, Kaiser, & Varese, 2003). Eisenman et al. (2003) also found that Latino clients in primary care settings reporting exposure to political violence had greater chronic pain, impaired physical functioning, and diminished health-related quality of life. The combination of exposure to violence, lack of screening by providers, and less access to health care has the potential to affect overall health, the detection of PTSD, and access to treatments among immigrant populations (Barcelona de Mendoza, 2001; Bauer et al., 2000; Elliot, Quinless, & Parietti, 2000).

Hinton et al. (2005b) described the phenomenon of neck-focused panic attacks among Cambodian refugees with histories of severe trauma such as physical torture and witnessing massacres. In a neck-focused panic attack, the individual fears death from rupture of the neck vessels, with prominent symptoms including a sore neck (*rooy gâ*), head symptoms (e.g., headache, tinnitus, blurry vision, dizziness), and general symptoms of autonomic arousal (e.g., cold extremities, palpitations, shortness of breath). The examples described here support the importance of screening for PTSD and political violence exposure, types of exposure, and both physical and psychological symptoms, as well as physical symptoms to evaluate treatment effectiveness.

There are at least three things to consider in addressing the issue of clients presenting with somatic symptoms potentially related to posttraumatic distress: (a) all clients who present for treatment with chronic somatic symptoms should be screened for history of trauma, including but not limited to political violence; (b) a full medical evaluation should be conducted, given that aside from psychosomatic symptoms related to PTSD, chronic medical conditions such as diabetes and heart disease are associated with exposure to severe or chronic stress; and (c) the use of health-related quality of life and daily functioning measures in monitoring treatment response should be considered in addition to measures of core PTSD symptoms and depression. The SF-36, derived from the Medical Outcomes Study, has been used in immigrant populations for this purpose (Eisenman et al., 2003; Stewart et al., 1989).

Because the expression of PTSD can vary, the question has been raised as to whether the symptom criteria for the diagnosis of PTSD are biased toward traditional Western expressions of distress and are not applicable cross-culturally (Cervantes, Padilla, & De Snyder, 1989; Marsella, Friedman, Gerrity, & Scurfield, 1996). Even with the current *Diagnostic and Statistical Manual of Mental Disorders* (4th ed.; *DSM–IV*; American Psychiatric Association, 1994) criteria for the diagnosis of PTSD, the disorder has often been noted to have a very heterogeneous presentation, as evident in attempts to develop additional diagnoses that capture complicated presentations, such as "complex PTSD" (Briere, 1984; M. W. Miller & Resick, 2007). However, when treating clients from diverse cultures there is the added need to be sensitive to how their language and conceptualization of illness or distress may reflect posttraumatic symptoms in addition to classic symptoms that define PTSD. For example, in a qualitative study of a postflood disaster in Mexico, Norris et al. (2001) found that event-related distress, hypervigilance, recurrent recollections, and avoiding reminders were described most often as trauma-related symptoms. However, 83% of Mexican victims also provided 109 separate expressions that could not be classified specifically as PTSD criterion symptoms. These expressions fit into categories including *ataques de nervios*, depression, lasting trauma, and somatic complaints.

PTSD can present as a type of culturally defined illness or problem. Hinton et al. (2005a) examined PTSD symptoms among Cambodian immigrants and found that the most frequently reported posttraumatic stress symptoms were recurrent intrusive memories of trauma, sleep paralysis, and night terrors. Further examination of this phenomenon has indicated that these experiences are believed to be caused by night hauntings from spirits of people killed back in the homeland and now tormenting the survivors (Hinton et al., 2005b).

Minority populations in the United States may also have unique patterns of trauma-related symptoms, cognitions, and social support that may be amenable to CR. For example, Pole et al. (2005) found that greater peritraumatic dissociation, greater wishful thinking and self-blame coping, lower social support, and greater perceived racism were important variables in explaining elevated PTSD symptoms among Latino police officers compared with their non-Latino counterparts. Similar stressors such as perceived racism and discrimination have been found to be related to higher distress in African Americans, and asking about these stressors can reveal other symptoms of PTSD populations (Alim et al., 2006). These findings underscore the importance of assessing the broad range of distressing experiences, cognitions, and symptoms in multicultural clients. Therapists should work together with clients to identify those concerns that are most relevant to client circumstances and that would be helpful to begin to address as part of PTSD treatment.

ENGAGING AND RETAINING DIVERSE POPULATIONS IN THE COGNITIVE RESTRUCTURING FOR POSTTRAUMATIC STRESS DISORDER PROGRAM

The process of engaging people in therapy is especially important for immigrant and other underserved populations. Minority populations in the United States are less likely to receive treatment for all mental health conditions, including PTSD (Alegria et al., 2004). Some of the primary identified barriers to care include lack of insurance and language barriers. Studies have shown that CR can be an effective modality of treatment for immigrant populations (Kataoka et al., 2003), but often there are lower retention rates for treatment among minority populations compared with Whites (Morris & Silove, 1992; Scharlach et al., 2006). It is important to remember that diverse racial and ethnic groups vary in their use of health services, and there can be tremendous within group variability in services use based on gender, socioeconomic status, education and level of acculturation (Alegria et al., 2004). However, the literature does indicate that minority populations in the United States receive fewer health and mental health services (Atdjian & Vega, 2005; Bauer et al., 2000; Fortuna et al., 2008). This suggests the importance of considering strategies for engaging and retaining minority clients in the CR for PTSD Program. The following are some specific considerations:

1. The psychoeducation component of the CR for PTSD Program is an introduction to a greater conversation about the potential emotional and physical impact of trauma. Therapists may need to spend some additional time with minority populations in conducting the psychoeducation modules of the program. First, the therapist may be introducing a psychological framework that is foreign to the client's understanding of stress or trauma, and time may be needed to both introduce the material and ensure that it can be integrated into the client's own conceptualization of his or her problems. Second, some minority communities have had poor access to health and mental health care, and this may be the first opportunity they have had to discuss PTSD, trauma, or any mental health issue with a clinician. It is important to take the time to ensure mutual understanding of PTSD and other concepts and expressions that will be addressed in later sessions.

2. Endorsement of PTSD symptoms may take some probing because most people, including ethnic and racial minorities, are not familiar with the language of *DSM–IV*. As with all clients, during the psychoeducation modules of the CR for PTSD program it is important to explore minority clients' understanding and experience of PTSD symptoms in their own words and language. For example, does the term *hyperarousal* resonate with the client? How do clients describe their experiences with this cluster of symptoms? Are there other words or concepts that they use to describe their symptoms of anxiety, anger, or tension? What do they associate with these symptoms (e.g., specific stressors, physical or spiritual connections)? In addition, as with all clients participating in the CR for PTSD program, it is important to explore the impact of trauma symptoms on role functioning (e.g., work, role as parent) as an important factor related to help seeking and treatment engagement. These can then be related to treatment goals that are then developed collaboratively with the client.

3. Family, role and social functioning difficulties may be chief complaint for many minority and immigrant clients, even more than distress related to PTSD symptoms. If so, then understanding the nature of the client's complaints or concerns about family life may be particularly important. For example, the client may have feelings of worthlessness, guilt, or failure in family roles, and instilling hope for addressing these concerns can

facilitate engagement in treatment. Some individuals will be open to including a support person, such as a family member, in the therapy. Careful attention should be played to who the client is comfortable with including in sessions while also preserving traditional family roles in the process.

4. The Western model of psychotherapy and treatment of mental illness has traditionally been a White, middle-class activity that values individualism, individual responsibility, and autonomy (Barcelona de Mendoza, 2001; Morris & Silove, 1992; Scharlach & Frenzel, 1986). In contrast, many other cultures value family and community interdependence over individualism. The CR for PTSD program does not stress one framework over another, but therapists should take care not to present a worldview that is incongruent with the client's and to support the integration of his or her values into the development of treatment goals. For example, at the beginning of treatment, one young Latina woman was very concerned that her therapist would challenge her need to focus on her role within the family rather than her own independence and personal needs. They were able to address this during a larger discussion of treatment goals because the therapist provided an opportunity to talk about the client's priorities.

5. Cultural issues should be addressed in supervision/training of clinicians. Supervisors should identify whether and how differences in cultural background between clinician and client might be influencing communication and case formulation. Consideration should be given to how new therapists can receive supervision regarding their clients' culture and collaborate with cultural brokers. Explicit supervision is needed on how cultural differences, power differences, and trust may be impacting client engagement and treatment.

Several additional considerations are important regarding the treatment settings in which minority and immigrant clients may be identified. Multicultural populations are more likely to present at primary care settings rather than specialized mental health services. Although primary care physicians can be an important source for the identification and referral of clients, they may need guidance in how to identify clients. The use of standard screening measures for trauma and PTSD (see chap. 2, this volume) may facilitate the identification of clients who may benefit from treatment, especially in clinics serving high numbers of multicultural populations. See chapter 16 of this volume for more information on treating PTSD in the primary care setting.

Culturally competent agencies that serve multicultural communities can also be important collaborators in building awareness in minority communities about trauma and PTSD without sending a message that patholo-gizes the difficult circumstances experienced by their clients. Agencies such as youth development agencies and family centers serving specific ethnic pop-ulations provide a range of social services, cultural events, and health promo-tion activities. Many cities and communities have local Latino, African American, or Asian community centers where a high density of ethnic minority members live. This approach to identifying individuals who may benefit from treatment for PTSD requires collaboration between clinicians and providers in these organizations. Key representatives from the organiza-tion may need to learn about the CR for PTSD program before feeling com-fortable referring clients. They may need to build their own trust and confidence in the clinician's ability to work respectfully and effectively within the context of clients' culture and circumstances.

Research indicates that some African Americans and Latinos rely pri-marily on clergy to address mental health problems (Neighbors, Musick, & Williams, 1998). In addition, clergy and other spiritual leaders often have an advantage over mental health service providers because they do not charge for services and are well integrated into the community (Taylor, Chatters, & Levin, 2004). Collaborations with clergy and religious or spiritual leaders may be helpful in engaging some minority populations.

Screening for PTSD can be facilitated by using measures that have been adapted or validated with these populations. Table 15.1 lists some of the trauma and PTSD screening measures that have been used in other languages and with varied populations.

Substance use disorders have a high rate of comorbidity with PSTD, and thus substance abuse treatment settings may be an important setting for iden-tifying clients with PTSD and engaging them in treatment. See chapter 13 of this volume for information on using this program in addiction settings.

The CR for PTSD program allows sufficient flexibility so that the pac-ing and content can be adapted to the needs of culturally diverse clients. Spe-cific considerations for cultural adaptations of this model are summarized in Table 15.2. The following examples briefly demonstrate how some of these recommendations are considered or implemented using the CR for PTSD program with multicultural populations.

CLINICAL EXAMPLES

Michael

Michael was a 19-year-old African American man with a history of exposure to multiple violent events, including physical abuse as a child, gang-related violence as an adolescent, and being assaulted when incarcerated as a young adult. One of the primary reasons Michael was referred for treatment

TABLE 15.1
Examples of Posttraumatic Stress Disorder Measures
Tested in Diverse or Specific Ethnic/Racial Groups

Measures and instruments	Population, uses, and validation
SF-36	The SF-36 has been translated into numerous languages. Measures physical, role, and social functioning; mental health; health perceptions; and/or bodily pain (Stewart et al., 1989). See http://www.sf-36.org/
The Hopkins Symptom Checklist Depression Scale (HSCL–D)	Has been used in international studies, particularly among refugees and conflict-affected populations (J. W. J. Williams, Stellato, Cornell, & Barrett, 2004). Available in multiple languages.
Harvard Trauma Questionnaire (HTQ)	Has been used in international studies, particularly among refugees and conflict-affected populations to identify PTSD (Kleijn, Hovens, & Rodenburg, 2001).
Comprehensive Trauma Inventory—104 (CTI–104)	Developed and designed empirically to improve assessment of traumatic war-related events; strong internal and test–retest reliability in community-dwelling Kurdish and Vietnamese refugees. Strong correlation with other measures of known outcomes of trauma (Hollifield et al., 2006).
PTSD Symptom Checklist—Civilian Version (PCL–C)	Sample of young adult survivors of community violence. English and Spanish versions of PCL–S showed general measurement equivalence (Weathers et al., 1993).
Distressing Event Questionnaire (DEQ)	Brief instrument for assessing PTSD according to *Diagnostic and Statistical Manual of Mental Disorders* (4th ed.) criteria. Has exhibited strong convergent validity with other PTSD measures and other indexes of adjustment and also exhibited strong convergent validity as a measure of PTSD across diverse ethnic groups in both a veteran sample and civilian women's sample (Kubany et al., 2000).
Civilian Mississippi Scale for PTSD	Demonstrated English–Spanish equivalence, evidence of scale reliability, and correlates in meaningful ways with known traumatic stressors (Norris & Kaniasty, 1996).

was his recurrent angry outbursts, which resulted in altercations with others, lost jobs, and lost partners and friendships. He was identified as potentially needing treatment by an outreach worker at a community-based organization that provided services primarily to Latino and African American youth and young adults in an urban neighborhood.

This agency had also worked collaboratively with mental health clinicians to identify clients in need of treatment and played the important role of initiating psychoeducation about PTSD and referrals. The agency received

TABLE 15.2
Potential Cultural Adaptations of Cognitive Restructuring for Posttraumatic Stress Disorder (PTSD) Program

Portion of program	Adaptation
Introduction and assessment	■ Information on PTSD readily available in client's language ■ Program description translated (or videos to assist clients with low literacy) to complement in-session discussions ■ Time spent understanding client's chief complaint, understanding of traumatic events, and response to stress ■ Assessment of education level, language preference, social supports, role functioning, family, religion, and other supports
Relaxation	■ Relaxation techniques such as breathing retraining can be used in most cases ■ Ask client about concerns regarding using techniques ■ Consider other helpful techniques that may be more amenable to client (e.g. prayer, meditation) or that have been useful to them
Psychoeducation	■ Educational handouts and worksheets translated ■ Incorporate some of client's insights and expressions into symptom descriptions and relevance to life circumstances ■ Possible need for additional information about the effects of trauma on physical problems
Cognitive restructuring	■ Check in with clients about their understanding of cognitive restructuring ■ Take care to avoid suggesting that current coping efforts are pathological ■ Use examples from client's life and understanding of common styles of thinking ■ Assist clients in generating their own alternative thoughts
Assessments/measures	■ Culturally and linguistically appropriate measures for monitoring core PTSD symptoms, depression, anxiety and general psychosocial functioning ■ Assess and consider how race or ethnic-related stressors like discrimination and racism may interact with trauma and other psychosocial stressors in contributing to client distress ■ Use ethnically relevant and validated measures to screen for PTSD and other trauma-related consequences ■ Consider client level of acculturation and treatment preferences

training in identifying the symptoms of PTSD and in using screening measures. Staff members were also introduced to the CR for PTSD program so that they would have an understanding of the approach and be able to judge the appropriateness for the population they served.

An assessment of Michael's symptoms indicated that he met criteria for PTSD. He struggled with a great deal of anxiety and felt that he could not trust anyone. He reported having particularly severe symptoms of nightmares, avoiding talking about past traumatic experiences, and experiencing hypervigilance and hyperarousal, including anger outbursts and jumpiness. In the past he had been given diagnoses of paranoid schizophrenia or paranoid personality disorder, which further added to his resistance to speaking with clinicians because he felt these diagnoses meant he was being labeled as "crazy."

Initially, Michael was concerned about being identified as having some type of mental problem, and this apprehension made engagement in treatment difficult. To address this, he was first involved in treatment through the community-based agency, which helped broker trust. Michael was able to engage with an African American clinician who was knowledgeable about the community and the criminal justice system, as well as Michael's experiences as a man of color. The introduction and psychoeducation parts of the program provided Michael with the opportunity to share his concerns. His anger, the primary reason that he was referred for treatment, clearly appeared to be a result of his traumatic experience. However, Michael was not motivated to focus on his anger, but he was motivated to work on his anxiety. Therefore, engagement initially focused on talking with Michael about how the CR for PTSD program could help reduce his anxiety.

During the psychoeducation component of the program Michael was given the opportunity to describe in his own words what he was experiencing. When asked, he eventually shared that he felt he had just "gone the wrong way" and he would "always be abused and used." He reflected on his experiences of racism and discrimination as evidence that he would not be able to make it in this world because of societal barriers. This made him feel hopeless about his future. Psychoeducation was helpful in assisting Michael in understanding the links among trauma, anger, and anxiety. He found it helpful to understand why he tended to "blow up," and he was relieved to know his symptoms were common and did not mean that he was crazy. Michael also found it helpful for his therapist to validate his stressful experiences with discrimination and its effects on his well-being, especially when combined with the other traumatic events in his life. The clinician emphasized that he understood that discrimination is a real and difficult challenge but that they could work together to consider how Michael could make progress toward his goals despite these barriers.

CR was presented as a tool for helping Michael achieve his goals of feeling less anxious, finding and maintaining employment, and improving how he felt in relationships. Michael had strong feelings of anger and resentment about his father's physical abusiveness toward him over many years. During the course of teaching the 5 Steps of CR, after considering all the evidence Michael concluded that his angry feelings were justified. When discussion turned to creating an action plan for dealing with his anger, Michael was able to consider how his anger was getting in the way of his daily functioning and relationships, and he contemplated whether it was worth letting go of some of his resentment toward his father or whether he could take other steps to improve his current relationships. He elected to try both strategies.

In subsequent sessions Michael also worked on the anxiety he experienced when starting new relationships. Using the 5 Steps of CR, he was able to identify thoughts and beliefs that underlay his anxious feelings, including "I will always be left alone" and "I am not a good person, I deserve to be alone." Michael was able to connect these thoughts and feelings to the isolation and sense of abandonment he felt as a child unable to escape or be rescued from his abusive father. Michael began to challenge these thoughts and to consider that he was worthy of relationships. He also made an action plan to talk to a friend about some of the stress they both felt regarding racial discrimination as a way of releasing some of the tension with someone who could understand.

Michael worked with the therapist to consider feelings of depression that were related to thoughts of defeat and that contributed to his social and employment difficulties. Here it was important for the therapist to validate his real difficulties in getting a job due to discrimination on the basis of his criminal record and possibly his race. He was encouraged to consider additional problems arising from trauma-related beliefs that he was helpless and incapable of overcoming his challenges. Using the 5 Steps of CR, Michael began to see that he had been powerless over his abuser as a child but that now, as a man, he had more control over his life—he was no longer the helpless, defeated child. The therapist also evaluated with Michael whether he had truly been "defeated" by the abuse he had experienced as a child. By exploring how he had coped with his father's abuse (e.g., initially retreating to a fantasyland, later joining a gang), Michael began to see that he had not been entirely defeated by his father's abuse but instead had used whatever personal resources he could to manage his difficult circumstances. Michael found these new ways of looking at himself and his life experiences as helpful in addressing his immediate needs and relationship difficulties. The clinician also worked collaboratively with a social worker who was able to assist Michael in getting vocational services at a supported employment program.

Michael completed treatment, his PTSD symptoms improved significantly, especially in regards to anxiety, and he also demonstrated fewer outbursts of anger.

Rita

Rita was a 20-year-old Latina woman of Puerto Rican heritage who was born and raised in the United States. She had a long history of sexual abuse and domestic violence exposure as a child and had been diagnosed with both bipolar disorder and PTSD. Rita had been attending a local church and told her pastor that she had "sick nerves" and that she just could not "deal with it" anymore. She also told the pastor that she was afraid that her bad childhood would affect her ability to be a good mother and that she had too much anxiety and too little energy to be a good parent. The minister provided pastoral support but also discussed a referral to mental health services for her nerves.

During Rita's assessment interview she disclosed her trauma history and reported a variety of PTSD symptoms, especially avoiding places that reminded her about past traumatic experiences and hyperarousal symptoms, including anxiety attacks, jitteriness, and hypervigilance. She also described symptoms of depression, including sadness and anhedonia. Rita experienced episodes of panic attacks and dissociative symptoms she called "sick nerves" and "*ataques*" or "attacks." These episodes were manifested by intense crying spells and anxious agitation. During these episodes she seemed unresponsive to others, and the episodes required that she be "sat down" and monitored by family until the agitation passed.

Rita was quite willing to consider therapy, although she was anxious that she might have to talk about her past trauma in detail. She was reassured that she would not have to provide any details and that the therapy would focus on helping her challenge trauma-related thoughts or beliefs that were leading to distress and impacting her functioning. Her therapy was delivered in a combination of English and Spanish because although she spoke English fluently, she often preferred to discuss salient emotional topics in Spanish or in a mixture of Spanish and English. She identified with being Latina and felt her culture to be very important for her identity.

Rita had a husband and a 2-year-old son. Planning for therapy and practicing relaxation techniques required some creativity and juggling of tasks because of her household responsibilities as a mother and wife. The clinician and client agreed to go over handouts together during sessions as she was not always able to do them at home because of a lack of privacy and time. However, she was able to practice relaxation techniques, bring current stressors and situations into the sessions, and use CR. Psychoeducation included discussion of Rita's understanding of her symptoms, what was working for her in her life, and what she most wanted to work on to improve her life circumstances. Part of the work also focused on her thoughts and anxiety regarding her transition to becoming a parent to her young son and building confidence to ask what she needed from family and friends while also respecting the importance of these relationships in her life.

When learning the 5 Steps of CR, Rita began to make connections between her *ataques*, distressing feelings and associated thoughts that contributed to her anxiety and depression. Through monitoring her feelings and using the 5 Steps of CR, she noticed that her nervous attacks occurred when she was overwhelmed and were triggered by thoughts such as "I am never able to control anything in my life" and "I am helpless and unprotected, and no one can understand." As Rita learned how to challenge these and other self-depreciating thoughts, she began to understand how her traumatic experiences had affected her self-image and her relationships. Challenging her thoughts gave Rita something she could control in her life while also encouraging her to consider that absolute control over everything was not necessary and that it could be helpful to be supported by others when she felt overwhelmed by her feelings. She requested that her husband attend some of the sessions so he could understand why she was so stressed. Rita reported that she found it helpful for him to learn about PTSD, relaxation, and CR and that he liked being able to be more helpful to her.

At the end of therapy Rita reported feeling equipped to challenge her distressing thoughts. She showed an improvement in both clinical depression and PTSD severity, and her panic attacks diminished to rare episodes. Rita was able to share more with her husband, including parenting tasks, and trust in him. This improved the quality of their relationship.

SUMMARY AND CONCLUSIONS

It is most important when using the CR for PTSD program with minority and immigrant clients to build a trusting environment that can clinically respond to the individual's needs and preferences, including help with outreach and language capacity. Clinicians need the ability to frame the model within the context of the clients' understanding of their symptoms and experiences as well as their current circumstances. The program is respectful of how clients perceive their own distress while also fostering their understanding of the effects of trauma and how CR can help. There is also room to respect the clients' expression of their experiences either in an actual foreign language or as personal expressions imbedded in a cultural context—the meaning of trauma in an individual's life.

Hinton et al. (2005b) addressed the importance of language in working with Cambodian refugees with severe trauma histories. They stated that in Cambodian culture, clients often refer to their emotional distress as "having a heavy heart." Hinton et al. found the appropriate language used within Cambodian culture to respond to this distress in telling clients that they were there to help "carry heavy hearts." The therapist helps by understanding the client's words and experiences and by joining with clients in forging an honorable path that reconciles the past with the present, engenders compassion for oneself and others, and leads into an enlightened and more hopeful future. In the end, this is the goal of trauma work with all clients, regardless of their origins.

The CR for PTSD program can be readily used with minority, immigrant, and refugee populations. Special consideration is necessary regarding issues of assessment, engagement, outreach, language, and variations in symptom expression. However, with sensitivity to these issues and a collaborative stance with clients, their families, and other providers, this program can be an effective treatment for clients of diverse racial and cultural backgrounds.

16

TREATMENT IN PRIMARY CARE SETTINGS

ANNABEL PRINS, DELIA CIMPEAN, AND PAULA P. SCHNURR

Since the mid-1990s, there has been tremendous interest in the delivery of primary health care, resulting in structural and organizational changes. Increasingly, civilian, military, and Veterans Health Administration (VHA) primary care providers are responsible for the overall health of their patients, including health promotion, disease prevention, management of acute and chronic medical conditions, and mental health. Supporting transformations in primary care is the emergence of integrated practices that include care managers (e.g., nurses, social workers), who monitor chronic conditions such as diabetes or depression, and behavioral health specialists (e.g., psychologists, psychiatrists), who provide evidence-based treatment for mental health conditions like posttraumatic stress disorder (PTSD). For example, in the VHA primary care enrollment was 38% in 1993. By 1999, 95% of patients were enrolled in a primary care clinic with an assigned primary care provider (Yano, Simon, Lanto, & Rubenstein, 2007). This profound change is associated with significant gains in the quality of VHA care and has resulted in the VHA being recognized as a potential model of health care delivery in the United States (Jha, Perlin,

Kizer, & Dudley, 2003; Perlin, Kolodner, & Roswell, 2004). Within VHA, close to 100 integrated practices were established in 2007, with special emphasis on helping primary care providers manage alcohol misuse and abuse, depression, and PTSD (Wray, 2007).

TRAUMA AND POSTTRAUMATIC STRESS DISORDER IN PRIMARY CARE

As a result of natural disasters (e.g., Hurricane Katrina) and the September 11 attacks at the World Trade Center as well as increased media attention to military conflicts in Iraq and Afghanistan, health care providers and the general public have become increasingly aware of exposure to trauma and its consequences. Indeed, exposure to traumatic events is common. Approximately 60% of men and 50% of women in the United States have been exposed to at least one traumatic event (Kessler et al., 1995). The prevalence of traumatic exposure reported in primary care settings may be even higher: One study of civilian patients found that 83% of primary care patients reported at least one traumatic event (Bruce et al., 2001). The types of events are varied. The most common and upsetting traumatic events reported in one study of civilian primary care patients were serious accidents, sudden injury or death to another, sexual molestation, sexual assault, and natural disasters (Stein, McQuaid, Pedrelli, Lenox, & McCahill, 2000). Exposure is especially high in veterans, who have exposure to military and war zone-related stressors in addition to civilian events. For example, Zinzow, Grubaugh, Frueh, and Magruder (2008) found that 90% of VHA primary care patients reported at least one traumatic event, with most reporting between two and five.

Despite the high prevalence of exposure to traumatic events, the lifetime prevalence of PTSD in the general population is relatively low, most recently estimated at 3.6% for men and 9.7% for women (Kessler, Bergland, et al., 2005). The prevalence of PTSD is higher in primary care patients, however. When limiting prevalence data to those obtained from gold standard diagnostic interviews like the Structured Clinical Interview for *DSM–IV* (Spitzer, Williams, Gibbon, & First, 1995) or the Clinician-Administered PTSD Scale (CAPS; Weathers, Keane, & Davidson, 2001), the prevalence of PTSD in primary care samples ranges from 8% to 36% (Dobie et al., 2002; Kroenke, Spitzer, Williams, Monahan, & Lowe, 2007; Magruder et al., 2005; Prins et al., 2004). In a recent study of 965 patients from 15 different primary care clinics, 8.6% met diagnostic criteria for PTSD compared with 7.6% for generalized anxiety disorder, 6.8% for panic disorder, and 6.2% for social anxiety disorder (Kroenke et al., 2007). Higher rates have been reported in primary care clinics within VHA. For example, Magruder et al. (2005) found that 11.5% of VHA primary care patients had PTSD.

PROBLEMS ASSOCIATED WITH POSTTRAUMATIC STRESS DISORDER

There is accumulating evidence that PTSD is a chronic condition associated with significant functional impairment and compromised physical health. About one third of patients with PTSD never remit, regardless of treatment (Kessler et al., 1995). PTSD is often associated with comorbid psychiatric disorders. In adults in the United States, 75% of individuals with PTSD have at least one additional psychiatric disorder (Kessler, Chiu, Demler, & Walters, 2005). Depression is particularly common, but other anxiety disorders and substance or alcohol abuse are prevalent as well. Among individuals with PTSD, the odds of depression are elevated 6.9-fold in men and 4.1-fold in women (Kessler et al., 1995). Kessler et al. (1995) also found that 52% of persons with a lifetime diagnosis of PTSD had a lifetime diagnosis of alcohol abuse or dependence, and 34% had a lifetime diagnosis of drug abuse or dependence. The association between PTSD and other disorders often results from other disorders developing after the onset of PTSD (Kessler et al., 1995), but also because prior psychiatric disorder is a risk factor for the development of PTSD (Brewin, Andrews, & Valentine, 2000; Ozer, Best, Lipsey, & Weiss, 2003).

PTSD is frequently associated with reduced quality of life and functional difficulties in psychosocial, occupational, and physical domains (Lunney & Schnurr, 2007; M. B. Stein et al., 1997). The extent of impairment can be substantial, comparable to that seen in other serious psychiatric disorders. One study found severe quality of life impairment in 59% of PTSD patients and 63% of patients with major depression (Rapaport, Clary, Fayyad, & Endicott, 2005). Functioning has important prognostic value: Initial PTSD predicts poor life quality at follow-up intervals (Holbrook, Hoyt, Stein, & Sieber, 2001; Zatzick, Jurkovich, Gentilello, Wisner, & Rivara, 2002). However, reductions in PTSD symptoms are associated with improved quality of life (Schnurr, Hayes, Lunney, McFall, & Uddo, 2006), and quality of life improves following PTSD treatment (Foa, Dancu, et al., 1999; Rapaport, Endicott, & Clary, 2002; Tucker et al., 2001).

The impaired physical functioning associated with PTSD is accompanied by elevated likelihood of poor self-reported health and morbidity (Green & Kimerling, 2004; Schnurr & Green, 2004; Schnurr & Jankowski, 1999). The etiology of physical health problems among individuals with PTSD is likely to result from a combination of biological and psychological changes associated with PTSD, but also behavioral changes (Schnurr & Green, 2004;

Schnurr & Jankowski, 1999). PTSD is associated with an increased likelihood of health risk behaviors and decreased likelihood of preventive care (Rheingold et al., 2004). For example, the prevalence of smoking in individuals with PTSD is 45%, compared with 23% in the adult population at large (Lasser et al., 2000).

The chronicity, comorbidity, and excess illness and physical impairment in PTSD have obvious relevance for practitioners in primary care settings. Patients with PTSD may present with medical problems not only as an expression of their distress but also because they in fact have a greater likelihood of being ill. To date, there is no conclusive evidence that treating PTSD successfully improves physical health and physical functioning, but only a few studies have been conducted. There is growing support, however, that treating health risk behaviors within the context of PTSD treatment improves outcome (McFall et al., 2005, 2006; Ouimette, Moos, & Finney, 2000).

SPECIAL PROBLEMS AND CHALLENGES IN TREATING PRIMARY CARE PATIENTS

As the primary care model becomes increasingly central to health care delivery in the United States, other pressures are also converging on providers. These include high patient loads, pressures for productivity, and ever-expanding expectations and suggestions to add screening procedures and interventions that go beyond treatment of patients' presenting complaints. Good arguments can be made for primary care providers assessing substance use, depression, exercise, smoking, diet, domestic violence, occupational stress, sexual risk behaviors, and multiple other risk factors and developing disorders. However, the total burden of dealing with all of these would render day-to-day practice extremely difficult, and physicians understandably resist adding too many mandates to their traditional set of responsibilities.

To date, primary care practice guidelines have not prioritized PTSD above these many other potential foci. It will require education, support, and persuasion to change practice patterns in primary care to include attention to posttraumatic disorders as a priority. This is particularly true because patients in primary care rarely mention posttraumatic symptoms in their presenting complaint and may not even be aware of PTSD as a disorder. Providers working with high-risk populations are more likely to be amenable to prioritizing posttraumatic issues because they are frequently confronted with the immediacy of trauma exposure and the symptoms and distress associated with this exposure. In any event, success in integrating identification and treatment of PTSD in primary care settings will likely require informing providers of the overall health and functional toll of the disorder; providing simple, effective tools for screening, diagnosis, and treatment; and providing ongoing support, training, and specialty consultation for patient management.

Identification of the Problem

Despite increased attention to trauma and its aftermath, trauma history and PTSD symptoms continue to be underidentified in primary care. In a recent study of urban primary care patients, only 11% of patients with PTSD had a PTSD diagnosis in their chart (Liebschutz et al., 2007). In Magruder et al.'s (2005) study of VHA primary care patients, only 46.5% of patients with PTSD had a PTSD diagnosis in their chart. Certain patients may be at greater risk of nondetection than others. For example, Borowsky et al. (2007) found that physicians were less likely to detect mental health problems among patients with depression if the patient was African American, male, or younger than 35.

The United States Preventive Health Task Force (1996; Pignone et al., 2002) recommends screening for substance abuse and depression only; however, the Veterans Affairs/Department of Defense Clinical Practice Guideline (2003) recommends screening for PTSD as well. A frequently used screen within the DoD and VHA is the Primary Care PTSD Screen (PC-PTSD; Prins et al., 2004). This brief 4-item questionnaire is in the public domain and is not specific to any one traumatic experience. It has good operating characteristics in both VHA primary care patients and soldiers returning from combat when a cutoff score of 3 or more is used (Bliese, Wright, Adler, & Cabrera, 2008; Prins et al., 2004).

Although the PC-PTSD still requires validation with civilian primary care samples, the 17-item PTSD Checklist (PCL; Weathers, Litz, Herman, Huska, & Keane, 1993) has been widely used and validated in primary care samples (Brewin, 2005). In civilian primary care settings, cutoff scores ranging from 30 to 44 yield adequate sensitivity and specificity (Brewin, 2005). The PCL offers the advantage of providing a score that allows for monitoring of symptom severity and response to treatment. Regardless of what instrument is used, standardized and routine screening for PTSD symptoms will likely identify those patients needing additional diagnostic assessment.

Identification of Treatment Options

Another challenge for treating PTSD patients in primary care is the lack of empirical support for what works in this setting. To date, there have been no randomized clinical trials of either pharmacological or psychotherapeutic treatments for PTSD in primary care. Practice guidelines recommend cognitive–behavioral (CBT) treatments as the best psychotherapeutic approach for PTSD (American Psychiatric Association, 2004; VA/DoD Clinical Practice Guideline Working Group, 2003), but these treatments typically require 10 to 15 weekly sessions of 60–90 minutes delivered by a trained mental health professional. Few primary care providers have the time or training to provide this level of care as part of their practice. When there is time for longer and more frequent primary care visits or when a primary care physician trained in CBT or colocated mental health professional is available, a modified treatment program might prove effective in primary care (see Strategies and Adaptations of CBT for PTSD section, below).

Given the training, expertise, and practice patterns more common among primary care providers, they are more likely to provide pharmacotherapy for clients with PTSD. Most systematic reviews and clinical practice guidelines support the use of a selective serotonin reuptake inhibitor (SSRI) as the first line of medication for PTSD, with sertraline and paroxetine receiving Food and Drug Administration approval. The low potential for SSRI abuse coupled with few side effects and easy dosing schedules makes these medications easy to prescribe in primary care. Although the effect size of SSRIs on PTSD is modest, medications are a good alternative for primary care providers who do not have access to behavioral health specialists and for patients who do not want psychotherapy.

Because PTSD can become chronic for so many patients, chronic care models represent a promising way to engage patients in treatment. These models emphasize specialty care consultation, patient education, self-monitoring, and frequent follow-ups by care managers (usually trained nurses or social workers) as adjunctive components to pharmacological treatments (Bodenheimer, Lorig, Holman, & Grumbach, 2002). Care managers are often colocated and focus on medication adherence, side effect monitoring, and referral to specialty care. Chronic care models have been shown to be quite successful in the treatment of depression in primary care (Katon et al., 1995; Rost, Nutting, Smith, Werner, & Duan, 2001).

In integrated care models, the colocated mental health professional (usually a psychologist) works collaboratively with the primary care team (which can include care managers). He or she is able to provide diagnostic assessments as well as evidence-based treatments for common conditions like depression or PTSD. Many of these mental health professionals are also trained in behavioral medicine or health psychology and are therefore able to address co-occurring behavioral health problems such as substance abuse, smoking, and inactivity. These integrated or blended models are being increasingly used within primary care, with several PTSD management programs being piloted and evaluated in these settings (Litz, Engel, Bryant,

& Papa, 2007; Sullivan et al., 2007). There is evidence that primary care providers prefer integrated models of care over enhanced referral models (Gallo et al., 2004).

Obstacles to Posttraumatic Stress Disorder Treatment Services in Primary Care

There are several other obstacles to the adequate delivery of PTSD services in primary care. Some of these obstacles are related to the infrastructure of many primary care clinics (e.g., large patient panels, short appointment times) as well as the availability of supportive resources (e.g., electronic records, automated screening reminders). Others are related to the clinical presentation of clients with PTSD, whereas still others pertain to provider knowledge of PTSD.

Like other patients with mental health problems, patients with PTSD are more likely to report symptoms of PTSD and problems in functioning to their primary care provider than a mental health professional (Butterfield & Becker, 2002). Often, presenting complaints are not easily tied to a traumatic event and include such nonspecific symptoms as difficulty falling or staying asleep, diminished interest in others or in activities, irritability, hyperarousal, as well as physical complaints such as tension headaches or upset stomach. Patients with childhood traumas or with delayed symptom onset may not tie these symptoms to the trauma they underwent. Symptoms that are more obviously tied to a traumatic event, such as flashbacks or dissociation, can be frightening for both the patient and the primary care provider. Certain medical procedures or exams may serve as reminders of the trauma and result in patient reactions that are unanticipated. For example, survivors of a sexual assault may be reminded of the assault during a routine pelvic exam and respond with fear and distrust. They may avoid preventive care as well. Farley, Golding, and Minkoff (2002) found that female sexual trauma survivors were less likely than women without such a history to obtain cervical cancer screening.

Provider knowledge of trauma and PTSD appears to be less complete than knowledge about other common conditions such as depression. In an analogue study using textbook clinical vignettes, primary care providers almost unanimously recognized and recommended adequate treatment for depression (Munro, Freeman, & Law, 2004). However, PTSD was recognized in only two thirds of cases, and recommendations for appropriate treatment occurred in less than half of cases. Only 10% of primary care providers were able to describe best practices for PTSD compared with 47.7% for depression. Clearly, additional educational efforts are needed on the detection, management, and treatment of PTSD in primary care.

STRATEGIES AND ADAPTATIONS OF
THE COGNITIVE RESTRUCTURING FOR
POSTTRAUMATIC STRESS DISORDER PROGRAM

The CBT–Primary Care (CBT-PC) program (Hamblen, Mueser, Rosenberg, & Rosenberg, 2005) is an adaptation of the Cognitive Restructuring (CR) for PTSD program for use in primary care clinics. It is a manualized, six-session intervention and includes both a detailed therapist manual and a patient workbook. The workbook, written on an 8th grade level for broad accessibility, provides basic information about PTSD and worksheets designed to help patients understand and use the skill of CR. Both the manual and patient workbook are based on those used in longer CR interventions that have proven efficacious in reducing the symptoms of PTSD and depression in multiple randomized trials in psychiatric settings (Bryant et al., 2003; Marks et al., 1998; Tarrier, Pilgrim, et al., 1999).

One issue of concern in adapting this intervention is that clients presenting in primary care are typically not seeking mental health referrals and frequently reject or do not follow through on such referrals. Neither providers nor clients in primary care tend to favor lengthy psychosocial interventions. Rather, clients with posttraumatic symptoms presenting in primary care settings are typically more focused on somatic concerns and prefer care to be brief and to be delivered by their regular medical providers.

The CBT-PC program takes these issues and preferences into account and has modified and condensed key elements of the CR for PTSD program, using strategies and language better suited to the context of primary care. First, CBT-PC is presented to clients as a brief, skills-based program, delivered at the site of primary medical care, to help them better deal with stress-related symptoms and problems. Therefore, it may be seen as more acceptable than specialty mental health care delivered in a different treatment setting. To maximize the feasibility of adopting the program, the manual was designed to be very explicit, containing detailed scripting of each session. Much of the key work of the program is guided by user-friendly client handouts provided at each session. The manual was designed so that it could readily be taught to non-mental health professionals such as primary care physicians or nurses, and it does not require that the therapist have prior experience with CR. To date, the major elements of the program have been successfully delivered by primary care providers and by master's level behavioral health clinicians, suggesting its feasibility for general health care settings.

The CBT-PC manual includes six sessions, each administered in about 1 hour. The first session is structured to sequentially accomplish six primary tasks, which are (a) overview of the program, (b) brief discussion of identified trauma(s), (c) review of PTSD symptoms and other reactions to trauma, (d) introduction to CR, (e) introduction to common styles of thinking, and (f) practicing skills.

This first session rapidly introduces not only the rationale of the treatment but also specific techniques of CR that can provide the client with skills to help him or her deal with upsetting feelings. The client is thus helped to engage in a paradigm shift: recognizing posttraumatic symptoms, tying them to previous trauma exposure, and beginning to recognize that improved quality of life and well-being can be achieved if these problems are addressed. Secondly, this condensation of CR provides the client with potential rapid relief (even if only very partial), enhancing motivation for continuing the treatment.

Homework is assigned at the first and each of the next four sessions and is reviewed early in the following session. The next four sessions focus on applying the skills of CR, and the last session reviews strategies for relapse prevention. Sessions 2–5 share a similar structure and include the following components: (a) check-in and agenda setting, (b) homework review, (c) practice and use of the 5 Steps of CR, (d) sum up and practice skills assignments. In the final session, in addition to reviewing the final homework, the therapist adds the following tasks and topics: (a) review of treatment, (b) relapse prevention, (c) termination, and (d) communication with referring physician.

The goals of CBT-PC are to improve knowledge about PTSD, decrease distorted beliefs about self and the world, reduce PTSD symptoms and diagnosis, and improve perceived health. In 2006–2007, we pretested the CBT-PC manual and then conducted a pilot study using a civilian primary care sample. Treatment was delivered by primary care providers on a general internal medicine service in a large rural medical center. The primary care providers were trained to use the manual over a couple of days and offered supervision by phone or direct contact with experts during the treatment delivery. Ten clients received CBT-PC in a primary care/general internal medicine treatment service, and 9 completed the treatment and posttreatment assessment. Clients were either referred by their medical providers or self-referred on the basis of information about treatments for PTSD available to people served by the practice. The intervention, delivered by a member of the client's treatment team, was well received and retention was high (1 client agreed to the treatment but did not attend the first session because of external complications).

There was significant improvement in PTSD symptoms and depression from pre- to posttreatment as measured by the PCL (Weathers et al., 1993), $t(8) = 2.82, p < .02$, and the Beck Depression Inventory—II (BDI; A. T. Beck, Steer, & Brown, 1996), $t(8) = 2.7, p < .03$. Initial PCL scores ($M = 56, SD = 13$) were above clinical cutoffs for PTSD (Brewin, 2005), with posttreatment scores at 6 weeks ($M = 34, SD = 7$) and at 3 months ($M = 28, SD = 9$) reflecting a clinically significant change for all patients. In addition to significant PCL changes, clients displayed significant improvement in all major symptom classes of PTSD (intrusion, avoidance, and arousal) as measured by the CAPS (Weathers et al., 2001).

The BDI was used to measure changes in depression. Initial BDI scores at baseline ($M = 25.0$, $SD = 5.5$) did not decline at 6 weeks ($M = 26.4$, $SD = 5.4$). There was a significant decrease at 3 months ($M = 19.0$, $SD = 3.5$). Clients displayed improvement in all major symptom classes of PTSD as measured by the CAPS: intrusive ($p = .05$), avoidant ($p = .02$), and arousal symptoms ($p = .04$).

CLINICAL EXAMPLE

Presenting Problem

Angela was a 55-year-old unemployed mother of three adult children, married to her third husband. Her presenting complaint to her primary care provider was chronic, severe headaches, which had become worse in recent months. Major features of her psychosocial history included the following: The patient had been an excellent student and had begun college work at a highly competitive university. However, she experienced considerable stress in the demanding academic environment; underwent an episode of marked depression; and following a medical leave of absence, dropped out. Her employment history was quite erratic, with Angela holding intermittent jobs that were not very challenging or rewarding. She reported a pattern of developing conflicts with supervisors, accompanied or triggered by a sense of feeling unfairly "singled out," at which point she would quit. Her last job had been a volunteer position assisting local businesses. For the past year, she had pursued numerous jobs but had not secured one.

Angela came from a large family (six siblings), with a mother who was described as passive and a father who was described as authoritarian, alcoholic, and violent. Her parents eventually separated, and her mother remarried. Over this period of family turbulence, the client was frequently sent to live with her maternal grandparents. In this period, she regarded her grandfather as the trustworthy adult in her life. However, when she was 12, her grandfather called her in the basement, locked the door, and asked her to take her clothes off. She initially resisted, but he held a gun to her head and molested her. Her memory of the incident is incomplete, but she knows that at some point she was able to rush out of the basement and refused to ever return to see her grandparents. She felt that she could not tell her parents about this event for fear of being blamed or punished, and indeed she never did tell anyone, including her psychiatric providers of many years.

Over multiple episodes of treatment, Angela's psychiatric history was characterized by recurrent major depression, and she had never been diagnosed with PTSD. Her primary care provider had placed her on bupropion, trazodone, and zolpidem. Angela referred herself to the CBT-PC program after finding information about PTSD and the trial in the clinic waiting room. At the intake assessment, Angela stated that she had largely "forgotten" about the incident in the basement until her first daughter turned 12, at which point she experienced vivid, intrusive memories. In reviewing her reactions to the childhood trauma, she acknowledged that she had a trust issue and that she had been unable to develop any long-term relationships with friends or family. She could not tolerate physical closeness, did not like hugging or being alone, and felt a need to always be vigilant (e.g., refused to have anesthesia during medical procedures, had to struggle to "let go" in order to fall sleep). Angela disclosed that in almost all new situations she needed to map out an escape route and that she could not tolerate being alone in the house or in a situation in which her car was not working properly. About a year before beginning the program, after her third husband confessed to having had a short affair, Angela again experienced flashbacks of the event with her grandfather, increased difficulty sleeping, and severe anxiety.

Formal assessments at intake indicated severe PTSD symptoms (PCL total = 69; CAPS severity = 64). Angela met *Diagnostic and Statistical Manual of Mental Disorders* (4th ed.; American Psychiatric Association, 1994) criteria for PTSD as well as for major depression, moderate, without suicidal ideation. Her baseline BDI was 23.

Angela experienced notable relief from the initial psychoeducational session, stating that she understood for the first time that many of her troubling experiences could be seen as reactions to her trauma and PTSD symptoms. For example, being able to identify her reactions when her daughter was 12 years old as "flashbacks" gave her a greater sense of control and counteracted her feeling of being "crazy" whenever she experienced intrusive memories.

After working to learn to identify and separate feelings from thoughts, some common cognitive biases became evident. In a variety of upsetting situations, Angela was able to identify feelings of self-loathing related to ideas of her own inadequacy and a belief that this inadequacy or badness was obvious to others around her, even virtual strangers. In more intimate relationships, she reported feeling sad, angry, and fearful, and the thoughts associated with these feelings were primarily thoughts of betrayal and distrust. She identified all-or-nothing thinking, emotional reasoning, and self-blame as her common styles of thinking when upset. Angela reported liking the program, particularly the way it provided her with ways of challenging her thoughts herself. She consistently completed worksheets at home between sessions and reviewed them in the meetings with the therapist.

Sample Dialogue

Therapist: What is an upsetting situation that you would like to discuss today?

Client: My last job interview and part of the test.

Therapist: What happened?

Client: The interview went well initially, the supervisor was nice, and I think I was presenting well. But then I had to undergo this transcription-typing test. I was very anxious. She didn't explain to me exactly what the different buttons were, and in the middle of the transcription I had to stop and ask her, and she didn't want to tell me, she told me to just go on.

Therapist: How did that make you feel?

Client: I was having this sense of failure, I was feeling completely inadequate, and I hated myself and her.

Therapist: What were your thoughts?

Client: I knew that I wasn't doing well, probably she didn't like me, she wanted me to fail, and I felt stupid.

Therapist: What thinking style do you think these thoughts reflect?

Client: I can identify all-or-nothing thinking (I am either the best or the worst), emotional reasoning (I feel stupid; therefore, I am stupid), and self-blame.

Therapist: These are several thoughts. Which one do you feel is the strongest, or which thought do you want to focus on?

Client: I am stupid.

Therapist: Okay, what is the evidence for that thought?

Client: I am failing all the job interviews. I feel stupid. I haven't accomplished much in my life. I start well, but I always lose the opportunity in the end.

Therapist: Okay, what is the evidence against your being stupid?

Client: I always did well in school and on big tests, like the SATs. I can do puzzles and games that other people can't do. But when it counts, I tend to mess up.

Therapist: What makes you mess up and act in a way that you think of as "stupid"?

Client: Well, when other people are judging me, my mind goes blank. I feel frozen, and I can't find the right answers.

Therapist:	Does that sound like somebody being stupid or like some other problem?
Client:	Well, when I start feeling pressure or feeling judged, I panic, I freeze up.
Therapist:	So is there another way to understand why your problem occurs in these situations?
Client:	Maybe it's not stupidity. Maybe it's anxiety that I feel.
Therapist:	Is there any other evidence that you may actually not be stupid?
Client:	I went to a great school. I had a few jobs that were important, even if I didn't keep them.
Therapist:	Can you replace the thought of being stupid with a more accurate thought?
Client:	Having a job interview makes me very anxious; I am interpreting anxiety as feeling stupid, which further paralyzes me. I feel anxious, I am not stupid.
Therapist:	How do you feel when you think this new thought rather than the old one?
Client:	Much better. I don't feel like a failure.

At the end of the six sessions, Angela reported high satisfaction with the treatment. Her PCL score was down to 37, and her BDI score was 18. At 3 months follow-up she reported that she continued to use CR in upsetting situations. Her PCL dropped further to 20 and her BDI to 5. She was hired by a local large nonprofit organization as a secretary. Following a stressful encounter at work, she asked for a single booster session and was still employed 1 year later. She reported that she was having headaches only occasionally, that the headaches were responsive to usual treatment, and that the depression had not recurred.

SUMMARY AND CONCLUSIONS

PTSD is strongly associated with health problems, resulting in higher rates of PTSD in primary care treatment settings compared with the general population. However, despite the high prevalence of PTSD in primary care services, trauma history and PTSD are not routinely screened in these settings, and therefore patients rarely receive treatment. The primary care setting may be ideal for screening and treating PTSD because of the ready access to a population of people who are more likely to have posttraumatic disorders and the ability to avoid the problem of poor follow-through on referrals for mental health treatment.

To address this need, we abbreviated the CR for PTSD program to make it suitable to implement in the primary care setting and conducted a pilot study to evaluate its feasibility and explore its clinical effects. The six-session CBT-PC program was feasible to implement, with 9 out of 10 clients completing it. Furthermore, clinical outcomes were positive, with significant improvements in PTSD symptoms and depression observed. The findings suggest that the CBT-PC program can be implemented successfully in the primary care setting and that participation is associated with expected improvements in PTSD symptoms and depression. More rigorous, controlled research is needed to evaluate the effects of the CR for PTSD program in primary care settings, including its impact on PTSD and depression, as well as to explore its potential effects on health and health service utilization.

APPENDIX: TESTS, HANDOUTS, AND WORKSHEETS

PTSD KNOWLEDGE TEST

Instructions: Please answer the following questions about trauma and PTSD. We do not expect people to get all the "right" answers, just try to answer the questions as well as you can. If you are not sure about the answer, you can use the "Do not know" response. Please circle only one answer for each question.

1. Is the following statement true or false? Most adults have had at least one traumatic event in their lives.
   A) True
   B) False
   C) Do not know

2. Which of the following can be a traumatic event?
   A) Car accident
   B) Child abuse
   C) Seeing someone else get seriously hurt
   D) Any of the above
   E) Do not know

3. What does PTSD stand for?
   A) Previous trauma symptom duress
   B) Partial trauma stress disease
   C) Preterminal substance disorder
   D) Posttraumatic stress disorder
   E) Do not know

4. What two things are needed for an experience to be considered a "traumatic event"?
   A) Upsetting event and feeling of sadness
   B) Head injury and passing out
   C) Life-threatening event and feeling of fear
   D) Combat and being wounded
   E) Do not know

From *Treatment of Posttraumatic Stress Disorder in Special Populations: A Cognitive Restructuring Program*, by K. T. Mueser, S. D. Rosenberg, and H. J. Rosenberg, 2009, Washington, DC: American Psychological Association. Copyright 2009 by the American Psychological Association.

5. Is the following statement true or false? Everyone who has experienced a traumatic event gets PTSD.
   A) True
   B) False
   C) Do not know

6. Is the following statement true or false? PTSD is the only bad effect of having experienced a traumatic event.
   A) True
   B) False
   C) Do not know

7. Select a way that people reexperience traumatic events.
   A) Nightmares
   B) Flashbacks
   C) Memories
   D) All of the above
   E) Do not know

8. Is the following statement true or false? People who have PTSD often have other problems like using too much alcohol or drugs.
   A) True
   B) False
   C) Do not know

9. Select a symptom of overarousal.
   A) Being upset all the time
   B) Sadness
   C) Irritability
   D) Weepiness
   E) Do not know

10. Is the following statement true or false? People who have PTSD often have relationship problems.
    A) True
    B) False
    C) Do not know

11. Select a symptom of avoidance.
    A) Being in a bad mood
    B) Not taking prescribed medications
    C) Staying away from things that remind you of the bad event
    D) Do not know

12. Select one way to treat PTSD.
    A) Getting away from stress
    B) Making a big change in life
    C) Exposure
    D) Engaging in strenuous exercise
    E) Do not know

13. Besides PTSD, what is another problem that people often have who have experienced a traumatic event?
    A) Drug/alcohol problems
    B) Depression
    C) Anger
    D) All of the above
    E) Do not know

14. Is the following statement true or false? There are currently no treatments for PTSD.
    A) True
    B) False
    C) Do not know

15. Is the following statement true or false? The only people who get PTSD are people who have been in a war.
    A) True
    B) False
    C) Do not know

Answer Key: 1-A; 2-D; 3-D; 4-D; 5-B; 6-B; 7-D; 8-A; 9-C; 10-A; 11-C; 12-C; 13-D; 14-B; 15-B

ORIENTATION TO THE CR FOR PTSD PROGRAM: HANDOUT #1

The Cognitive Restructuring for Posttraumatic Stress Disorder (CR for PTSD) program includes learning about *breathing retraining, common reactions to trauma,* and developing *skills for managing upsetting thoughts and feelings.* These techniques can help reduce PTSD and other posttraumatic symptoms such as anxiety, distress, irritability and high levels of body tension. Each technique is briefly described below.

- *Breathing retraining:* This skill involves learning a new way to breathe that can help you to relax. Over time and with practice, you will learn how to use breathing retraining to relax in stressful situations and reduce your anxiety. By the end of the program, you will develop an improved sense of control over your anxiety and distress.
- *Education:* You will be taught about the common reactions to trauma. PTSD symptoms are learned responses that can be unlearned and the CR for PTSD program can teach you ways to change these learned responses.
- *Cognitive restructuring:* This skill involves learning how to identify and then challenge thoughts and beliefs that contribute to distress. You will learn ways to increase your awareness of distressing thoughts. You will learn to identify patterns in your thinking that contribute to negative feelings, and how to challenge and change your thinking to make you feel better.

Homework

Putting aside some time to practice your skills is an important part of this program. Each week there will be a homework assignment that you and your therapist agree on, such as monitoring your responses to upsetting situations. Daily practice is necessary to really benefit from the program. Your therapist will explain each assignment and help you develop a plan to practice and use the skills in your everyday life.

CRISIS PLAN CHECKLIST WORKSHEET: HANDOUT #2

What type of crisis would be difficult for you to handle? In what situations do you feel out of control, unsafe, or afraid of harm to yourself or others?

- Suicidal thinking
- Self-injurious behavior
- Increased anxiety or depression
- Increased other symptoms (such as voices)
- Withdrawing and isolating from other people
- Starting to use alcohol or drugs again, or increasing use
- Other (describe)

What are your warning signs of an approaching crisis?

A) _____

B) _____

C) _____

D) _____

Who might you go to for help if a crisis should occur?

                              Name   *Phone Number*

A) Friends and family:

B) Providers you trust:

What other individuals, groups, or organizations might give you support in a crisis?

A) _____

B) _____

C) _____

D) _____

What is your crisis plan? Different plans may be necessary for different crisis situations. List the different steps:

1. _____

2. _____

3. _____

From *Treatment of Posttraumatic Stress Disorder in Special Populations: A Cognitive Restructuring Program,* by K. T. Mueser, S. D. Rosenberg, and H. J. Rosenberg, 2009, Washington, DC: American Psychological Association. Copyright 2009 by the American Psychological Association.

BREATHING RETRAINING: HANDOUT #3

Breathing fast and taking deep breaths (*hyperventilating*) are common responses to feeling stressed. However, breathing too fast increases the flow of oxygen to the brain, which can lead to feeling lightheaded and more anxious. *Breathing retraining* is a skill that helps you slow down your breathing, and decrease the amount of oxygen going to your brain, which can make you more relaxed. Learning breathing retraining takes daily practice, but once you get good at it you can use it in any situation you feel stressed or anxious. Try following the steps below.

Instructions:
1. Choose a word that you find relaxing, such as *calm*, *relax*, or *peaceful*.
2. Take a normal breath (not a deep one) in through your nose and exhale slowly through your mouth.
3. While you exhale, say the relaxing word you have chosen very slowly: "calm" or "relax."
4. Pause briefly before taking your next breath. You can count to four before taking in each new breath.
5. Practice this exercise several times a day, taking 10 to 15 breaths at each practice.

Some people like to combine breathing retraining with other relaxation exercises, such as focusing on the cool air going into your nose and the warm air going out of your mouth, picturing peaceful and restful scenes or places, or tensing and relaxing your muscles. Some people prefer using a different exercise than breathing retraining to relax. What is important is that you learn what relaxation strategies work best for you.

From *Treatment of Posttraumatic Stress Disorder in Special Populations: A Cognitive Restructuring Program*, by K. T. Mueser, S. D. Rosenberg, and H. J. Rosenberg, 2009, Washington, DC: American Psychological Association. Copyright 2009 by the American Psychological Association.

COMMON REACTIONS TO TRAUMA I: PTSD SYMPTOMS: HANDOUT #4

When a person experiences a traumatic event, it is common to have many distressing feelings as a result, even long after the event. Although each person responds to trauma in a unique way, there are also a number of common reactions. In order to learn how to manage these symptoms, it is helpful to understand what they are and why they occur. This handout describes the symptoms of posttraumatic stress disorder (PTSD). The core symptoms of PTSD are:

- *Reexperiencing* the traumatic event or events
- *Avoiding* things that remind the person of the trauma
- Being *overaroused*

Reexperiencing the Trauma

A very common way that people reexperience traumatic events is by having unwanted *memories, images,* or *pictures* of part of the trauma suddenly pop into one's mind. Sometimes a memory is so vivid that it temporarily feels like the event is actually happening again (a *flashback*). These memories may be triggered by external things (such as a smell, a noise, or a TV commercial), or internal things (such as a thought or feeling). Sometimes the memories seem to come out of nowhere. The person may also have *bad dreams* or *nightmares* about the trauma itself or other frightening situations. When these experiences happen, people may feel they have no control over what they are feeling, thinking, and experiencing.

Avoidance

People often *avoid other people, places, or things* that remind them of their traumatic events. Distressing thoughts and feelings about the events are also often avoided. This is quite natural, since thinking about traumatic experiences can be upsetting. However, the avoidance is usually only partially successful. It is difficult to avoid every possible reminder of trauma, and many people find that the more they try to avoid, the more that new triggers that can evoke their traumatic memories.

Sometimes people avoid memories and feelings about the trauma without even being aware of it, such as *forgetting important parts of what happened*. Avoiding painful feelings and thoughts about the trauma can also lead to *feeling emotionally numb, empty,* or *detached and cut off from other people*. It is common for people to *lose interest* in things they once enjoyed.

From *Treatment of Posttraumatic Stress Disorder in Special Populations: A Cognitive Restructuring Program*, by K. T. Mueser, S. D. Rosenberg, and H. J. Rosenberg, 2009, Washington, DC: American Psychological Association. Copyright 2009 by the American Psychological Association.

Overarousal

Another common reaction to trauma is to be overaroused or hyperalert. People may feel *tense*, *agitated*, *jumpy*, or *hypervigilant*. The person may have a *racing heart*, *tense muscles*, and *perspire easily*. People may also be *easily startled* and have *trouble sleeping*. All of these problems can lead to *irritable feelings* and *anger outbursts*.

These changes in your body are the result of fear. When people (and animals) are threatened by something, they react by fleeing or fighting—a normal response. This response requires a burst of adrenaline to mobilize the body and help it respond to the danger. When people have experienced traumatic events, they may come to think of the world as dangerous and want to be ready for it. Their body may respond by being in a constant state of preparedness and arousal, so they are ready to react immediately to the danger. This response may be easily triggered and can affect many areas of the person's life.

REEXPERIENCING SYMPTOMS WORKSHEET

Reexperiencing symptoms include:

- Recurrent memories or images of event
- Distressing dreams/nightmares
- Acting or feeling like event is occurring again (flashbacks)
- Intense distress or feeling upset when reminded of event
- Intense bodily reactions (heart racing, headache, stomachache, sweating) when reminded

Instructions: Describe some of the reexperiencing symptoms that have troubled you in the space below:

Images:

_____

_____

Intrusive Thoughts or Memories:

_____

_____

Nightmares:

_____

_____

Flashbacks:

_____

_____

Upsetting Reminders and Triggers:

_____

_____

Body Reactions to Memories and Triggers:

_____

_____

Which of these intrusive symptoms is most upsetting to you?

_____

_____

Which is most frequent?

_____

_____

AVOIDANCE SYMPTOMS WORKSHEET

Avoidance symptoms include:

- Avoiding thoughts or feelings associated with the traumatic event
- Avoiding talking with people about what happened to you
- Avoiding activities, places, or people that remind you of the trauma
- Forgetting important parts of the traumatic event
- Losing interest in activities
- Feeling detached or disconnected from others
- Feeling numb or not being able to be happy or have a full range of feelings
- Not seeing yourself as having a future

Instructions: Describe some of the avoidance symptoms that have troubled you in the space below:

People I avoid:

_____

_____

Places I avoid:

_____

_____

Situations I avoid:

_____

_____

Feelings I avoid:

_____

_____

Thoughts I avoid:

_____

_____

Which of these avoidance symptoms is most disruptive or upsetting to you?

_____

_____

Which is most frequent?

_____

_____

OVERAROUSAL SYMPTOMS WORKSHEET

Instructions: In the space below, check off how your body reacts to the signs of overarousal.

_____ Heart pounding
_____ Trembling/shaking
_____ Sweating
_____ Hot flashes
_____ Trouble falling asleep
_____ Tense muscles
_____ Jitteriness
_____ Restlessness
_____ Feeling tense or uptight
_____ Dry mouth
_____ Lump in throat
_____ Chest pain or discomfort
_____ Nausea or stomachache
_____ Dizziness
_____ Jumpiness
_____ Quick temper
_____ Always on guard
_____ Irritable
_____ Other (describe):

Put an asterisk (*) next to those overarousal signs that are most disruptive or upsetting to you.

Which is most frequent?

COMMON REACTIONS TO TRAUMA II: ASSOCIATED PROBLEMS: HANDOUT #5

Many people with PTSD also experience other reactions or problems that interfere with their lives, such as upsetting feelings and relationship problems. Understanding why these problems occur after traumatic events can prepare the person for learning how to cope, and eventually overcome them. This handout addresses the nature of three common associated problems in trauma survivors:

- Distressing feelings
- Problems in relationships with others
- Using too much alcohol or other drugs

Distressing Feelings

Common upsetting feelings include fear and anxiety, sadness and depression, guilt and shame, and anger.

Fear and anxiety. Anxiety and fear are common feelings after a traumatic event. As described in the handout on PTSD symptoms, these feelings may arise when memories of traumatic events are triggered by something, such as by a certain place, smell, or thought. Another common symptom of PTSD is avoiding places, people, or other things that remind the person of his/her trauma and make him/her feel afraid. These feelings can spread to many different situations, including ones not clearly related to the trauma, to the point where the person feels anxious and fearful much of the time. The person may view the world as an unsafe place, and never feel comfortable and safe.

Sadness and depression. Another common reaction to experiencing a traumatic event is *sadness*. Sadness can be experienced as *feeling blue, depressed,* or *hopeless about the future.* When people are depressed they sometimes *cry,* have *thoughts about self-harm or death,* and may even think about *suicide.* They may find it hard to concentrate, and their *appetite* and *sleep* patterns may be disturbed, either by eating or sleeping too much or too little. People often *lose interest* in previously enjoyable activities, so that nothing seems fun to them anymore. Sadness and depression may occur in people with PTSD because of the frequent memories of their traumatic experiences that are stirred up, thoughts about their losses related to the trauma, or because their fear and avoidance prevents them from being involved in or appreciating rewarding activities, such as close relationships, work, school, parenting, or leisure pursuits.

Guilt and shame. People often have feelings of *guilt* or *shame* related to something they did (or did not do) during or after their traumatic experiences. It is common for people to second-guess their reactions and blame themselves. For example, people who have been assaulted, either sexually or physically, may blame themselves for not having prevented the assault in the first place, or for not having successfully fought off the attacker. People may also feel ashamed simply because they have PTSD; they may believe that having symptoms such as recurrent memories of the trauma or nightmares for a long time means they are weak or inferior because they should have "gotten over" the trauma.

Anger. Feelings of anger are also common reactions to trauma. The anger may be directed at someone who hurt the person, but it can be also stirred up in the presence of other people, such as loved ones or even strangers. The anger may be so strong that the person lashes out at others, either verbally or physically. Angry feelings may occur for a variety of reasons, such as feeling frustrated by having PTSD, misperceiving threats or insults from other people, or overreacting to situations due to hypervigilance. Sometimes people get angry with themselves because of something they did or failed to do during or after their traumatic experiences.

Relationship Difficulties

People with PTSD often have difficulty with relationships. These problems may be partly a result of strong feelings of depression, anxiety, sadness, or anger, which can get in the way of getting along with others. People who have been victimized by another person (like being attacked, raped, or abused) may find it very hard to trust others or allow themselves to feel close to someone else. Situations that involve intimacy and closeness can stir up distressing emotions and memories. This may lead people withdraw and avoid spending time with others.

Traumatic experiences and PTSD symptoms can also lead to sexual difficulties for people who have intimate relationships. They may be less interested in sex because of depression, or they may avoid it because it reminds them of their trauma or makes them feel vulnerable. Sexual relations may also be uncomfortable because they bring on feelings of shame or guilt.

Family relationships can be a source of joy and support, but they can also be affected when trauma has touched the life of a family member. For example, family relationships may be strained or broken when one member abuses another, or when a child or adolescent reports being abused to a parent, but is not believed. Family members often do not know how to support a relative with PTSD, and they may be unable or unwilling to listen to them talk about their traumatic experiences. People with PTSD may also feel inferior around their family because they have not accomplished what they hoped to, or they think their relatives do not understand why they have not "gotten over" what happened to them yet.

Drug and Alcohol Problems

Sometimes people with traumatic experiences use alcohol or drugs to avoid thinking about their traumatic experiences or to sleep better. Although drinking or using drugs can provide a temporary escape from distressing thoughts and feelings, using substances to cope with symptoms usually ends up making them worse. Similarly, alcohol or drugs may help people get to sleep faster, but substances disrupt the natural sleep cycle, resulting in more sleep problems in the long run. The CR for PTSD program helps people learn skills for dealing with distressing feelings and traumatic experiences without using substances. However, in order to learn these skills, it is important that the person practice them each day and while sober.

DISTRESSING FEELINGS WORKSHEET

Fear and Anxiety

Instructions: Anxious and fearful feelings may come and go on their own or they may be triggered by thoughts, people, places, or other reminders of traumatic experiences.

In the space below, write down the kinds of things that make you afraid:

- Places:

- People:

- Activities:

- Sounds, smells, sensations:

The way my body feels when I am afraid:

My thoughts when I am afraid (check all that apply):

_____ Something terrible is going to happen
_____ I am going to be attacked or hurt
_____ I am going to be rejected or abandoned
_____ I am going to lose control or go crazy
_____ Other:

Sadness and Depression

Instructions: Common symptoms of depression include feeling "blue" or "down"; feeling worthless, hopeless, or helpless; low self-esteem; thinking about death or life not being worth living; difficulty sleeping; loss of appetite or weight; and difficulty concentrating.

In the space below, write down any symptoms of depression you experience:

My thoughts when I am sad or depressed (check all that apply):

     _____ I am worthless
     _____ I don't have anyone I can depend on
     _____ Nothing will ever get better
     _____ My life is not worth living
     _____ Other:

Guilt and Shame

Instructions: Many people blame themselves for something they did or did not do to survive or cope with the trauma.

In the space below, describe any feelings of guilt and/or shame you may have had:

My thoughts when I feel guilty or ashamed (check all that apply):

     _____ I am inadequate
     _____ I am a bad person
     _____ I am a failure
     _____ I am to blame for what happened to me
     _____ If only I hadn't done _____, this wouldn't have happened to me
     _____ Other:

Anger

Instructions: Angry feelings may be directed at a specific person involved in your traumatic experience. They can also be directed at people you love the most. Your anger may seem too intense or seem like an overreaction to the situation.

In the space below, describe difficulties with anger you have had, including the situations, events, and people that trigger your anger:

Situations/events:

People:

Memories:

My thoughts when I am angry (check all that apply):

     _____ I am being treated unfairly
     _____ I am being taken advantage of
     _____ This situation is unfair
     _____ I am weak or incompetent
     _____ Other:

RELATIONSHIP DIFFICULTIES WORKSHEET

Problems in your relationships may be related to upsetting feelings you have such as fear, sadness, guilt, or anger. It may be difficult for you to trust other people or feel close to them. People who love you may have a hard time hearing about your experiences.

Instructions: In the space below, check the types of relationship problems that you are having:

_____ Conflict with spouse/significant other
_____ Conflict with other family members
_____ Violence in relationships/fear for safety
_____ Difficulty establishing relationships
_____ Difficulty maintaining relationships
_____ Difficulty being emotionally close to others
_____ Difficulty trusting others
_____ Sexual difficulties
_____ Other:

DRUG AND ALCOHOL PROBLEMS WORKSHEET

Alcohol or drugs may be used to try to avoid thinking about trauma, to escape upsetting feelings, or to try to sleep better. Using these substances usually makes things worse in the long-run.

Instructions: Describe your use of alcohol and drugs by completing the questions below.

Has there ever been a period of time when (circle your answer):

You felt that you used too much?	No	Yes
Your use led to problems (such as relationships, work, legal, health)?	No	Yes
Your use was out of your own control?	No	Yes
Someone else was concerned about your use?	No	Yes

If you circled "Yes" for any of these questions, indicate which substances you were using:

_____ Alcohol
_____ Marijuana
_____ Cocaine
_____ Amphetamines
_____ Heroin or other narcotics (such as Vicodin)
_____ Sedatives (such as Klonopin, Xanax, Ambien)
_____ Other

Do you use any of these substances on a regular basis?   Yes   No

Do you use more of any of these substances when your PTSD symptoms are worse?

If so, what happens? Does it help? Does it make you feel worse?

HOW TRAUMA AFFECTS THOUGHTS AND FEELINGS: HANDOUT #6

Trauma and PTSD often lead to negative thoughts about oneself, other people, or the world. Thoughts related to traumatic experiences can have very personal meanings to the individual, but are often not truly accurate. How do the traumatic events you've experienced affect how you think about yourself?

Do you tend to blame yourself or are you very critical of yourself?

Yes   No

If yes, give examples of these types of critical thoughts:

Do you tend to distrust other people?

Yes   No

If yes, give examples of these types of thoughts:

Are you generally very fearful or think the world is an unsafe place?

Yes   No

If yes, give examples of these types of thoughts:

Look at Handout #7 to learn about Common Styles of Thinking: All-or-Nothing Thinking; Overgeneralization; "Must," "Should," or "Never" Statements; Catastrophizing, Emotional Reasoning; Overestimation of Risk, Inaccurate or Excessive Self-Blame; or Mental Filter.

Which of your thoughts appears to reflect a Common Style of Thinking? Examples:
>   Self-critical or self-blaming thoughts
>   Thoughts about distrusting other people
>   Thoughts about not feeling safe

Write your own thoughts here:

From *Treatment of Posttraumatic Stress Disorder in Special Populations: A Cognitive Restructuring Program*, by K. T. Mueser, S. D. Rosenberg, and H. J. Rosenberg, 2009, Washington, DC: American Psychological Association. Copyright 2009 by the American Psychological Association.

Catastrophizing

These thoughts occur when one focuses on the most extreme and distressing possible outcome. The thoughts often come out of the blue or following a minor problem when the person assumes the very worst will happen.
- "What if I'm attacked on my way to work?"
- "I didn't do well on this exam, so I know I'm going to flunk the class."
- "What if this cough means I have lung cancer?"

Overgeneralization

The person jumps to conclusions by assuming that when something bad happens, it will happen again and again.
- "Once a victim, always a victim"
- "I was unable to keep myself safe before, therefore I will always be unable to protect myself in the future."

"Must," "Should," or "Never" Statements

These are unwritten rules or expectations for how people think they should behave that are not based on facts. These "rules" may have been learned when growing up and they may seem unchangeable. When they cannot be followed, they are distressing.
- "I never should have let it happen."
- "I must stop thinking about my abusive experiences."

All-or-Nothing Thinking

The world is seen in extremes with nothing in between. For example:
- "Since I'm not perfect, I'm a failure."
- "The world is a totally dangerous place."

Common Styles of Thinking is based on the concept of cognitive distortions developed for cognitive–behavioral therapy for depression and anxiety (see, e.g., A.T. Beck, 1963; A.T. Beck et al., 1979; Burns, 1999; Ellis, 1962; Leahy, 2003).

From *Treatment of Posttraumatic Stress Disorder in Special Populations: A Cognitive Restructuring Program*, by K. T. Mueser, S. D. Rosenberg, and H. J. Rosenberg, 2009, Washington, DC: American Psychological Association. Copyright 2009 by the American Psychological Association.

Emotional Reasoning	This occurs when the person's feelings determine what he or she thinks or believes, even when there is no "hard" evidence to support it. Just because a person feels something, it doesn't mean it's true. ■ "I feel anxious and afraid, so I must be in danger." ■ "I feel ashamed, so I must be a bad person." ■ "I feel sad, so my life must be hopeless." ■ "I feel angry, so somebody must have wronged me."
Overestimation of Risk	The person thinks the risk of something bad happening is much greater than evidence supports. ■ "I'm not going to take a walk because I might be attacked." ■ "I'm not going to drive because I might get into a car accident."
Inaccurate or Excessive Self-Blame	The person blames him- or herself for something he or she had little or no control over or responsibility for. ■ "It's my fault that I let the abuse go on for so long." ■ "I'm responsible because my child got into a fight."
Mental Filter	These thoughts occur when the person focuses only on negative aspects of something and ignores the positive aspects. By focusing on the negative, the person does not see the "whole picture" and feels worse than necessary. ■ After fumbling for words in a conversation, you tell yourself, "I'm such a screw-up, I made a total fool of myself." ■ After missing the turn to the highway entrance, you tell yourself, "That was such a stupid move, I shouldn't be allowed to drive a car." ■ Your boss gives you positive feedback about your work, but then recommends improving one area. You think, "My boss is unhappy with my performance."

COMMON STYLES OF THINKING WORKSHEET: HANDOUT #8

Directions: When you begin to feel distressed or upset, ask yourself, "What am I thinking right now that is causing this feeling?" Identify whether the upsetting thought is a Common Style of Thinking, and come up with a more helpful or realistic thought.* Use this sheet to write down your thoughts.

Situation	Upsetting Thought/Feeling	Common Style of Thinking*	More Helpful or Realistic Thought
Example: On Friday at noon I was walking down the street when I saw a friend, but she did not say hello to me.	She must not like me anymore./Sad	Catastrophizing	Maybe she did not really see me. Maybe she was distracted and was thinking about something else.

*More than one Common Style of Thinking may be related to the distressing feeling.

THE 5 STEPS OF CR WORKSHEET: HANDOUT #9

1. Situation

Ask yourself, "What happened that made me upset?" Write down a brief description of the situation.

Situation: _____

2. Feeling

Circle your strongest feeling(s):

Fear/Anxiety   Sadness/Depression   Guilt/Shame   Anger

3. Thought

Ask yourself, "What am I thinking that is leading me to feel this way?" Use your Guide to Thoughts and Feelings handout to identify thoughts related to the feeling(s) circled above. You may identify more than one thought related to the feeling. Write down your thoughts below, and circle the thought most strongly related to the feeling.

Thoughts:_____

_____

Is this thought a Common Style of Thinking? If yes, circle which one(s):

All-or-Nothing   Emotional Reasoning
Overgeneralizing   Overestimation of Risk
Must/Should/Never   Self-Blame
Catastrophizing   Mental Filter

4. Evaluate Your Thought

Ask yourself, "What evidence do I have for this thought?" "Is there another way to look at this situation?" "How would someone else think about this situation?" Write down the answers that *do* support your thought and the answers that *do not* support your thought.

Things that DO support my thought:_____

_____

Things that DO NOT support my thought:_____

_____

5. Take Action!

Next, ask yourself, "Do things mostly support my thought or mostly NOT support my thought?"

☐ **YES,** the evidence *does* support my thought.
☐ **NO,** the evidence does *not* support my thought.

If the evidence does NOT support your thought, come up with a new thought that is supported by the evidence. These thoughts are usually more accurate, balanced, and helpful. Write your new, more helpful thought in the space below. And remember, when you encounter this upsetting situation in the future, replace your unhelpful automatic thought with your new, more accurate thought.

New Thought: _____

If the evidence DOES support your thought, decide what you need to do next in order to deal with the situation. Ask yourself, "Do I need to get more information about what to do?" "Do I need to get some help?" "Do I need to take steps to make sure I am safe?" Write down the steps of your Action Plan for dealing with the upsetting situation below or complete the Action Plan Worksheet (Handout #11).

1. _____
2. _____
3. _____
4. _____

THE 5 STEPS OF CR
ALTERNATIVE WORKSHEET: HANDOUT #10

1. Situation

Ask yourself, "What happened that made me upset?" Write down a brief description of the situation.

Situation: _____

2. Feeling

Circle your strongest feeling:

Fear/Anxiety   Sadness/Depression   Guilt/Shame   Anger

3. Thought

Ask yourself, "What am I thinking that is leading me to feel this way?" Use Guide to Thoughts and Feelings (Handout #12) to identify thoughts related to the feeling circled above. You may identify more than one thought related to the feeling. Write down your thoughts below, and circle the thought most strongly related to the feeling.

Thoughts:_____
_____

Is this thought a Common Style of Thinking? If yes, circle which one or ones:
All-or-Nothing   Emotional Reasoning
Overgeneralizing   Overestimation of Risk
Must/Should/Never   Self-Blame
Catastrophizing   Mental Filter

Belief rating: How accurate is the thought? _____ (0 = definitely untrue, 100 = definitely true)

Distress rating: How upsetting is the thought? _____(0 = not upsetting, 100 = extremely upsetting)

4. Evaluate Your Thought

Ask yourself, "What evidence do I have for this thought?" "Is there another way to look at this situation?" "How would someone else think about this situation?" Write down the answers that *do* support your thought and the answers that *do not* support your thought.

From *Treatment of Posttraumatic Stress Disorder in Special Populations: A Cognitive Restructuring Program*, by K. T. Mueser, S. D. Rosenberg, and H. J. Rosenberg, 2009, Washington, DC: American Psychological Association. Copyright 2009 by the American Psychological Association.

Things that DO support my thought:_____
_____
_____

Things that DO NOT support my thought:_____
_____
_____

5. Take Action!

Considering all the evidence FOR and AGAINST your thought, now how accurate do you believe your thought is?

Belief rating:_____ (0 = *definitely not accurate*, 100 = *definitely accurate*)

Does the evidence completely support the thought? Is your belief as strong as before? (Step 3)

☐ **YES,** the evidence *does* support my thought—my belief is just as strong as before.

☐ **NO,** the evidence does *not* completely support my thought—my belief is lower than before.

If the evidence does NOT completely support your thought, come up with a new thought that is supported by the evidence. These thoughts are usually more balanced and helpful. Write your new, more helpful thought in the space below. And remember, when you think of this upsetting situation in the future, replace your unhelpful automatic thought with your new, more accurate thought.

New Thought: _____

How accurate is this new thought? Make sure it is more accurate than the old thought.

Belief rating:_____ (0 = definitely not accurate, 100 = definitely accurate)

How much distress do you feel when you think of this new thought? Most people find replacing incorrect, unhelpful thoughts with more accurate and helpful ones reduces their distress.

Distress rating:_____ (0 = not upsetting, 100 = extremely upsetting)

If the evidence DOES support your thought, decide what you need to do next in order to deal with the situation. Ask yourself, "Do I need to get more information about what to do?" "Do I need to get some help?" "Do I need to take steps to make sure I am safe?" Write down the steps of your Action Plan for dealing with the upsetting situation below or complete the Action Plan Worksheet (Handout #11).

1. _____
2. _____
3. _____
4. _____

ACTION PLAN WORKSHEET: HANDOUT #11

Instructions: Follow the steps below to develop a detailed Action Plan.

1. *Define the goal.* What situation requires action?

Consider what change you would like to see in the problem situation. Be as specific as possible.

_____

_____

2. *Brainstorm possible strategies.* What can you do to change the situation?

Using your creative problem-solving skills, think of all the possible ways of achieving your goal. Then, when you have identified a list of different strategies, evaluate each one and place an asterisk (*) next to the best ones.

_____   _____

_____   _____

_____   _____

3. *Plan how to implement the strategies you chose.* What steps can you take to make this happen?

Consider these questions:

What information do you need to have? Do you need to get some help? Who is going to support you in taking this action? What obstacles could interfere with the plan? How could I prevent or deal with these obstacles?

Then, write down the plan below:

I will take the following actions:

_____

_____

_____

4. *Set a time or a situation to follow up your plan.* When and how are you going to take this action?

Ask yourself: What is the situation or type of situation where you want to use your plan? When is it likely to come up again next?

_____

_____

GUIDE TO THOUGHTS AND FEELINGS: HANDOUT #12

Feelings	Ask Yourself	Related Thoughts
Fear or anxiety	What bad thing do I expect to happen? What am I scared is going to happen?	Thoughts that something bad will happen, such as: ■ Some terrible thing is going to happen ■ I am going to be attacked or hurt ■ I am going to be rejected or abandoned ■ I am going to lose control or go crazy
Sadness or depression	What have I lost? What is missing in me or in my life?	Thoughts of loss, such as: ■ I am worthless ■ I don't have anyone I can depend on ■ Nothing will ever get better
Guilt or shame	What bad thing have I done? What is wrong with me?	Thoughts of having done something wrong or lacking in some way, such as: ■ I am a failure ■ I am to blame for what happened to me ■ I am a bad person
Anger	What is unfair about this situation? Who has wronged me?	Thoughts of being treated unfairly or having been wronged, such as: ■ I am being treated unfairly ■ I am being taken advantage of ■ Someone has done something wrong to me

From *Treatment of Posttraumatic Stress Disorder in Special Populations: A Cognitive Restructuring Program*, by K. T. Mueser, S. D. Rosenberg, and H. J. Rosenberg, 2009, Washington, DC: American Psychological Association. Copyright 2009 by the American Psychological Association.

MY MOST DISTRESSING PTSD SYMPTOMS: HANDOUT #13

Trauma-Related Experiences and Responses	Related Distressing Feeling	Underlying Thought/ Common Style of Thinking	New Thought/ Action Plan

From *Treatment of Posttraumatic Stress Disorder in Special Populations: A Cognitive Restructuring Program*, by K. T. Mueser, S. D. Rosenberg, and H. J. Rosenberg, 2009, Washington, DC: American Psychological Association. Copyright 2009 by the American Psychological Association.

SUMMING UP: HANDOUT #14

Skills covered in CR for PTSD program

- Education about PTSD and related symptoms
- Breathing retraining or other relaxation skills
- Cognitive restructuring

What things have gotten better since I started the CR for PTSD Program?

1. _____
2. _____
3. _____

What things do I still want to work on after the program ends?

1. _____
2. _____
3. _____

Which skills from the CR for PTSD program will help me to work on these things?

1. _____
2. _____
3. _____

What can help me to remember to use my new skills in these situations?

1. _____
2. _____
3. _____

PAYOFF MATRIX: HANDOUT #15

Instructions: List the advantages and disadvantages of keeping your thought or belief versus changing it to a more accurate one. Be as specific as possible.

Advantages of *Keeping* Thought or Belief	Advantages of *Changing* Thought or Belief
How does *holding onto* your thought or belief make your life seem more manageable, safer, or easier to handle? Does the thought or belief provide you with a sense of control, security, or predictability of the future?	How could *changing* your thought or belief improve your life? Consider whether changing your thought or belief would reduce distressing feelings and free you of concerns about past events.
Disadvantages of *Keeping* Thought or Belief	**Disadvantages of *Changing* Thought or Belief**
How does *holding onto* your thought or belief make your life more difficult? Consider the role of the thought or belief in creating upsetting feelings for you and in restricting you from doing things you would like to do.	What are the possible disadvantages of *changing* your thought or belief? Would changing the thought or belief lead to your feeling less control, security, or ability to predict the future?

REFERENCES

Abram, K. M., Teplin, L. A., Charles, D. R., Longworth, S. L., McClelland, G. M., & Dulcan, M. K. (2004). Posttraumatic stress disorder and trauma in youth in juvenile detention. *Archives of General Psychiatry, 61,* 403–410.

Alegria, M., Takeuchi, D., Canino, G., Duan, N., Shrout, P., Meng, X.-L., et al. (2004). Considering context, place and culture: The National Latino and Asian American Study. *International Journal of Methods in Psychiatric Research, 13,* 208–220.

Alim, T. N., Graves, E., Mellman, T. A., Aigbogun, N., Gray, E., Lawson, W., & Charney, D. S. (2006). Trauma exposure, posttraumatic stress disorder and depression in an African-American primary care population. *Journal of the National Medical Association, 98,* 1630–1636.

Allen, J. G. (2005). *Coping with trauma: A guide to understanding* (2nd ed.). Washington, DC: American Psychiatric Association Press.

American Academy of Child and Adolescent Psychiatry. (1998). Summary of the practice parameters for the assessment and treatment of children and adolescents with posttraumatic stress disorder. *Journal of the American Academy of Child and Adolescent Psychiatry, 37,* 997–1001.

American Psychiatric Association. (1952). *Diagnostic and statistical manual of mental disorders.* Washington, DC: American Psychiatric Association.

American Psychiatric Association. (1968). *Diagnostic and statistical manual of mental disorders* (2nd ed.). Washington, DC: American Psychiatric Association.

American Psychiatric Association. (1980). *Diagnostic and statistical manual of mental disorders* (3rd ed.). Washington, DC: American Psychiatric Association.

American Psychiatric Association. (1994). *Diagnostic and statistical manual of mental disorders* (4th ed.). Washington, DC: American Psychiatric Association.

American Psychiatric Association. (2004, May). *Should the RRC requirement for competence in psychodynamic psychotherapy be dropped? A debate.* Paper presented at the 157th Annual Meeting of the American Psychiatric Association, New York.

Anderson, C. M., Reiss, D. J., & Hogarty, G. E. (1986). *Schizophrenia and the family.* New York: Guilford Press.

Arata, C. M. (2002). Child sexual abuse and sexual revictimization. *Clinical Psychology: Science and Practice, 9,* 135–164.

Armbruster, P., & Kazdin, A. E. (1994). Attrition in child psychotherapy. *Advances in Clinical Psychology, 16,* 81–108.

Ascher-Svanum, H., & Krause, A. A. (1991). *Psychoeducational groups for patients with schizophrenia: A guide for practitioners.* Gaithersburg, MD: Aspen.

Atdjian, S., & Vega, W. A. (2005). Disparities in mental health treatment in U.S. racial and ethnic minority groups: Implications for psychiatrists. *Psychiatric Services, 56,* 1600–1602.

Avison, W. R., & Gotlib, I. H. (Eds.). (1994). *Stress and mental health: Contemporary issues and prospects for the future*. New York: Plenum Press.

Back, S., Dansky, B. S., Coffey, S. F., Saladin, M. E., Sonne, S., & Brady, K. T. (2000). Cocaine dependence with and without post-traumatic stress disorder: A comparison of substance use, trauma history and psychiatric comorbidity. *American Journal on Addictions, 9*, 51–62.

Barcelona de Mendoza, V. B. (2001). Culturally appropriate care for pregnant Latina women who are victims of domestic violence. *Journal of Obstetric, Gynecologic, and Neonatal Nursing, 30*, 579–588.

Barlow, D. H., & Craske, M. G. (1994). *Mastery of your anxiety and panic: II*. Albany, NY: Graywind.

Barrett, D. H., Green, M. L., Morris, R., Giles, W. H., & Croft, J. B. (1996). Cognitive functioning and posttraumatic stress disorder. *American Journal of Psychiatry, 153*, 1492–1494.

Basoglu, M., Livanou, M., & Salcioglu, E. (2003). A single session with an earthquake simulator for traumatic stress in earthquake survivors. *American Journal of Psychiatry, 160*, 788–790.

Basoglu, M., Livanou, M., Salcioglu, E., & Kalender, D. (2003). A brief behavioural treatment of chronic post-traumatic stress disorder in earthquake survivors: Results from an open clinical trial. *Psychological Medicine, 33*, 647–654.

Basoglu, M., Salcioglu, E., & Livanou, M. (2007). A randomized controlled study of single-session behavioral treatment of earthquake-related post-traumatic stress disorder using an earthquake simulator. *Psychological Medicine, 37*, 203–213.

Basoglu, M., Salcioglu, E., Livanou, M., & Acar, G. (2005). Single-session behavioral treatment of earthquake-related post-traumatic stress disorder: A randomized waiting list controlled trial. *Journal of Traumatic Stress, 18*, 1–11.

Bauer, H. M., Rodriguez, M. A., Quiroga, S. S., & Flores-Ortiz, Y. G. (2000). Barriers to health care for abused Latina and Asian immigrant women. *Journal of Health Care for the Poor and Underserved, 11*, 33–44.

Bebbington, P. E., Bhugra, D., Brugha, T., Singleton, N., Farrell, M., Jenkins, R., et al. (2004). Psychosis, victimisation and childhood disadvantage: Evidence from the second British National Survey of Psychiatric Morbidity. *British Journal of Psychiatry, 185*, 220–226.

Beck, A. T. (1963). Thinking and depression: Idiosyncratic content and cognitive distortions. *Archives of General Psychiatry, 9*, 324–333.

Beck, A. T., Rector, N. A., Stolar, N., & Grant, P. (2009). *Schizophrenia: Cognitive theory, research, and therapy*. New York: Guilford Press.

Beck, A. T., Rush, A. J., Shaw, B. F., & Emery, G. (1979). *Cognitive therapy of depression*. New York: Guilford Press.

Beck, A. T., Steer, R. A., & Brown, G. K. (1996). *Manual for the Beck Depression Inventory—II*. San Antonio, TX: Psychological Corporation.

Beck, A. T., Wright, F. D., Newman, C. F., & Liese, B. S. (1993). *Cognitive therapy of substance abuse.* New York: Guilford Press.

Beck, J. S. (1995). *Cognitive therapy: Basics and beyond.* New York: Guilford Press.

Beck, J. S. (2005). *Cognitive therapy for challenging problems.* New York: Guilford Press.

Becker, C. B., Zayfert, C., & Anderson, E. (2004). A survey of psychologists' attitudes towards and utilization of exposure therapy for PTSD. *Behaviour Research and Therapy, 42,* 277–292.

Beitchman, J. H., Zucker, K. J., Hood, J. E., de Costa, G. A., Akman, D., & Cassavia, E. (1992). A review of the long term effects of child sexual abuse. *Child Abuse and Neglect, 16,* 101–118.

Bellack, A. S., Mueser, K. T., Gingerich, S., & Agresta, J. (2004). *Social skills training for schizophrenia: A step-by-step guide* (2nd ed.). New York: Guilford Press.

Benish, S. G., Imel, Z. E., & Wampold, B. E. (2008). The relative efficacy of bona fide psychotherapies for treating post-traumatic stress disorder: A meta-analysis of direct comparisons. *Clinical Psychology Review, 28,* 746–758.

Berthold, S. M. (1999). The effects of exposure to community violence on Khmer refugee adolescents. *Journal of Traumatic Stress, 12,* 455–471.

Birmes, P., Hatton, L., Brunet, A., & Schmitt, L. (2003). Early historical literature for post-traumatic symptomatology. *Stress and Health, 19,* 17–26.

Bisson, J. I., & Andrew, M. (2007). Psychological treatment of post-traumatic stress disorder (PTSD). *Cochrane Database of Systematic Reviews, April 18*(2), Art No. CD003388. Available at http://mrw.interscience.wiley.com/cochrane.clsysrev/articles/CD003388/pdf_fs.html

Bisson, J. I., Ehlers, A., Matthews, R., Pilling, S., Richards, D., & Turner, S. (2007). Psychological treatments for chronic post-traumatic stress disorder. Systematic review and meta-analysis. *British Journal of Psychiatry, 190,* 97–104.

Blake, D. D., Weathers, F. W., Nagy, L. M., Kaloupek, D. G., Charney, D. S., & Keane, T. M. (1995). *Clinician administered PTSD Scale for* DSM–IV. Boston: National Center for Posttraumatic Stress Disorder.

Blanchard, E. P., Jones-Alexander, J., Buckley, T. C., & Forneris, C. A. (1996). Psychometric properties of the PTSD Checklist. *Behavior Therapy, 34,* 669–673.

Bliese, P. D., Wright, K. M., Adler, A. B., & Cabrera, O. (2008). Validating the PC-PTSD and the PTSD checklist with soldiers returning from combat. *Journal of Consulting and Clinical Psychology, 76,* 272–281.

Bodenheimer, T., Lorig, K., Holman, H., & Grumbach, K. (2002). Patient self-management of chronic disease in primary care. *JAMA, 288,* 2469–2475.

Bolton, E. E., Mueser, K. T., & Rosenberg, S. D. (2006). Symptom correlates of post-traumatic stress disorder in clients with borderline personality disorder. *Comprehensive Psychiatry, 47,* 357–361.

Boney-McCoy, S., & Finkelhor, D. (1995). Psychosocial sequelae of violent victimization in a national youth sample. *Journal of Consulting and Clinical Psychology, 63,* 726–736.

Borkovec, T. D., & Whisman, M. A. (1996). Psychosocial treatment for generalized anxiety disorder. In M. Mavissakalian & R. F. Prien (Eds.), *Anxiety disorders: Psychological and pharmacological treatments* (pp. 171–199). Washington, DC: American Psychiatric Press.

Borowsky, S. J., Rubenstein, L. V., Meredith, L. S., Camp, P., Jackson-Triche, M., & Wells, K. B. (2007). Who is at risk of nondetection of mental health problems in primary care? *Journal of General Internal Medicine, 15,* 381–388.

Boudewyns, P. A., & Shipley, R. H. (1983). *Flooding and implosive therapy: Direct therapeutic exposure in clinical practice.* New York: Plenum Press.

Bourne, E. J. (1998). *Overcoming specific phobias: A hierarchy and exposure-based protocol for the treatment of all specific phobias—Therapist protocol.* Oakland, CA: New Harbinger.

Bowman, E. S. (1993). Etiology and clinical course of pseudoseizures: Relationship to trauma, depression, and dissociation. *Psychosomatics, 34,* 333–342.

Bracken, P. J. (2001). Post-modernity and posttraumatic stress disorder. *Social Science and Medicine, 53,* 733–743.

Bradley, R., Greene, J., Russ, E., Dutra, L., & Westen, D. (2005). A multidimensional meta-analysis of psychotherapy for PTSD. *American Journal of Psychiatry, 162,* 214–227.

Brady, K. T., Back, S. E., & Coffey, S. F. (2004). Substance abuse and posttraumatic stress disorder. *Current Directions in Psychological Science, 13,* 206–209.

Brady, K. T., Dansky, B. S., Back, S. E., Foa, E. B., & Carroll, K. M. (2001). Exposure therapy in the treatment of PTSD among cocaine-dependent individuals: Preliminary findings. *Journal of Substance Abuse Treatment, 21,* 47–54.

Brady, K. T., Killeen, T. K., Brewerton, T., & Lucerini, S. (2000). Comorbidity of psychiatric disorders and posttraumatic stress disorder. *Journal of Clinical Psychiatry, 61*(Suppl. 7), 22–32.

Brady, K. T., Killeen, T., Saladin, M. E., & Dansky, B. S. (1994). Comorbid substance abuse and posttraumatic stress disorder: Characteristics of women in treatment. *American Journal on Addictions, 3,* 160–164.

Brady, S., Rierdan, J., Penk, W., Losardo, M., & Meschede, T. (2003). Post-traumatic stress disorder in adults with serious mental illness and substance abuse. *Journal of Trauma and Dissociation, 4*(4), 77–90.

Brandes, D., Ben-Schachar, G., Gilboa, A., Bonne, O., Freedman, S., & Shalev, A. Y. (2002). PTSD symptoms and cognitive performance in recent trauma survivors. *Psychiatry Research, 110,* 231–238.

Brandon, S., Boakes, J., Glaser, D., & Green, R. (1998). Recovered memories of childhood sexual abuse: Implications for clinical practice. *British Journal of Psychiatry, 172,* 296–307.

Brehm, J. W. (1966). *A theory of psychological reactance.* New York: Academic Press.

Breslau, N., Davis, G. C., Andreski, P., & Peterson, E. (1991). Traumatic events and posttraumatic stress disorder in an urban population of young adults. *Archives of General Psychiatry, 48,* 216–222.

Breslau, N., Davis, G. C., Peterson, E. L., & Schultz, L. (1997). Psychiatric sequelae of posttraumatic stress disorder in women. *Archives of General Psychiatry, 54,* 81–87.

Breslau, N., Davis, G. C., Peterson, E. L., & Schultz, L. R. (2000). A second look at comorbidity in victims of trauma: The posttraumatic stress disorder–major depression connection. *Biological Psychiatry, 48,* 902–909.

Breslau, N., Davis, G. C., & Schultz, L. R. (2003). Posttraumatic stress disorder and the incidence of nicotine, alcohol, and other drug disorders in persons who have experienced trauma. *Archives of General Psychiatry, 60,* 289–294.

Breslau, N., Peterson, E. L., Poisson, L. M., Schultz, L. R., & Lucia, V. C. (2004). Estimating post-traumatic stress disorder in the community: Lifetime perspective and impact of typical traumatic events. *Psychological Medicine, 34,* 889–898.

Brewin, C. R. (2003). *Post-traumatic stress disorder: Malady or myth?* New Haven, CT: Yale University Press.

Brewin, C. R. (2005). Systematic review of screening instruments for adults at risk of PTSD. *Journal of Traumatic Stress, 18,* 53–62.

Brewin, C. R., Andrews, B., & Valentine, J. D. (2000). Meta-analysis of risk factors for posttraumatic stress disorder in trauma-exposed adults. *Journal of Consulting and Clinical Psychology, 68,* 748–766.

Brewin, C. R., & Holmes, E. A. (2003). Psychological theories of posttraumatic stress disorder. *Clinical Psychology Review, 23,* 339–376.

Brewin, C. R., Kleiner, J. S., Vasterling, J. J., & Field, A. P. (2007). Memory for emotionally neutral information in posttraumatic stress disorder: A meta-analytic investigation. *Journal of Abnormal Psychology, 116,* 448–463.

Briere, J. (1984, April). *The effects of childhood sexual abuse on later psychological functioning: Defining a "post-sexual-abuse syndrome."* Paper presented at the Third National Conference on Sexual Victimization of Children, Washington, DC.

Briere, J. (1992). *Child abuse trauma: Theory and treatment of the lasting effects.* Newbury Park, CA: Sage.

Briere, J., Woo, R., McRae, B., Foltz, J., & Sitzman, R. (1997). Lifetime victimization history, demographics, and clinical status in female psychiatric emergency room patients. *Journal of Nervous and Mental Disease, 185,* 95–101.

Brown, D., Scheflin, A. W., & Hammond, D. C. (1998). *Memory, trauma, treatment, and the law.* New York: Norton.

Brown, P. J., Recupero, P. R., & Stout, R. (1995). PTSD substance abuse comorbidity and treatment utilization. *Addictive Behaviors, 20,* 251–254.

Brown, P. J., Stout, R. L., & Mueller, T. (1999). Substance use disorder and posttraumatic stress disorder comorbidity: Addiction and psychiatric treatment rates. *Psychology of Addictive Behaviors, 13,* 115–122.

Brown, S. (1985). *Treating the alcoholic.* New York: Wiley.

Bruce, S. E., Weisberg, R. B., Dolan, R. T., Machan, J. T., Manchester, G., Kessler, R. C., et al. (2001). Trauma and posttraumatic stress disorder in primary care patients. *Primary Care Companion to the Journal of Clinical Psychiatry, 3,* 211–217.

Bryant, R. A., Moulds, M. L., Guthrie, R. M., Dang, S. T., Mastrodomenico, J., Nixon, R. D. V., et al. (2008). A randomized controlled trial of exposure therapy and cognitive restructuring for posttraumatic stress disorder. *Journal of Consulting and Clinical Psychology, 76,* 695–703.

Bryant, R. A., Moulds, M. L., Guthrie, R. M., Dang, S. T., & Nixon, R. D. V. (2003). Imaginal exposure alone and imaginal exposure with cognitive restructuring in treatment of posttraumatic stress disorder. *Journal of Consulting and Clinical Psychology, 71,* 706–712.

Buckley, T. C., Blanchard, E. B., & Neill, W. T. (1990). Information processing and PTSD: A review of the empirical literature. *Clinical Psychology Review, 20,* 1041–1065.

Buka, S. L., Stichick, T. L., Birdthistle, I., & Earls, F. J. (2001). Youth exposure to violence: Prevalence, risks, and consequences. *American Journal of Orthopsychiatry, 71,* 298–310.

Burns, D. D. (1999). *Feeling good: The new mood therapy* (Rev. ed.). New York: Avon.

Burton, D., Foy, D. W., Bwanausi, C., Johnson, J., & Moore, L. (1994). The relationship between traumatic exposure, family dysfunction, and post-traumatic stress symptoms in male juvenile offenders. *Journal of Traumatic Stress, 7,* 83–93.

Buss, A. H., & Perry, M. (1992). The aggression questionnaire. *Journal of Personality and Social Psychology, 63,* 452–459.

Bustamante, V., Mellman, T. A., David, D., & Fins, A. I. (2001). Cognitive functioning and the early development of PTSD. *Journal of Traumatic Stress, 14,* 791–797.

Butler, R. W., Mueser, K. T., Sprock, J., & Braff, D. L. (1996). Positive symptoms of psychosis in posttraumatic stress disorder. *Biological Psychiatry, 39,* 839–844.

Butterfield, M. I., & Becker, M. E. (2002). Posttraumatic stress disorder in women: Assessment and treatment in primary care. *Primary Care: Clinics in Office Practice, 29,* 151–170.

Cacciola, J. S., Alterman, A. I., McKay, J. R., & Rutherford, M. J. (2001). Psychiatric comorbidity in clients with substance use disorders: Do not forget Axis II disorders. *Psychiatric Annals, 31,* 321–331.

Calhoun, P. S., Stechuchak, K. M., Strauss, J., Bosworth, H. B., Marx, C. E., & Butterfield, M. I. (2007). Interpersonal trauma, war zone exposure, and posttraumatic stress disorder among veterans with schizophrenia. *Schizophrenia Research, 91,* 210–216.

Callaghan, P., & Morrissey, J. (1993). Social support and health: A review. *Journal of Advanced Nursing, 18,* 203–210.

Canterbury, R., & Yule, W. (1999). Planning a psychosocial response to a disaster. In W. Yule (Ed.), *Post-traumatic stress disorders: Concepts and therapy* (pp. 285–296). New York: Wiley.

Cardena, E., & Spiegel, D. (1993). Dissociative reactions to the San Francisco Bay area earthquake of 1989. *American Journal of Psychiatry, 150*, 474–478.

Carmen, E., Rieker, P. P., & Mills, T. (1984). Victims of violence and psychiatric illness. *American Journal of Psychiatry, 141*, 378–383.

Cascardi, M., Mueser, K. T., DeGiralomo, J., & Murrin, M. (1996). Physical aggression against psychiatric inpatients by family members and partners: A descriptive study. *Psychiatric Services, 47*, 531–533.

Cauffman, E., Feldman, S. S., Waterman, J., & Steiner, H. (1998). Posttraumatic stress disorder among female juvenile offenders. *Journal of the American Academy of Child & Adolescent Psychiatry, 37*, 1209–1216.

Cervantes, R. C., Padilla, A. M., & De Snyder, N. S. (1989). Reliability and validity of the Hispanic Stress Inventory. *Hispanic Journal of Behavioral Sciences, 12*, 76–82.

Chadwick, P. (2006). *Person-based cognitive therapy for distressing psychosis.* Chichester, England: Wiley.

Charcot, J. M. (1872–1873). *Lecons sur les maladies du système nerveux faites à la Salpêtrière* [Lessons on the illnesses of the nervous system held at the Salpêtrière]. Paris: Delahaye.

Charcot, J. M. (1895). *Oeuvres complètes.* [Complete works]. Paris: Bureau du Progrès Mèdical.

Chard, K. M. (2005). An evaluation of cognitive processing therapy for the treatment of posttraumatic stress disorder related to childhood sexual abuse. *Journal of Consulting and Clinical Psychology, 73*, 965–971.

Chard, K. M., Weaver, T. L., & Resick, P. A. (1997). Adapting cognitive processing therapy for child sexual abuse survivors. *Cognitive and Behavioral Practice, 4*, 31–52.

Charney, M. E., & Keane, T. M. (2007). Psychometric analyses of the Clinician-Administered PTSD Scale (CAPS)—Bosnian translation. *Cultural Diversity and Ethnic Minority Psychology, 13*, 161–168.

Chemtob, C. M., Novaco, R., Hamada, R. S., Gross, D. M., & Smith, G. (1997). Anger regulation deficits in combat-related posttraumatic stress disorder. *Journal of Traumatic Stress, 10*, 17–36.

Chemtob, C. M., Tomas, S., Law, W., & Cremniter, D. (1997). Postdisaster psychosocial intervention: A field study of the impact of debriefing on psychological distress. *American Journal of Psychiatry, 154*, 415–417.

Chilcoat, H. D., & Breslau, N. (1998). Posttraumatic stress disorder and drug disorders: Testing causal pathways. *Archives of General Psychiatry, 55*, 913–917.

Clark, D. A. (2004). *Cognitive–behavioral therapy for OCD.* New York: Guilford Press.

Clark, D. M. (1989). Anxiety states: Panic and generalized anxiety. In K. Hawton, P. Salkovskis, J. Kirk, & D. M. Clark (Eds.). *Cognitive behavioural therapy for psychiatric problems: A practical guide* (pp. 52–96). Oxford, England: Oxford University Press.

Clark, D. M., & Ehlers, A. (2005). Posttraumatic stress disorder: From cognitive theory to therapy. In R. L. Leahy (Ed.), *Contemporary cognitive therapy* (pp. 141–160). New York: Guilford Press.

Clark, D. M., Salkovskis, P., & Chalkley, A. (1985). Respiratory control as a treatment for panic attacks. *Journal of Behavior Therapy and Experimental Psychiatry, 16,* 23–30.

Clark, H. W., Masson, C. L., Delucchi, K. L., Hall, S. M., & Sees, K. L. (2001). Violent traumatic events and drug abuse severity. *Journal of Substance Abuse Treatment, 20,* 121–127.

Clear, P. J., Vincent, J. P., & Harris, G. E. (2006). Ethnic differences in symptom presentation of sexually abused girls. *Journal of Child Sexual Abuse, 15,* 79–98.

Cloitre, M., Cohen, L. R., & Koenen, K. C. (2006). *Treating survivors of childhood abuse: Psychotherapy for the interrupted life.* New York: Guilford Press.

Cloitre, M., Miranda, R., Stovall-McClough, K. C., & Han, H. (2005). Beyond PTSD: Emotion regulation and interpersonal problems as predictors of functional impairment in survivors of childhood abuse. *Behavior Therapy, 36,* 119–124.

Cobb, S. (1976). Social support as a moderator of life stress. *Psychosomatic Medicine, 38,* 3000–3314.

Cohen, J. A., Berliner, L., & March, J. S. (2000). Treatment of children and adolescents. In E. B. Foa, T. M. Keane, & M. J. Friedman (Eds.), *Effective treatments for PTSD* (pp. 106–138). New York: Guilford Press.

Cohen, J. A., Deblinger, E., Mannarino, A. P., & Steer, R. A. (2004). A multisite, randomized controlled trial for children with sexual abuse–related PTSD symptoms. *Journal of the American Academy of Child & Adolescent Psychiatry, 43,* 393–402.

Cohen, J. A., Mannarino, A. P., & Deblinger, E. (2006). *Treating trauma and traumatic grief in children and adolescents.* New York: Guilford Press.

Cohen, L. R., & Hien, D. A. (2006). Treatment outcomes for women with substance abuse and PTSD who have experienced complex trauma. *Psychiatric Services, 57,* 100–106.

Cohen, M. L., & Quintner, J. L. (1996). The derailment of railway spine: A timely lesson for post-traumatic fibromyalgia syndrome. *Pain Reviews, 3,* 181–202.

Connor, K. M., Davidson, J. R. T., Hughes, D. C., Swartz, M. S., Blazer, D. G., & George, L. K. (2002). The impact of borderline personality disorder on posttraumatic stress in the community: A study of health status, health utilization, and functioning. *Comprehensive Psychiatry, 43,* 41–48.

Coon, D. W., & Thompson, L. W. (2003). The relationship between homework compliance and treatment outcomes among older adult outpatients with mild-to-moderate depression. *American Journal of Geriatric Psychiatry, 11,* 53–61.

Copeland, M. E., & Harris, M. (2000). *Healing the trauma of abuse: A woman's workbook.* Oakland, CA: New Harbinger.

Copeland, W. E., Keeler, G., Angold, A., & Costello, E. J. (2007). Traumatic events and posttraumatic stress in childhood. *Archives of General Psychiatry, 64*, 577–584.

Costello, E. J., Erkanli, A., Fairbank, J. A., & Angold, A. (2002). The prevalence of potentially traumatic events in childhood and adolescence. *Journal of Traumatic Stress, 15*, 99–112.

Cottler, L. B., Compton, W. M., III, Mager, D., Spitznagel, E. L., & Janca, A. (1992). Posttraumatic stress disorder among substance users from the general population. *American Journal of Psychiatry, 149*, 664–670.

Coverdale, J. H., & Grunebaum, H. (1998). Sexuality and family planning. In K. T. Mueser & N. Tarrier (Eds.), *Handbook of social functioning in schizophrenia* (pp. 224–237). Needham Heights, MA: Allyn & Bacon.

Craine, L. S., Henson, C. E., Colliver, J. A., & MacLean, D. G. (1988). Prevalence of a history of sexual abuse among female psychiatric patients in a state hospital system. *Hospital and Community Psychiatry, 39*, 300–304.

Crane, S. (1895). *The red badge of courage.* New York: Appleton.

Craske, M. G., Barlow, D. H., & Meadows, E. A. (2000). *Mastery of your anxiety and panic: Therapist guide for anxiety, panic, and agoraphobia MAP–3* (3rd ed.). San Antonio, TX: The Psychological Corporation.

Craske, M. G., & Lewin, M. R. (1998). Cognitive–behavioral treatment of panic disorders. In V. E. Caballo (Ed.), *International handbook of cognitive and behavioural treatments for psychological disorders* (pp. 105–128). Oxford, England: Pergamon.

Crescenzi, A., Ketzer, E., Van Ommeren, M., Phuntsok, K., Komproe, I., & de Jong, J. T. (2002). Effect of political imprisonment and trauma history on recent Tibetan refugees in India. *Journal of Traumatic Stress, 15*, 369–375.

Cuffe, S. P., Addy, C. L., Garrison, C. Z., Waller, J. L., Jackson, K. L., McKeown, R. E., et al. (1998). Prevalence of PTSD in a community sample of older adolescents. *Journal of the American Academy of Child and Adolescent Psychiatry, 37*, 147–154.

Cusack, K. J., Frueh, B. C., & Brady, K. T. (2004). Trauma history screening in a community mental health center. *Psychiatric Services, 55*, 157–162.

Dalgleish, T. (2004). Cognitive approaches to posttraumatic stress disorder: The evolution of multirepresentational theorizing. *Psychological Bulletin, 130*, 228–260.

Daly, R. J. (1983). Samuel Pepys and post-traumatic stress disorder. *British Journal of Psychiatry, 143*, 64–68.

Dansky, B. S., Brady, K. T., Saladin, M. E., Killeen, T., Becker, S., & Roitzsch, J. C. (1996). Victimization and PTSD in individuals with substance use disorders: Gender and racial differences. *American Journal of Drug and Alcohol Abuse, 22*, 75–93.

Dansky, B. S., Roitzsch, J. C., Brady, K. T., & Saladin, M. E. (1997). Posttraumatic stress disorder and substance abuse: Use of research in a clinical setting. *Journal of Traumatic Stress, 10*, 141–148.

Dansky, B. S., Saladin, M. E., Brady, K. T., Kilpatrick, D. G., & Resnick, H. S. (1995). Prevalence of victimization and posttraumatic stress disorder among women with substance use disorders: Comparison of telephone and in-person assessment samples. *International Journal of the Addictions, 30*, 1079–1099.

Dartmouth Trauma Interventions Research Center. (2006). *The coping with stress handbook*. Unpublished handbook.

Deblinger, E., McLeer, S. V., Atkins, M. S., Ralphe, D., & Foa, E. B. (1989). Posttraumatic stress in sexually abused, physically abused, and nonabused children. *Child Abuse and Neglect, 13*, 403–408.

Deegan, P. (1996, September). *Recovery and the conspiracy of hope*. Paper presented at the Sixth Annual Mental Health Conference of Australia and New Zealand, Brisbane, Australia.

Deters, P. T., Novins, D. K., Fickenscher, A., & Beals, J. (2006). Trauma and posttraumatic stress disorder symptomatology: Patterns among American Indian adolescents in substance abuse treatment. *American Journal of Orthopsychiatry, 76*, 335–345.

Deykin, E. Y., & Buka, S. L. (1997). Prevalence and risk factors for posttraumatic stress disorder among chemically dependent adolescents. *American Journal of Psychiatry, 154*, 752–757.

Dixon, A., Howie, P., & Starling, J. (2005). Trauma exposure, posttraumatic stress, and psychiatric comorbidity in female juvenile offenders. *Journal of the Academy of Child and Adolescent Psychiatry, 44*, 798–806.

Dobie, D. J., Kivlahan, D. R., Maynard, C., Bush, K. R., McFall, M., Epler, A. J., et al. (2002). Screening for post-traumatic stress disorder in female Veteran's Affairs patients: Validation of the PTSD checklist. *General Hospital Psychiatry, 21*, 367–374.

Donahue, S., Jackson, C., Shear, M. K., Felton, C., & Essock, S. M. (2006). Outcomes of enhanced counseling services provided to adults through Project Liberty. *Psychiatric Services, 57*, 1298–1303.

Donnelly, C. L., & Amaya-Jackson, L. (2002). Post-traumatic stress disorder in children and adolescents: Epidemiology, diagnosis and treatment options. *Pediatric Drugs, 4*, 159–170.

Downs, W. R., & Harrison, L. (1998). Childhood maltreatment and the risk of substance Problems in later life. *Health and Social Care in the Community, 6*, 35–48.

Dreessen, L., & Arntz, A. (1998). The impact of personality disorders on treatment outcome of anxiety disorders: Best-evidence synthesis. *Behaviour Research and Therapy, 36*, 483–504.

Drossman, D. A., Leserman, J., Nachman, G., Li, Z., Gluck, H., Toomey, T. C., et al. (1990). Sexual and physical abuse in women with functional or organic gastrointestinal disorders. *Annals of Internal Medicine, 113*, 828–833.

Duffy, M., Gillespie, K., & Clark, D. M. (2007). Post-traumatic stress disorder in the context of terrorism and other civil conflict in Northern Ireland: Randomised controlled trial. *British Medical Journal, 334*, 1147–1150.

Dunmore, E., Clark, D. M., & Ehlers, A. (2001). A prospective investigation of the role of cognitive factors in persistent posttraumatic stress disorder (PTSD) after physical or sexual assault. *Behaviour Research and Therapy, 39*, 1063–1084.

Edelman, R. E., & Chambless, D. L. (1995). Adherence during sessions and home-work in cognitive–behavioral group treatment of social phobia. *Behaviour Research and Therapy, 33*, 573–577.

Edwards, V. J., Holden, G. W., Felitti, V. J., & Anda, R. F. (2003). Relationship between multiple forms of childhood maltreatment and adult mental health in community respondents: Results from the adverse childhood experiences study. *American Journal of Psychiatry, 160*, 1453–1460.

Ehlers, A., & Clark, D. M. (2000). A cognitive model of posttraumatic stress disor-der. *Behaviour Research and Therapy, 38*, 319–345.

Ehlers, A., Clark, D. M., Hackmann, A., McManus, F., & Fennell, M. (2005). Cog-nitive therapy for post-traumatic stress disorder: Development and evaluation. *Behaviour Research and Therapy, 43*, 413–431.

Ehlers, A., Clark, D. M., Hackmann, A., McManus, F., Fennell, M., Herbert, C., et al. (2003). A randomized controlled trial of cognitive therapy, a self-help booklet, and repeated assessments as early interventions for posttraumatic stress disorder. *Archives of General Psychiatry, 60*, 1024–1032.

Ehlers, A., Hackmann, A., & Michael, T. (2004). Intrusive re-experiencing in post-traumatic stress disorder: Phenomenology, theory, and therapy. *Memory, 12*, 403–415.

Ehlers, A., Maercker, A., & Boos, A. (2000). Posttraumatic stress disorder following political imprisonment: The role of mental defeat, alienation, and perceived per-manent change. *Journal of Abnormal Psychology, 109*, 45–55.

Ehlers, A., Mayou, R. A., & Bryant, B. (1998). Psychological predictors of chronic posttraumatic stress disorder after motor vehicle accidents. *Journal of Abnormal Psychology, 107*, 508–519.

Ehlers, A., Mayou, R. A., & Bryant, B. (2003). Cognitive predictors of posttraumatic stress disorder in children: Results of a prospective longitudinal study. *Behaviour Research and Therapy, 41*, 1–10.

Ehring, T., Ehlers, A., Cleare, A. J., & Glucksman, E. (2008). Do acute psychologi-cal and psychobiological responses to trauma predict subsequent symptom sever-ities of PTSD and depression? *Psychiatry Research, 161*, 67–75.

Eisenman, D. P., Gelberg, L., Liu, H., & Shapiro, M. F. (2003). Mental health and health-related quality of life among adult Latino primary care patients living in the United States with previous exposure to political violence. *JAMA, 290*, 667–670.

Elklit, A. (2002). Victimization and PTSD in a Danish national youth probability sam-ple. *Journal of the American Academy of Child & Adolescent Psychiatry, 41*, 174–181.

Elliot, N. L., Quinless, F. W., & Parietti, E. S. (2000). Assessment of a Newark neigh-borhood: Process and outcomes. *Journal of Community Health Nursing, 17*, 211–224.

Ellis, A. (1962). *Reason and emotion in psychotherapy.* New York: Lyle Stuart.

Enright, R. D., & Fitzgibbons, R. P. (2000). *Helping clients forgive: An empirical guide for resolving anger and restoring hope.* Washington, DC: American Psychological Association.

Erichsen, J. E. (1866). *On railway and other injuries to the nervous system*. London: Walton & Maberly.

Erikson, E. (1968). *Identity: Youth and crisis*. New York: Norton.

Eriksson, C. B., Van De Kemp, H., Gorsuch, R., Hokke, S., & Foy, D. W. (2001). Trauma exposure and PTSD symptoms in international relief and development personnel. *Journal of Traumatic Stress, 14*, 205–219.

Farley, M., Golding, J. M., & Minkoff, J. R. (2002). Is a history of trauma associated with a reduced likelihood of cervical cancer screening? *Journal of Family Practice, 51*, 827–831.

Feeny, N. C., Zoellner, L. A., & Foa, E. B. (2002). Treatment outcome for chronic PTSD among female assault victims with borderline personality characteristics: A preliminary examination. *Journal of Personality Disorders, 16*, 30–40.

Figueroa, E. F., Silk, K. R., Huth, A., & Lohr, N. E. (1997). History of childhood sexual abuse and general psychopathology. *Comprehensive Psychiatry, 38*, 23–30.

Finkelhor, D., Hotaling, G., Lewis, I. A., & Smith, C. (1990). Sexual abuse in a national survey of adult men and women: Prevalence, characteristics, risk factors. *Child Abuse and Neglect, 14*, 19–28.

Flynn, P. M., & Brown, B. S. (2008). Co-occurring disorders in substance abuse treatment: Issues and prospects. *Journal of Substance Abuse Treatment, 34*, 36–47.

Foa, E. B., Dancu, C. V., Hembree, E. A., Jaycox, L. H., Meadows, E. A., & Street, G. P. (1999). A comparison of exposure therapy, stress inoculation training, and their combination for reducing posttraumatic stress disorder in female assault victims. *Journal of Consulting and Clinical Psychology, 67*, 194–200.

Foa, E. B., Ehlers, A., Clark, D. M., Tolin, D. F., & Orsillo, S. M. (1999). The Posttraumatic Cognitions Inventory (PTCI): Development and validation. *Psychological Assessment, 11*, 303–314.

Foa, E. B., Hembree, E. A., Cahill, S. P., Rauch, S. A. M., Riggs, D. S., Feeny, N. C., et al. (2005). Randomized trial of prolonged exposure for posttraumatic stress disorder with and without cognitive restructuring: Outcome at academic and community clinics. *Journal of Consulting and Clinical Psychology, 73*, 953–564.

Foa, E. B., Hembree, E. A., & Rothbaum, B. O. (2007). *Prolonged exposure therapy for PTSD*. New York: Oxford University Press.

Foa, E. B., Johnson, K. M., Feeny, N. C., & Treadwell, K. R. H. (2001). The Child PTSD Symptom Scale: A preliminary examination of its psychometric properties. *Journal of Clinical Child Psychology, 30*, 376–384.

Foa, E. B., Keane, T. M., & Friedman, M. J. (2000). Guidelines for the treatment of PTSD. *Journal of Traumatic Stress, 13*, 539–555.

Foa, E. B., & Kozak, M. J. (1986). Emotional processing of fear: Exposure to corrective information. *Psychological Bulletin, 99*, 20–35.

Foa, E. B., & Riggs, D. S. (1993). Post-traumatic stress disorder in rape victims. In J. Oldham, M. B. Riba, & A. Tasman (Eds.), *American Psychiatric Press review of psychiatry* (Vol. 12, pp. 273–303). Washington, DC: American Psychiatric Press.

Foa, E. B., Riggs, D. S., Massie, E., & Yarczower, M. (1995). The impact of fear activation and anger on the efficacy of exposure treatment for posttraumatic stress disorder. *Behavior Therapy, 26*, 487–499.

Foa, E. B., & Rothbaum, B. O. (1998). *Treating the trauma of rape: Cognitive–behavioral therapy for PTSD*. New York: Guilford Press.

Foa, E. B., Steketee, G., & Rothbaum, B. O. (1989). Behavioral/cognitive conceptualization of post-traumatic stress disorder. *Behavior Therapy, 20*, 155–176.

Foa, E. B., & Tolin, D. F. (2000). Comparison of the PTSD Symptom Scale—Interview Version and the Clinician-Administered PTSD Scale. *Journal of Traumatic Stress, 13*, 181–191.

Follette, V. M., & Pistorello, J. (2007). *Finding life beyond trauma: Using acceptance and commitment therapy to heal from post-traumatic stress and trauma-related problems*. Oakland, CA: New Harbinger.

Forbes, D., Creamer, M., Hawthorne, G., Allen, N., & McHugh, T. (2003). Comorbidity as a predictor of symptom change after treatment in combat-related posttraumatic stress disorder. *Journal of Nervous and Mental Disease, 191*, 93–99.

Ford, J. D., Fisher, P., & Arson, L. (1997). Object relations as a predictor of treatment outcome with chronic posttraumatic stress disorder. *Journal of Consulting and Clinical Psychology, 65*, 547–559.

Ford, J. D., & Kidd, P. (1998). Early childhood trauma and disorders of extreme stress as predictors of treatment outcome with chronic posttraumatic stress disorder. *Journal of Traumatic Stress, 4*, 743–761.

Fortuna, L. R., Porche, M. V., & Alegria, M. (2008). Political violence, psychosocial trauma, and the context of mental health services use among immigrant Latinos in the United States. *Ethnicity & Health, 13*, 435–463.

Fox, P. G., Burns, K. R., Popovich, J. M., & Ilg, M. M. (2001). Depression among immigrant Mexican women and Southeast Asian refugee women in the U. S. *International Journal of Psychiatric Nursing Research, 7*, 778–792.

Foy, D. W., Kagan, B. L., McDermott, C., Leskin, G., Sipprelle, R. C., & Paz, G. (1996). Practical parameters in the use of flooding for treating chronic PTSD. *Clinical Psychology and Psychotherapy, 3*, 169–175.

Freedman, S. R., & Enright, R. D. (1996). Forgiveness as an intervention goal with incest survivors. *Journal of Consulting and Clinical Psychology, 64*, 983–992.

Freedy, J. R., Resnick, H. S., Kilpatrick, D. G., Dansky, B. S., & Tidwell, R. P. (1994). The psychological adjustment of recent crime victims in the criminal justice system. *Journal of Interpersonal Violence, 9*, 450–468.

Freud, S. (1954). *New introductory lectures on psychoanalysis* (J. Strachey, Trans.). London: Allen & Unwin. (Original work published 1933)

Freud, S. (1956). Memorandum on the electrical treatment of war neurotics (1920). *International Journal of Psychoanalysis, 37*, 16–18. (Original work published 1920)

Freud, S. (1957). Remembering, repeating, and working through. In J. Strachey (Ed. & Trans.), *The standard edition of the complete psychological works of Sigmund*

Freud (Vol. 12, pp. 147–156). London: Hogarth Press. (Original work published 1914)

Freud, S. (1962). The aetiology of hysteria. In J. Strachey (Ed. & Trans.), *The standard edition of the complete psychological works of Sigmund Freud* (Vol. 3, pp. 189–224). London: Hogarth Press. (Original work published 1896)

Freud, S. (1989). *Introductory lectures on psychoanalysis* (J. Strachey, Trans.). New York: Norton. (Original work published 1917)

Freud, S. (2001). *The standard edition of the complete works of Sigmund Freud* (J. Strachey, Ed. & Trans.). London: Hogarth Press. (Original work published 1893–1899)

Freud, S., & Brewer, J. (1895). *Studies on hysteria* (J. Strachey, Ed. & Trans.). London: Hogarth Press.

Friedman, L., Samet, J., Roberts, M., Hudlin, M., & Hans, P. (1992). Inquiry about victimization experiences: A survey of patient preferences and physician practices. *Archives of Internal Medicine, 152,* 1186–1190.

Fullilove, M. T., Fullilove, R. E., III, Smith, M., Winkler, K., Michael, C., Panzer, P. G., et al. (1993). Violence, trauma, and post-traumatic stress disorder among women drug users. *Journal of Traumatic Stress, 6,* 533–543.

Galea, S., Nandi, A., & Vlahov, D. (2005). The epidemiology of post-traumatic stress disorder after disasters. *Epidemiologic Reviews, 27,* 78–91.

Gallo, J. J., Zubritsky, C., Maxwell, J., Nazar, M., Bogner, H. R., Quijano, L. M., et al. (2004). Primary care clinicians evaluate integrated and referral models of behavioral health care for older adults: Results from a multisite effectiveness trial (PRISM–E). *Annals of Family Medicine, 2,* 305–309.

Gearon, J. S., & Bellack, A. S. (1999). Women with schizophrenia and co-occurring substance use disorders: An increased risk for violent victimization and HIV. *Community Mental Health Journal, 35,* 401–419.

Gershuny, B. S., Cloitre, M., & Otto, M. W. (2003). Peritraumatic dissociation and PTSD severity: Do event-related fears about death and control mediate their relation? *Behaviour Research and Therapy, 41,* 157–166.

Gersons, B. P. R., & Carlier, I. V. E. (1992). Post-traumatic stress disorder: History of a recent concept. *British Journal of Psychiatry, 161,* 742–748.

Giaconia, R. M., Reinherz, H. Z., Silverman, A. B., Pakiz, B., Frost, A. K., & Cohen, E. (1995). Traumas and posttraumatic stress disorder in a community population of older adolescents. *Journal of the American Academy of Child & Adolescent Psychiatry, 34,* 1369–1380.

Gilbert, P. (2005). Compassion and cruelty: A biopsychosocial approach. In P. Gilbert (Ed.), *Compassion: Conceptualisations, research and use in psychotherapy* (pp. 9–71). London: Routledge.

Gilbert, P., & Irons, C. (2005). Focused therapies and compassionate mind training for shame and self-attacking. In P. Gilbert (Ed.), *Compassion: Conceptualisations, research and use in psychotherapy* (pp. 263–325). London: Routledge.

Gilbertson, M. W., Paulus, L. A., Williston, S. K., Gurvits, T. V., Lasko, N. B., Pitman, R. K., et al. (2006). Neurocognitive function in monozygotic twins discordant for combat exposure: Relationship to posttraumatic stress disorder. *Journal of Abnormal Psychology, 115,* 484–495.

Gillespie, K., Duffy, M., Hackman, A., & Clark, D. M. (2002). Community based cognitive therapy in the treatment of post-traumatic stress disorder following the Omagh bomb. *Behaviour Research and Therapy, 40,* 345–357.

Gloaguen, V., Cottraux, J., Cucherat, M., & Blackburn, I. M. (1998). A meta-analysis of the effects of cognitive therapy in depressed patients. *Journal of Affective Disorders, 62,* 59–72.

Gold, J., & Harvey, P. (1993). Cognitive deficits in schizophrenia. *Psychiatric Clinics of North America, 16,* 295–313.

Golding, J. M., Stein, J. A., Siegel, J. M., Burnam, M. A., & Sorenson, S. B. (1988). Sexual assault history and use of health and mental health services. *American Journal of Community Psychology, 16,* 625–643.

Goldman, C. R., & Quinn, F. L. (1988). Effects of a patient education program in the treatment of schizophrenia. *Hospital and Community Psychiatry, 39,* 282–286.

Golier, J. A., Yehuda, R., Bierer, L. M., Mitropoulou, V., New, A. S., Schmeidler, J., et al. (2003). The relationship of borderline personality disorder to posttraumatic stress disorder and traumatic events. *American Journal of Psychiatry, 160,* 2018–2024.

Goodman, L. A., Dutton, M. A., & Harris, M. (1995). Physical and sexual assault prevalence among episodically homeless women with serious mental illness. *American Journal of Orthopsychiatry, 65,* 468–478.

Goodman, L. A., Rosenberg, S. D., Mueser, K. T., & Drake, R. E. (1997). Physical and sexual assault history in women with serious mental illness: Prevalence, correlates, treatment, and future research directions. *Schizophrenia Bulletin, 23,* 685–696.

Goodman, L. A., Salyers, M. P., Mueser, K. T., Rosenberg, S. D., Swartz, M., Essock, S. M., et al. (2001). Recent victimization in women and men with severe mental illness: Prevalence and correlates. *Journal of Traumatic Stress, 14,* 615–632.

Goodman, L. A., Thompson, K. M., Weinfurt, K., Corl, S., Acker, P., Mueser, K. T., et al. (1999). Reliability of reports of violent victimization and PTSD among men and women with SMI. *Journal of Traumatic Stress, 12,* 587–599.

Granholm, E., McQuaid, J. R., McClure, F. S., Auslander, L. A., Perivoliotis, D., Pedrelli, P., et al. (2005). A randomized, controlled trial of cognitive behavioral social skills training for middle-aged and older outpatients with chronic schizophrenia. *American Journal of Psychiatry, 162,* 520–529.

Green, B. L. (1996). Trauma History Questionnaire. In B. H. Stamm (Ed.), *Measurement of stress, self-report trauma, and adaptation* (pp. 366–368). Lutherville, MD: Sidran Press.

Green, B. L., & Kimerling, R. (2004). Trauma, posttraumatic stress disorder, and health status. In P. P. Schnurr & B. L. Green (Eds.), *Trauma and health: Physical health consequences of exposure to extreme stress* (pp. 13–42). Washington, DC: American Psychological Association.

Grubaugh, A. L., Elhai, J. D., Cusack, K. J., Wells, C., & Frueh, B. C. (2007). Screening for PTSD in public-sector mental health settings: The diagnostic utility of the PTSD checklist. *Depression and Anxiety, 24,* 124–129.

Gunderson, J. G., & Sabo, A. N. (1993). The phenomenological and conceptual interface between borderline personality disorder and PTSD. *American Journal of Psychiatry, 150,* 19–27.

Gwadz, M. V., Nish, D., Leonard, N. R., & Strauss, S. M. (2007). Gender differences in traumatic events and rates of post-traumatic stress disorder among homeless youth. *Journal of Adolescence, 30,* 117–129.

Halligan, S. L., Michael, T., Clark, D. M., & Ehlers, A. (2003). Posttraumatic stress disorder following assault: The role of cognitive processing, traumatic memory, and appraisals. *Journal of Consulting and Clinical Psychology, 71,* 419–431.

Hamblen, J. L., Gibson, L. E., Mueser, K. T., & Norris, F. H. (2006). Cognitive behavioral therapy for prolonged postdisaster distress. *Journal of Clinical Psychology: In Session, 62,* 1043–1052.

Hamblen, J. L., Jankowski, M. K., Rosenberg, S. D., & Mueser, K. T. (2004). Cognitive–behavioral treatment for PTSD in people with severe mental illness: Three case studies. *American Journal of Psychiatric Rehabilitation, 7,* 147–170.

Hamblen, J. L., Mueser, K. T., Rosenberg, S. D., & Rosenberg, H. J. (2005). *Brief cognitive behavioral treatment for PTSD: Treatment manual and handouts.* Lebanon, NH: Dartmouth Trauma Interventions Research Center.

Hamblen, J. L., & Norris, F. H. (2007). *Project recovery evaluation: CBT for postdisaster distress.* White River Junction, VT: National Center for PTSD.

Hamblen, J. L., Norris, F. H., Pietruszkiewicz, S., Gibson, L., Naturale, A., & Louis, C. (in press). Cognitive behavioral therapy for postdisaster distress: A community based treatment program for survivors of Hurricane Katrina. *American Journal of Disaster Medicine.*

Harned, M. S., & Linehan, M. M. (2008). Integrating dialectical behavior therapy and prolonged exposure to treat co-occurring borderline personality disorder and PTSD: Two case studies. *Cognitive and Behavioral Practice, 15,* 263–276.

Harpaz-Rotem, I., Leslie, D., & Rosenheck, R. A. (2004). Treatment retention among children entering a new episode of mental health care. *Psychiatric Services, 55,* 225–237.

Hasanovic, M., Sinanovic, O., & Pavlovic, S. (2005). Acculturation and psychological problems of adolescents from Bosnia and Herzegovina during exile and repatriation. *Croatian Medical Journal, 46,* 105–115.

Hayes, S. C., Strosahl, K. D., & Wilson, K. G. (1999). *Acceptance and commitment therapy: An experiential approach to behavior change.* New York: Guilford Press.

Heaton, R., Paulsen, J. S., McAdams, L. A., Kuck, J., Zisook, S., Braff, D., et al. (1994). Neuropsychological deficits in schizophrenics: Relationship to age, chronicity, and dementia. *Archives of General Psychiatry, 51*, 469–476.

Heffernan, K., & Cloitre, M. (2000). A comparison of posttraumatic stress disorder with and without borderline personality disorder among women with a history of childhood sexual abuse: Etiological and clinical characteristics. *Journal of Nervous and Mental Disease, 188*, 589–595.

Heimberg, R. G., & Becker, R. E. (2002). *Cognitive–behavioral group therapy for social phobia.* New York: Guilford Press.

Hein, D. A., Cohen, L. R., Miele, G. M., Litt, L. C., & Capstick, C. (2004). Promising treatments for women with comorbid PTSD and substance use disorders. *American Journal of Psychiatry, 161*, 1426–1432.

Hein, D. A., Nunes, E., Levin, F. R., & Fraser, D. (2000). Posttraumatic stress disorder and short-term outcome in early methadone treatment. *Journal of Substance Abuse Treatment, 19*, 31–37.

Heinrichs, R. W. (2001). *In search of madness: Schizophrenia and neuroscience.* New York: Oxford University Press.

Hembree, E. A., Cahill, S. P., & Foa, E. B. (2004). Impact of personality disorders on treatment outcome for female assault survivors with chronic posttraumatic stress disorder. *Journal of Personality Disorders, 18*, 117–127.

Hemingway, E. (1940). *For whom the bell tolls.* New York: Scribner.

Herbert, J. D., & Sageman, M. (2004). "First do no harm:" Emerging guidelines for the treatment of posttraumatic reactions. In G. M. Rosen (Ed.), *Posttraumatic stress disorder: Issues and controversies* (pp. 213–232). New York: Wiley.

Herman, J. L. (1992a). Complex PTSD: A syndrome in survivors of prolonged and repeated trauma. *Journal of Traumatic Stress, 5*, 377–391.

Herman, J. L. (1992b). *Trauma and recovery.* New York: Basic Books.

Hinton, D. E., Chhean, D., Pich, V., Pollack, M. H., Orr, S. P., & Pitman, R. K. (2006). Assessment of posttraumatic stress disorder in Cambodian refugees using the clinician-administered PTSD scale: Psychometric properties and symptom severity. *Journal of Traumatic Stress, 19*, 405–440.

Hinton, D. E., Pich, V., Chhean, D., Pollack, M. H., & McNally, R. J. (2005a). "The ghost pushes you down": Sleep paralysis panic attacks in Khmer Refugee population. *Transcultural Psychiatry, 42*, 46–77.

Hinton, D. E., Pich, V., Chhean, D., Pollack, M. H., & McNally, R. J. (2005b). Sleep paralysis among Cambodian refugees: Association with PTSD diagnosis and severity. *Depression and Anxiety, 22*, 47–51.

Hjern, A., Angel, B., & Jeppson, O. (1998). Political violence, family stress and mental health of refugee children in exile. *Scandinavian Journal of Social Medicine, 26*, 18–25.

Hodgkinson, P., & Stewart, M. (1998). *Coping with catastrophe: A handbook of post-disaster psychosocial aftercare* (2nd ed.). London: Routledge.

Holbrook, T. L., Hoyt, D. B., Stein, M. B., & Sieber, W. J. (2001). Perceived threat to life predicts posttraumatic stress disorder after major trauma: Risk factors and functional outcome. *Journal of Traumatic Stress, 51*, 287–293.

Hollifield, V., Eckert, T., Warner, J., Jenkins, B., Krakow, J., Ruiz, J., et al. (2006). Development of an inventory for measuring war-related events in refugees. *Comprehensive Psychiatry, 6*, 67–80.

Horowitz, M. J. (1975). Intrusive and repetitive thoughts after stress. *Archives of General Psychiatry, 32*, 1457–1463.

Horowitz, M. J. (1979). Psychological response to serious life events. In V. Hamilton & D. M. Warburton (Eds.), *Human stress and cognition: An information processing approach* (pp. 235–263). New York: Wiley.

Horowitz, M. J. (1986). *Stress response syndromes* (2nd ed.). New York: Jason Aronson.

Hout, A. C. (2000). Fifty years of psychiatric nomenclature: Reflections on the 1943 War Department Technical Bulletin, Medical 203. *Journal of Clinical Psychology, 56*, 935–967.

Howgego, I. M., Owen, C., Meldrum, L., Yellowlees, P., Dark, F., & Parslow, R. (2005). Posttraumatic stress disorder: An exploratory study examining rates of trauma and PTSD and its effect on client outcomes in community mental health. *BMC Psychiatry, 5*(21). doi:10.1186/1471-244X-5-21

Institute of Medicine. (2006). *Improving the quality of health care for mental and substance-use conditions*. Washington, DC: Author.

International Federation of Red Cross and Red Crescent Societies. (2000). *World disaster report*. Dordrecht, The Netherlands: Martinus Nijhoff.

Jablensky, A. (1997). The 100-year epidemiology of schizophrenia. *Schizophrenia Research, 28*, 111–125.

Jacobson, L. K., Southwick, S. M., & Kosten, T. R. (2001). Substance use disorders in patients with posttraumatic stress disorder: A review of the literature. *American Journal of Psychiatry, 158*, 1184–1190.

Jamil, H., Hakim-Larson, J., Farrag, M., Kafaji, T., Duqum, I., & Jamil, L. H. (2002). A retrospective study of Arab American mental health clients: Trauma and the Iraqi refugees. *American Journal of Orthopsychiatry, 72*, 355–361.

Janet, P. (1898). *Névroses et idées fixes* [Neurosis and fixed ideas]. Paris: Alcan.

Janet, P. (1925). *Psychological healing* (Vols. I–II). New York: Arno Press.

Jankowski, M. K., Rosenberg, H. J., Mueser, K. T., Rosenberg, S. D., & Hamblen, J. L. (2005). *Cognitive behavioral therapy for PTSD in adolescents*. Unpublished manual.

Janoff-Bulman, R. (1992). *Shattered assumptions: Towards a new psychology of trauma*. New York: Free Press.

Jayasinghe, N., Giosan, C., Difende, J., Spielman, L., & Robin, L. (2006). Predictors of responses to psychotherapy referral of WTC utility disaster workers. *Journal of Traumatic Stress, 19*, 307–312.

Jaycox, L. H., & Foa, E. B. (1996). Obstacles in implementing exposure therapy for PTSD: Case discussions and practical solutions. *Clinical Psychology and Psychotherapy, 3*, 176–184.

Jaycox, L. H., Stein, B. D., Kataoka, S. H., Wong, M., Fink, A., Escudero, P., et al. (2002). Violence exposure, posttraumatic stress disorder, and depressive symptoms among recent immigrant schoolchildren. *Journal of the American Academy of Child & Adolescent Psychiatry, 41,* 1104–1110.

Jelinek, J. M., & Williams, T. (1984). Post-traumatic stress disorder and substance abuse in Vietnam combat veterans: Treatment problems, strategies and recommendations. *Journal of Substance Abuse Treatment, 1,* 87–97.

Jeon, W. T., Hong, C., Lee, C., Kim, D. K., Han, M., & Min, S. (2005). Correlation between traumatic events and posttraumatic stress disorder among North Korean defectors in South Korea. *Journal of Traumatic Stress, 18,* 147–154.

Jha, A. K., Perlin, J. B., Kizer, K. W., & Dudley, R. A. (2003). Effect of the transformation of the Veterans Affairs Health Care System on the quality of care. *New England Journal of Medicine, 348,* 2218–2227.

Kataoka, S. H., Stein, B. D., Jaycox, L. H., Wong, W., Escudero, P., Tu, W., et al. (2003). A school-based mental health program for traumatized Latino immigrant children. *Journal of the American Academy of Child & Adolescent Psychiatry, 42,* 311–318.

Katon, W., Von Korff, M., Lin, E., Walker, E., Simon, G. E., Bush, T., et al. (1995). Collaborative management to achieve treatment guidelines: Impact on depression in primary care. *JAMA, 273,* 1026–1031.

Kendall, P. C. (Ed.). (2000). *Child and adolescent therapy: Cognitive–behavioral procedures.* New York: Guilford Press.

Kessler, R. C. (2000). Posttraumatic stress disorder: The burden to the individual and to society. *Journal of Clinical Psychiatry, 61*(Suppl. 5), 4–12.

Kessler, R. C., Bergland, P., Demler, O., Jin, R., Merikangas, K. R., & Walters, E. E. (2005). Lifetime prevalence and age-of-onset distributions of *DSM–IV* disorders in the National Comorbidity Survey Replication. *Archives of General Psychiatry, 62,* 593–602.

Kessler, R. C., Chiu, W. T., Demler, O., & Walters, E. E. (2005). Prevalence, severity, and comorbidity of 12-month *DSM–IV* disorders in the National Comorbidity Survey Replication. *Archives of General Psychiatry, 62,* 617–627.

Kessler, R. C., Sonnega, A., Bromet, E., Hughes, M., & Nelson, C. B. (1995). Posttraumatic stress disorder in the National Comorbidity Survey. *Archives of General Psychiatry, 52,* 1048–1060.

Kessler, R. C., & Zhao, S. (1999). Overview of descriptive epidemiology of mental disorders. In C. S. Aneshensel & J. C. Phelan (Eds.), *Handbook of sociology of mental health* (pp. 127–150). Dordrecht, The Netherlands: Kluwer Academic.

Kessler, R. C., Zhao, S., Katz, S. J., Kouzis, A. C., Frank, R. G., Edlund, M., et al. (1999). Past-year use of outpatient services for psychiatric problems in the National Comorbidity Study. *American Journal of Psychiatry, 156,* 115–123.

Kilpatrick, D. G., Acierno, R., Saunders, B., Resnick, H. S., Best, C. L., & Schnurr, P. P. (2000). Risk factors for adolescent substance abuse and dependence: Data from a national sample. *Journal of Consulting and Clinical Psychology, 68,* 19–30.

Kilpatrick, D. G., & Best, C. L. (1984). Some cautionary remarks on treating sexual assault victims with implosion. *Behavior Therapy, 15,* 421–423.

Kilpatrick, D. G., Ruggiero, K. J., Acierno, R., Saunders, B. E., Resnick, H. S., & Best, C. L. (2003). Violence and risk of PTSD, major depression, substance abuse/dependence, and comorbidity: Results from the National Survey of Adolescents. *Journal of Consulting and Clinical Psychology, 71,* 692–700.

Kilpatrick, D. G., & Saunders, B. E. (1999). *Prevalence and consequences of child victimization: Results from the National Survey of Adolescents.* Washington, DC: National Institute of Justice.

Kindt, M., & Engelhard, I. M. (2005). Trauma processing and the development of posttraumatic stress disorder. *Journal of Behavior Therapy and Experimental Psychiatry, 36,* 69–76.

King, L. A., King, D. W., Fairbank, J. A., Keane, T. M., & Adams, G. A. (1998). Resilience–recovery factors in post-traumatic stress disorder among female and male Vietnam veterans: Hardiness, postwar social support, and additional stressful life events. *Journal of Personality and Social Psychology, 74,* 420–434.

King, N. J., Tonge, B. J., Mullen, P., Myerson, N., Heyne, D., Rollings, S., et al. (2002). Treating sexually abused children with posttraumatic stress symptoms: A randomized clinical trial. *Journal of the American Academy of Child & Adolescent Psychiatry, 39,* 1347–1355.

Kingdon, D. G., & Turkington, D. (2004). *Cognitive therapy of schizophrenia.* New York: Guilford Press.

Klaus, P., & Rennison, C. M. (2002). *Age patterns in violent victimization, 1973–2000* (Document No. NCJ 190104). Washington, DC: U.S. Department of Justice, Office of Justice Programs.

Kleijn, W. C., Hovens, J. E., & Rodenburg, J. J. (2001). Posttraumatic stress symptoms in refugees: assessments with the Harvard Trauma Questionnaire and the Hopkins Symptom Checklist-25 in different languages. *Psychological Reports, 88,* 527–532.

Knight, J., Sherritt, L., Shrier, L., Harris, S. K., & Change, G. (2002). Validity of the CRAFFT substance abuse screening test among adolescent clinic patients. *Archives of Pediatric and Adolescent Medicine, 156,* 607–614.

Koppenhaver, J. M., Caccioloa, J. S., Alterman, A. I., McKay, J. R., Rutherford, M. J., & Mulvaney, F. (2007). *Posttraumatic stress disorder and other psychopathology in substance abusing patients.* Unpublished manuscript.

Kroenke, K., Spitzer, R. L., Williams, J. B., Monahan, P. O., & Lowe, B. (2007). Anxiety disorders in primary care: Prevalence, impairment, comorbidity, and detection. *Annals of Internal Medicine, 146,* 317–325.

Krystal, H. (1988). *Integration and healing.* Hillsdale, NJ: Analytic Press.

Kubany, E. S., Haynes, S. N., Leisen, M. B., Owens, J. A., Kaplan, A. S., Watson, S. B., et al. (2000). Development and preliminary validation of a brief broad-spectrum measure of trauma exposure: The Traumatic Life Events Questionnaire. *Psychological Assessment, 12,* 210–224.

Kubany, E. S., & Ralston, T. C. (2008). *Treating PTSD in battered women: A step-by-step manual for therapists and counselors.* Oakland, CA: New Harbinger.

Kuhn, E., Blanchard, E. B., & Hickling, E. J. (2003). Posttraumatic stress disorder and psychosocial functioning within two samples of MVA survivors. *Behaviour Research and Therapy, 41,* 1105–1112.

Kulka, R. A., Schlenger, W. E., Fairbank, J. A., Hough, R. L., Jordan, B. K., & Marmar, C. R. (1990). *Trauma and the Vietnam War generation.* New York: Brunner/Mazel.

Kushner, M. G., & Mueser, K. T. (1993). Psychiatric co-morbidity with alcohol use disorders. In *Eighth special report to the U.S. Congress on alcohol and health* (NIH Pub. No. 94-3699, pp. 37–59). Rockville, MD: U.S. Department of Health and Human Services.

Lang, A. J., & Stein, M. B. (2005). An abbreviated PTSD checklist for use as a screening instrument in primary care. *Behaviour Research and Therapy, 43,* 585–594.

Lanou, F. (1993). Coordinating private and public mental health resources in a disaster. *Journal of Social Behavior and Personality, 8,* 255–260.

Lasser, K., Boyd, J. W., Woolhandler, S., Himmelstein, D. U., McCormick, D., & Bor, D. H. (2000). Smoking and mental illness: A population-based prevalence study. *JAMA, 284,* 2606–2610.

Lauterbach, D., & Vrana, S. (1996). Three studies on the reliability and validity of a self-report measure of posttraumatic stress disorder. *Assessment, 3,* 17–26.

Leahy, R. L. (2003a). *Cognitive therapy techniques: A practitioner's guide.* New York: Guilford Press.

Leahy, R. L. (Ed.). (2003b). *Roadblocks in cognitive–behavioral therapy.* New York: Guilford Press.

Lee, D. A. (2005). The perfect nurturer: A model to develop a compassionate mind within the context of cognitive therapy. In P. Gilbert (Ed.), *Compassion: Conceptualisations, research and use in psychotherapy* (pp. 326–351). London: Routledge.

Lewis-Fernandez, R., Garrido-Castillo, P., Bennasar, M. C., Parrilla, E. M., Laria, A. J., Ma, G., et al. (2002). Dissociation, childhood trauma, and *ataque de nervios* among Puerto Rican psychiatric outpatients. *American Journal of Psychiatry, 159,* 1603–1605.

Lieb, K., Zanarini, M. C., Schmahl, C., Linehan, M. M., & Bohus, M. (2004). Borderline personality disorder. *Lancet, 364,* 453–461.

Liebschutz, J., Saitz, R., Brower, V., Keane, T. M., Lloyd-Travaglini, C., Averbuch, T., et al. (2007). PTSD in urban primary care: High prevalence and low physician detection. *Journal of General Internal Medicine, 22,* 719–726.

Lifton, R. J. (1967). *Death in life: The survivors of Hiroshima.* New York: Simon & Schuster.

Linehan, M. M. (1993). *Cognitive–behavioral treatment of borderline personality disorder.* New York: Guilford Press.

Lipschitz, D. S., Kaplan, M. L., Sorkenn, J. B., Faedda, G. L., Chorney, P., & Asnis, G. M. (1996). Prevalence and characteristics of physical and sexual abuse among psychiatric outpatients. *Psychiatric Services, 47*, 189–191.

Litz, B. T., Blake, D. D., Gerardi, R. G., & Keane, T. M. (1990). Decision making guidelines for the use of direct therapeutic exposure in the treatment of post-traumatic stress disorder. *The Behavior Therapist, 13*, 91–93.

Litz, B. T., Engel, C. C., Bryant, R. A., & Papa, A. (2007). A randomized, controlled proof-of-concept trial of an Internet-based, therapist-assisted self-management treatment for posttraumatic stress disorder. *American Journal of Psychiatry, 164*, 1676–1684.

Loftus, E., & Ketcham, K. (1994). *The myth of repressed memory*. New York: St. Martin's Press.

Loo, C. M. (1994). Race-related PTSD: The Asian American Vietnam veteran. *Journal of Traumatic Stress, 7*, 637–656.

Lovallo, W. R. (2005). *Stress & health: Biological and psychological interactions* (2nd ed.). Thousand Oaks, CA: Sage.

Lu, W., Fite, R., Kim, E., Hyer, L., Yanos, P. T., Mueser, K. T., et al. (2009). Cognitive–behavioral treatment of PTSD in severe mental illness: Pilot study replication in an ethnically diverse population. *American Journal of Psychiatric Rehabilitation, 12*, 73–91.

Luborsky, L., Crits-Christoph, P., Alexander, L., Margolis, M., & Cohen, M. (1983). Two helping alliance methods for predicting outcomes of psychotherapy. A counting signs vs. a global rating method. *Journal of Nervous and Mental Disease, 171*, 480–491.

Lukoff, D., Nuechterlein, K. H., & Ventura, J. (1986). Manual for the Expanded Brief Psychiatric Rating Scale (BPRS). *Schizophrenia Bulletin, 12*, 594–602.

Lunney, C. A., & Schnurr, P. P. (2007). Domains of quality of life and symptoms in male veterans treated for posttraumatic stress disorder. *Journal of Traumatic Stress, 20*, 955–964.

Luxenberg, T., Spinazzola, J., Hidalgo, J., Hunt, C., & van der Kolk, B. A. (2001). Complex trauma and disorders of extreme stress (DESNOS) diagnosis, Part II: Treatment. *Directions in Psychiatry, 21*, 395–414.

Lysaker, P. H., Meyer, P. S., Evans, J. D., Clements, C. A., & Marks, K. A. (2001). Childhood sexual trauma and psychosocial functioning in adults with schizophrenia. *Psychiatric Services, 52*, 1485–1488.

Magruder, K. M., Frueh, B. C., Knapp, R. G., Davis, L., Hamner, M. B., Martin, R. H., et al. (2005). Prevalence of posttraumatic stress disorder in VA primary care clinics. *General Hospital Psychiatry, 27*, 169–179.

Marks, I., Lovell, K., Noshirvani, H., Livanou, M., & Thrasher, S. (1998). Treatment of posttraumatic stress disorder by exposure and/or cognitive restructuring. *Archives of General Psychiatry, 55*, 317–325.

Marsella, A. J., Friedman, M. J., Gerrity, E. T., & Scurfield, R. M. (Eds.). (1996). *Ethnocultural aspects of posttraumatic stress disorder: Issues, research, and clinical applications*. Washington, DC: American Psychological Association.

Marshall, R. D., Amsel, L., Neria, Y., & Jung Suh, E. (2006). Strategies for determination of evidence-based treatments: Training clinicians after large-scale disasters. In F. H. Norris, S. Galea, M. J. Friedman, & P. J. Watson (Eds.), *Research methods for studying mental health after disasters and terrorism* (pp. 226–242). New York: Guilford Press.

Martin-Baro, I., & Canas, J. S. (1989). Political violence and war as causes of psychosocial trauma in El Salvador. *International Journal of Mental Health, 18*, 3–20.

Masson, J. M. (2003). *The assault on truth: Freud's suppression of the seduction theory.* New York: Farrar, Strauss, & Giroux.

Matsakis, A. (1996). *I can't get over it: A handbook for trauma survivors* (2nd ed.). Oakland, CA: New Harbinger.

Matsakis, A. (2003). *The rape recovery handbook: Step-by-step help for survivors of sexual assault.* Oakland, CA: New Harbinger.

McCloskey, L., Southwick, K., Fernandez-Esquer, M. E., & Locke, C. (1995). The psychological effects of political and domestic violence on Central American and Mexican immigrant mothers and children. *Journal of Community Psychology, 23*, 95–116.

McFall, M., Atkins, D. C., Yoshimoto, D., Thompson, C. E., Kanter, E., Malte, C. A., et al. (2006). Integrating tobacco cessation treatment into mental health care for patients with posttraumatic stress disorder. *American Journal of Addictions, 15*, 336–344.

McFall, M., Saxon, A. J., Thompson, C. E., Yoshimoto, D., Malte, C., Straits-Troster, K., et al. (2005). Improving the rates of quitting smoking for veterans with posttraumatic stress disorder. *American Journal of Psychiatry, 162*, 1311–1319.

McFarlane, A. C., Bookless, C., & Air, T. (2001). Posttraumatic stress disorder in a general psychiatric inpatient population. *Journal of Traumatic Stress, 14*, 633–645.

McGovern, M. P., Drake, K. M., & Weiss, R. D. (2005, June). *Co-occurring PTSD and substance use disorders in community addiction treatment: Prevalence, retention and treatment outcomes.* Paper presented at the 67th Annual Meeting of the College on Problems of Drug Dependence, Orlando, FL.

McGovern, M. P., Fox, T. S., Xie, H., & Drake, R. E. (2004). A survey of clinical practices and readiness to adopt evidence-based practices: Dissemination research in an addiction treatment system. *Journal of Substance Abuse Treatment, 26*, 305–312.

McGovern, M. P., Lambert-Harris, C., Acquilano, S., Weiss, R. D., & Xie, H. (in press). A promising cognitive behavioral therapy for co-occurring substance use and posttraumatic stress disorders. *Addictive Behaviors.*

McLeer, S. V., Callaghan, M., Henry, D., & Wallen, J. (1994). Psychiatric disorders in sexually abused children. *Journal of the American Academy of Child & Adolescent Psychiatry, 33*, 313–319.

McLeer, S. V., Deblinger, E., Henry, D., & Orvaschel, H. (1992). Sexually abused children at high risk for post-traumatic stress disorder. *Journal of the American Academy of Child & Adolescent Psychiatry, 31*, 875–879.

McNally, R. J. (2003). *Remembering trauma*. Cambridge, MA: Belknap Press.

McNally, R. J., & Shin, L. M. (1995). Association of intelligence with severity of posttraumatic stress disorder symptoms in Vietnam combat veterans. *American Journal of Psychiatry, 152,* 936–938.

Meyer, I. H., Muenzenmaier, K., Cancienne, J., & Struening, E. L. (1996). Reliability and validity of a measure of sexual and physical abuse histories among women with serious mental illness. *Child Abuse and Neglect, 20,* 213–219.

Miller, D. (2003). *Your surviving spirit: A spiritual workbook for coping with trauma.* Oakland, CA: New Harbinger.

Miller, M. W., & Resick, P. A. (2007). Internalizing and externalizing subtypes in female sexual assault survivors: Implications for the understanding of complex PTSD. *Behavior Therapy, 38,* 58–71.

Mills, K. L., Lynskey, M., Teesson, M., Ross, J., & Darke, S. (2005). Post-traumatic stress disorder among people with heroin dependence in the Australian treatment outcome study (ATOS): Prevalence and correlates. *Drug and Alcohol Dependence, 77,* 243–249.

Milton, F., Patwa, V. K., & Hafner, R. J. (1978). Confrontation vs. belief modification in persistently deluded patients. *British Journal of Medical Psychology, 51,* 127–130.

Moeller, T. P., Bachman, G. A., & Moeller, J. R. (1993). The combined effects of physical, sexual, and emotional abuse during childhood: Long-term health consequences for women. *Child Abuse & Neglect, 17,* 623–640.

Monson, C. M., Schnurr, P. P., Resick, P. A., Friedman, M. J., Young-Xu, Y., & Stevens, S. P. (2006). Cognitive processing therapy for veterans with military-related posttraumatic stress disorder. *Journal of Consulting and Clinical Psychology, 74,* 898–907.

Monti, P. M., Abrams, D. B., Kadden, R. M., & Cooney, N. L. (2002). *Treating alcohol dependence* (2nd ed.). New York: Guilford Press.

Montoya, I., Haertzen, C., Hess, J., Covi, L., Fudala, P., Johnson, R., & Gorelick, D. A. (1995). Comparison of psychological symptoms between drug abusers seeking and not seeking treatment. *Journal of Nervous and Mental Disease, 183,* 50–53.

Morris, P., & Silove, D. (1992). Cultural influences in psychotherapy with refugee survivors of torture and trauma. *Hospital and Community Psychiatry, 43,* 820–824.

Morrison, A. P., Renton, J. C., Dunn, H., Williams, S., & Bentall, R. P. (2004). *Cognitive therapy for psychosis: A formulation-based approach.* New York: Brunner-Routledge.

Morrissey-Kane, E., & Prinz, R. J. (1999). Engagement in child and adolescent treatment: The role of parental cognitions and attributions. *Clinical Child and Family Psychology Review, 2,* 183–198.

Mueser, K. T., Bolton, E. E., Carty, P. C., Bradley, M. J., Ahlgren, K. F., DiStaso, D. R., et al. (2007). The trauma recovery group: A cognitive–behavioral program for PTSD in persons with severe mental illness. *Community Mental Health Journal, 43,* 281–304.

Mueser, K. T., & Butler, R. W. (1987). Auditory hallucinations in combat-related chronic posttraumatic stress disorder. *American Journal of Psychiatry, 144,* 299–302.

Mueser, K. T., Essock, S. M., Haines, M., Wolfe, R., & Xie, H. (2004). Posttraumatic stress disorder, supported employment, and outcomes in people with severe mental illness. *CNS Spectrums, 9,* 913–925.

Mueser, K. T., Goodman, L. A., Trumbetta, S. L., Rosenberg, S. D., Osher, F. C., Vidaver, R., et al. (1998). Trauma and posttraumatic stress disorder in severe mental illness. *Journal of Consulting and Clinical Psychology, 66,* 493–499.

Mueser, K. T., Rosenberg, S. D., Goodman, L. A., & Trumbetta, S. L. (2002). Trauma, PTSD, and the course of schizophrenia: An interactive model. *Schizophrenia Research, 53,* 123–143.

Mueser, K. T., Rosenberg, S. D., Jankowski, M. K., Hamblen, J. L., & Descamps, M. (2004). A cognitive–behavioral treatment program for posttraumatic stress disorder in severe mental illness. *American Journal of Psychiatric Rehabilitation, 7,* 107–146.

Mueser, K. T., Rosenberg, S. R., Xie, H., Jankowski, M. K., Bolton, E. E., Lu, W., et al. (2008). A randomized controlled trial of cognitive–behavioral treatment of posttraumatic stress disorder in severe mental illness. *Journal of Consulting and Clinical Psychology, 76,* 259–271.

Mueser, K. T., Salyers, M. P., Rosenberg, S. D., Ford, J. D., Fox, L., & Carty, P. (2001). A psychometric evaluation of trauma and PTSD assessments in persons with severe mental illness. *Psychological Assessment, 13,* 110–117.

Mueser, K. T., Salyers, M. P., Rosenberg, S. D., Goodman, L. A., Essock, S. M., Osher, F. C., et al. (2004). Interpersonal trauma and posttraumatic stress disorder in patients with severe mental illness: Demographic, clinical, and health correlates. *Schizophrenia Bulletin, 30,* 45–57.

Mueser, K. T., & Taub, J. (2008). Trauma and PTSD in adolescents with severe emotional disorders involved in multiple service systems. *Psychiatric Services, 59,* 627–634.

Mueser, K. T., & Taylor, K. L. (1997). A cognitive–behavioral approach. In M. Harris & C. L. Landis (Eds.), *Sexual abuse in the lives of women diagnosed with serious mental illness* (pp. 67–90). Amsterdam: Harwood Academic.

Mulvihill, D. (2005). The health impact of childhood trauma: An interdisciplinary review. *Issues in Comprehensive Pediatric Nursing, 28,* 115–136.

Mumford, D. B. (1992). Emotional distress in the Hebrew Bible: Somatic or psychological? *British Journal of Psychiatry, 160,* 92–97.

Munro, C. G., Freeman, C. P., & Law, R. (2004). General practitioners' knowledge of post-traumatic stress disorder: A controlled study. *British Journal of General Practice, 54,* 843–847.

Najavits, L. M. (2002). *Seeking safety: A treatment manual for PTSD and substance abuse.* New York: Guilford Press.

Najavits, L. M., Weiss, R. D., Shaw, S. R., & Muenz, L. R. (1998). "Seeking safety": Outcome of a new cognitive behavioral psychotherapy for women with posttraumatic stress disorder and substance dependence. *Journal of Traumatic Stress, 11,* 437–456.

Naparstek, B. (2005). *Invisible heroes: Survivors of trauma and how they heal.* New York: Bantam.

National Institute of Mental Health. (2002). *Mental health and mass violence: Evidence based early psychological intervention for victims/survivors of mass violence: A workshop to reach consensus on best practices* (NIH Publication No. 02-5138). Washington, DC: U.S. Government Printing Office.

Neighbors, H. W., Musick, M. A., & Williams, D. R. (1998). The African American minister as a source of help for serious personal crises: Bridge or barrier to mental health care? *Health Education & Behavior, 25,* 759–777.

Neria, Y., Bormet, E. J., Sievers, S., Lavelle, J., & Fochtmann, L. J. (2002). Trauma exposure and posttraumatic stress disorder in psychosis: Findings from a first-admission cohort. *Journal of Consulting and Clinical Psychology, 70,* 246–251.

Neria, Y., Solomon, Z., & Dekel, R. (1998). An eighteen-year follow-up study of Israeli prisoners of war and combat veterans. *Journal of Nervous and Mental Disease, 186,* 174–182.

Neuner, F., Schauer, M., Karunakara, U., Klaschik, C., Robert, C., & Elbert , T. (2004). Psychological trauma and evidence for enhanced vulnerability for posttraumatic stress disorder through previous trauma among West Nile refugees. *BMC Psychiatry, 4*(34). doi:10.1186/1471-244X-4-34

Nishith, P., Resick, P. A., & Mueser, K. T. (2001). Sleep disturbances and alcohol use motives in female rape victims with posttraumatic stress disorder. *Journal of Traumatic Stress, 14,* 469–479.

Norris, F. H. (1992). Epidemiology of trauma: Frequency and impact of different potentially traumatic events on different demographic groups. *Journal of Consulting and Clinical Psychology, 60,* 409–418.

Norris, F. H., Donahue, S., Felton, C., Watson, P., Hamblen, J. L., & Marshall, R. (2006). A psychometric analysis of Project Liberty's Adult Enhanced Services Referral Tool. *Psychiatric Services, 57,* 1328–1334.

Norris, F. H., & Elrod, C. L. (2006). Psychosocial consequences of disaster: A review of past research. In F. H. Norris, S. Galea, M. J. Friedman & P. J. Watson (Eds.), *Research methods for studying mental health after disasters and terrorism* (pp. 20–44). New York: Guilford Press.

Norris, F. H., & Kaniasty, K. Z. (1996). Received and perceived social support in times of stress: A test of the social support deterioration deterrence model. *Journal of Personality and Social Psychology, 71,* 498–511.

Norris, F. H., Perilla, J. L., & Murphy, A. D. (2001). Postdisaster stress in the United States and Mexico: A cross-cultural test of the multicriterion conceptual model of posttraumatic stress disorder. *Journal of Abnormal Psychology, 110,* 553–563.

Norris, F. H., Watson, P. J., Hamblen, J. L., & Pfefferbaum, B. J. (2005). Provider perspectives on disaster mental health services in Oklahoma City. In Y. Danieli, D. Brom, & J. B. Sills (Eds.), *The trauma of terrorism: Sharing knowledge and shared care* (pp. 649–662). Binghamton, NY: Haworth Press.

North, C. N., Nixon, S. J., Shariat, S., Mallonee, S., McMillen, J. C., Spitznagel, E. L., et al. (1999). Psychiatric disorders among survivors of the Oklahoma City bombing. *JAMA, 282,* 755–762.

North, J. (1987). Wrongdoing and forgiveness. *Philosophy, 62,* 499–508.

O'Brien, T. (1990). *The things they carried.* Boston: Houghton Mifflin.

Oetzel, K. B., & Scherer, D. G. (2003). Therapeutic engagement with adolescents in psychotherapy. *Psychotherapy Theory, Research, Practice, Training, 40,* 215–225.

Ogata, S. N., Silk, K. R., Goodrich, S., Lohr, N. E., Westen, D., & Hill, E. M. (1990). Childhood sexual and physical abuse in adult patients with borderline personality disorder. *American Journal of Psychiatry, 147,* 1008–1013.

Oruc, L., & Bell, P. (1995). Multiple rape trauma followed by delusional parasitosis: A case report from the Bosnian war. *Schizophrenia Research, 16,* 173–174.

Ouimette, P. C., Ahrens, C., Moos, R. H., & Finney, J. W. (1997). Posttraumatic stress disorder in substance abuse clients: Relationship to 1-year posttreatment outcomes. *Psychology of Addictive Behaviors, 11,* 34–47.

Ouimette, P. C., Finney, J. W., & Moos, R. H. (1999). Two-year posttreatment functioning and coping of substance abuse clients with posttraumatic stress disorder. *Psychology of Addictive Behaviors, 13,* 105–114.

Ouimette, P. C., Goodwin, E., & Brown, P. J. (2006). Health and well being of substance use disorder clients with and without posttraumatic stress disorder. *Addictive Behaviors, 31,* 1415–1423.

Ouimette, P. C., Moos, R. H., & Finney, J. W. (2000). Two-year mental health service use and course of remission in patients with substance use and posttraumatic stress disorders. *Journal of Studies on Alcohol, 61,* 247–253.

Ozer, E. J., Best, S. R., Lipsey, T. L., & Weiss, D. S. (2003). Predictors of posttraumatic stress disorder and symptoms in adults: A meta-analysis. *Psychological Bulletin, 129,* 52–73.

Paunovic, N., & Öst, L.-G. (2001). Cognitive–behavior therapy vs. exposure therapy in the treatment of PTSD in refugees. *Behaviour Research and Therapy, 39,* 1183–1197.

Pedersen, D. (2002). Political violence, ethnic conflict, and contemporary wars: Broad implications for health and social well-being. *Social Science & Medicine, 55,* 175–190.

Pelcovitz, D., van der Kolk, B., Roth, S., Mandel, F., Kaplan, S., & Resick, P. (1997). Development of a criteria set and a structured interview for disorders of extreme stress (SIDES). *Journal of Traumatic Stress, 10,* 3–16.

Pennebaker, J. W. (2004). *Writing to heal: A guided journal for recovering from trauma and emotional upheaval.* Oakland, CA: New Harbinger.

Perlin, J. B., Kolodner, R. M., & Roswell, R. H. (2004). The Veterans Health Administration: Quality, value, accountability, and information as transforming strategies for patient-centered care. *American Journal of Managed Care, 10,* 828–836.

Pfammatter, M., Junghan, U. M., & Brenner, H. D. (2006). Efficacy of psychological therapy in schizophrenia: Conclusions from meta-analyses. *Schizophrenia Bulletin, 32*(Suppl. 1), S64–S68.

Pham, P. N., Weinstein, H. M., & Longman, T. (2004). Trauma and PTSD symptoms in Rwanda: implications for attitudes toward justice and reconciliation. *JAMA, 292,* 602–612.

Pignone, M. P., Gaynes, B. N., Rushton, J. L., Burchell, C. M., Orleans, C. T., Mulrow, C. D., et al. (2002). Screening for depression in adults: A summary of the evidence for the US Preventive Services Task Force. *Annals of Internal Medicine, 136,* 765–776.

Pitman, R. K., Altman, B., Greenwald, E., Longpre, R. E., Macklin, M. L., Poire, R., et al. (1991). Psychiatric complications during flooding therapy for posttraumatic stress disorder. *Journal of Clinical Psychiatry, 52,* 17–20.

Pole, N., Best, S. R., Metzler, T., & Marmar, C. R. (2005). Why are Hispanics at greater risk for PTSD? *Cultural Diversity and Ethnic Minority Psychology, 11,* 144–161.

Polusny, M. A., & Follette, V. M. (1995). Long-term correlates of child sexual abuse: Theory and review of the empirical literature. *Applied and Preventive Psychology, 4,* 143–166.

Pope, H. G., Jr., & Hudson, J. I. (1995). Can memories of childhood sexual abuse be repressed? *Psychological Medicine, 25,* 121–126.

Pratt, S. I., Rosenberg, S. D., Mueser, K. T., Brancato, J., Salyers, M. P., Jankowski, M. K., et al. (2005). Evaluation of a PTSD psychoeducational program for psychiatric inpatients. *Journal of Mental Health, 14,* 121–127.

Prins, A., Ouimette, P., Kimerling, R., Cameron, R. P., Hugelshofer, D. S., Shaw-Hegwer, J., et al. (2004). The primary care PTSD screen: Development and operating characteristics. *Primary Care Psychiatry, 9,* 9–14.

Rapaport, M. H., Clary, C. M., Fayyad, R., & Endicott, J. (2005). Quality-of-life impairment in depressive and anxiety disorders. *American Journal of Psychiatry, 162,* 1171–1178.

Rapaport, M. H., Endicott, J., & Clary, C. M. (2002). Posttraumatic stress disorder and quality of life: Results across 64 weeks of sertraline treatment. *Journal of Clinical Psychiatry, 63,* 59–65.

Rapkin, A. J., Kames, L. D., Darke, L. L., Stampler, F. M., & Naliboff, B. D. (1990). History of physical and sexual abuse in women with chronic pelvic pain. *Obstetrics & Gynecology, 76,* 92.

Read, J., van Os, J., Morrison, A. P., & Ross, C. A. (2005). Childhood trauma, psychosis and schizophrenia: A literature review with theoretical and clinical implications. *Acta Psychiatrica Scandinavica, 112,* 330–350.

Read, J. P., Brown, P. J., & Kahler, C. W. (2004). Substance use and posttraumatic stress disorders: Symptom interplay and effects on outcome. *Addictive Behaviors, 29,* 1665–1672.

Reed, G. L., & Enright, R. D. (2006). The effects of forgiveness therapy on depression, anxiety, and posttraumatic stress for women after spousal emotional abuse. *Journal of Consulting and Clinical Psychology, 74,* 920–929.

Remarque, E. M. (1929). *All quiet on the western front.* Boston: Little, Brown.

Resick, P. A., Galovski, T. E., Uhlmansiek, M. O., Scher, C. D., Clum, G. A., & Young-Xu, Y. (2008). A randomized clinical trial to dismantle components of cognitive processing therapy for posttraumatic stress disorder in female victims of interpersonal violence. *Journal of Consulting and Clinical Psychology, 76,* 243–258.

Resick, P. A., Monson, C. M., & Chard, K. M. (2006). *Cognitive processing therapy: Veteran/Military Version.* Boston: VA Boston Healthcare System.

Resick, P. A., Nishith, P., Weaver, T. L., Astin, M. C., & Feuer, C. A. (2002). A comparison of cognitive processing therapy with prolonged exposure and a waiting condition for the treatment of posttraumatic stress disorder in female rape victims. *Journal of Consulting and Clinical Psychology, 70,* 867–879.

Resick, P. A., & Schnicke, M. K. (1993). *Cognitive processing therapy for rape victims: A treatment manual.* Newbury Park, CA: Sage.

Resnick, S. G., Bond, G. R., & Mueser, K. T. (2003). Trauma and posttraumatic stress disorder in people with schizophrenia. *Journal of Abnormal Psychology, 112,* 415–423.

Rheingold, A. A., Acierno, R., & Resnick, H. S. (2004). Trauma, posttraumatic stress disorder, and health risk behaviors. In P. P. Schnurr & B. L. Green (Eds.), *Trauma and health: Physical health consequences of exposure to extreme stress* (pp. 217–243). Washington, DC: American Psychological Association.

Rivers, W. H. R. (1918). The repression of war experience. *Proceedings of the Royal Society of Medicine, 11*(Sect Psychiat), 1–20.

Roberts, T. A., & Klein, J. (2003). Intimate partner abuse and high-risk behavior in adolescents. *Archives of Pediatrics & Adolescent Medicine, 157,* 375–380.

Romans, S. E., Martin, J. L., Anderson, J. C., O'Shea, M. L., & Mullen, P. E. (1995). Factors that mediate between child sexual abuse and adult psychological outcome. *Psychological Medicine, 25,* 127–142.

Rosenberg, H. J., Rosenberg, S. D., Williamson, P. J., & Wolford, G. L. (2000). A comparative study of trauma and PTSD prevalence in epileptic and psychogenic non-epileptic seizure patients. *Epilepsia, 41,* 447–452.

Rosenberg, H. J., Rosenberg, S. D., Wolford, G. L., Manganiello, P. D., Brunette, M. F., & Boynton, R. A. (2000). The relationship between trauma, PTSD and medical utilization in three high risk medical populations. *Psychiatry in Medicine, 30,* 247–259.

Rosenberg, S. D., Mueser, K. T., Jankowski, M. K., Salyers, M. P., & Acker, K. (2004). Cognitive–behavioral treatment of posttraumatic stress disorder in severe mental illness: Results of a pilot study. *American Journal of Psychiatric Rehabilitation, 7*, 171–186.

Rost, K., Nutting, P., Smith, J., Werner, J., & Duan, N. (2001). Improving depression outcomes in community primary care practice: A randomized trial of the quEST intervention. Quality Enhancement by Strategic Teaming. *Journal of General Internal Medicine, 16*, 143–149.

Roth, G., Ekblad, S., & Agren, H. (2006). A longitudinal study of PTSD in a sample of adult mass-evacuated Kosovars, some of whom returned to their home country. *European Psychiatry, 21*, 152–159.

Roth, S., Newman, E., Pelcovitz, D., van der Kolk, B., & Mandel, F. S. (1997). Complex PTSD in victims exposed to sexual and physical abuse: Results from the DSM–IV field trial for posttraumatic stress disorder. *Journal of Traumatic Stress, 10*, 539–555.

Rousseau, C., & Drapeau, A. (2004). Premigration exposure to political violence among independent immigrants and its association with emotional distress. *Journal of Nervous and Mental Disease, 192*, 852–856.

Rygh, J. L., & Sanderson, W. C. (2004). *Treating generalized anxiety disorder: Evidence-based strategies, tools, and techniques.* New York: Guilford Press.

Sabin, M., Cardozo, B. L., Nackerud, L., Kaiser, R., & Varese, L. (2003). Factors associated with poor mental health among Guatemalan refugees living in Mexico twenty years after civil conflict. *JAMA, 290*, 635–642.

Salyers, M. P., Evans, L. J., Bond, G. R., & Meyer, P. S. (2004). Barriers to assessment and treatment of posttraumatic stress disorder and other trauma-related problems in people with severe mental illness: Clinician perspectives. *Community Mental Health Journal, 40*, 17–31.

Sandars, N. K. (1972). *The epic of Gilgamesh.* New York: Penguin.

Saunders, B. E., Villeponteaux, L. A., Lipovsky, J. A., Kilpatrick, D. G., & Veronen, L. J. (1992). Child sexual assault as a risk factor for mental disorders among women: A community survey. *Journal of Interpersonal Violence, 7*, 189–204.

Sautter, F. J., Cornwell, J., Johnson, J. J., Wiley, J., & Faraone, S. V. (2002). Family history study of posttraumatic stress disorder with secondary psychotic symptoms. *American Journal of Psychiatry, 159*, 1775–1777.

Savoca, E., & Rosenheck, R. (2000). The civilian labor market experiences of Vietnam-era veterans: The influence of psychiatric disorders. *Journal of Mental Health Policy and Economics, 3*, 199–207.

Scharlach, A. E., & Frenzel, C. (1986). An evaluation of institution-based respite care. *The Gerontologist, 26*(1), 77–82.

Scharlach, A. E., Kellam, R., Ong, N., Baskin, A., Goldstein, C., & Fox, P. J. (2006). Cultural attitudes and caregiver service use: Lessons from focus groups with racially and ethnically diverse family caregivers. *Journal of Gerontology Social Work, 47*, 133–156.

Schiraldi, G. R. (2000). *The post-traumatic stress disorder sourcebook: A guide to healing, recovery, and growth.* Los Angeles: Lowell House.

Schnurr, P. P., & Green, B. L. (2004). Understanding relationships among trauma, PTSD, and health outcomes. In P. P. Schnurr & B. L. Green (Eds.), *Trauma and health: Physical health consequences of exposure to extreme stress* (pp. 247–275). Washington, DC: American Psychological Association.

Schnurr, P. P., Hayes, A. F., Lunney, C. A., McFall, M., & Uddo, M. (2006). Longitudinal analysis of the relationship between symptoms and quality of life in veterans treated for posttraumatic stress disorder. *Journal of Consulting and Clinical Psychology, 74,* 707–713.

Schnurr, P. P., & Jankowski, M. K. (1999). Physical health and posttraumatic stress disorder: Review and synthesis. *Seminars in Clinical Neuropsychiatry, 4,* 295–304.

Schnurr, P. P., Vielhauer, M. J., Weathers, F., & Findler, M. (1999). *The Brief Trauma Questionnaire.* White River Junction, VT: National Center for PTSD.

Schoenfeld, F. B., Marmar, C. R., & Neylan, T. C. (2004). Current concepts in pharmacotherapy for posttraumatic stress disorder. *Psychiatric Services, 55,* 519–531.

Schwab-Stone, M. E., Ayers, T. S., Kasprow, W., Voyce, C., Barone, C., Shriver, T., et al. (1995). No safe haven: A study of violence exposure in an urban community. *Journal of the American Academy of Child and Adolescent Psychiatry, 34,* 1343–1352.

Scott, M. J., & Stradling, S. G. (1997). Client compliance with exposure treatments for posttraumatic stress disorder. *Journal of Traumatic Stress, 10,* 523–526.

Scott, M. J., & Stradling, S. G. (2006). *Counselling for post-traumatic stress disorder* (3rd ed.). London: Sage.

Seedat, S., Nyamai, C., Njenga, F., Vythilingum, B., & Stein, D. (2004). Trauma exposure and post-traumatic stress symptoms in urban African schools. Survey in Cape Town and Nairobi. *British Journal of Psychiatry, 184,* 169–175.

Seedat, S., Stein, M. B., Oosthuizen, P. P., Emsley, R. A., & Stein, D. J. (2003). Linking posttraumatic stress disorder and psychosis: A look at epidemiology, phenomenology, and treatment. *Journal of Nervous and Mental Disease, 191,* 675–681.

Segal, Z. V., Williams, J. M. G., & Teasdale, J. D. (2002). *Mindfulness-based cognitive therapy for depression.* New York: Guilford Press.

Seng, J. S., Graham-Bermann, S. A., Clark, M. K., McCarthy, A. M., & Ronis, D. L. (2005). Posttraumatic stress disorder and physical comorbidity among female children and adolescents: Results from service-use data. *Pediatrics, 116,* 767–776.

Shafer, A. (2005). Meta-analysis of the Brief Psychiatric Rating Scale factor structure. *Psychological Assessment, 17,* 324–335.

Shalev, A. Y., Freedman, S., Peri, T., Brandes, D., Sahar, T., Orr, S. P., et al. (1998). Prospective study of posttraumatic stress disorder and depression following trauma. *American Journal of Psychiatry, 155,* 630–637.

Shay, J. (1995). *Achilles in Vietnam: Combat trauma and the undoing of character.* New York: Simon & Schuster.

Shay, J. (2000). *Odysseus in America.* New York: Scribner.

REFERENCES   *379*

Simpson, T. L., & Miller, W. R. (2002). Concomitance between childhood sexual and physical abuse and substance abuse problems: A review. *Clinical Psychology Review, 22,* 27–77.

Sitterle, K., & Gurwich, R. (1998). The terrorist bombing in Oklahoma City. In E. Zinner & M. Williams (Eds.), *When a community weeps: Case studies in group survivorship* (pp. 161–189). Philadelphia: Brunner/Mazel.

Smith, G. E., & Pear, T. H. (1917). *Shell shock and its lessons.* Manchester, England: Manchester University Press.

Smucker, M. R., Grunert, B. K., & Weis, J. M. (2003). Posttraumatic stress disorder: A new algorithm treatment model. In R. L. Leahy (Ed.), *Roadblocks in cognitive–behavioral therapy: Transforming challenges into opportunities for change* (pp. 175–194). New York: Guilford Press.

Smyth, L. (1999). *Overcoming post-traumatic stress disorder: A cognitive–behavioral exposure-based protocol for the treatment of PTSD and other anxiety disorders—Therapist protocol.* Oakland, CA: New Harbinger.

Solinsky, S. A. (2002). *Act it out: 25 expressive ways to help you heal from childhood abuse.* Oakland, CA: New Harbinger.

Spinazzola, J., Blaustein, M., & van der Kolk, B. A. (2005). Posttraumatic stress disorder treatment outcome research: The study of unrepresentative samples? *Journal of Traumatic Stress, 18,* 425–436.

Spitzer, R. L., Williams, J. B., Gibbon, M., & First, M. B. (1995). *Structured Clinical Interview for DSM–IV—Patient Version (SCID–P, Version 2.0).* Washington, DC: American Psychiatric Press.

Stampfl, T. G., & Levis, D. J. (1967). Essentials of implosion therapy: A learning theory based psychodynamic behavioral therapy. *Journal of Abnormal Psychology, 72,* 496–503.

Stanovich, K. E. (2001). *How to think straight about psychology* (6th ed.). Needham Heights, MA: Allyn & Bacon.

Stein, B., Comer, D., Gardner, W., & Kelleher, K. (1999). Prospective study of displaced children's symptoms in wartime Bosnia. *Social Psychiatry and Psychiatric Epidemiology, 34,* 464–469.

Stein, B., Jaycox, L. H., Kataoka, S., Wong, M., Tu, W., Elliott, M., et al. (2003). A mental health intervention for schoolchildren exposed to violence. *JAMA, 290,* 603–611.

Stein, M. B., McQuaid, J. R., Pedrelli, P., Lenox, R., & McCahill, M. E. (2000). Posttraumatic stress disorder in the primary care medical setting. *General Hospital Psychiatry, 22,* 261–269.

Stein, M. B., Walker, J., & Forde, D. (2000). Gender differences in susceptibility to posttraumatic stress disorder. *Behaviour and Research Therapy, 38,* 619–628.

Stein, M. B., Walker, J. R., Hazen, A. L., & Forde, D. R. (1997). Full and partial posttraumatic stress disorder: Findings from a community survey. *American Journal of Psychiatry, 154,* 1114–1119.

Steiner, H., Garcia, I. G., & Matthews, Z. (1997). Posttraumatic stress disorder in incarcerated juvenile delinquents. *Journal of the American Academy of Child & Adolescent Psychiatry, 36,* 357–365.

Steketee, G. (1999). *Overcoming obsessive–compulsive disorder: A behavioral and cognitive protocol for the treatment of OCD—Therapist protocol.* Oakland, CA: New Harbinger.

Stevens, T. N., Ruggiero, K. J., Kilpatrick, D. G., Resnick, H. S., & Saunders, B. E. (2005). Variables differentiating singly and multiply victimized youth: Results from the National Survey of Adolescents and implications for secondary prevention. *Child Maltreatment, 10,* 211–223.

Stewart, A. L., Greenfield, S., Hays, R. D., Wells, K., Rogers, W. H., Berry, S. D., et al. (1989). Functional status and well-being of patients with chronic conditions. Results from the Medical Outcomes Study. *JAMA, 262,* 907–913.

Stewart, S. H., Pihl, R. O., Conrod, P. J., & Dongier, M. (1998). Functional associations among trauma, PTSD, and substance-related disorders. *Addictive Behaviors, 6,* 797–812.

Strauss, J. L., Calhoun, P. S., Marx, C. E., Stechuchak, K. M., Oddone, E. Z., Swartz, M. S., et al. (2006). Comorbid posttraumatic stress disorder is associated with suicidality in male veterans with schizophrenia or schizoaffective disorder. *Schizophrenia Research, 84,* 165–169.

Street, A. E., Gibson, L. E., & Holohan, D. R. (2005). The impact of childhood traumatic experiences, trauma-related guilt, and avoidant coping strategies on PTSD symptoms in female survivors of domestic violence. *Journal of Traumatic Stress, 18,* 245–252.

Stuber, J., & Galea, S. (2005). Barriers to mental health treatment after disasters. *Psychiatric Services, 56,* 1157–1158.

Suarez, R., Mills, R. C., & Stewart, D. G. (1987). *Sanity, insanity, and common sense: The groundbreaking new approach to happiness.* New York: Fawcett Columbine.

Substance Abuse and Mental Health Services Administration. (2002). *Report to Congress on the prevention and treatment of co-occurring substance abuse disorders and mental disorders.* Rockville, MD: Author.

Sullivan, G., Craske, M. G., Sherbourne, C., Edlund, M. J., Rose, R. D., Golinelli, D., et al. (2007). Design of the Coordinated Anxiety Learning and Management (CALM) study: Innovations in collaborative care for anxiety disorders. *General Hospital Psychiatry, 29,* 379–387.

Switzer, G. E., Dew, M. A., Thompson, K., Goycoolea, J. M., Derricott, T., & Mullins, S. D. (1999). Posttraumatic stress disorder and service utilization among urban mental health center clients. *Journal of Traumatic Stress, 12,* 25–39.

Tarrier, N., Pilgrim, H., Sommerfield, C., Faragher, B., Reynolds, M., Graham, E., et al. (1999). Cognitive and exposure therapy in the treatment of PTSD. *Journal of Consulting and Clinical Psychology, 67,* 13–18.

Tarrier, N., & Sommerfield, C. (2004). Treatment of chronic PTSD by cognitive therapy with exposure: 5-year follow-up. *Behavior Therapy, 35,* 231–246.

Tarrier, N., Sommerfield, C., & Pilgrim, H. (1999). Relatives expressed emotion (EE) and PTSD treatment outcome. *Psychological Medicine, 29*, 801–811.

Taylor, R. J., Chatters, L. M., & Levin, J. (2004). *Religion in the lives of African Americans: Social, psychological and health perspectives.* Thousand Oaks, CA: Sage.

Thapa, S. B., Van Ommeren, M., Sharma, B., de Jong, J. T., & Hauff, E. (2003). Psychiatric disability among tortured Bhutanese refugees in Nepal. *American Journal of Psychiatry, 160*, 2032–2037.

Thompson, M. P., Kaslow, N. J., Kingree, J. B., Rashid, A., Puett, R., Jacobs, D., et al. (2000). Partner violence, social support, and distress among inner-city African American women. *American Journal of Community Psychology, 28*, 127–143.

Thompson, S. J. (2005). Factors associated with trauma symptoms among runaway/homeless adolescents. *Stress, Trauma, and Crisis, 8*, 143–156.

Trafton, J. A., Minkel, J., & Humphreys, K. (2006). Opioid substitution treatment reduces substance use equivalently in clients with and without posttraumatic stress disorder. *Journal of Studies on Alcohol, 67*, 228–235.

Triffleman, E. G., Marmar, C. R., Delucchi, K. L., & Ronfeldt, H. (1995). Childhood trauma and posttraumatic stress disorder in substance abuse inpatients. *Journal of Nervous and Mental Disease, 183*, 172–176.

Trimble, M. R. (1985). Post-traumatic stress disorder: History of a concept. In C. R. Figley (Ed.), *Trauma and its wake: The study and treatment of post-traumatic stress disorder* (pp. 5–35). New York: Brunner Mazel.

Tucker, P. M., Zaninelli, R., Yehuda, R., Ruggiero, L., Dillingham, K., & Pitts, C. D. (2001). Paroxetine in the treatment of chronic posttraumatic stress disorder: Results of a placebo-controlled, flexible-dosage trial. *Journal of Clinical Psychiatry, 62*, 860–868.

Ullman, S. E., & Filipas, H. H. (2001). Predictors of PTSD symptom severity and social reactions in sexual assault victims. *Journal of Traumatic Stress, 14*, 369–389.

U.S. Department of Veterans Affairs, National Center for PTSD Assessments. (2007). *Chart—Trauma exposure measures.* Retrieved January 29, 2009, from http://ncptsd.va.gov/ncmain/ncdocs/assmnts/nc_chart_trauma_exp.html

U.S. Preventive Services Task Force. (1996). *Guide to clinical prevention services* (2nd ed.). Baltimore: Williams & Wilkins.

VA/DoD Clinical Practice Guideline Working Group. (2003). *Management of posttraumatic stress* (Office of Quality and Performance Publication 10QCPG/PTSD-04). Washington, DC: Veterans Health Administration, Department of Veterans Affairs and Health Affairs, Department of Defense.

van Minnen, A., Arntz, A., & Keijsers, G. P. J. (2002). Prolonged exposure in patients with chronic PTSD: Predictors of treatment and dropout. *Behaviour Research and Therapy, 40*, 439–457.

Veiel, H. O. F., & Baumann, U. (1992). The many meanings of social support. In H. O. F. Veiel & U. Baumann (Eds.), *The meaning and measurement of social support* (pp. 193–216). New York: Hemisphere.

Wagner, A. W., Rizvi, S., L., & Harned, M. S. (2007). Applications of dialectical behavior therapy to the treatment of complex trauma-related problems: When one case formulation does not fit all. *Journal of Traumatic Stress, 20*, 391–400.

Waldfogel, S., & Mueser, K. T. (1988). Another case of chronic PTSD with auditory hallucinations. *American Journal of Psychiatry, 145*, 1314.

Wason, P. C. (1960). On the failure to eliminate hypotheses in a conceptual task. *Quarterly Journal of Experimental Psychology, 12*, 129–140.

Wasserman, D. A., Havassy, B. E., & Boles, S. M. (1997). Traumatic events and post-traumatic stress disorder in cocaine users entering private treatment. *Drug and Alcohol Dependence, 46*, 1–8.

Weathers, F. W., Keane, T. M., & Davidson, J. R. T. (2001). Clinician-Administered PTSD Scale: A review of the first ten years of research. *Depression and Anxiety, 13*, 132–156.

Weathers, F. W., Litz, B. T., Herman, D. S., Huska, J. A., & Keane, T. M. (1993, October). *The PTSD Checklist (PCL): Reliability, validity, and diagnostic utility.* Paper presented at the Ninth Annual Meeting of the International Society for Traumatic Stress Studies, San Antonio, TX.

Wells, A. (2009). *Metacognitive therapy for anxiety and depression.* New York: Guilford Press.

Whitbeck, L. B., Adams, G. W., Hoyt, D. R., & Chen, X. (2004). Conceptualizing and measuring historical trauma among American Indian people. *American Journal of Community Psychology, 33*, 119–130.

White, C. N., Gunderson, J. G., Zanarini, M. C., & Hudson, J. I. (2003). Family studies of borderline personality disorder: A review. *Harvard Review of Psychiatry, 1*, 8–19.

Widom, C. S. (1999). Posttraumatic stress disorder in abused and neglected children grown up. *American Journal of Psychiatry, 156*, 1223–1229.

Williams, J. W. J., Stellato, C. P., Cornell, J., & Barrett, J. (2004). The 13- and 20-item Hopkins Symptom Checklist Depression Scale: Psychometric properties in primary care patients with minor depression or dysthymia. *International Journal of Psychiatry in Medicine, 34*, 37–50.

Williams, L. M., & Banyard, V. L. (1998). *Trauma & memory.* New York: Wiley.

Williams, M. B., & Poijula, S. (2002). *The PTSD workbook: Simple, effective techniques for overcoming traumatic stress symptoms.* Oakland, CA: New Harbinger.

Wilson, A. E., Calhoun, K. S., & Bernat, J. A. (1999). Risk recognition and trauma-related symptoms among sexually revictimized women. *Journal of Consulting and Clinical Psychology, 67*, 705–710.

Wilson, J. P., & Keane, T. M. (Eds.). (2004). *Assessing psychological trauma and PTSD* (2nd ed.). New York: Guilford Press.

Wolford, G., Rosenberg, S. D., Rosenberg, H. J., Swartz, M. S., Butterfield, M. I., Swanson, J. W., et al. (2008). A clinical trial comparing interviewer and computer-assisted assessment in clients with severe mental illness. *Psychiatric Services, 59*, 769–775.

World Health Organization. (2004). *International statistical classification of diseases and related health problems: Tenth revision* (2nd ed.). Geneva, Switzerland: Author.

Wray, L. O. (2007). Primary care–mental health integration at the VA national mental health conference. *Department of Veterans Affairs, Mental Illness Research, Education, and Clinical Centers, 8*, 1–5.

Wright, J., Friedrich, W., Cinq-Mars, C., Cyr, M., & McDuff, P. (2004). Self-destructive and delinquent behaviors of adolescent female victims of child sexual abuse: Rates and covariates in clinical and nonclinical samples. *Violence and Victims, 19*, 627–643.

Yano, E. M., Simon, B. F., Lanto, A. B., & Rubenstein, L. V. (2007). The evolution of changes in primary care delivery underlying the Veterans Health Administration's quality transformation. *American Journal of Public Health, 97*, 2151–2159.

Yehuda, R., Golier, J. A., Halligan, S. L., & Harvey, P. D. (2004). Learning and memory in Holocaust survivors with posttraumatic stress disorder. *Biological Psychiatry, 55*, 291–295.

Yen, S., Shea, M. T., Battle, C. L., Johnson, D. M., Zlotnick, C., Dolan-Sewell, R., et al. (2002). Traumatic exposure and posttraumatic stress disorder in borderline, schizotypal, avoidant, and obsessive-compulsive personality disorders: Findings from the collaborative longitudinal personality disorders study. *Journal of Nervous and Mental Disease, 190*, 510–518.

Zanarini, M. C., Frankenburg, F. R., Dubo, E. D., Sickel, A. E., Trikha, A., Levin, A., et al. (1998). Axis I comorbidity of borderline personality disorder. *American Journal of Psychiatry, 155*, 1733–1739.

Zanarini, M. C., Williams, A. A., Lewis, R. E., Reich, R. B., Vera, S. C., Marino, M. F., et al. (1997). Reported pathological childhood experiences associated with the development of borderline personality disorder. *American Journal of Psychiatry, 154*, 1101–1106.

Zatzick, D. F., Jurkovich, G. J., Gentilello, L. M., Wisner, D., & Rivara, F. P. (2002). Posttraumatic stress, problem drinking, and functioning after injury. *Archives of Surgery, 137*, 200–205.

Zayfert, C., & Becker, C. B. (2000). Implementing of empirically supported treatment for PTSD: Obstacles and innovations. *The Behavior Therapist, 23*, 161–168.

Zayfert, C., & Becker, C. B. (2007). *Cognitive–behavioral therapy for PTSD: A case formulation approach.* New York: Guilford Press.

Zimmermann, G., Favrod, J., Trieu, V. H., & Pomini, V. (2005). The effect of cognitive behavioral treatment on the positive symptoms of schizophrenia spectrum disorders: A meta-analysis. *Schizophrenia Research, 77*, 1–9.

Zinzow, H. M., Grubaugh, A. L., Frueh, B. C., & Magruder, K. M. (2008). Sexual assault, mental health, and service use among male and female veterans seen in Veterans Affairs primary care clinics: A multi-site study. *Psychiatry Research, 159*, 226–236.

Zlotnick, C., Bruce, S., Weisberg, R. B., Shea, M. T., Machan, J., & Keller, M. (2003). Social and health functioning in female primary care patients with posttraumatic stress disorder with and without comorbid substance abuse. *Comprehensive Psychiatry, 44,* 177–183.

Zlotnick, C., Franklin, C. L., & Zimmerman, M. (2002). Is comorbidity of posttraumatic stress disorder and borderline personality disorder related to greater pathology and impairment? *American Journal of Psychiatry, 159,* 1940–1943.

Zlotnick, C., Johnson, D. M., Yen, S., Battle, C. L., Sanislow, C. A., Skodol, A. E., et al. (2003). Clinical features and impairment in women with borderline personality disorder (BPD) with posttraumatic stress disorder (PTSD), BPD without PTSD, and other personality disorders with PTSD. *Journal of Nervous and Mental Disease, 191,* 706–713.

INDEX

American Academy of Child and
        Adolescent Psychiatry, 257, 262
Amnesia, 19, 25
Amsel, L., 271
Amygdala, 24
Anger
    action plans for dealing with,
        179–180
    as associated problem, 90–91, 329
    in clients with BPD, 227
    as cue for initiating CR, 165, 166
    and maladaptive behavior, 182–183
    personal goals related to, 198
    residual, 180–182
    strategies to address, 178–179
    thoughts associated with, 125
    as unresolved feeling, 154
Anhedonia, 211
Anxiety
    as associated problem, 88
    and breathing retraining, 55–56, 77, 79
    as cue for initiating CR, 165
    and exposure therapy, 29–31
    and memory, 164
    thoughts associated with, 125
Apathy, 211
Appraisals, of traumatic events, 27–28
Asian American Vietnam veterans, 286
Asian clients, 286, 287, 289, 290
Assessing Psychological Trauma and PTSD
        (J. P. Wilson & T. M. Keane),
        41–42
Assessment(s)
    of adolescents, 261–262
    in CBT for Postdisaster Distress
        program, 274
    of clients in addiction treatment
        programs, 245–246
    of clients' other domains, 49–52
    during cognitive restructuring
        sessions, 101
    of culturally diverse clients, 289, 295
    and diagnosis of PTSD, 37–39, 47–49
    and screening for PTSD symptoms,
        44–47
    for special populations, 39–40
    of trauma exposure, 42–44

Associated problems (with PTSD),
        88–95
    bipolar disorder, 94–95
    in cognitive functioning, 94
    delusions, 94
    dissociation, x, 25, 94, 183–184
    drug and alcohol problems, 92–94
    hallucinations, 94
    negative feelings, 88–91
    relationship difficulties, 91–92
    schizophrenia-spectrum disorders,
        94–95
Avoidance symptoms, 85–86, 323
    coping strategies for, 150
    in diagnosis of PTSD, 23, 47
    and exposure therapy, 29, 30
    persistent, 197
Avoidance Symptoms Worksheet, 326

Barriers to treatment
    for clients with psychosis, 211
    for culturally diverse clients, 290
    for disaster survivors, 272–273
BDI. *See* Beck Depression Inventory—II
Beck Anxiety Interview—Primary Care,
        47
Beck Depression Inventory—II (BDI),
        50, 60, 101, 262
Behavioral activation, 274
Behaviors
    as cues for initiating CR, 165–166
    maladaptive, 182–183
    self-destructive, 232–233
    self-injurious, 256, 258
Beliefs
    clinging to, 172–174
    of therapists following disasters,
        276–277
    trauma-related, 155–159
Belief scale, 114–116, 164
Believability, of alternative thoughts
    for clients with psychosis, 222–223
    strategies to increase, 142–143, 164,
        167–168
Bereavement, 37
Bible, 16
"Big four" feelings, 125

Psychiatric disorders, 94–95. *See also* Mental illness
Psychoanalysis, 19
Psychodynamic approach, to PTSD, 26
Psychodynamic therapy, 35
Psychoeducation, 81–97
    about associated problems, 88–95
    about posttraumatic disorders, 56–57
    about symptoms of PTSD, 83–88
    in CBT for Postdisaster Distress, 274
    for clients in addiction treatment programs, 248
    for culturally diverse clients, 291, 295
    and functional goals for treatment, 95–97
    teaching techniques of, 82–83
Psychological hardiness, 38
Psychological reactance, 160
Psychosis, 209–224. *See also* Schizophrenia-spectrum disorders
    addressing challenges of, 213–217
    challenges in treating, 211–213
    clinical example of, 217–223
    in crisis planning, 75
    impact of trauma and PTSD on, 210–211
    measuring progress for, 216–217
    prevalence of trauma and PTSD in, 210
    and trauma assessment, 39
    understanding population with, 209–210
Psychosocial functioning, 211
Psychotherapeutic interventions, 24
Psychotic symptoms, 212, 213–214
PTSD. *See* Posttraumatic stress disorder
PTSD Checklist (PCL), 40
    monitoring symptoms with, 60, 101
    in primary care settings, 305
    screening with, 44–49
PTSD Checklist—Civilian Version, 45
PTSD Checklist—Specific Version, 46, 294
PTSD Knowledge Test, 51, 317–319
Purdue PTSD Scale, 47

Race, as risk factor for PTSD, 286
Racism, as stressor, 287, 290

Railroad crash survivors, 17–18
Reading and writing proficiency, clients with limited, 215
Recreation, goals related to, 96
Recurrent trauma-related thoughts, 118–119
The Red Badge of Courage (Stephen Crane), 17
Reductions in distress, modest, 138, 168–169
Reexperiencing symptoms, 84–85, 149, 323
    coping strategies for, 150
    in diagnosis of PTSD, 23, 47
    persistent, 196–197
    and personal goals, 198
Reexperiencing Symptoms Worksheet, 325
Referrals, from primary care settings, 292, 308
Refugee populations, 11, 14. *See also* Culturally diverse clients
Reinforcement
    of 5 Steps of CR, 139
    of common styles of thinking, 114
    of small gains, 161
Relationship difficulties, 91–92, 329
Relationship Difficulties Worksheet, 333
Relaxation breathing, 260
Reliving, 25
Remarque, Erich, 17
"Remembering, Repeating, and Working Through" (Sigmund Freud), 20
Resick, P. A., 32
Residual anger, 180–182
Resilience, 38
Responsibility, unrealistic beliefs about, 170–171
Retention
    of adolescents, 258–259
    of clients in addiction treatment programs, 242–244
    of culturally diverse clients, 290–295
Revictimization
    and anger, 181, 182
    preventing, 121–122, 152

Reviewing progress, 161
Revised Civilian Mississippi Scale for PTSD, 47
Risk, overestimation of, 116, 133, 337
Rivers, W. H. R., 21–22
Roberts, M., 39
Role functioning
    as chief complaint, 291–292
    goals related to, 96
Role play, 146, 166, 168, 180, 183, 204, 205, 214
Romeo and Juliet (William Shakespeare), 17

Samet, J., 39
Schemas, xi, 25, 27, 99–100
Schizo-affective disorder, 210
Schizophrenia-spectrum disorders, 94–95, 210
Schizophreniform disorder, 210
Schizotypal personality disorder, 210
Screen for Posttraumatic Stress Symptoms, 47
Screening
    of culturally diverse clients, 293, 294
    for postdisaster distress, 272
    in primary care settings, 39, 305
    for PTSD symptoms, 44–47
    for substance abuse, 50
Seeking Safety (intervention), 242, 243
Selective serotonin reuptake inhibitor (SSRI), 306
Self-blame, excessive, 170–171, 337
Self-care, 96
Self-destructive behaviors, 232–233
Self-efficacy, reinforcement of, 203–205
Self-harm, 229, 231–232
Self-injurious behavior, 256, 258
Self-management skill, CR as, 33, 57, 100, 160
Self-reporting, in assessments, 41
Self-statements, 182–183
Sensations, as cues for initiating Cognitive Restructuring, 165–166
September 11 terrorist attacks, 34, 271–273
Sertraline, 306

Sexual assault, 11
Sexual risk taking, by adolescents, 258
SF-36. *See* Medical Outcomes Study, Short Form 36
Shakespeare, William, 17
Shame
    as associated problem, 89–90, 328–329
    as cue for initiating CR, 165, 166
    psychoeducation to reduce, 81
    as underlying feeling of anger, 88
    as unresolved feeling, 133, 154
Shaping, 188
Shell shock, 20–21
Shielding, 184
Short Form of the PTSD Checklist, 47
Short PTSD Rating Interview (SPRINT), 47
Short Screening Scale for PTSD, 47
"Should" statements, 336
SIDES (Structural Interview for Disorders of Extreme Stress), 51
Significant others, support from, 61–63, 191–193
Skill practice, 74
Sleep hygiene, 150, 151, 177, 197
Sleeping, difficulty, 17, 21–23, 47, 69, 87, 93, 149–151, 176–177, 192, 218, 258, 264, 274, 277, 307, 311
SLESQ (Stressful Life Events Screening Questionnaire), 45
Smith, Grafton, 21
Smoking, co-occurrence of PTSD and, 304
Social functioning, as chief complaint, 291–292
Social isolation, 14–15
Social skills training, 183
Social support. *See also* Environmental supports
    for clients with BPD, 230
    for clients with psychosis, 214
    in CR for PTSD program, 61–63
    in crisis planning, 76–77
    of culturally diverse clients, 292
    for disaster survivors, 269
    families of adolescent clients as, 259
Socratic method, 131, 133, 179, 222, 276

SPAN (startle, physical upset, anger, numbness), 47
Special populations
   assessments for, 39–40
   trauma in, 11–15
Spiritual leaders, as collaborators with mental health providers, 293
Spouses. *See* Significant Others
SPRINT (Short PTSD Rating Interview), 47
SPRINT-E, 272
SSRI (selective serotonin reuptake inhibitor), 306
Stigma, as barrier to treatment, 273
Stress, hypersensitivity to, 212
Stressful Life Events Screening Questionnaire (SLESQ), 45
Structural Interview for Disorders of Extreme Stress (SIDES), 51
Substance abuse
   by adolescents, 257, 258
   as associated problem, 92–94, 330
   and nightmares, 176
   screening for, 50
Substance dependence PTSD therapy treatment, 243
Substance-induced psychotic disorder, 37–38
Substance use disorder. *See* Addiction treatment programs
Summing Up handout, 347
Suppression, of memories, 21
Symptoms of PTSD
   action plans to manage, 149–151
   in adolescents, 258
   avoidance symptoms, 23, 47, 85–86
   descriptions of, by culturally diverse clients, 291
   in diagnosis, 23, 47–49
   monitoring of, 60
   onset of, 38
   overarousal symptoms, 23, 47, 87, 149
   persistent, 196–199
   physical symptoms as, 287–289
   in primary care settings, 307
   problematic, 176–184

psychoeducation about, 83–88
psychotic, 212, 213–214
reexperiencing symptoms, 23, 47, 84–85, 149
screening for, 44–47

TAA (Trauma Assessment for Adults), 45
Taking action, 133–137, 143
Teaching Cognitive Restructuring for PTSD, 57–59. *See also* Challenges in teaching Cognitive Restructuring for PTSD
   to cognitively impaired clients, 193–195
   describing upsetting situations, 139–140
   development of action plans, 146–148
   examining evidence, 141–142
   identifying most distressing thoughts, 140–141
   identifying strongest emotions, 140
   making decisions and taking action, 142–143
   and psychoeducation, 82–83
   sample worksheet for, 144–145
   strategies for, 138–145
   tips for, 160–162
Technological accidents, 267–268
TEQ (Traumatic Events Questionnaire), 45
Termination, of program, 199–205
   coordinating with other professionals in, 203–205
   general approach to, 200–203
   preparing for, 59
Terrorism survivors. *See* Disaster survivors
Test–retest reliability, 40
Themes, trauma-related, 157–158
Therapeutic alliances, x, 247, 259
Therapeutic frame, 247
Therapeutic relationship
   for adolescents, 259
   for clients in addiction treatment programs, 246–247
   conflict in, 233

Veterans
  in literary accounts of trauma, 17
  trauma exposure rates of, 302
  and traumatic neuroses, 19–21
Veterans Administration, 22
Veterans Affairs/Department of Defense
    Clinical Practice Guideline, 305
Veterans Health Administration
    (VHA), 301–302
Vietnam War, 22, 286
Vulnerability, 178

"Walking down the street" scenario,
    103–104
War, trauma from, 16–17, 19–21

Wilson, J. P., 42
Women
  addiction treatment programs for,
    241
  hysterical symptoms of, 19
Work, 49, 70, 71, 72, 94, 96, 178, 192,
    198, 212, 223, 230, 231, 234,
    240, 245, 249–252, 268, 273,
    278, 288, 291, 297, 310, 313, 328
Worksheets, reducing reliance on,
    190–191
World War I, 20–21, 26
World War II, 22
Writing proficiency, clients with
    limited, 215

ABOUT THE AUTHORS

Kim T. Mueser, PhD, received a doctorate in clinical psychology from the University of Illinois at Chicago. He is currently on the faculty of Dartmouth Medical School, Hanover, New Hampshire, where he is a professor in the Departments of Psychiatry and of Community and Family Medicine. Dr. Mueser's clinical and research interests focus on the treatment of posttraumatic stress disorder in vulnerable populations and in psychiatric rehabilitation for persons with severe mental illness. He has given numerous workshops on his work, both nationally and internationally, and has coauthored more than 10 books and more than 300 journal articles and book chapters. He has received a number of awards, including the Armin Loeb Research Award and the Emily Mumford Medal for Distinguished Contributions to Social Science in Medicine.

Stanley D. Rosenberg, PhD, is a professor of psychiatry and community and family medicine at Dartmouth Medical School, Hanover, New Hampshire, and director of the Dartmouth Trauma Interventions Research Center. He directs the New Hampshire Project for Adolescent Trauma Treatment (National Child Traumatic Stress Network) and has served as a consultant for multiple state mental health authorities, federal agencies, health provider organizations, and Fortune 500 corporations. He also has served as a reviewer for the National Institutes of Health, National Institute of Drug Addiction, National Cancer Institute, and multiple professional journals. He is currently on the editorial board of the *Journal of Traumatic Stress* and has authored several books and more than 150 journal articles and book chapters

Harriet J. Rosenberg, MA, received a bachelor of science degree from Cornell University, Ithaca, New York, and a master of arts degree from Columbia University, New York, New York. She is an instructor in psychiatry at Dartmouth Medical School, Hanover, New Hampshire. As a research scientist at the Dartmouth Trauma Interventions Research Center, she has been a coinvestigator on numerous sponsored research projects involving the study of people with posttraumatic stress disorder (PTSD), including individuals with severe mental illness, medical populations such as people with seizure disorders and prostate cancer, children and adolescents with trauma and PTSD, and veterans. Ms. Rosenberg has specialized in the clinical assessment of psychiatric disorders, particularly the assessment of PTSD in special and multiply diagnosed populations. She has authored and coauthored numerous articles and book chapters on trauma and posttraumatic disorders.